Information Structure

Language, Context, and Cognition

Edited by
Anita Steube

Volume 1

Walter de Gruyter · Berlin · New York

Information Structure

Theoretical and Empirical Aspects

Edited by
Anita Steube

Walter de Gruyter · Berlin · New York

♾ Printed on acid-free paper which falls within the guidelines
of the ANSI to ensure permanence and durability.

ISBN 3-11-017934-2

Bibliographic information published by Die Deutsche Bibliothek

Die Deutsche Bibliothek lists this publication in the Deutsche Nationalbibliografie;
detailed bibliographic data is available in the Internet at <http://dnb.ddb.de>.

Printed in Germany
Cover design: Christopher Schneider, Berlin
Printing and binding: Hubert & Co., Göttingen

Contents

Contents

Introduction

"Information Structure: Theoretical and Empirical Aspects" is the first volume in the series "Language, Context, and Cognition". The series was established as the organ of the Research Group "Linguistic Foundations of Cognitive Science: Linguistic and Conceptual Knowledge" at the University of Leipzig, sponsored by the German Research Foundation as Research Group 349.

Several projects in the research group have been concerned with information structure already from 1999 to 2002. They are especially responsible for this volume:

Ewald Lang and Gerhild Zybatow (Marcela Adamíková, Dorothee Fehrmann): *CONTRAST and CORRECTION in the interaction of the lexicon, syntax, information structure and prosody with special attention on the Slavonic languages*
Ingolf Max (Claudia Henning, Werner Wolff, Nils Kürbis): *Multidimensional representations of linguistic and world knowledge: studies on presupposition and negation in discourse*
Anita Steube und Kai Alter (Carla Umbach, Andreas Späth, Stefan Sudhoff): *Intonation and meaning in information structure*
Gerhild Zybatow (Dieter Wirth, Rolf Meyer, Klaus Abels): *Russian information structure*

The first publication of work done in these projects appeared in 2001 under the title "Kontrast – lexikalisch, semantisch, intonatorisch" (Contrast – lexical, semantic, and prosodic), in: "Linguistische Arbeitsberichte" 77, Leipzig. In February 2002, the four projects organized an international workshop on "Contrast and Information Structure“. Before this workshop, we sent our results - documented in "Linguistische Arbeitsberichte" 79, Leipzig 2002 under the heading "Contrast" and "Information Structure and Grammatical Modularity" - to our partners in Berlin, Bonn, Budapest, Edinburgh, Eindhoven, Konstanz, Lund, Prague, Stuttgart, Tübingen asking for their comments and for their own approaches to information structure. We are happy to publish three of the feed-back contributions here: Petr Sgall and Eva Hajičová from Prague, Beáta Gyuris from Budapest, and Brigitta Haftka from Potsdam.

Although there are already syntactic descriptions of nearly all phenomena of German information structure in different models now, and although there is a Minimalist description of Russian information structure of declarative matrix clauses as well, investigations on the impact of information structure on semantics and experiments on modern German and Russian prosody have only just begun. The few phonological parameters delimited so far are highly context dependent. Many more experiments will be necessary. Therefore, this volume mainly presents models for information structural descriptions, semantic contributions, contributions on the processing of prosody, and evidence coming from Neuroscience. The papers by Ulrike Toepel and Kai Alter, Claudia Hruska and Kai Alter, and Britta Stolterfoht and Markus Bader document the close cooperation of the research group with the Max Planck Institute of Cognitive Neuroscience in Leipzig. The text-structural influence on the topic, the influence of focus sensitive particles on information structure, and the topic-focus structure in Russian non-declarative clauses and dependent clauses is left for research in the second three years' period of the research group which began in 2003.

We will now introduce the papers of this volume individually.

First the Praguian Functional Generative Model and the Generative Model used in Leipzig for the description of German are presented as the background for the description of modular grammar, information structure, and prosodic contrast. The contributions on the semantic, syntactic and prosodic components of grammar respectively, as in the model proposed by Steube, Alter, and Späth, then follow. The second part of the book is devoted to the problem of contrast in a broader sense accompanied by prosodic tests on the realization of sentences containing German *aber*, and Polish, Czech and Slovak *ale* (engl. *but*).

I. Modular grammar, information structure and prosodic contrast

Petr Sgall and **Eva Hajičová** make use of the framework of the Praguian Functional Generative Description which includes a description of the topic-focus articulation to explain phenomena connected with contrast and degrees of its intensity. The semantic basis for the articulation of a sentence into T(opic) and F(ocus) is understood as the relation of aboutness: in a prototypical declarative sentence F holds about its T. Normally the finite verb is F, the DPs and PPs preceding it are topics, and those following it are focus.

According to the context (1), only *one of his friends* is in the focus in (2).

(1) *Whom was your brother visiting yesterday?*

(2) *My*.t *brother*.t *was visiting*.t *one*.f *of his*.t *friends*.f. *yesterday*.t

Thus, within the Praguian Functional framework the topic-focus articulation is not conceived of as a separate level of grammatical structure formation.

The authors take their examples from the syntactically annotated Prague Dependency Treebank. In Czech, lexical and phonological strategies for expressing focus and contrast are the so-called strong pronominal forms (as opposed to weak pronominal forms as used in bound contexts) and pitch accent.

When in M. Rooth 1985 focus is characterized as a choice from a set of alternatives, F always has a contrastive value. Since - in contrast to German - it is also possible in Czech to use (3) as well as (4) to answer (5), a grammatical value distinguishing CF (contrastive focus) from F seems not to exist. In German, *Buch* in (3) expresses contrastive accent. It answers (5) but (4) does not.

(3) *Hans hat das BUCH dem Schüler gegeben.*
Lit.: Hans has the BOOK to the student given.
(4) *Hans hat dem SCHÜler das Buch gegeben.*
Lit.: Hans has to the STUDENT the book given.
(5) *Hat Hans dem Schüler das Buch oder das Bild gegeben?*
Lit.: Has Hans to the student the book or the picture given?

The distinctiveness of contrastive accent in German as well as in Russian is also shown by Ulrike Toepel and Kai Alter as well as by Grit Mehlhorn in this volume.

If more than one accented (contrasted) item is present in Czech, they get distributed among T and F. More numerous are the cases with a contrastive part of T. Sentence (7) has two contrasted topics in each of the conjuncts. In Steube, Alter and Späth these constructions are called Bridge Contours with the I-Topic as a contextually known part which semantically is part of the focus domain.

(6) *Rodiče odjeli na dovolenou a děti svěřili příbuzným.*
– The parents left for a leave and entrusted their children to their relatives.
(7) *Syna.*c *ve čtvrtek.*c *zavezli.*f *do PARdubic.*f, *a dceru.*c *v sobotu.*c *do HRADce.*f.

The paper further differentiates several degrees of intensity of contrast and argues that different dimensions have to be distinguished.

Anita Steube, Kai Alter and **Andreas Späth** consider information structure as one of the late pragmatic factors that mark the pieces of propositional structure as being a topic, a background constituent (Haftka's 'anaphoric topic') or the focus constituent or rheme before they are realized in the grammatical module of a modular generative grammar (when the process is analysed as speaking). This means that information structure is considered to be of pragmatic origin but that it will be made visible and understood by the joint interaction of the different grammatical modules. It is not a separate module of grammar.

Using the lexicon as an interface level between the cognitive model (with information structural pragmatics as one of its parts) and the grammatical model, grammatical computation begins with the semantic level of a two-level semantics. It maps its structures onto a generative surface syntax from where the structure becomes the input to phonology / prosody. This way the pragmatic features T and F or CF are handed over into grammar and are realized on each grammatical level in the respective way.

The paper uses the model to describe German categorical sentences, correction sentences, and Bridge Contours. The constructions are characterized by their semantic, syntactic and prosodic properties. As there have not been enough prosodic experiments on Bridge Contours, the reader is asked to consider the contribution of Hruska and Alter and that of Mehlhorn on the realization and perceptive value of the contrastive accent in combination with the focus accent in this volume.

Andreas Späth and **Martin Trautwein** discuss what is negated in negative sentences, or, in other words, what negative sentences denote. This is very important for information structure because categorical sentences presuppose objects, times, and places, and the corresponding DPs have referential (i.e. specific, in-group, or partitive) interpretations.

(1) *What about the child.*

(2) *The child does not sleep.*

'The child' is anchored in context (1) and therefore presupposed. It exists independently of whether there is a positive or negative predicate on it. And the existing child can only take part in an existing situation. The proposition of which the situation is an instance is negative in (2). It is the propositions which are positive or negative, but not the events. The meaning of (2) is formalized as in (3).

(3) ∃x [[CHILD, x] & [∃e NOT [SLEEP, x](e)]

At the same time, (3) expresses the information structure of sentence (2) by representing the presupposed background constituent *the child* as the restrictor and the focus *does not sleep* as the nuclear scope of the construction. When there are no sentence adverbials such as *vielleicht, tatsächlich,* etc. in German sentences, negation also marks the border of the focus domain.

The paper does not consider sentences with a contrastive accent. It rather provides further ontological evidence on situations expressed by negative propositions.

Ingolf Max proposes a two-dimensional explication of the semantics expounded in Steube, Alter and Späth and in earlier papers of the authors. A general two-dimensional form of a sentence S is as in (1):

(1) $\lambda x_n \ldots \lambda x_1$ ☼ $\left|\begin{matrix}\alpha \\ \beta\end{matrix}\right|$

in which: α represents the proper ordinary meaning of S
β represents the background of S
α and β have a conjunctive form.
☼ is the placeholder that marks the position of negation.

By specifying the format in (1) Ingolf Max can explicate many semantic notions and can create a model for a series of linguistic phenomena: semantic presupposition, entailment, assertion; correction sentence, Bridge Contour and the thetic sentence as a sentence with tautological presuppositions. This two-dimensional reconstruction brings to light hitherto unclear notions in information structure.

Beáta Gyuris describes Hungarian Bridge Contours the I-Topics of which are monotone increasing, monotone decreasing, or non-monotonic DPs. The author discusses in which question contexts these sentences are correct. A parallel English example with a non-monotonic DP is (2).

(1) *Did you talk to five teachers?*
(2) [$_{CF}$ */To five teachers*] *I* [$_F$ *\ DIDn't*] *talk.*

After examining Büring's (1997, 1999) theory on Bridge Contours in detail, Beáta Gyuris argues that Kadmon's (2001) theory of discourse congruence is superior. She increases Kadmon's conditions on I-Topics and concludes that there is no evidence to support the binary division within DPs into those which can be licensed by the appearance of the same DP in the preceding discourse only (as in (1) and (2)) and those which can be licensed by other DPs as well. The paper convincingly shows that a declarative sentence with a contrastive topic DP has to satisfy the following three conditions to be licensed:

(i) The last question under discussion for the declarative and the question preceding it overtly must be members of the topic value associated with the declarative.
(ii) The two questions must be capable of serving as subquestions of the same superquestion in the discourse (determined by the topic value of the declarative).
(iii) If the overt question is not identical to the last QUD for the declarative, the declarative must entail a complete answer to the overt question.

Since the phenomenon under review has hardly been described as yet, the paper makes an important contribution to the semantics and pragmatics of Bridge Contours far beyond those in Hungarian.

Brigitta Haftka's paper can be regarded as the volume's reference system on the syntactic order in the middlefield of German categorical sentences (without contrastive pitch accent). Having worked on the problems of German word order and information structure for years, Brigitta Haftka lays down all the observations in the present paper and explains them in a framework. She distinguishes between 'proper topic', 'aboutness topic' and 'theme of the sentence' (which are considered to be synonymous) as well as between anaphoric and stressless constituents called 'anaphoric topics'. The former dominate the latter. So, in order to make a proper topic, a constituent must be familiar in terms of information structure, and it must be predicated on by the rest of the sentence (including the anaphoric topic constituents). This is considered to be a rule of textual structure.

The constituents in the German middle field are ordered by seven constraints which, in turn, are defined by c-command relations. In the last part of the paper the constraints are included in an Optimality Theoretic (henceforth OT) ranking system.

When word formation is achieved in the lexicon and the lexicon is the input to each of the grammatical subsystems, **Rosemarie Lühr**'s paper on the accent pattern of Vedic compounds represents the starting point of the prosodic rules that lead to information structural focussing.

Rosemarie Lühr also uses an optimality based framework to clarify the accent positions of those endocentric and exocentric Vedic compounds that hitherto counted as counterexamples to known rules. But the combination of prosodic constraints with faithfulness constraints concerning the underlying stress of the compound as a whole [MAX (wf)] and of the members as single words [MAX $(w)_{In;}$ MAX $(w)_{Fin}$] was not recognized. Nor was the importance of prosodic constraints understood. Admittedly, there are many lexicalizations, but the following constraint is absolutely clear: The more a vowel which functions as the nucleus is unmarked, the more unmarked it is as the nucleus in stressed syllables, too. As demonstrated in the paper, in compounds this constraint concerns the avoidance of stressed *ú* and *í*. Yet, there are further prosodic constraints.

Prosodically determinated stressing and those stresses which fulfill faithfulness constraints can be overridden by contrastive stress. Firstly, the well known stress shifts to differentiate parts of speech must be mentioned. Secondly, contrastive word stress appears within a compound as well.

Thomas Weskott's paper goes over from the more theoretical to the more empirical aspects. It makes use of a scalar notion of information structural markedness to generate empirical hypotheses to which experimental studies have direct access. The notion of markedness is understood in a naïve Jakobsonian way.

Information structural markedness is achieved by deviations from canonical orders: (i) The basic order of arguments is determined by the order in the argument structure of the verbal head; (ii) accent assignment is done in accordance with Cinque's null-hypothesis. A third type of deviation originates in the constraints which context puts on the information structure (topic-comment and background-focus structures) of the sentence. A simultaneous violation of these two orders and of the information structural constraints is additive and increases the degree of markedness. Thus, for the sentence *Der KELLner beleidigte den Gast* the order of background and focus is reversed, and the assumption about the default-accent placement is violated. *Den GAST beleidigte der Kellner* is marked threefold. The scale of markedness is put into a formal framework.

But the scale of markedness should not be considered merely as a descriptive generalization of intuitive judgements about the contextual adequacy of a sentence. It also serves as a basis for predicting processing difficulties of information structural variants relative to a given context. Several experimental studies show that German OVS structures are more difficult to process than canonical SVO structures as long as the context is rich enough.

Claudia Hruska and **Kai Alter** discuss the influence of prosody on sentence perception in online ERPs (event-related potentials). The result of their experiments on dialogues is as follows: As reflected by frontal effects, listeners pay more attention to the positions of expected new information. New information has to be integrated into already given context information maintained in working memory. Inappropriate accentuation in dialogues leads to disturbed comprehension, especially when focus accents are missed. Superfluous highlighting by accentuation, on the other hand, does not lead to a special brain reaction and seems to be ignored in some cases during speech perception.

When the same sentences were presented out of context, the system preferably used the prosodic cues of intonational phrase boundaries for an efficient evaluation of the underlying syntactic structure.

Ulrike Toepel and **Kai Alter** show that it is useful to split up the concept of narrow focus into (i) narrow new information focus and (ii) contrastive focus. New information accents and contrastive accents differ with respect to their acoustic properties in prominence and type. The acoustic analyses show that new information is accented with a bitonal L+H* pattern. For contrastive information, the pertinent pattern is more complicated: L+H*L-. The slightly differing peak heights might play a role in the interpretation of the focus accents as well, since only in the contrastive condition are there no pre-focal accents. Hence the prominence of the contrastive accent is further enhanced by the surrounding prosodic pattern.

The behavioral and electrophysiological data provide evidence for the human brain's ability to detect these focus accents whenever they occur in an inadequate focus environment.

The authors show that not only the dichotomy of given vs. new information as well as that of broad vs. narrow focus is reflected in electrophysiological data, but also the more subtle difference between new and contrastive information. Prosodically underspecified (focus) accents in discourse generally lead to processing difficulties, whereas overspecified accents do so only under certain task requirements. This agrees with the results of Claudia Hruska and Kai Alter's paper.

The dissertation by **Grit Mehlhorn** is one of the first publications on modern Russian prosody. She provides the fundamental prosodic representations of Russian sentences with New Information Focus (NIF) and with Contrastive Focus in correction sentences as well as in Bridge Contours. In production as well as in perception experiments contrastive pitch accent was identified (in the respective contexts) by the subjects to nearly hundred percent, whereas the NIF was identified only by nearly 55 %. This finding proves that CF is a separate pitch accent with its own function in a Russian sentence. The paper describes the kind of the experiments and the relevant accent patterns. Similarities are found between Russian and German intonation as far as the accent types are concerned.

Britta Stolterfoht and **Markus Bader** focus on scrambling in German. They found two cases where focus structure is not fully determined by syntactic structure but also by context (cf. (1)) and by the type of the moved constituent (cf. (2)):

(1) focus scrambling
Maria hat behauptet daß [die Tante]$_F$ *die Nichten* t_i *begrüßt haben.*

(2) scrambled pronominal objects co-referring to the subject of the main clause
Maria hat behauptet, daß sie$_i$ *[die Nichten* t_i *begrüßt haben]*$_F$

Stolterfoht and Bader investigate on the scrambled referential DPs in ERP experiments and found effects of focus structural and prosodic revision in (1). But when focus particles are inserted as in (3)

(3) *Maria hat behauptet, daß die Tante*$_i$ *nur [die Nichten]*$_F$ t_i *begrüßt haben.*

the focus structural effects disappear. A focus particle assigns focus to its adjacent constituent and makes a focus structural revision unnecessary. Further experiments will clarify whether the ERP effects reflect the interaction of syntactic and focus structural processes.

II. Contrast and correction

In a series of papers, **Ewald Lang**[1] deals with the role of contrast in grammar, specifically in terms of conditions between the various modules. As regards the relation of syntax and semantics to prosodically designated information structure, he observes that syntactically constant coordinate constructions like those in (1) – (6) below allow for a range of readings that (i) draw on whether or not the conjuncts display parallel structure in terms of prosody and Topic/Focus articulation, (ii) suggest interpretations, cf. (4) – (6), that come close to those overtly expressed by inherently asymmetric connectives like *obwohl/although, deshalb/therefore* etc., cf. (4') – (6'). Here is a briefly annotated summary of Lang's observations that have stimulated various follow-up studies.

(context): Was machen denn deine Eltern? How are your parents doing?

L*H H*L L% L*H H*L L%

(1) [[[*Mein Vater* ↗]$_T$ [*ist KRANK* ↘]$_F$ ^{IP}] ^{U}] [Ø [*meine MUtter* ↗]$_T$ [*geht ARbeiten* ↘]$_F$ ^{IP}]^U]

My dad is ill↘ my mom goes out to work\

<pure contrastive reading, 1st & 2nd conjunct can be reordered without change in interpretation>

L*H L*H H% L L*H H*L L%

(2) [[[*Mein Vater* ↗]$_T$ [*ist KRANK* ↗]$_F$ ^{IP}] [*und* [*meine MUtter* ↗]$_T$ [*geht ARbeiten* ↘]$_F$ ^{IP}]^U]

My dad is ill↗ and my mom goes out to work↘

<connected contrastive reading. L*H pitch accent at the end of the 1st conjunct obligatory>

---

[1] Ewald Lang 2001: Kontrastiv vs. implikativ: Interpretationeseffekte intonatorischer Distinktionen bei Koordination. In: A. Steube, C. Umbach (eds): Kontrast- lexikalisch, semantisch, intonatorisch. Linguistische Arbeitsberichte 77, Leipzig, 113 – 138.
Ewald Lang 2002: Kontrastiv vs. implikativ II: Intonationseffekte einer intonatorischen Distinktion bei elliptischen Sprichwörtern. In: A. Steube (ed): Sprachtheoretische Grundlagen der Kognitionswissenschaft: sprachliches und nichtsprachliches Wissen. Linguistische Arbeitsberichte 79, Leipzig, 187-212.
Ewald Lang (forthcoming): Contrasts in Grammar. Their roles, sources, and ways of realisation.

L*H L*H H% L L*H H*L L%

(3) [[[*Mein Vater* ↗$]_T$ [*ist KRANK* ↗ $]_F{}^{IP}$] [*aber* [*meine MUtter* ↗ $]_T$ [*geht ARbeiten* ↘$]_F{}^{IP}]^U$]

My dad is ill but my mom goes out to work

<contrastive reading with added adversative evaluation of the conjuncts>

L*H H H* H*L L%

(4) [*Mein Vater* [*ist KRANK* ↗ $]_F$ [*aber meine MUtter geht ARbeiten* \\$]_F{}^U$]

My dad is ill but (nevertheless) my mom goes out to work

<implicative concessive reading, 2nd conjunct via *aber* in contrast to assumed inference from 1st conjunct>

(4) has an interpretation that comes close to that in (4') with an overt concessive connective like *obwohl* 'although':

(4') Obwohl mein Vater krank ist, geht meine Mutter arbeiten.

Although my dad is ill, my mom goes out to work'

L*H H H* ↑H*L L%

(5) [*Mein Vater* [*ist KRANK* ↗ $]_F$ [*und meine MUtter geht ARbeiten* ↘ $]_F{}^U$]

My dad is ill and my mom goes out to work (= (5'))

<implicative concessive reading, 2nd conjunct via ↑H*L on VP in contrast to assumed inference from 1st conjunct>

(5) has an interpretation that comes close to that in (5') with an overt concessive connective like *dennoch* 'nevertheless':

(5') Mein Vater ist krank Dennoch geht meine Mutter arbeiten

My dad is ill. Nevertheless, my mom goes out to work.

L*H H ↑H*L L%

(6) [*Mein Vater* [*ist KRANK* /$]_F$ [*und meine MUtter* ↘ *geht arbeiten*$]_F{}^U$]

My dad is ill and my mom goes out to work

<implicative causal reading, 2nd conjunct via ↑H*L on subject in contrast to assumed inference from 1st conjunct>

(6) has an interpretation that comes close to that in (6') with an overt causal connective like *deshalb* 'therefore':

(6') Mein Vater ist krank (und) deshalb geht statt seiner meine Mutter arbeiten.

My dad is ill / (and) therefore my mom goes out to work instead

Apart from the connectives, the variants (1) – (6) do not differ in their syntax and truth conditional semantics but do differ remarkably in prosodic patterning and information structure. Following Lang, the major distinction between contrastive vs. implicative readings crucially rests on the prosodic and information structural symmetry vs. asymmetry of the conjuncts. The relevant distinctive features involved may be summarized as follows:

(1) – (3)
- Subjects marked by ↗ as contrastive Topics
- each conjunct forms an IP within the domain Utterance
- 2nd conjunct starts with low tone
- Topic-Focus articulation parallel in both conjuncts, i.e. $[[\text{Subject}]_T\ [\text{VP}]_F]$
- the meaning of 1st and 2nd conjunct interchangeably exemplify (K)

(3) – (6)
- Subjects are deaccented, form part of the Background
- no clearly marked internal IPs within the domain Utterance
- 2nd conjunct starts with high tone
- Topic-Focus articulation in the conjuncts non-parallel:
  narrow F vs. wide F in (4)
  narrow vs. emphatic contrastive F on VP in (5)
  narrow vs. emphatic contrastive F on Subject in (6)
- the meaning of 1st conjunct exemplifies (K), the meaning of the 2nd conjunct relates to an inference drawable from the 1st conjunct

Following Lang, it is the features of parallel structuring that are responsible for the "contrastive" reading in (1) – (3), whereas those of non-parallel structure induce "implicative" readings in (4) – (6), readings which are comparable to those otherwise induced by explicit asymmetric connectives like *obwohl/although, dennoch/nevertheless* or *deshalb/therefore,* cf. in (4') – (6'). What we observe here is a kind of compensatory trade-off between syntax/semantics and contextualized prosody and information structure. The connectives involved determine the way the conjuncts are related to (K) in terms of Discourse Linking. While ø , based on parallel-structured conjuncts, signals just exemplification (1), *und/and* cover a broader range of connections (2, 5, 6), depending on the prosodic make-up of the conjuncts. (3, 4) show the conditions on which *aber/but* may induce either adversativity (3) or concession (4).

Other researchers in the group, notably Carla Umbach, Marcela Adamíková, and Dorothee Fehrmann take up and modify Ewald Lang's approach. **Carla Umbach** herself[2] presents a different semantic explanation of *aber/but* which

[2] Cf. also Ewald Lang, Carla Umbach 2002: Kontrast in der Grammatik: spezifische Realisierungen und übergreifender Konnex. In: A. Steube (ed): Sprachtheoretische Grundlagen der Kognitionswissenschaft: Sprachliches und nichtsprachliches Wissen. Linguistische Arbeitsberichte 79, Leipzig, 145-186, and Ewald Lang 2004: Schnittstellen bei der Konnektoren-Beschreibung. In:

has also been made use of in this volume: (i) The contrast evoked by *aber/but* relates to the alternatives evoked by focus. (ii) An *aber/but*–sentence comprises a confirmation and a denial with respect to an explicit question referring to the alternatives under discussion. The meaning of *aber/but* can be characterized as both additive and excluding.

(7) Adam: *Did John clean up his room and wash the dishes?*

(8) Ben: *Bill cleaned up his room, but he didn't wash the dishes.*

There is no clear separation of contrast in the sense of adversativity and of concession. The concessive interpretation is induced by causal overinterpretation (which, due to the inherent negation of *aber/but,* results in incausativity, i.e. concession). (9) can be interpreted as (10).

(9) *It is raining but Mary is happy.*

(10) *It is raining but it is not the case that Mary is not happy because if that.*

Whereas in Lang's account prosodic symmetry of conjuncts is coupled with adversative and asymmetry with concessive readings, the account of Umbach 2002 and Umbach et al. in this volume sees concessive readings in all of these cases. Still, both Lang and Umbach predict that symmetric and asymmetric cases differ in intonation. **Carla Umbach, Ina Mleinek, Christine Lehmann, Thomas Weskott, Kai Alter, and Anita Steube** examine *aber/but* sentences along the lines of Lang in order to see whether his clear predictions concerning intonational patternings can be verified. Umbach et al. conduct a speech production experiment accompanied by acoustic analyses and perceptual evaluation. The acoustic analysis of the production study illustrate that in German a prosodic distinction between the adversative and the concessive versions in Lang's hypothesis could not be verified. The perceptive evaluation of the experiment did not give decisive insights either, so that a more sophisticated experimental design will be needed to test Lang's and Umbach's prosodic hypotheses.

Marcela Adamíková and Dorothee Fehrmann have been concerned with the adversative conjunction *ale* (engl. *but*) in Polish, Czech and Slovak. In her paper, **Dorothee Fehrmann** comes to the conclusion that the Polish conjunction *ale* is lexically and syntactically underspecified and thus covers interpretations that in other languages are associated with distinct connectives. Thus, *ale* may either indicate CONTRAST (adversativity) like German *aber* (English *but*) without deletion of the non-focussed material, cf. (11a), or else – in con-

H. Blühdorn et al. (eds.): Brücken schlagen. Grundlagen der Konnektoren-Semantik. Berlin-New York: de Gruyter (in press).

struction with negation – CORRECTION like German *sondern* or English *but* with obligatory deletion (cf. (11b)).

(11a): (Context suggesting a CONTRAST reading)

A: *How are you getting to the station?*

B: *Peter is taking me there.*

A: *Really? But he hasn't got a car!*

B: *Piotr nie ma samochodu, ale motocykl.*

'Peter hasn't got a car, but he's got a motorbike.

(11b): (Context suggesting a CORRECTION reading)

A: *Peter has a new Honda.*

B: *Really? Peter's got a new car?*

A: *Listen, dad.*

Piotr nie ma samochodu, ale motocykl.

'Peter hasn't got a car, but a motorbike'.

The Polish data under review have a sentence negation in the first conjunct and an elliptic second conjunct. The aim of the paper was to look for prosodic features that might indicate the CONTRAST/CORRECTION distinction. Fehrmann's experiments so far did not show intonation contours that would clearly distinguish the two readings of *ale*. Instead, she found a default continuative intonation contour in Polish. Markers indicating IP boundaries between the two conjuncts were mostly missing. There are two pitch accents in the first conjunct. In the CONTRAST context the one on the XP was slightly more prominent than the one on $[_{Neg^\circ}$ Neg° V°], whereas in the CORRECTION context the prominence marking was mostly the other way round. So far, neither the German intonation contours (with two separate conjunctions *aber, sondern,* (see Umbach et al.) nor the Polish ones show the expected parallelisms. But further research is needed in both languages.

More promising results concerning the problem illustrated by ambiguous data like (11) have been offered by **Marcela Adamíková** (2004). Based on production and perception experiments with native speakers of Slovak, Czech, and Polish, Adamíková investigates the full range of prosodic variations associated with data sets like (11). She takes into account the multifarious role of Negation (Foreground ~ vs. Background ~, focussing ~ vs. non-focussing ~ , sentence ~ vs. replacive ~) as well as the ways in which Focus assignment interacts with the scope of certain operators. Based on this, Adamíková singles out prosodic factors that actually distinguish CONTRAST vs. CORRECTION readings with data like (11) by showing that prosodic disambiguation takes place within the 1st conjunct, which contains the negation operator (normally prefixed to the finite verb). We illustrate two of the relevant patterns A, B by means of the annotated Slovak data in (12a – b):

(12) (Context: Your husband plans to open a haulage firm. Does he at least have a car?)

!H* L% H (L+)H* L%

a. *Môj muž* [***ne****-má*]F_{ASS} *auto* ↘. *Ale má* [***motorku***]F_{ASS}

'My husband does not have a car. But he has a motor cycle.' < CONTRAST >

Pattern A
- non-focussing wide-scope negation
- low boundary tone (↘) at the end of 1st conjunct
- intonational break between the conjuncts

(12) (Context: I am sure your husband has a car. – You are wrong.)

L+H* L*H H (L+)H* L%

b. *Môj muž* [***ne****-má*]F_{ASS} [*auto*]F_{NEG}, *ale má* [***motorku***]F_{ASS}

'My husband doesn't have a car but a motor cycle' < CORRECTION >

Pattern B
- focussing narrow scope negation
- high phrasal tone at the end of the 1st conjunct
- no intonational break between the conjuncts

Hence the prosodic differentiation of CONTRAST (12a) vs. CORRECTION (12b) readings is shown to correlate with differences in negation scope, focus assignment, and falling or raising tones at the end of the 1st conjunct. Though concerning a facet of adversativity that differs from the one illustrated by (1) – (6) above, Adamíková's work is on par with Lang's approach in showing that lacking lexical and/or syntactic distinctions can, to a certain extend, be compensated by prosodic patterns.

I warmly thank all those who helped to evaluate the results of the information structure projects in the research group. First it is the experts of the German Research Foundation who evaluated the projects and their outcomes several times and stimulated the interactive efforts of the group. It is the atmosphere of an ongoing lively discussion which the papers presented here have grown out of. There are at least four different weekly colloquia in Leipzig in cooperation with the Graduiertenkolleg "Universality and Differentiality: Linguistic Structures and Processes"; there were the national and international workshops in Leipzig, Berlin, and Lund, and the e-mail based discussions with partners who also commented on the papers of doctoral and habilitation candidates.

I also thank Kai Alter and Uwe Junghanns for special comments on this volume. Sebastian Hellman did the layout, and Stefan Sudhoff and Andreas Späth took care of further technical details. My warmest thanks also for their cooperation and for Rachel Grenon's efforts to bring the different stages of

English into a homogeneous form. Last but not least I want to thank the Publishing House Walter de Gruyter for initiating the series "Language, Context and Cognition" just at this time.

Leipzig, July 2004 Anita Steube

Books of the research group and of its associated scholars since 2000

Marcela Adamíková 2004: KONTRAST oder KORREKTUR? Prosodische Disambiguierung bei negationshaltigen Adversativkonstruktionen in den Westslavinen. Phil. Diss., Humboldt-University Berlin

Kai Alter 2002: Prosodie zwischen Sprachproduktion und –perzeption. Habilitation Thesis, University Leipzig

Irene Balles 2004: Die altindische Cvi-Konstruktion. Form, Funktion, Ursprung. Phil. Diss., Friedrich-Schiller University Jena

Nicole Dehé 2002: Particle Verbs in English. Syntax, Information Structure, and Intonation. In: Linguistik Aktuell /Linguistics Today 59. Amsterdam, Philadelphia: John Benjamins

Johannes Dölling, Thomas Pechmann (eds): Prosodie – Struktur – Interpretation. Linguistische Arbeitsberichte 74, Leipzig 2000, 306 p.

Johannes Dölling 2001: Systematische Bedeutungsvariationen: Semantische Form und kontextuelle Interpretation. Linguistische Arbeitsberichte 78, Leipzig, 252 p.

Johannes Dölling, Tatjana Zybatow (eds.): Ereignisstrukturen. Linguistische Arbeitsberichte 76. Leipzig 2001, 218 p.

Uwe Junghanns 2002: Untersuchungen zur Syntax und Informationsstruktur slawischer Deklarativsätze. Linguistische Arbeitsberichte 80, Leipzig, 193 p.

Grit Mehlhorn 2002: Kontrastierte Konstituenten im Russischen: Experimentelle Untersuchungen zur Informationsstruktur. Frankfurt/M.: Peter Lang

Sandra Muckel 2002: Wortstellungseffekte beim Satzverstehen: zur Rolle syntaktischer, lexikalischer und prosodischer Informationen. Wiesbaden: Deutscher Universitätsverlag

Andreas Späth 2004: Determination im Satzkontext. Grammatische Voraussetzungen der Nominalreferenz in den artikellosen slawischen Sprachen im Vergleich zum Deutschen. Habilitation Thesis, University of Leipzig

Anita Steube und Carla Umbach (eds): Kontrast – lexikalisch, semantisch, intonatorisch. Linguistische Arbeitsberichte 77, Leipzig 2001, 219 p.

Anita Steube (ed.): Sprachtheoretische Grundlagen der Kognitionswissenschaft: Sprachliches und nichtsprachliches Wissen. Linguistische Arbeitsberichte 79, Leipzig 2002, 325 p.

Luka Szucsich 2002: Nominale Adverbiale im Russischen. Syntax, Semantik und Informationsstruktur. München: Otto Sager

Martin Trautwein 2003: The Time Window of Language: The Interaction between Linguistic and Non-linguistic Knowledge in the Temporal Interpretation of German and English Texts. Phil. Diss., University Leipzig

Valja Werkmann 2003: Objektklitika im Bulgarischen. studia grammatica 57 Berlin: Akademie Verlag

Thomas Weskott 2002: The Left Periphery of German Verb-Second Sentences and its Interpretation in Context. Phil. Diss., Leipzig 2003

Tatjana Zybatow 2001: Grammatische Determinatoren von Zeit- und Sachverhaltsverlauf im Deutschen. Phil. Diss., University Leipzig

Eva Hajičová and Petr Sgall (Prague)

Degrees of Contrast and the Topic-Focus Articulation

1 Introduction

The aim of the present contribution is to present several hypotheses that may help to characterize and identify contrast as such and degrees of its intensity, and to point out how the phenomena connected with contrast can be handled in a descriptive framework that uses a dependency based syntax and includes a description of the topic-focus articulation (TFA) as one of the aspects of the underlying sentence structure. We also illustrate how the chosen descriptive framework is tested in a syntactic annotation of a large corpus. First we examine the chosen description of TFA (Section 1), then the means of expression of contrast are discussed (Section 2), as well as issues of contrast in focus (Section 3), and especially in topic (Section 4).

2 Topic-focus articulation

2.1 Topic, focus, and contextual boundness in a linguistic description

In the theoretical framework of the Praguian Functional Generative Description (FGD, see Sgall et al. 1986, Hajičová et al. 1998), the semantic basis of the articulation of the sentence into **T**(opic) and **F**(ocus) is understood as the relation of **aboutness**: a prototypical declarative sentence asserts that its F holds (or, with negation, does not hold) about its T. Thus, the core of the semantico-pragmatic interpretation of a declarative sentence might be based on a formula such as F(T) or, for a negative sentence, as non-F(T), if for the aim of the present discussion issues such as those of intension, lambda calculus and type theory are put aside. Within both T and F, an opposition of **contextually bound (CB)** and **non-bound (NB)** nodes is distinguished, which is understood as a grammatically patterned opposition, rather than in the literal sense of the term. In the underlying left-to-right order, NB dependents follow and CB dependents precede their heads.

In unmarked cases, the main verb (V) and those of its direct dependents that on the surface follow it belong to F, and the items preceding V are parts of T.

In marked (non-prototypical) cases, V can be CB, i.e. in T, or (a part of) F may precede V; usually the intonation centre (sentence stress) then marks F, occupying a marked position. The dependents of nouns primarily are NB.

Let us illustrate this view with a typical example (we understand the intonation center, in the prototypical case expressed by a falling pitch, to be placed at the end of the sentence; in other, marked positions it is denoted by capitals (which we use also in some other cases, to avoid a possible misunderstanding); let us recall that, in our underlying representations, the counterparts of function words are just indices of node labels, not occupying independent syntactic positions:

(1) My.t brother.t was visiting.t/f one.f of his.t friends.f yesterday.t.
focus: (*was visiting*) *one of his friends* (intonation center on *friends*)

Here and in the sequel, t denotes a CB item, f denotes a NB one, and c is used to denote a contrastive CB item.

The verb in (1) is ambiguous in that it is NB (and thus a part of F) on one reading and CB (a part of T) on another; while the former is an appropriate "full" answer to (2), the latter answers (3).

(2) What was your brother DOING yesterday?

(3) Whom was your brother VISITING yesterday?

This view, the motivation of which has been published several times, makes it possible to analyze similar sentences (with an ambiguous part that may contain other words, not only verbs) with a **single opposition** of T and F. Thus the discrepancy between the single relationship of aboutness and two dichotomies assumed to constitute the information structure (e.g. by Junghanns and Zybatow 1997, ex. (2), p. 290) can be avoided and the T-F articulation (TFA) of the sentence can be assigned a specific position within the system of language (de Saussure's *langue*, Chomsky's *linguistic competence*), namely that of one of the basic aspects of the underlying, **tectogrammatical** representations of sentences (TRs). No separate level of information structure is needed.

The TRs contain no nonterminal symbols; each of their nodes is labelled by a complex symbol composed of a **lexical** and a **morphological** part (values of morphological categories such as number, tense, modalities), and each edge is labelled by the symbol indicating a **syntactic** relation (i.e. the type of the dependency relation).

2.2 TFA and contrast in a large corpus

The approach of FGD makes it possible to capture TFA and contrast in sentences of various degrees of complexity. The chosen descriptive framework, FGD, is being checked with examples taken from the **syntactically annotated Prague Dependency Treebank** (PDT), in which sentences from running text, from the Czech National Corpus (CNC, which contains hundreds of millions of word occurrences in journalistic fiction and other texts) are analyzed by a semi-automatic procedure.

In the PDT scenario, three layers of annotation are present, with TFA and contrast being represented (together with underlying dependency relations) on the underlying syntactic level. The resulting sentence representations have the form of tectogrammatical tree structures (TGTSs), with the following characteristic properties:

(a) only autosemantic words are represented as separate nodes, with the exception of the coordinating conjunctions (in this point, TGTSs differ from the theoretically based TRs),
(b) nodes deleted on the surface are restored,
(c) the condition of projectivity is met (i.e. no discontinuity of sentence parts is allowed),
(d) tectogrammatical functions ('functors'), i.e. kinds of the dependency relation such as (i) arguments: Actor/Bearer, Patient, Addressee, Origin, Effect and (ii) different kinds of adjuncts (temporal, local, condition, manner, etc.) are assigned as labels of the edges of the tree (or, equivalently, as indices in the labels of the dependents),
(e) basic features of TFA are introduced (f, t, c, see Sect. 1.1 above).

Let us note that in the present experimental phase, 2000 sentences have been annotated in what concerns their underlying syntactic structure itself (‘**large** collection‘), with only 200 sentences having been annotated in full detail (the so-called ‘**model** collection‘), and the annotations of 2000 sentences contain a treatment of TFA).

In the sequel, after a more general discussion of the phenomena of contrast, the checking of our descriptive framework on the material from PDT is illustrated by the Czech examples (30), (31), (33) and (34).

3 The means of expression of contrast

Several typical means of expression of contrast can be distinguished:
(i) E.g. in Czech, **strong pronominal forms** are used with certain pronouns; the typical cases of opposition of weak and strong forms are:

Czech *ho – jeho* 'him-Gen,Acc', *mu – jemu* 'him-Dat',
tě – tebe 'you-Gen,Acc', *ti – tobě* 'you-Dat',
se – sebe 'Refl.Gen,Acc', *si – sobě* 'Refl.Dat'.

The strong forms are used to express NB pronominal forms, or CB contrastive forms as *ona* and *jeho* in (4)(a), respectively; they are also used in prepositional case forms and in coordination, cf. *tebe* in (5) and *tobě* in (6).

(4) (a) (Petr ji nazval konzervativcem.) Potom.t jeho.c urazila.t ona.f.
(Petr called her a conservative). Then him insulted she.
Then he was insulted by HER.
(b) (Petr ji nazval konzervativcem.) Potom.t ho.t opustila.f.
(Petr called her a conservative.) The she LEFT him.

(5) Na tebe jsem se celý týden těšil.
for you I-have-been Refl (the) whole week looking-forward
I have been looking FORWARD to you for the whole week.

(6) Tobě nebo Martinovi to pošlu zítra.
to-you or to-Martin it I-will-send tomorrow
I will send it to you or to Martin tomorrow.

The corresponding weak ("short") forms are used only as CB, without contrast, cf. *ho* in (4)(b); it should be noted that Czech, a pro-drop language, has a zero form in the Nominative of all the personal pronouns, which occurs as their weak form (this is the case of the counterpart of *she* in (4)(b) or of *I* in (5) and (6)), although the „strong" forms *já, ty, on, my*, etc., may also occur without contrastive function, esp. in colloquial speech.

In German, English and many other languages (and also in Czech with pronominal forms such as *je* 'them.Acc', *ji* 'her.Acc'), only an opposition of accented and unaccented forms is present as expressing that of contrastive (and NB) vs. non-contrastive use.

Following up Koktová's (1999) observation that weak forms of pronouns in Czech cannot be used in certain positions in T, we use the opposition of strong and weak personal pronouns as an **operational test** for the contrastive use in T. Thus, *jeho* in (4)(a) is contrasted with *she*; there is no such contrast in (b). However, the application of this test is limited, since not only in coordination or with a preposition, but also when used as NB, in **focus**, is the pronominal form similar to that expressing a contrastive (part of) topic (marked with c), as is the case of *ona* in (4)(a), and also of *jeho* in (7)(b):

(7) (a) Jeho.c jsme viděli včera.f. – Him we saw yesterday.
(b) Včera.c jsme viděli jeho.f – Yesterday we saw HIM.

(ii) Rising stress (or, perhaps, falling-rising), having the form of L^*H, falls – perhaps optionally – on a contrastive (part of) topic in examples such as *jeho* in (7)(a) or *včera* in (7)(b); cf. also *jeho* in (4)(a). In the sequel we indicate such a "phrasal" or contrastive stress by italics. It would be interesting to check to what extent such examples can be characterized as bearing a **hat contour**, and under which conditions the hat contour can be taken as a criterion for contrastive T.

Steube (2001) examines similar examples in relation to the concept of I-topic, cf. also Jacobs (1997). Specific pragmatic properties accompany such accentuation at least in German (bound with specific illocutionary types and scope effects). If observations of this kind are valid for other languages as well, this would be significant for a further analysis of relationships between TFA, contrast, illocution and scopes of operators (now cf. also Umbach (2001). It would be important to also check examples such as the following, known from preceding dicussions:

(8) An *American*.c farmer met a CANADIAN.f farmer.

However, it has to be noticed that such (or a similar) rising stress (marked by italics) is also used for an **open continuation** in various cases:

(a) This stress can occur in the middle of a longer sentence (without contrast, marking the ends of certain segments):

(9) Naši mladší kolegové, kteří nedávno *dostudovali*, dokončují své disertace.
Our younger colleagues, who recently finished-studies, are-completing their dissertations.

Perhaps this is the case also in coordinated clauses, e.g. in some languages, cf. the Slovak ex. given here as (10) (presented by Adamíková and Fehrmann 2001 without distinguishing the two kinds of accentuation, the presence of which we would assume):

(10) Robert nie je HLÚpy, ale LEnivý. – Robert is not stupid, but lazy.

Slovak is far from isolated in such issues. Not only is the situation in Czech similar, but, e.g., also the English equivalent sentence can probably be pronounced as given in (11):

(11) Robert is not *stupid*, but LAZY.

It would be difficult to speak of hat acccentuation in such examples. Rather, we would understand them as cases in which the two kinds of accent express the focus (an NB item), since it is often supposed (appropriately, as we are convinced) that each of the coordinated clauses in a compound sentence has its own TFA. The NB value of the rising stress in a non-final clause under coordination might then be understood as being marked, non-prototypical.

(b) Rising stress also occurs at the end of the sentence, similarly as with a yes/no question:

(12) Here are my *documents*... (... is there everything you are looking for in them?)

We differ from M. Steedman (2000), who has analyzed such sentences, in understanding this kind of stress (often indicated by „..." and having something in common with the intonation prototypically marked by a semicolon) as expressing **focus**, although a marked means of expression is used in such cases.

4 Contrast in focus

Focus as such has been characterized as a choice from **a set of alternatives**, esp. by M. Rooth (1985). This can only be understood so that F as such has a contrastive value. It might be claimed that if a sentence contains a single contrastive item, then this item constitutes the F. Only if more than one contrastive item is present, are they distributed among T and F. Thus, while a single contrast may be seen in sentences such as (13), both *Mike* and *Mary* are contrastive in (14).

(13) Mike met Mary.

(14) (Jim and Mike were looking for their classmates.)
Mike met MARY.
(*Jim* found ROBIN.)

This would mean that every F is contrastive. However, esp. in German studies, linguists often distinguish between contrastive and non-contrastive focus; perhaps it would be more exact to speak about two degrees of contrast, which are distinguished by the structure of German, as the following observations indicate:

Sentences such as (15) are appropriate only for contexts which can be characterized by questions similar to (17), rather than by (18), i.e. in (15) *das Buch* is contrastive. On the other hand, (16) is acceptable both after (19) and (20), i.e. in (16) *Schüler* is either contrastive or not; cf. e.g. (in the framework of Optimality Theory) Hye-Won Choi (1996), discussed in Hajičová (2000).

(15) Hans hat das BUCH dem Schüler gegeben .
Lit.: Hans has the BOOK to the student given.

(16) Hans hat dem SCHÜLER das Buch gegeben .
Lit.: Hans has to the STUDENT the book given.

(17) Hat Hans dem Schüler das Buch oder das Bild gegeben?
Lit.: Has Hans to the student the book or the picture given?

(18) Was hat Hans dem Schüler gegeben?
Lit.: What has Hans to student given?

(19) Hat Hans das Buch dem Schüler oder dem Lehrer gegeben?
Lit.: Hans has the book to the student or to the teacher given?

(20) Wem hat Hans das Buch gegeben?
Lit.: Who has Hans the book given?

It seems that in Czech it is quite possible to use (15) as well as (16) as an answer to (17); this would mean that in Czech contrastive (part of) F does not constitute a specific grammatical value. It would than be interesting to investigate what the situation in English and in other languages is.

5 Contrast in topic (on a CB item)

Hajičová et al. (1998, 151) introduce the notion of **contrastive (part of) T** in connection with the occurrences of the so-called focusing particles in T, cf. (21):

(21) (Who criticized even MOTHER TERESA as a tool of the capitalists?) JOHN criticized even Mother Theresa as a tool of the capitalists.

To see how our criterion with the use of strong pronominal forms works, cf. a parallel Czech sentence with a corresponding noun of the masculine gender, (22). Note that the wording with the weak pronominal form is excluded: **I ho kritizoval Martin.*

(22) (Kdo kritizoval i PAPEŽE jako nástroj kapitalismu?) I *jeho* kritizoval MARTIN. (Who criticized even the POPE as a tool of the capitalists?) MARTIN criticized even *him*.

The notion of contrastive T, however, should not be restricted to cases with focalizers, as we have seen with (4)(a), and as (23) confirms (with (23') as its simplified underlying representation).

(23) (Mluví se česky v Česku nebo na Slovensku?) *Česky* se mluví v ČESKU, *na Slovensku* se mluví SLOVENSKY. (Is Czech spoken in Czechia or in Slovakia?) Czech is spoken in Czechia, (while) in Slovakia, SLOVAK is spoken.

(23') Česky.*t* se-mluví.*t* v-Česku.*f*, na-Slovensku.*c* se-mluví.*t* slovensky.*f*.

Let us note that (23) is a compound sentence, in which each of the coordinated clauses exhibits its own TFA; *Česky*, as a part of the topic of the first conjunct, is contrasted as being chosen from the set of the two languages, and, in the second conjunct, *na-Slovensku* is contrasted with the focus part of the first conjunct.

It is possible to find two contrastive parts in T of a sentence:

(24) (Rodiče odjeli na dovolenou a děti svěřili příbuzným.) *Syna*.c ve *čtvrtek*.c zavezli.f DO PARDUBIC.f, a *dceru*.c *v sobotu*.c DO HRADCE.f

Lit.: (The parents left for a vacation and entrusted their children to their relatives.) Their *son* on *Thursday* they-brought to P. and their *daughter* on *Saturday* to H.

(25) (Včerejší utkání bylo dramatické.) Po *gólu*.c SIEGLA.f se *Sparta*.c už.f ve třetí.f minutě.f dostala.f hladce.f DO VEDENÍ.f.

Lit.: (Yesterday's match was dramatic.) After *goal* SIEGL'S *Sparta* already in the third minute got smoothly in the LEAD.

If the **degrees** of intensity of contrast are examined, it is possible to see that different dimensions are to be distinguished:

A. The **narrower** F is, the stronger the contrast:

The highest degree of contrast can be seen in the cases of **correction**, cf. Steube (2002). It may be asked whether correction differs from "second instance," as discussed for a long time especially in Czech linguistics. Another question is whether there are sentences occurring only as corrections; as was discussed already in Sgall et al. (1973, 36f), this may concern sentences with stressed items that cannot bear regular stress. However, at least in Czech, two degrees have to be distinguished:

(i) endings or affixes can only bear stress in corrections:

(26) He carried out the analySES (not just one analysis).

(27) Er sagt er hätte die Nachricht ERfasst, nicht VERfasst.

(ii) function words may bear stress not only in corrections, but also as constituting a narrow focus; thus, in (28), the tense value is in F, everything else belongs to T:

(28) Er WIRD das tun.
Lit.: He WILL do it.

Such an extremely **narrow F** can be seen as bearing a strong contrast.

B. The **set of alternatives** underlying the contrast in T is conditioned by various factors, both cotextual and contextual (situational). A scale (or a partial ordering) concerning the **explicitness** of the set of alternatives underlying the contrast, which appears to be weaker in case the set is not delimited explicitly.

The set of alternatives is **explicitly** enumerated:

(29) (Jakým jazykem se mluví v Rakousku a jakým na Moravě?) *V Rakousku*.c se mluví.t NĚMECKY.f, *na Moravě*.c se mluví.t ČESKY.f.
(Which language is spoken in Austria and which in Moravia?)
In Austria, GERMAN is spoken, *in Moravia*, CZECH is spoken.

The following relevant examples have been found in a set of sentence sequences from running texts in the Prague Dependency Treebank (PDT, see Sect. 1.2 above), examined by K. Veselá:

(30) (Včera se hrál zápas mezi Brnem a Ostravou.) Ze začátku.b se dařilo.f DOMÁCÍM.f. *Hosté*.c se začali.f prosazovat.f až.f ve DRUHÉM.f POLOČASE.f. – (Yesterday, the match between B. and O. took place.) At the beginning, the LOCAL TEAM was successful. The *guests* started to succeed only in the SECOND HALF.

In (30), the set of alternatives is clearly delimited. However, the contrast is felt even stronger in case the sentences (clauses) are structured as parallel:

(31) *Domácím*.c se dařilo.f ZE ZAČÁTKU.f. *Hostům*.c se povedl.f až.f DRUHÝ.f. POLOČAS.f. – *The local team* was successful AT THE BEGINNING. The *guests* succeeded only in the SECOND HALF.

In other cases, the alternatives are not quite clearly delimited, being determined just by the **set** being referred to:

(32) (Terry has many friends.) My.t *brother*.c is.f one.f of his.t closest.f SCHOOLMATES.f.

There is also a possibility for the alternatives to stay **implicit**, just inferred from context. This can be illustrated by two subsequent sentences from PDT (from a newspaper article describing the feelings of the journalists when they saw and tested a new type of Toyota car, which was supposed to be suitable both for driving on roads and on the terrain):

(33) Už.f první.c pohled.t na atypickou.f karosérii.f potvrzuje.f, že se jim.t jejich.t
Lit. Already first glance at atypical body confirms that Refl. them their
zámĕr.t podařilo.f naplnit.f.
intention managed to-accomplish

Already the first glance at the atypical body confirms that they managed to accomplish their intention.

(34) Pro pohon.c byl zvolen.f dvoulitrový.f motor.f osvĕdčený.f v Toyotĕ.f. Cari.f. E.f ...
Lit. For drive was chosen two-liter engine well-tried with Toyota Cari E ...

As for the drive, a two-liter engine was chosen well-tried with Toyota Cari E. In (33), *první* 'first' is chosen among different possible steps of observation (more or less thorough); in (34), *pohon* 'drive' is chosen among the attributes of the car.

C. A third dimension concerns the **range** of the set: it may be a (i) **pair** – cf. (4), (23), (29), (30), (31) above, – which is connected with a relatively strong contrast, or (ii) **larger** – cf. (32) above, – with a weaker contrast, or (iii) it has a **single** member, as is the case in the following cases:

(i) the contrastive item is coreferential with an item of the F of the preceding utterance, rather than with one of its T, i.e. a "new T" is present; it seems that the opposition between "new" and "old" T (i.e. between a (part of the) T that has not occurred in the T in the preceding co-text and a (part of the) T that has, respectively, comes close to the opposition of T proper and temporal or local setting):

(35) (Kde se mluví česky?) Česky.c se mluví.t v Česku.f.
(Where is Czech spoken?) Czech is spoken in Czechia.

(ii) cases with a focusing particle in T, as in (21) above,

(iii) the contrast is being newly established, as in (36), in which *já* 'I' is presented as being in contrast to other individuals.

(36) Přiznám.f se, že já.c osobnĕ.f to.t dost.f prožívám.f.
Lit.: I-admit that I personally it quite live-through.
I admit that I personally live through this quite intensely.

To be more exact, we should note that in example (36) the contrastive item is not in T, but, rather, it is a **CB item in F**. Typically, CB items stand in T while NB ones are in F; however, elements deeply embedded (i.e. dependent on an item that differs from the main verb) may occur as NB (contrastive or not) items within T, or as CB items in F of the whole sentence. In (36), the subject of the main clause, having a zero form, is CB and constitutes the T (the values of its grammatemes are expressed, on the morphemic level, by the agreeing personal ending of the verb). The verb together with the embedded clause constitute the F. The subject of this clause, expressed by the pronoun in its strong form, is a contrastive CB item, and together with the CB pronoun *to* 'it' it belongs to the F, since both the pronouns depend on an item in Focus different from the main verb (namely on the embedded verb).

If the patterning of a discourse is examined taking into account the TFA of the subsequent sentences, then the **prototypical** case may be found in those sequences of two sentences S_0 and S_1 in which the T of S_1 is referentially identical to T of S_0, and the F of S_1 is chosen among the alternatives of what can be asserted about T; cf. Weil's (1844) *la marche parallèle,* and Daneš's (1974) first alternative of 'thematic progression', $T_2 = T_1$.

In **marked** cases, there are the following possibilities for the choice of T_1 :

(a) associative relations with accommodation are present, rather than the referential identity of T_0 and T_1,

(b) T_2 is coreferential with F1, rather than to T1 (Weil's *progression,* Daneš's $\mathbf{T_2 = F_1}$,

(c) T_1 is chosen from another part of the set of established items than from those referred to in S_0 or from those associated with these referents.

While case (a) is directly related to the protoypical situation, in cases (b) and (c) T_1 is **chosen** from a set of alternatives, i.e. a may be seen as a contrastive item. Since T may include more than one item, it is more precise to speak of **CB items.**

Thus, often also (a part of the) topic can be considered as a choice from a set of alternatives (cf. Steedman's 2002 'theme alternative set', with 'theme' marked by the L+H* pitch accent, cf. R. Jackendoff's 'B contour'). It should be noted that in a compound sentence the focus stress (intonation centre) in the non-final coordinated clause(s) primarily is rising, rather than falling. A similar kind of pitch probably can be observed in the middle of longer sentences of other types, without expressing focus or even contrast, see Sect. 1.2.(ii) above.

Other interesting examples, known from older discussions without such an interpretation, were analyzed as containing a contrastive (part of) T by Hajičová et al. (1998, 155-157):

(37) Farmers.t that.t grow.c rice.t often.t only.f eat.f rice.c.

Here the focusing particle *only* is connected with the CB occurrence of *rice* at the end of the sentence, and a hat contour (rising pitch on *grow*) is present.

(38) (Niemand liest Goethes Gedichte heute.)
Sogar.f Peter.f kennt.t nur.f einen Roman.c von Goethe.t.
Lit.: (Nobody reads Goethe's poems nowadays.) Even Peter knows only a novel by Goethe.

6 Conclusion

The view presented and illustrated in the present paper makes it possible to analyze the information structure of sentences with the use of a **single opposition** of T and F, if also the difference between contextually bound and non-bound items is observed, as well as that between contrastive and non-contrastive items in T. Thus the discrepancy between the single relationship of **aboutness** and two dichotomies often assumed to constitute the information structure can be avoided and the T-F articulation of the sentence can be assigned a specific position within the system of language, namely that of one of the basic aspects of the underlying, **tectogrammatical** representations of sentences. No separate level of information structure is needed.

7 References

Adamíková, M. and D. Fehrmann (2001): Prosodische Differenzierung von Kontrast- und Korrekturkonstruktionen im Slovakischen und Polnischen. Linguistische Arbeitsberichte 77, Leipzig, 81-112.

Daneš, F. (1974): Functional sentence perspective and the organization of the text. In: F. Daneš (ed): Papers on Functional sentence perspective. Prague: Academia (1974), 106-128.

Hajičová, E. (2000): Teorie optimality a aktuální členění věty [Optimality theory and the topic-focus articulation]. Slovo a slovesnost 61, 161-169.

Hajičová, E., B. H. Partee, and P. Sgall (1998): Topic-focus articulation, tripartite structures, and semantic content. Dordrecht: Kluwer.

Hye-Won, C. (1996): Optimizing structure in context: Scrambling and information structure. PhD Thesis. Stanford University.

Jacobs, J. (1997): I-Topikalisierung. Linguistische Berichte 168, 91-133.

Junghanns, U. and G. Zybatow (1997): Syntax and information structure of Russian clauses. In: E. W. Browne, E. Dornisch, N. Kondrashova, and D. Zec (eds): Annual Workshop on Formal Approaches to Slavic Linguistics. The Cornell Meeting 1995. Ann Arbor, Mi : Michigan Slavic Publications.

Koktová, E. (1999): Word-order based grammar. Berlin/New York: Mouton de Gruyter. Pražský závislostní korpus [Prague Dependency Treebank] (2001): http://ufal.mff.cuni.cz/pdt .

Rooth, M. (1985): Association with focus. PhD. dissertation. University of Massachusetts, Amherst.

Sgall, P., E. Hajičová, and E. Benešová (1973): Topic, focus and Generative semantics. Kronberg/Taunus:Scriptor.

Sgall, P., E. Hajičová, and J. Panevová (1986): In: J. L. Mey (ed): The Meaning of the Sentence in its Semantic and Pragmatic Aspects, Dordrecht: Reidel - Prague: Academia.

Steedman, M. (2000): Information structure and the syntax-phonology interface. Linguistic Inquiry 31, 649-689.

Steedman, M. (2002): The surface grammar of intonation and information structure. Paper delivered at the workshop on Contrast and Information Structure, Leipzig, February 2002.

Steube, A. (2001): Grammatik und Pragmatik von Hutkonturen. Linguistische Arbeitsberichte 77, Leipzig, 7-30.

Steube, A. (2002): Correction by contrastive focus. In: Theoretical Linguistics 27, 2-3, 215-49.

Umbach, C. (2001): Restriktion der Alternativen. Linguistische Arbeitsberichte 77, Leipzig, 165-198.

Weil H. (1844): De l'ordre des mots dans les langues anciennes comparées aux langues modernes. Paris. Translated as The order of words in the ancient languages compared with that of the modern languages. Boston 1887, reedited in Amsterdam: Benjamins 1978.

* **Acknowledgement**. The work reported on in this paper has been carried out under the project GAČR 405/03/0377 and the project of the Czech Ministry of Education LN00A063.

Anita Steube, Kai Alter, and Andreas Späth (Leipzig)

Information Structure and Modular Grammar

1 Information Structure and its pragmatic categories

Isolated grammatically correct sentences do not fulfill the pragmatic functions that sentences in coherent texts of certain types and subtypes do. It is information structure that selects the grammatical forms and constructions that embed sentences in a text. As far as known nowadays this is achieved by two pairs of pragmatic categories: the background–focus~ and the topic–comment partitions. By means of the background–focus partition, a sequence of sentences becomes coherent by the phenomenon that the subsequent sentences are anaphorically enchained with the ones preceding them. By means of the topic–comment partition, longer texts are subdivided into paragraphs each dealing with one object or event. At the same time, the realization of topics can e.g. characterize the subtype of a narrative text, such as a tale versus a news report.

All four pragmatic categories must be realized by grammatical means in order to get expressed. However, languages also differ in the grammatical level and structure of expression as a function of language specificity. It is thus not enough to give exclusively pragmatic definitions of the information structural categories. We must also know how the corresponding language maps them on its grammatical forms and their combinations. Hypothesizing that pragmatic definitions are universally comparable, their mappings on the grammatical forms and structures will not only differ from language to language but will even depend on the theory of grammar used.

Background Constituents express familiar information belonging to the common ground of both the speaker and the hearer. It has either been verbalized immediately before, can be derived from the communicative situation, is part of the common knowledge of the communication partners, or can be inferred from different kinds of holistic linguistic and/or non-linguistic knowledge. Therefore, Background Constituents can be said to be anchored in context. They are represented by the marking [-F(okus)]. One sentence may contain one or more Background Constituents. But no pragmatically expressive sentence may consist of Background Constituents only.

(1) [*Es war einmal ein alter KÖnig*]$_F$
There once was an old king.
Der [*hatte drei SÖHne*]$_F$
[-F]
He had three sons.
Ihre Burgen [*standen entlang einer wichtigen HANdelsstrasse*]$_F$[1]
[-F]
Their castles stood along an important trade route.

Focus Constituents express non-familiar information which, correspondingly, is new information for the hearer, has not been verbalized before in the communicative situation, and is not givenby the context. Thus, when it is expressed, it is communicatively new or important.

Focus constituents are represented by the marking [+F]. A sentence may contain one or more focus constituents, or it may consist of focused information only. Sentences of the latter type are called fully focused sentences. Short fully focused sentences of mostly one constituent besides the finite verb are called thetic sentences. The focus constituents form the focus domain which, correspondingly, can be a minimal domain, a middle wide, or a maximal domain.

Focus constituents can be subdivided into Representative Focus (also called New Information Focus) and Contrastive Focus. Contrastive Focus partly shares the pragmatic characteristics of Representational Focus, but is used in sentences with additional communicative functions: in Correction Sentences and in the so called Bridge Contours (cf. § 4). We will represent contrastive focus by [CF]. The focus domain of contrastive focus may have all the degrees of width that New Information Focus has, but it tends to have narrow focus.[2]

Fully Focused Sentences are normally introductory sentences (cf. the first sentence in (1)). They are used when no common ground has yet been established between the communicative partners. The partition between Background and Focus in a sentence can be decided upon by means of context only. In German, the default sequence of Information Structure is: Background Constituents before Focus Constituents.

In the literature, we very often find the name "Background Constituent" replaced by Topic. Other authors differentiate between Familiarity Topics (designating our Backgound Constituents) and Aboutness Topics (or Topics proper). In this paper, only Aboutness Topics are called Topics. One sentence thus has got one topic. This topic expresses what the rest of the sentence (i.e.

[1] The pronoun *die* and the DP *ihre Burgen* are Background Constituents. Whereas the pronoun is lexically anchored, the DP must be inferred by means of world knowledge.

[2] The focus domain is bracketed by indexed angled brackets [...]$_F$. The position of the focus accent in the focus domain is represented by CAPITALS.

the Comment) is about. In a descriptive text, the chain of Topics is built by the elements of the set constituting the Theme (i.e. Topic of the text), (cf. (2) with its Theme *Thüringen*). Topics were thought to always be a subset of Background Constituents for a long time. (In (2), the area, the number of inhabitants, and the capital belong to the political elements constituting a country. These elements belong to the common ground.) But when texts were inspected more closely with respect to their substructure, focused and even contrastively focused constituents had to be analyzed as Topics as well (cf. (3)).

(2) *Thüringen ist*$_1$ [*seit 1990 ein neues Bundesland der Bundesrepublik DEUTSCHland* t_1]$_F$
Die Bodenfläche des Freistaates beträgt$_1$ [*16 251 QuadRATkilometer* t_1]$_F$
Seine Bevölkerungszahl ist t_1 [*2,7 Millionen EINwohner* t_1]$_F$
Die Landeshauptstadt ist$_1$ [*Erfurt* t_1]$_F$[3]
Thuringia has been a new federal state of the Federal Republic of Germany since 1990.
The area of the Freestate is 16 251 million square kilometres.
Its population is 2,7 million inhabitants.
The federal capital is Erfurt.

(3) *Aldi unterm Zeltdach*
a) Vor zwei Monaten$_3$ *begann*$_i$ *Aldi*$_2$ [t_3 t_2 *seine Verhandlungen mit dem Rat der Stadt LEIPzig* t_i]$_F$ [-F]
b) [*Ein GeLÄNde*]$_F$ *wollte der Konzern in Leipzig pachten.*
c) [*Ein GROSSzelt*]$_F$ *wurde auf dem Gelände errichtet.*
d) [*Voll von WAren*]$_F$ *ist der Supermarkt, aber* [*sehr primitiv EINgerichtet*]$_F$ *ist er.*
Aldi under a tent
Two months ago Aldi began negotiations with the Council of The Town of Leipzig.
It was an area which the trust wanted to rent.
A big tent was erected on the lot.
Full of goods is the super-market is but it is very primitively furnished.

(3) is a news report. *Aldi unterm Zeltdach* constitutes the Theme. In all sentences of the text the Focus is placed before the Background. This is untypical for tales but typical for news stories which tend to mention what is new as soon as possible. Nevertheless, sentence b) speaks about an area, sentence c) about a tent, and sentence d) speaks about the make-up of the supermarket twice. It is the focused Topics here which constitute the internal structure of the text. Extending the notion of Topic to focused constituents, we can include even the so called I-Topics of Bridge Contours in the notion of Topic. These are also used to promote text (3):

[3] The Topics are underlined.

(3) e) */Einfach ge**STA**pelt sind [die in KarTON verpackten Waren]$_F$.*
[CS]
Simply piled up are all the goods packed in cartons.

f) */In Re**GA**len steht [das ZerBRECHliche]$_F$.*
[CS]
On shelves stands what is breakable.

The elaboration of sentence 3d) by the sentences e) and f) continues the pattern of news reports by avoiding to topicalize the subject which is the default Topic[4]. Bridge Contours have two pitch accent positions. The rising pitch accent on the so-called I-Topic is additionally marked by "/", and the accentuated syllable is written in bold face. (This accent will be characterized as a contrastive pitch accent in § 4.3. In 3e) it is indexed by [CS]). The second pitch accent is the normal representational pitch accent. What the two sentences in 3e) and f) are about is how and where the goods are arranged in the supermarket, and this is what we call their topic-hood. Accepting this pragmatic definition of Topics, they are the Background- or Focus- or even contrastively focused constituents in the prefield of a German sentence, or – according to the certain particulars exemplified in § 3 – in the position immediately after C°.

The **Comment** of a sentence can be defined negatively as the part of the information structure of a sentence minus its Topic.

2 On the modularity of grammar

Information structure is doubtlessly pragmatically grounded. But there are many different points of view on whether and how it is connected with grammar. Chomsky (1995) excludes information-structurally driven syntactic movement from grammar. This way, a big part of German surface structure would not belong to syntax but – according to Chomsky - to stylistics. Rosengren (1993) and Haider and Rosengren (1998) but include scrambling and topicalization in syntax. However, they address these phenomena from the view of an autonomous syntax only and regard them as optional grammatical movements. According to Rosengren (1993), the information structural interpretation is achieved on an independent pragmatic level. In our research project "Intonation und Meaning of Information Structure" at the University of

[4] If the subject had become the I-Topic, we would have two Bridge Contours, too. Cf. § 4.
/Die in KarTON verpackten Waren sind [einfach geSTApelt]$_F$
/Das ZerBRECHliche steht [in ReGAlen]$_F$.
The semantics of Bridge Contours which is explained in § 4, cannot be the reason for the journalist to change the inner sequence of the two sentences. We assume instead that the change effects a property of the type of text. Cf. the paper of Th. Weskott in this volume.

Leipzig, however, we differentiate between grammatically and pragmatically driven movement to surface structure (cf. § 3).

Similarly, different approaches to information structure are found in semantics. Many authors restrict semantics to the truth conditions of sentences despite the fact that it was already shown in Hajičová (1993) that some information structural phenomena have an impact on truth conditions. Similar observations have been made by Akmajian and Jackendoff (1970; influences of pitch accent shift on binding relations), Dretske (1972; pitch accent shift in *if – then* sentences changes their truth conditions), Büring (1996; the (de)focusing of negation transforms categorical sentences into Bridge Contours). In their paper "The Meaning of the Sentence in its Semantic and Pragmatic Aspects" Sgall, Hajičová and Panevová (1986) enlarged the object of semantics and included the conditions of use so that correct answers (cf. (4)(a)) can be separated from incorrect ones (cf. (4)(b)):

(4) Was hat sich Peter gekauft?
What did Peter buy for himself?
a) *Peter hat sich ein AUTO gekauft.*
Peter bought himself a car.
b) *Ein Auto hat sich PETER gekauft.*
A car was bought by PETER.

Answer (4b), in fact, is a syntactically and semantically well-formed sentence. But within the restricted context of question (4), the sentence can not be used, because sentence (4b) is not a congruent answer to this question context. The explicit question provides a presupposition skeleton where the referent of *Peter* is presupposed within the discourse context. At the same time, it is assumed that *Peter* is the agent of an event that is a description resulting from the predicate *buy (x, y)*. The wh-interrogative sentence abstracts from the referential value of the internal argument. The answer has to provide the referent as its focus semantic value. This congruence-requirement is fulfilled by answer (4a) only. The focus of the sentence corresponds with the presupposition which the proposition of the question can not fulfil. In sentence (4b), however, the external argument bears the focus semantic value. But the referent of the external argument is already introduced by the current discourse model. At the same time, the existence of an object *car* is stated. Although both answers are composed of the same lexical entries, the two utterances establish different discourse models. Furthermore, within the restricted context of question (4), reference as a speech act fails with respect to the answer (4b). The referent of the DP *car* is stated as a presupposed discourse referent, whereas the discourse model of the question does not contain such a discourse object. If the trigger of presuppositions of discourse objects was not part of the compositional meaning of the sentence, both sentences would have to be possible answers in identical discourse contexts. This is why the semantic reflex of information structure has to be compositionally integrated into the meaning of sentences.

The semantic relevance of information structure was observed by other authors from the late sixties onward (Halliday 1967, Fodor 1979, Givón 1978). Hajičová, Partee, and Sgall (1998: 110) evaluate relevant data with regard to the truth-conditional relevance of information structure. They take different degrees of the truth-conditional validity of information structure into consideration:

(5) a) *KENNEDY has been killed.*
    b) *Kennedy has been KILLED.*

For the semantic analysis of sentences like (5) it is assumed that there are "differences in contextual felicity with respect to verbal and non-verbal context with no differences in presupposition or truth-conditions proper" (Hajičová, Partee, and Sgall 1998: 110). If so, both sentences would have identical semantic representations and truth conditions. Why is it then that both sentences can not be used in the same context? Both sentences have a different context-changing potential. Every sentence in (5) establishes reference to different discourse models and situations in the real world.

(6) a) *This time John's cousin didn't cause our defeat.*
    b) *This time our defeat was not caused by John's cousin.*

For example (6), Hajičová, Partee, and Sgall (ibid.) state that there are no differences in truth conditions proper, because "in a given situation one may be true and the other undefined, or one undefined and one false, but not true and the other false" (ibid.).

Further, truth-conditional relevance of information structure appears, "if 'invited' 'exhaustive listing' is included in truth-conditional content, and/or differences in truth conditions with respect to some contexts of evaluation but not others" (ibid.). This is the case in example (7):

(7) (a) *Sorbisch wird in SACHSEN gesprochen.*
    Sorbian is spoken in Saxony.
    (b) *In Sachsen wird SORBISCH gesprochen.*
    In Saxony they speak Sorbian.

With regard to the local context of evaluation fixed by the frame setting adverbial *in Saxony*, only sentence (7a) is an extra-linguistically correct statement. Utterance (7b), however, asserts that the Sorbian language is used in the whole territory of Saxony.

Differences in truth conditions proper appear in the case of example (8) taken from Rooth (1985):

(8) a) *John only introduced Bill to SUE.*
b) *John only introduced BILL to Sue.*

Both sentences establish reference to different situations: "there can be situations in which one assertion is definitely true and the other definitely false" (Hajičová, Partee, and Sgall, ibid.). In sentence (8a), the scope of the focus-sensitive particle *only* triggers the assumption that John did not do anything but the action described by the proposition of the sentence, whereas the utterance (8b) excludes that John introduced another person to Sue.

The examples given clearly support that information structure determines sentence meaning with respect to its truth and context conditions. This way, information structure provides conditions for the use of a sentence within a restricted context. So, the syntactic and prosodic variance of information structure establishes reference to different situations in the real world.

After the different examples have made clear that information structure must be realized on all levels of grammar we want to explicate a corresponding grammatical model.

(9) Survey of a modular grammar of German

Lexicon

↓

S(emantic) F(orm)

↓

S-Structure

↓

P(honological) F(orm)

The grammatical elements project from the lexicon. Each element is characterized by its grammatical, semantic and phonological features and by its combinatorial potential on each of the three levels of grammar. SF- and S-Structure representations can be mapped onto each other at each step of the process of projection / combination. Our model generates SF-representations and maps them onto syntactic surface structures which, in turn, are the basis for PF-representations. In the field of PF-representations, our paper only pays attention to the intonation contours. The lexicon is regarded as the interface to the conceptual system, and PF is regarded as the interface to the phonetic perception and/or realization in acoustic terms. We now turn to the intonational realization of information structure.

In intonational languages such as English, Dutch, and German, focus is realized also by phonological means related to the concept of highlighting of focused material inside a sentence. In these languages, focused constituents are mostly highlighted via phonological association with global and local variations (cf. Pierrehumbert; 1980). In speech production, these tonal variations are expressed by pitch variations and are supposed to be relevant for speech perception. The variation of tonal alignment triggered by information structure can vary among different phonological parameters, e.g., for prominence realization and boundary marking. Boundary marking, however, seems to be less important for the phonological realisation of focus in German (cf. Féry; 1993; in our interpretation, her boundary markers do not provide general evidence for focus-induced phrase markers). Other approaches claim that a universal boundary marking results from information structure (cf. Truckenbrodt; 1999).

An overall summary of the prosodic parameters involved in focus marking would comprise phonological as well as concrete acoustic features: the position of the most prominent pitch accent relative to other pitch accents called nuclear accent, the comparison of pre-, and postnuclear pitch accents and the tonal interpolation between the accents. Nevertheless, if we agree with the notion of highlighting by accentuation rather than by boundary marking, tonal alignment in German is supposed to be associated to accents.

The value of F-features is important for the phonological and semantic interpretation as well. The phonological structure can be derived from the S-structure in two steps: First, the assignment of [+F] and [–F] features is decisive for the distribution of prominence for the sentence. Lexical items assigned [+F] carry more prominence then constituents which are associated with [–F]. The concept of prominence suggests that not the whole lexical item is highlighted but only a part of it – namely a syllable. A prominent syllable is also said to be accented at sentence level.

Second, prominent positions within the sentence are then subject to tonal assignment rules. These rules ensure that prominent syllables or larger domains are aligned with tonal features (in an intonational language such as German). The phonological interpretation is realized by tonal feature alignment. Tonal alignment is subject to a long sustaining debate in the phonological and phonetic literature (cf. e.g. Atterer and Ladd (to appear)). Tonal phenomena appear to respond to information structure and reflect structural distinctions for the distribution of F-features. Nevertheless, the clear association of information structural-specific tonal features, i.e., different accent types, is not very well established. A relatively simple account of the theoretical and empirical framework (see also Silverman & Pierrehumbert; 1990) would involve the fact that accented syllables are realized including phonological contexts such as pre-nuclear tones, segmental anchoring of F0, nuclear tone realization and tonal association with boundaries. This still is a subject for ongoing empirically-based research.

3 On the modularity of cognition

The grammatical model in (10) is one of the cognitive components. In Levelt (1989), the grammatical model is called Formulation. It is preceded by two cognitive components. Cognition 1 is responsible for the pre-structuring of the contents with respect to the type of text selected and with respect to the knowledge and the social status of the communicative partners. Cognition 2 brings about the information structurally relevant pre-structuring which means that propositionally coded structures are built up that can be verbalized sentence by sentence. These propositional structures already contain the information upon which conceptual content will serve as the Background and as the Focus of the next sentence.

(10) Survey of a conceptual model

Cognition	Phase 1	Conceptual pre-selection and pre-structuring 1
	Phase 2	Conceptual pre-selection and pre-structuring 2
Formulation	A modular grammar of German according to (10)	
Realization	Phonetic realization[5]	

Similar cognitive models have been proposed by Bierwisch and Schreuder (1992) and by Herweg and Maienborn (1992).

The interface between grammar and cognition that is important for the purpose of this paper is Cognition 2. When the concepts are mapped onto the SF-representations of lexical items they are enriched by the pragmatic features [+F] or [-F] and [Top(ic)] which trigger the realization of the information structural information in the process of semantic composition and carry it over from the SF-representations of the sentences to the syntactic and phonological representations where they influence the way in which the lexical elements project and are phonologically interpreted. § 4 will exemplify in detail how pragmatics influences the grammatical formulation. Before turning to this point, we will list by which grammatical means on the different levels of grammar the pragmatic features Background, Focus and Topic are realized.
Background Constituents:

[5] In § 4 we concentrate on the acoustic realization of the prosody of the sentences.

- The mapping onto lexical elements and SF-representations:

Referential as well as non-referential elements (e.g. verbs and verb phrases) can be anchored in context. Background Constituents are mostly anaphoric DPs and PPs (among them pronouns and proadverbials). The German articles in their specific or generic interpretation (which is influenced by the context) are an important precondition for being a Background Constituent.

In the composition of the SF-representation of the sentences, the Background Constituents become the restrictor, and the Focus Constituents become the Nuclear Scope of the constructions.

- The mapping onto S-Structure representations:

In the default case, the German Background Constituents are moved out of the focus domain, their left border being formed by the attitudinal adverbials: pronouns go into the so-called Wackernagel position (cf. (11)), and contextually anchored DPs and PPs are scrambled (cf. (12)). Pronouns and scrambled elements are adjuncted to VP^{max} in this surface order from left to right. But there are exceptions where Background Constituents remain in the focus domain (13). These are pronouns, proadverbials which are cliticized to a DP^{nom}. To be identifiable as Background Constituents in the focus domain, they must be marked [-F] (cf. *davon* in (13)). In any case, no Background Constituents are marked by representational or contrastive pitch accents. For detailed information on information structurally influenced word order cf. Haftka (in this volume).

(11) *Ich weiß, dass er*$_1$ *es*$_3$ *ihm*$_2$ *wahrscheinlich* [t_1 t_2 t_3 *gesagt hat*]$_F$
[-F][-F][-F]
I know that he has probably said it to him.

(12) *Ich weiß, dass Friedrich*$_1$ *dem Vater*$_2$ *davon*$_3$ *wahrscheinlich* [t_1 t_2 t_3 *erzählt hat*]$_F$
[-F][-F][-F]
I know that Friedrich has probgably told the father about it.

(13) *Ich weiß, dass ihm*$_1$ *wahrscheinlich* [*Heinrich* t_1 *davon erzählt hat*]$_F$
[-F] [-F]
I know that Heinrich has probably told him about it.

The movements of Background Constituents are information structurally driven. But German also shows grammatically driven movement: moved wh-elements go into the prefield, the finite verbs of assertive main clauses go into the C°-position (verb-second position) irrespective of whether they are anchored in context or not. Therefore, non-anaphoric finite verbs must be marked [+F] in their C° position in order to be compositionally constructed in the nuclear scope of the construction. In assertive main clauses, the prefield must be filled. A non-contextually anchored prefield constituent must be marked [+F].

(14) *Heinrich*$_1$ *hat ihm*$_2$ *wahrscheinlich* [t_1 t_2 *davon erzählt*]$_F$.
[+F] [+F] [-F] [-F]
Heinrich has him probably told him about it.

- The mapping onto prosodic representations:

Background Constituents are non-focused by what kind of focusing ever.

For Focus Constituents then, the following conditions evolve:

- The mapping onto lexical elements and SF-representations:

Focus Constituents express new information and are not anchored in context. In the default case, they are represented by non-referential constituents.

- The mapping onto S-Structure representations:

Focus Constituents are normally placed in the focus domain and need not be marked by [+F] because the brackets of the focus domain are focus-marked. However, as already mentioned, there are grammatically driven movements of Focus Constituents out of the focus domain, and there is also Topic movement into the prefield, whereby Topics may also be focused and even contrastively focused. Therefore, Focus Constituents outside the focus domain must be marked [+F] (cf. (14)). The so-called Bridge Contours have their I-Topic (a contrastively focused constituent) in different positions outside the focus domain (cf. (4.3)) and a focused constituent (with representational pitch-accent) in the focus domain (cf. (15)).

(15) *Heute*$_1$ *hat*$_4$ */**den**$_2$ *ihm*$_3$ [t_1 *der ZEUge* t_3 t_2 *gezeigt* t_4]$_F$.
[CF] [CF]
Today has this one him the witness shown.

- The mapping onto prosodic representations:

The representational pitch accent is normally a high or falling tone: H*(L). In German, an accent-organizing language, it is placed on a lexically and (in phrases syntactically) dominating position of a word. The representational pitch accent is normally found in the position of the deepest embedded argument or adjunct of the verb.

The contrastive pitch accent is a rising tone: L*H. Contrastive pitch accents can be found on any syllable (even on grammatical endings) and even on words which normally can not be focused: pronouns, articles, auxiliaries (cf. (15), (16)).

(16) */Mit Semmelnknödeln [ist NICHT korrekt]$_F$, /mit Semmelknödeln [IST korrekt]$_F$*
With Semmelnknödeln is not correct, with Semmelknödeln is correct.

Topics:

The notion of Topic is not well defined yet. Hence, it should be explored whether a narrow definition restricting Topics to subsets of Background Constituents is needed as proposed in earlier papers of our project. If so, we would have to introduce a further notion – possibly that of the Theme of a sentence – to fulfill the pragmatic function of continuing a text of a certain type. Should, on the other hand, Topics be considered within the concept of aboutness (as in this paper) the question emerges whether this idea is suitable in all cases and whether Topic can be considered as a synonym of Theme. In this paper, the second option is taken. But as we yet do not know well enough what the textual functions of topics are, our semantic formalizations in § 4 are restricted to the background-focus partition.[6]

- The mapping onto lexical elements and on SF-representations:

In this paper, we accept Topics belonging to the Background- (cf. (13) *'ihm'*) as well as to the Focused Constituents (cf. (14) *'Heinrich'*).

- The mapping onto S-Structure representations:

German Topics are placed in the prefield of assertive main clauses, and in assertive sub-clauses they are immediately following C° (cf. (13)). In cases where the prefield of a main clause houses a non-Topic (words like *jedoch, auch,* e.g.) the Topic is found to the left of C°, too.

(17) *Jedoch wird$_1$ Sachsen$_2$ wahrscheinlich*
[Top]
[t$_2$ *als das nördlichste deutsche Weinanbaugebiet zu betrachten sein* t$_1$]$_F$
However Saxony will probably have to be regarded as the northernmost German wine district.

- The mapping onto prosodic representations:

Assertive main clauses normally provide a high tone on an accented syllable of a word or phrase in the prefield. By doing so, preconditions for the (downstep) modulation of the fundamental frequency are brought about. This tone does not express information structural meaning, however. Contrastive pitch

[6] Werner Frey presently follows a third path: He tries to derive the movement into the German prefield from the syntactic and pragmatic abilities of middlefield topics. Cf. his paper "Syntaktische und funktionale Aspekte der Vorfeldbesetzung im Deutschen" read on April 23, 2003.

accents are by themselves rising tones and block the high frequency onset of sentences. Their fundamental frequency is higher than that of normal introductory rising tones on Background Constituents constituting the Topic. The tones of the contrastively accented Topics as well as those of I-Topics express information structural meaning.

In § 4, we will exemplify which kinds of information structural meaning we are able to differentiate, what syntactic structures the sample sentences have and what their acoustic representations look like. Our information-structural candidates are a categoric sentence, a correction sentence and a Bridge Contour.

4 A modular analysis of sentences in coherent texts

4.1 Categoric sentences

We begin with the syntactic analysis on the basis of a survey on the information structurally important positions in the S-Structure of German (cf. (18)).

(18) Survey of the information-structurally important positions in a German categoric S-Structure[7]

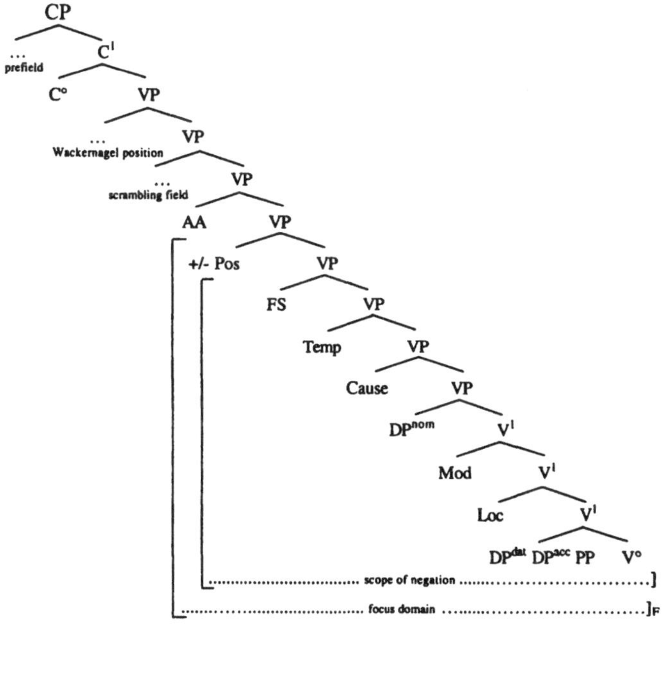

[7] AA = attitudinal adverbials, Pos = positional operator, FS = frame setting adverbials, Temp = temporal adverbials, Cause = causal adverbials, Mod = modal adverbials, Loc = local adverbials

What is striking at first glance is that the German V-projection only needs one functional category: C°. Secondly, the adverbials are base-generated in fixed positions (cf. Frey 2000)[8]. Thirdly, German categoric sentences are subdivided into two parts: Normally, the focus domain is dedicated to focus information. It begins on the right of the attitudinal adverbials[9]. But the focus domain is not identical with the focus of the sentence, because it is not the constituents base-generated in the focus domain which are Focal Constituents but those remaining there in S-Structure representations (with the exception of the Background Constituents of (14) which are in the focus domain): Pronouns normally move into the Wackernagel positions, background-DPs or –PPs move into the scrambling field[10]. Both can be governed there by the German verb[11]. When Background Constituents are marked as Topics they move into the prefield of assertive main clauses (which, however, can be taken up by Focused Constituents as well) or in front of the other Background Constituents in subordinate clauses.

However, in Frey (2000), and Haftka (2003)[12] it was shown that the focus domain and the scope of negation need not to be identical. (Cf. (19)(a) and (b)).

(19)(a) Weißt du etwas Neues von Ilona?
Do you know anything new about Ilona?
Sie$_i$ *wird*$_j$ *wahrscheinlich* [*den Millionär*$_k$ *NICHT* t_i t_k *heiraten* t_j, *den sie im Urlaub kennengelernt hat.*]$_F$
She will probably not marry the millionaire with whom she became acquainted during the vacation.

(b) Weißt du etwas Neues von Ilona und ihrem Millionär?
Do you know anything new about Inona and her millionaire?
Sie$_i$ *wird*$_j$ *ihn*$_k$ / *den Millionär*$_k$ *wahrscheinlich* [*NICHT* t_i t_k *heiraten* t_j]$_F$
She will him / the millionaire probably not marry.

That the scope of negation and the focus domain differ becomes visible only when both categories are present and the non-negated information is not con-

[8] Cf. (14)

[9] AA – attitudinal adverbial (*wahrscheinlich* – probably; *möglicherweise* – possibly; *tatsächlich* – really, in fact); cf. Lang (1979).

[10] This will say that we are of opinion that the German adverbials scramble, too.

[11] Cf. Haider (1997), and Haider & Rosengren (1998) who except the adverbials from scrambling, however.

[12] Cf. *Gibt es etwas neues von Paul? Man erzählt, dass Paul wahrscheinlich die Tochter des Bürgermeisters doch nicht HEIratet. Paul* is anchored in context and must be scrambled whereas *die Tochter des Bürgermeisters* is not. Nevertheless, *die Tochter des Bürgermeisters* is a referential constituent which is out of the scope of negation. Therefore, referentiality is not the only condition Background Constituents have to fulfill.

textually anchored (cf. (19) (a)). See also Trautwein and Späth (in this volume).

Let us now turn to the analysis of the categoric sentence which is underlined in (20)[13].

(20) *Am Sonntag morgen packte Martina ihre Reisetasche. <u>Sie fuhr zum Bahnhof.</u> Dort kaufte sie eine Fahrkarte nach Paris und setzte sich in die Wartehalle.*[14]
On Sunday Martina packed her bag. She went to the station. There she bought a ticket to Paris and sat down in the waiting room.

The relevant categoric sentence in (20a) only contains the subject, the finite verb, a prepositional phrase dominated by V^1, and the +Pos-phrase. *Sie* is a topicalized Background Constituent. *Fuhr* was moved out of the focus domain and is placed in C° for syntactic reasons only. Therefore, this constituent is [+F] and must be compositionally constructed in the focus domain of its SF structure.

(20) a) <u>*Sie$_i$ fuhr$_j$*</u> [Pos t_i <u>*zum BAHNhof*</u> t_j $]_F$
[-F] [+F] [-F] [+F]

(20a) expresses a categoric sentence. It is an assertion about a well known person, *she.* In the example given, the focus and the comment of the sentence coincide. The focus of the sentence is the informational unit that asserts what is the true case with respect to the presuppositional constituents of the Background. In the given example, the focus function is applied to the referent of the external argument-DP *she.* The syntax-semantic mapping for the sentence is based on the syntactic assumptions given in context (20). First, the VP is composed from the PP and the finite verb. Since the verb was moved out of the VP for grammatical reasons, the trace of the verb left in situ is marked by the discourse pragmatic feature [+F]. The trace therefore is semantically relevant, and the copy of the finite verb is of no semantic relevance. Traces of constituents which are not semantically relevant, [-F], are treated as identical mappings and have no descriptive content:

(21) Semantic composition of the VP:

a) Semantic composition of the PP:
$\lambda\mathfrak{R}\ \lambda x\ [\mathfrak{R}\ (\lambda y\ [FIN\ [LOC\ (x) \subseteq LOC\ (y)]])]\ (\lambda Q\ [\exists!y\ [[STATION\ (y)] \wedge [Q\ (y)]]])$
$\equiv \lambda x\ [\exists!y\ [[STATION\ (y)] \wedge [FIN\ [LOC\ (x) \subseteq LOC\ (y)]]]]$

[13] Cf. K. Alter, I. Mleinek, T. Rohe, A. Steube, C. Umbach (2001).

[14] The sample sentences (20) an (23) have been used in an experiment on the prosody of categorical sentences and corrections. Cf. K. Alter, I. Mleinek, T. Rohe, A. Steube, C. Umbach (2001).

b) Semantic composition of the VP:
$\lambda P\ \lambda x\ \lambda e$ [e INST [MOVE (x)]:[P (x)]] (λx [$\exists$!y [[STATION (y)]$\wedge$[FIN [LOC (x) $\subseteq$ LOC (y)]]]])
$\equiv \lambda x\ \lambda e$ [e INST [MOVE (x)]:[$\exists$!y [[STATION (y)]$\wedge$[FIN [LOC (x) $\subseteq$ LOC (y)]]]]]

In the next step of semantic composition the result (21b) combines with the positional operator. In accordance with Haftka (2003), the operator is adjoined to VP. Since the sentence is not a negated one, the positive operator takes scope over the focus functions and introduces the assertion that the Background of the sentence is true with respect to the property described by the focus. The positive and the negative operator, respectively, closes the focus function:

c) Semantic integration of the positional operator:
λp [POS [p]] ($\lambda x\ \lambda e$ [e INST [MOVE (x)]:[$\exists$!y [[STATION (y)]$\wedge$[FIN [LOC (x) $\subseteq$ LOC (y)]]]]])
$\equiv \lambda x\ \lambda e$ [POS [e INST [MOVE (x)]:[$\exists$!y [[STATION (y)]$\wedge$[FIN [LOC (x) $\subseteq$ LOC (y)]]]]]

In the following steps, the SF-representation (21a) combines with the sentence mood operator in C^0. The event role of the verb will be existentially bound. In Spec CP the topic of the sentence will be integrated into the Semantic Form of the sentence. The Semantic Form in (d) represents the sentence meaning of (20a):

d) $\exists$!x [[[PERSON (x)]:[FEMALE (x)]]$\wedge$[$\exists$e [POS [e INST [MOVE (x)]:
[$\exists$!y [[STATION (y)]$\wedge$[FIN [LOC (x) $\subseteq$ LOC (y)]]]]]]]]

In the semantic form (21d) its discourse pragmatic interpretation has been frozen. When it is mapped on the syntactic surface structure, the pragmatic marker [-F] and information structurally independent syntactic rules (of the finite verb) drive the syntactic movements into the surface positions. When surface structure is mapped on PF, the same pragmatic markers are active in ascribing the intonation contour: [-F] strings are de-accented; [+F] strings are highlighted. In the PF of sentence (20a), the sentence accent falls on the most deeply embedded argument of the verb, the PP *zum Bahnhof*, which gets the falling tone H*L.

4.2 Correction sentences

Corrections are rarely fully focused sentences, but they may be as seen in the second conjunct of (22b) and in (22c).

(22) Do you know where our colleagues are?

a) *[Albert went to POland]*$_F$.

b) *I [am still here]*$_F$*, but [FRED is on tour]*$_{CF}$

c) *[Peter is in BELfast.]*$_{CF}$

More often corrections are categorial sentences which correct only one constituent of the context like in (23a).

(23) Studentin am Telefon:
Martina? Die habe ich am Sonntag noch im Bus gesehen. Wo sie hingefahren ist?
Nein, nicht in die Innenstadt. Sie fuhr zum BAHNhof.
Female Student at the phone:
Martina? On Sunday I saw her in the bus. Where she went?
No, not to the inner city. She went to the station.

(23) a) *Sie*$_i$ *fuhr*$_j$ [Pos t_i [*zum BAHNhof*]$_{CF}$ t_j]$_F$.
[-F] [+F] [CF] [+F]

„Nicht in die Innenstadt“ as an anaphor of „Sie fuhr nicht in die Innenstadt“ is the typical antecedent context. On the other hand, there are the typical postcedent contexts denying the not-wanted alternative: "Sie fuhr zum Bahnhof und nicht die Innenstadt" [She went to the station and not into the Inner City]. But the correction sentences of German dialogical texts mostly do not mention the not-wanted alternative in the correction itself at all. The correcting speaker simply replaces the (supposedly) wrong constituent mentioned by an earlier speaker by the one he considers to be not correct (cf. (25b)).

(24) You know what the others want to study?

a) *Peter studies [mathematics]*$_F$.

b) *He studies [information science]*$_{CF}$

Sentence (24b) corrects (24a). Both differ only in the corrected constituent and in their tones: *Information science* under a CF-tone replaces *mathematics* under a F-tone. If (24b) was corrected again by e.g. *[applied linguistics]*$_{CF}$ the CF-tone of *applied linguistics* might even follow a CF-tone. What is important after all, is that the replacement bears a CF-tone. The CF-tone shows a considerably higher fundamental frequency than that of an F-tone, and the CF-tone is audible as that. It is the CF-tone that signals that its bearer is to be selected from the set of alternatives and not any other one in the set. Therefore the audible higher fundamental frequency is considered a lexical entry with a meaning counterpart.

Let us come back to (23a). Its meaning differs from that of (20a) as follows:

• The lexicalized part of sentence (23a) is the same as that of the presentationally focused categorial sentence (20a)[15],

> *Sie$_i$ fuhr$_j$* [Pos t_i zum BAHNhof t_{j-}]$_F$.
> [-F] [+F] [+F]

• But (23a) has the additional meaning of the CF-tone:

> $\lambda p\ [p]\ \&\ \exists!\ \Phi, s_1\ \ [s_1$ represented by $S_1 = (s \ldots[\ \Psi/\Phi]_{\text{focus domain}}\ )]$.
> Whereby
> p = compositionally constructed SF of the assertive part of the correction
> s_1 = the situation represented by the corrigendum
> S_1 = corrigendum sentence
> S = corrigens sentence
> Ψ = the entity in the corrigens realizing contrastive pitch-accent and replacing Φ
> Φ = the entity in the corrigendum that has to be replaced
> Φ, Ψ have a CI.[16]

• Therefore, the total meaning of (23a) is a conjunction of the lexicalised and of the additional part like in (23b):

(23) b) $\exists!$x {[[[PERSON (x)]:[FEMALE (x)]]$\wedge$[$\exists$e [POS [e INST [MOVE (x)]:
[$\exists!$y [[STATION (y)]$\wedge$[FIN [LOC (x) $\subseteq$ LOC (y)]]]]]]]] : & $\exists!\ \Phi$, s_1
[s_1 represented by S_1 = (s ...[y/Φ]$_{\text{focus domain}}$)]}

The SF representation of (23b), *Sie$_i$ fuhr$_j$* [Pos t_i [zum BAHNhof]$_{CF}$ t_{j-}]$_F$, says: She went to the station and not to another place of the same syntactic and semantic class and the same semantic domain. In the context sentence, there was the inner city mentioned as an alternative. It has to be derived from a pragmatic principle[17] that the alternative is not taken but the finally mentioned and not itself corrected place *zum Bahnhof.* When corrigendum and corrigens are alike except for the alternating constituents, the communicative partners want to establish a common ground even in this respect, and they accept the last mentioned constituent with the CF-tone as a member of their common ground.

---

[15] When [...]$_{CF}$ is a contrastively focused sentence the first part of the SF representation, a coordination, is the equivalent of the fully focused sentence [...]$_F$, the second part is the statement that the context contains an alternative represented by the constituent bearing the CF-tone.

[16] CI is the Common Integrator which says that the Ψ, Φ must belong to the same syntactic and semantic classes, and they must belong to the same semantic domain.

[17] Cf. A. Steube (2003a)

The mapping of the SF representation on the syntactic surface form of (23a) does not differ from the surface form of (20a). What differs is their intonation contour. Contrary to the categorial sentence in (20a), corrections require a special tone, a CF-tone. In (23a) it is associated with the corrigendum *zum Bahnhof.* The CF-tone is clearly related to the semantic-pragmatic level and ignores structural syntactic properties. As it has been proposed in Alter et al. (2002), the so called contrastive accents in comparison to [+F]-pitch accents do not necessarily need the syllable as their minimal domain for tonal association. CF-tonal accents can even be phonologically associated with sub-syllabic material. Their phonetic realization, however, might correspond to other spreading parts of their tonal realization onto neighbouring material. The important point for the differentiation between CF-tones and [+F]-pitch accents is therefore the domain of association.

In example (23a), the CF-tone clearly differs from the pitch accent assigned to the same constituent in (20a). The difference of the CF-tone has been established in the 'scaling' of the F0-peak being higher for the CF-tone. The rise of the CF-tone is further marked by a lower starting point resulting in a higher tonal slope. Other possible prosodic candidates such as fine grained anchoring of tonal variations to segments, i.e. F0 peak latencies, prenuclear and postnuclear tonal variations, are subject to further analysis. The difference in the tonal variation is a sufficient factor for auditory categorization of the sentences (23a) versus (20a) (cf. Alter et al.; 2002). In Alter et al. (2002) the perceptive relevance of CF-tones and [+F]-pitch accents in different contexts has been tested. It has been shown that a CF-tone embedded in a context bearing a reading with the finite verb and the PP bearing new information, the listener's judgement of the prosodic appropriateness is very high. In contrast, if the context demands a correction, and a [+F]-pitch item is associaated with the item to be corrected, e.g. "BAHNhof" (see example (23a) above), listeners rated these examples as unacceptable.

To summarize, a highlighting of the tonal peak (among other tonal parameters) seems to be less important even when the context does not require such a tonal specification. On the other hand, a tonal underspecification in a context where a CF-tone is necessary for listeners' sentence processing leads to a prosodic mismatch. A similar picture can be drawn from the data presented in Hruska & Alter (in this volume). A superfluous accent is ignored during the processing of question – answer pairs which indicate clearly, by presence of wh-pronouns in questions, where in the answer a [+F]-pitch accent has to be placed. A missing accent on a [+F]-constituent, however, leads to a strong mismatch reaction by the listener's brain. These data have been partially replicated in the studies presented by Toepel & Alter (in this volume) where subjects listened to sentences embedded in contexts that are either specified for [+F]- or CF-interpretations. Nevertheless, their data also propose differences in the mismatch reaction on the CF-tone specification related to its task relevance in the experiment.

Our interpretation of the data presented in this volume is based on the specific function of prosodic parameters related to accent positions and accent types: An over-specification of prosodic parameters such as additional accents or highlighting of tonal variance is more easily accepted by the hearer. An underspecification of prosodic parameters, - i.e., when an accent on a certain accent type is expected by the listener due to the preceding context information – leads to specific brain responses related to the detection of a prosodic mismatch. (Please note that in Hruska and Alter, in this volume, we found also brain reactions to expected accents. These expectations are marked by frontal negativities in the event-related brain potentials.) This prosodic mismatch can be expressed in terms of a missing or failing tonal association to [-F] or CF-marked constituents.

4.3 Bridge Contours

Bridge constructions have two pitch accents, a rising pitch accent on the so-called I-Topic, and a falling pitch accent in the position of the normal presentational focus. The accentuated syllable of the I-Topic is written in bold-face and with the sign for the rise "/" before the referring constituent. The accentuated syllable in the focus domain is written in capital letters. I-Topics are anchored in the context. They denote members of a set (cf. *Peter – Anne* as members of *the children*).

(25) What did the children do?

a) */**Pe**ter [repaired his CYcle]*$_F$

b) */**An**ne [combed her DOGS]*$_F$

The rising pitch accent states the existence of an alternative to the meaning / grammatical form / phonological form / connotation / etc. of the Theme.

(26) a) */**An**na hat es [den KINdern gegeben]* $_F$ – alternative to the meaning of the theme

/**An**ne has it given to the children.

b) */Frie**der**helm ist [nicht korREKT]*$_F$ – alternative to the grammatical form

/Frie**der**helm is not correct.

c) */**An**ne hat es [den KINdern gegeben]*$_F$ – alternative to PF or to the connotation

/**An**ne has it given to the children.

I-Topics may be found (a) in the Wackernagel position, (b) in the Scrambling field of the sentence. As shown in (c), the prefield may contain I-Topics which are Background Constituents or (d) Focus Constituents. Besides, there are two non-referential I-Topic positions after C°, (e) immediately before the Wackernagel position, and (f) at the end, between the two AA positions:

(27) a) *Heute hat /**den** ihm [der ZEUge gezeigt]*$_F$
Today has him /this one the witness shown.
b) *Heute hat ihn /mein **Vater** [ins KIno begleitet]*$_F$
Today /my father has accompanied him to the cinema.
c) */**Heute** hat ihn mein Vater [ins KIno begleitet]*$_F$
/Today has my father accompanied him to the cinema.
d) */**Angezogen** hat es ihm mein Vater [schon am MORgen]*$_F$
My father has it /dressed him already in the morning.
e) *Leider hat /**zurückgeben** können es ihm Karlchen [noch NICHT]*$_F$
Unfortunately Karlchen has not yet /been able to give it back to him.
f) *Karlchen wird es ihm vielleicht /**zurückgegeben** tatsächlich [HAben]*$_F$
Karlchen will probably have really given it back to him.

What is remarkable semantically, is that there is no correspondence between the syntactic position (outside the focus domain) and the semantic potential of the I-topic:

(28) *[Die Politiker **sind**$_2$ nicht ORDnung* $t_2]_F$
The politicians are not o.k.

(28) a) */**AL**le Politiker*$_1$ *sind*$_2$ *NICHT* [t_1 *korrupt* t_2]$_F$[18]
[CF] [CF] [-F]
/All politicians are not corrupt.

/ALle Polikers is contrastively focused. Since a constituent with a CF-tone is a focus constituent, it is part of the focus domain. But at the same time *alle Politiker* is anchored in the text and could very well be in the Background. So, by their non-prosodic properties the I-Topics of Bridge Contours are Background Constituents, and by their prosodic properties they are made part of the focus domain and must be compositionally constructed there. The reality of this is proved by the next examples:

(29) *[Alle Politiker sind im FERNsehen]*$_F$
All the politicians are on TV.

(29) a) /**ALle** *Politiker*$_1$ *sind*$_2$ *[SELten* t_1 *zu sehen* $t_2]_F$.
[CF] [CF]
/All politicians are seldom visible.

[18] *Alle Politiker* is semantically amalgamated in its base position which is in the scope of negation.

(30) Was schenkst du deinen Eltern zu Weihnachten?
What are you presenting your parents with at Christmas?

a) /*Der **Mutter**$_1$ schenke$_2$ ich$_3$* [t_3 t_1 *eine REIse* t_2]$_F$
CF [-F] [CF] [-F]
/Mother I am presenting with a journey.

b) /*Der **Vater**$_1$* [möchte$_2$ t_1 *einen FELDstecher* t_2]$_F$
[CF] [CF]
/Father would like a field glass.

(30b) becomes our sample sentence.

(30)(b)

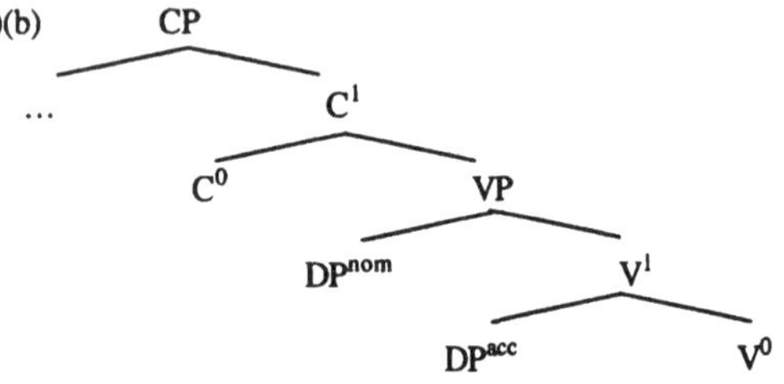

/*Der VAter*$_1$ [möchte$_2$ [t_1 *einen FELDstecher* t_2]$_F$
[CF] [+F] [CF] [+F]

(30b) is an all-focus sentence. /*Der **Vater**,* in addition, bears the rising tone of the I-Topic and signals an additional meaning: that there is an alternative to the I-Topic (and in this case, it is an alternative to its meaning) in the set of meanings of which the I-Topic itself is a subset. Contrary to corrections, which explicitly point out the alternative to the context, Bridge Contours need not name it. In (29a) the alternative(s) are only to be derived from the common set: few politicians, some politicians, ..., the ministers, ..., the federal politicians, ... The set from which the alternatives are derivable is rather big in (29), but in (30) the set consists only of the two alternatives mentioned in (30a) and b): *the mother, the father*. And if only one Bridge Contour (say (30a)) was mentioned, the sentence constitutes only half an answer to question (30).

The Bridge Contours looked at here but have a second, a presentational focus in the sentence which signals new information. In the several Bridge Contour constructions presented here this leads to the expectation that all the presentational foci express focus information. However, even these focus constituents belong to a common set. The meaning of (30b) is that of an all-focus sentence with the additional meaning of the CF-tone. The assertive lexicalised first part of the SF of (30b) is (30c).

(30)(c) $\exists s\ [[Ts = T' : \neg[Ts < t^o]] : [s\ inst\ [GETS, \iota x\ [FATHER, x], \varepsilon y\ [FIELD\text{-}GLASS, y]]]]$

(30d) is the meaning of the CF-tone, but note that the CF-tone of Bridge Contours differs in grammatical context from the CF-tone of corrections: the Bridge Contour consist of the already mentioned additional presentational focus accent.

(30) d) $\lambda p\ [p]\ \&\ \lambda x\ \exists!y, s_l\ [s_l$ is represented by $\{\ _{sl} \ldots [x]_{CF}\ [\ldots]^k\ /\ \ldots [y]_{CF}\ [\ldots]^k\ \}]$

- p = assertive lexicalised first part of the SF of the sentence
- x = SF of the grammatical form or phonological form or connotation of the I-Topic for which the existence of an alternative is stated
- z = alternative to x [here: x = SF of *der Vater*], z = a conceptual structure (to be interpreted in this case as *die Mutter*).
- s_l = situation s_l represented by sentence S_l. S_l"predicates" on the alternative to $x._x\ldots\ /\ _y\ldots$ replace x by z. Both constitutents have the same syntactic and semantic category and belong to the same semantic domain.

The total SF of the Bridge Contour (30e) is:

(30) e) $\exists s\ [[Ts = T' : \neg[Ts < t°]] : [s\ inst\ [GETS, \iota x\ [FATHER, x], \varepsilon y\ [FIELD\text{-}GLASS, y]]]$
$\&\ \exists!z, s_l\ [s_l$ is represented by $\{\ _{sl} \ldots [x]_{(C)F}\ [\ldots]^k\ /\ \ldots [z]_{CF}\ [\ldots]^k\ \}]\ ]$ [19]

(30e) is again a very under-specified SF-representation. It merely says that *father* will get a field-glass and that there is an alternative to *father*. In order to correspond to context (30), the alternative can only be mother. It would be semantically and pragmatically incorrect, if *mother* would get the same present. Mother's present is mentioned in (30)(a). But even a Bridge Contour with one member only would not allow the inference that the alternative (to, e.g., *mother*) was presented with the same thing, since the constituent bearing the presentational pitch accent cannot express already known information.
Finally, we want to sum up the prosodic properties of Bridge Contours. We claim that their peculiarity lies in their compositionality of two tones interacting via semantics.
Let us first consider the CF-tone. It is assigned to a constituent moved out of the focus domain (cf. 27a-f). The meaning of the CF-tone is exemplified in (30d). The bridge contour is therefore an overwhelming example for the interplay between prosody and semantics, the CF-tone being crucial for semantic interpretation. While the CF-tone is a rising tonal contour, the bridge contour is additionally followed by a high level tone and ending with a fall. This fall is then associated with the focused constituent.

A CF-tone alone cannot bear the interpretation in (30e). Its meaning is the result of an interaction between two tones: the CF and the falling pitch accent

[19] Index k says that both the representational focus-constituents belong to the same set. Cf. A. Steube (2003b)

on the focused item. Taking a rising tone alone, at least a triple set of interpretation of the prosodic realizations can evolve:

(i) a rising CF-tone followed by a falling focus pitch accent as described for the bridge contour in (30a). This contour could also arise from the expression of extended scope of negation elements.

(ii) a rising CF-tone followed by a continuously falling F0-contour as might be the case in sentences such as (31a) with one corrected element.

(31) *Does mother get a field-glass for Chrismas?*

(31) a) *[VAter]$_{CF}$ bekommt einen Feldstecher.*
Father will get a field glass.

(iii) a rising CF-tone followed by another rising CF-tone in the case of two corrected elements within one clause.

Taken together, only the interaction of the first accent with possible follow-up accents determines the correct meaning. The interpretation of minimal pairs such as derived from (i) and (iii) here is only possible by semantic compositional (re-) construction. However, a clear phonetic distinction between the three cases (i-iii above) needs more empirical research. Perhaps, such a specification of CF-tones can be disentangled by means of phonetic parameters such as the F0-peak alignment, F0 excursion and the anchoring of preceding and subsequent F0 valleys. Perceptually, the question also arises whether CF-tones on I-Topics can be differentiated from CF-tones on semantically focused material in corresponding contexts at all since they share at least some common prosodic properties. Preliminary data (Toepel; in preparation) suggest that listeners are indeed able to decide whether a certain accent is appropriate to a preceding context or not.

5 References

Alter, K., I. Mleinek, T. Rohe, A. Steube, and C. Umbach (2001): Kontrastprosodie in Sprachproduktion und -perzeption. In: Linguistische Arbeitsberichte 77, Leipzig, 59-79.

Akmajian, A. and R. Jackendoff (1970): Coreferentiality and Stress. In: Linguistic Inquiry 1.1, 124-126.

Atterer, M. and R. D. Ladd (to appear): On the phonetics and phonology of "Segmental Anchoring" of F0: Evidence from German. Journal of Phonetics.

Bierwisch, M. and E. Lang (1987) (eds): Grammatische und konzeptuelle Aspekte von Dimensionsadjektiven. studiagrammatica XXVI-XXVII, Berlin

Bierwisch, M. and R. Schreuder (1992): From Concepts To Lexical Items. In: Cognition 42, 23-60.

Büring, D. (1996): The 59th Street Bridge Accent. On the Meaning of Topic and Focus. Universität Tübingen. SFS-Report

Cinque, G. (1993): A null theory of phrase and compound stress. Linguistic Inquiry 24. 239-297.

Chomsky, N. (1995): The Minimalist Program. Cambridge/Ma.: MIT-Press

Dretske, F. J. (1972): Contrastive Statement. In: Philosophical Review, 411-437.

Fanselow, G. (1991): Minimale Syntax. In: W. Abraham (ed): Groninger Arbeiten zur germanistischen Linguistik (GAGL) 32, Groningen.

Féry, C. (1993): German intonational patterns. Tübingen, Germany.

Fodor, J. D. (1979): In defense of the truth-value gap. In: C.-K. Oh and D. A. Dineen (eds), 199–294.

Frey, W. (2000): Syntactic Requirements on Adjuncts. In: ZAS Papers in Linguistics 17, Berlin, 107-134.

Frey, W. (2000): Über die syntaktische Position der Satztopics in Deutschen. In: ZAS Papers in Linguistics 20, Berlin, 137-172.

Frey, W. (2003): Syntaktische und funktionale Aspekte der Vorfeldbesetzung im Deutschen, paper read in Leipzig on April 23, 2003.

Givón, T. (1978): Negation in Language. Pragmatics, Function, Ontology. in: P. Cole (ed), 69–112.

Haftka, B. (2003): Möglicherweise tatsächlich nicht immer. Beobachtungen zur Adverbialreihenfolge an der Spitze des Rhemas. In: W. Abraham and I. Molnár (eds): Optionality in Syntactic Discourse Structure - Aspects of Word Order Variation in (West-) Germanic and other Indo-European Languages. Folia Linguistica.

Haftka, B. (this volume): Topic Constraints in the German Middle Field.

Haider, H. (1997): Projective Economy. On the Minimal Functional Structure of the German Clause: In W. Abraham and E. van Gelderen (eds): Syntactic Problems – Problematic Syntax. Tübingen: Niemeyer, 83-103.

Haider, H. and I. Rosengren (1998): Scrambling. In: Sprache & Pragmatik 49, Lund, 1-104.

Hajičová, E. (1993): Issues of Sentence Structure and Discourse Patterns. Prague: Charles University.

Hajičová, E., B. H. Partee, and P. Sgall (1998): Topic-Focus Articulation, Tripartite Structures and Semantic Content. Studies in Linguistics and Philosophy 71. Dordrecht/Boston/London.

Halliday, M. A. K. (1967): Intonation and Grammar in British English. The Hague.

Herweg, M. and C. Maienborn (1992): Konzept, Kontext und Bedeutung – Zur Rolle der Zweiebenensemantik in einem Modell der Sprachproduktion. In: M. Herweg (ed): Hamburger Papiere zur Sprachproduktion 1, 7-81.

Hruska, C. and K. Alter (this volume): How Prosody can Influence Sentence Perception.

Lang, E. (1979): Zum Status der Satzadverbiale. In: Slovo a slovesnost XL, Praha, 200-213.

Levelt, W. (1989): Speaking. From Intention to Articulation. Cambridge/Mass., London: MIT-Press.

Maienborn, C. (2000): Modification and Underspecification: A Free Variable Account of Locative Modifiers. In: ZAS Papers in Linguistics 17, Berlin, 153-177.

Maienborn, C. (2001): On the Position and Interpretation of Locative Modifiers. In: Natural Language Semantics 9, 191-240.

Pierrehumbert, J. B. (1980): The Phonology and Phonetics of English Intonation. PhD dissertation, MIT.

Rosengren, I. (1993): Wahlfreiheit mit Konsequenzen – Scrambling, Topikalisierung und FHG im Dienst der Informationsstrukturierung. In: M. Reis (ed): Wortstellung und Informationsstrukturierung. Tübingen: Niemeyer, 251-312.

Silverman, K. and J. B. Pierrehumbert (1990): The timing of pre-nuclear high accents in English. In: J. Kingston and M. E. Beckman (eds): Papers in Laboratory Phonology I. Cambridge, 72-106.

Sgall, P., E. Hajičová, and J. Panevová (1986): The Meaning of the Sentence and Its Semantic and Pragmatic Aspects. Prague.

Steube, A. (2000): Ein kognitionswissenschaftlich basiertes Modell für Informationsstrukturierung. In: Ch. Römer and J. Bayer (ed): Von der Philologie zur Grammatiktheorie. P. Suchsland zum 65. Geburtstag. Tübingen: Niemeyer, 213-238.

Steube, A. (2003a): Correction by Contrastive Focus. In: Theoretical Linguistics 27 (2/3), 215-249.

Steube, A. (2003b): Bridge Contours in German Assertive Main Clauses. In: W. Abraham and I. Molnárfi (ed): Optionality in Syntactic Discourse Structure - Aspects of Word Order Variation in (West-) Germanic and other Indo-European Languages. Folia Linguistica 37/1-2,163-190.

Steube, A. and A. Späth (2002): Semantik, Informationsstruktur und grammatische Modularität. In: A. Steube (ed): Sprachtheoretische Grundlagen der Kognitionswissenschaft: Sprachliches und nichtsprachliches Wissen. Linguistische Arbeitsberichte 79, Leipzig, 235-254.

Toepel, U. and K. Alter (this volume): On the independence of information structural processing from prosody.

Truckenbrodt, H. (1999): On the relation between syntactic phrases and phonological phrases. Linguistic Inquiry 30, 219-255.

Weskott, Th. (2003): Information Structuring as a Processing Guide. Dissertation. Universität Leipzig.

Weskott, Th. (this volume): Towards a Scalar Notion of Information-Structural Markedness.

Wunderlich, D. (1991): Bedeutung und Gebrauch. In: A. von Stechow, D. Wunderlich (eds): Semantik. Ein internationales Handbuch der zeitgenössischen Forschung. Handbücher zur Sprach- und Kommunikationswissenschaft Bd. 6. Berlin/New York 32-52.

Andreas Späth and Martin Trautwein (Leipzig)

Negative Descriptions of Events: Semantic and Conceptual Aspects of Sentence Negation and its Relevance for Information Structure [1]

1 Event descriptions, discourse linking, and truth-making

Talking about the world always involves matching the meaning of what we communicate with an evaluation context, i.e. the part of the world we are speaking about. Otherwise, Formal Semantics would not be able to equate the semantic meaning of a sentence with the truth conditions that the sentence shows in possible contexts of utterance. Sentence meaning would instead resemble just logical propositions whose truth or falseness is purely hypothetical. Sentences of natural language express assertions, questions, orders, or wishes, whose types have their specific ways of establishing truth-conditions in a coherent discourse and linking these truth conditions to the evaluation context. Thus truth is – besides object reference – the main function of natural language that connects meaning to the being. Inspired by Seuren/Capretta/Geuvers (2001: p. 7), we propose the model (1) as our methodic framework.

(1) A model of the system of reference and truth

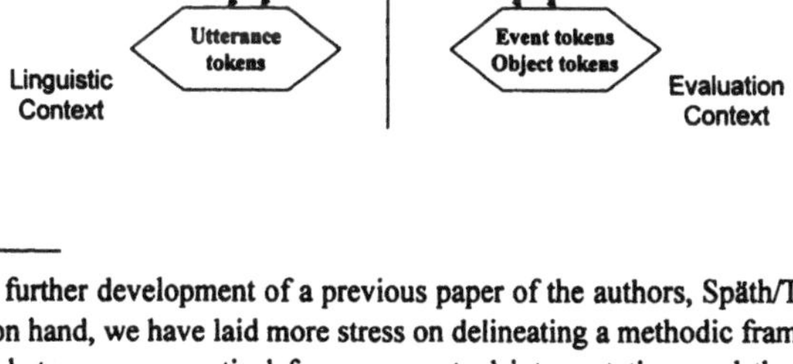

[1] This paper is a further development of a previous paper of the authors, Späth/Trautwein (2003). In the version on hand, we have laid more stress on delineating a methodic framework to explain the connection between grammatical form, conceptual interpretation, and the world. We have furthermore extended and sharpened the discussion about the ontological basis of the truth of positive and negative sentences.

Truth and reference connect linguistic forms to entities in the world context. Both linguistic forms and world entities are *tokens*, i.e., they are concrete, not abstract. Linguistic forms are always token realizations of *types* of sentences and nominal descriptions. Hence truth and object reference are mediated by the *cognitive discourse domain*, which is the domain of *type* knowledge and its various grammaticalizations. In language processing, we abstract types of linguistic descriptions from token utterances and integrate them into a larger context of type knowledge which constitutes the relevant *coherent discourse model*. This cognitive act, called *contextual anchoring*, especially has to consider all kinds of grammatical means such as anaphoric expressions, triggers of presuppositions, or information structure, which mark how the semantic meaning of the sentence currently processed relates to the discourse. Contextual anchoring determines the truth and reference conditions of a sentence, which then have to be matched with an extra-linguistic evaluation context (i.e. the act of *referential keying*).[2] Just as objects (or some kind of spatial entity) are the ontological antecedents of nominal descriptions which link descriptions to the world context, it is well-accepted that events[3] (or some kind of spatio-temporal entity) are the ontological antecedents of sentential descriptions. This parallel suggests a unified treatment of reference and truth (as supported, for instance, by Smith/Mulligan, forthcoming) and enables us to speak about the world of objects and events as the ontological basis of semantic meaning.

The strong claim that truth-conditions are ontologically grounded in the set of possible evaluation contexts goes far beyond the rather pragmatic assumption of event arguments as put forward by the pioneers of Event Semantics. Their presumptions are still valid though: the meaning of verbs and verbal projections reifies some spatio-temporal entities to which further grammatical constituents and operations such as verb nominalization (cf. Reichenbach 1947), modification (cf. Davidson 1967), and tense (cf. Bennett/Partee 1976) may co-refer. Beyond this, we assume that sentences generally encode propositions that describe events. Such propositional event descriptions are built in accord with the rules of compositionality. They provide the conditions for identifying events in the relevant context and consist generally of sortal

[2] Seuren/Capretta/Geuvers (2001) take an exclusively realist view on evaluation context by claiming that, matching the discourse domain with the evaluation context, we only attribute truth and reference values to sentences with realist content, whereas we cannot assign such values to sentences expressing fictive content. Nonetheless, all kinds of truth conditions or reference conditions somehow derive from acts of reference and truth. Even in fiction, we derive the 'meaning' of a text from our experience of how non-fictive sentences can be linked to the real world and its spatio-temporal structure. Otherwise the entire conception of truth-conditional semantics would become questionable since truth conditions then would resemble nothing but mental constructions.

[3] Throughout this paper, we will often use the term *event*. To avoid any confusion, we would like to mention in advance that we regard *events* as the ontological category of spatiotemporal entities. This category reflects the ontological notions of *eventualities* or *occurrents* and is completely neutral with respect to the aspectual classes of any linguistic descriptions.

identifying events in the relevant context and consist generally of sortal information and a referential marker. Also in this respect propositional event descriptions parallel nominal descriptions of objects.

(2) The bipartite organization of information in linguistic descriptions

	Referential marking	Sortal selection
Nominal descriptions	DP: $\lambda Q\, \exists x\, .\, Nx \wedge Qx$	
	D°: $\lambda P\, \lambda Q\, \exists x\, .\, Px \wedge Qx$	NP: $\lambda x\, .\, Nx$
Propositional descriptions (e.g. declarative)	CP: $\exists e\, .\, Ve$	
	C°: $\lambda P\, \exists e\, .\, Pe$	VP: $\lambda e\, .\, Ve$

In nominal descriptions, determiners act as referential markers which indicate that the reference-making object(s) can be found in the evaluation context relevant for the discourse situation. The nominal phrase provides the sortal information which additionally delineates the set of possible referents in this context. In analogy, declarative sentence mood in a propositional description marks that the truth-making event can be found in the relevant evaluation context, while the sortal information carried by the VP restricts the set of possible truth-makers. The different specifications of the sentence mood demonstrate that there are distinct ways of linking the truth-conditions to events in the evaluation domain. Assertions maintain the existence of an event of the special type described by the VP, whereas questions imply that it is undecided whether such an event exists. Orders, finally, could be seen as being made true or false by events that follow the utterance. All sentence types share, nonetheless, that the entire proposition is not true or false until it has been anchored in an evaluation context.

(3) (a) *You gave him 5€.*
(b) *Did you give him 5€?*
(c) *Give him 5€!*

The contrast of assertions, questions, and orders shows furthermore that the sortal part of the event description may be shared by sentences of different sentence types. In all sentences in (3), the type of event described is a situation in which someone gives a male person 5€. Thus we conclude that every sentence describes an event and that the semantic representation of every sentence has to contain an event argument.[4]

[4] We even defend this rigorous claim against theories that assume that sentences interpreted as tautologies, analytical judgments, generic truths, or individual-level judgments should not comprise event arguments. On the one hand, the decision of whether a sentence expresses an episodic truth or, in contrast, a judgment of the former kinds is not an issue of sentence semantics

So far we have only considered positive sentences. What does the claim that every sentence has a truth-maker mean for negative sentences, i.e. sentences with sentence negation? Are there events that prove a negative sentences false? Or do we then have to turn our argument upside down, saying that negative descriptions are true if we cannot find a truth-maker for their positive counterparts? Given the case that negative sentences are true if the positive sentence does not correspond to any truth-maker in the evaluation context, how can negative event descriptions be related to the evaluation context at all? What do we know about the world when we have understood such a negative description? We will try to give detailed answers to these questions throughout the discussion in section 0, but it is obvious already at this point that negative descriptions and the truth-conditional function of sentence negation are a touchstone of every ontologically founded formal theory of truth and reference. It illuminates a range of problems, such as, for instance, the ontology of non-existence, that we do not see as long as we are dealing with positive assertive sentences only.

The characteristic of negative sentences of exaggerating the problems of reference and truth also shows some interesting reflections on the grammatical side. Sentences are internally structured, and this information structure regulates how sentences and their phrases are anchored in a coherent discourse and linked to the world context. In the syntax-semantics mapping, sentence negation reveals the specific properties of certain syntactic domains relative to the syntactic position of sentence negation, which often remain hidden in positive sentences. Let us turn to these grammatical phenomena first. It is a commonly accepted assumption that presuppositions remain constant under negation. This holds both for the semantic presuppositions carried by verbs (cf. (4)) and the existential presuppositions carried by nominal expressions (cf. (5)).

(4) *Das Auto hält (nicht) an.* → The car is moving.
'The car stopped (did not stop).'

(5) *Das Kind schläft (nicht).* → The child exists.
'The child is (not) sleeping.'

---

but can only be decided by considering all relevant contextual aspects. So how could we ever, without knowing the concrete context, decide whether
(i) *Am Montag trinkt Gregor Tee.* 'Gregor drinks tea on Monday.'
(ii) *Ein Löwe frisst eine Antilope.* 'A lion eats an antelope.'
expresses an episodic or a habitual or a generic truth?
We do not exclude, on the other hand, that events may coincide with the universe, or the lifetime of objects and persons, such that these events could serve as the truth-makers of sentences with non-episodic readings. The decision on whether the context of utterance intended by the speaker is a 'small' or a 'big' one, and, concluding on this, the decision on whether the truth-making event is a 'small' or a 'big' one lies far beyond sentence semantics.

The presupposed information of a sentence type has to be matched with the relevant discourse model. In contrast, the truth-relevant parts of verbal semantic information and the reference-relevant parts of nominal semantic information which are not presupposed are subject to the communicative type predefined by sentence mood. In the declarative sentences in (4) and (5), they are part of assertions and thus have to be matched with the relevant evaluation context. We conclude that a formal-semantic representation of the truth-conditions of negative sentences has to take into account how information structure organizes presupposed and non-presupposed information in a sentence in relation to sentence negation.

2 How to read DPs: presuppositions as anchors for contextual anchoring

Among other things, the readings of DPs in negative sentences are suitable indicators for this internal organization. The particular reading of a DP depends on its syntactic position relative to the syntactic position of (a possible) sentence negation. The definitions of presupposition commonly used in semantic and pragmatic literature do not normally consider this crucial point. (6) represents a straightforward but familiar definition which uses the fact that the validity of presuppositions is not touched by negation. The definition is exemplified by the sentences pair and its existential presuppositions in (7a) and (7b).

(6) "A is a presupposition of B, if B entails A and not-B entails A".(Hajičová 1984: p. 156)

(7) (a) *Das Kind schläft.* → The child exists.
'The child is sleeping.'

(b) *Das Kind schläft nicht.* → The child exists.
'The child is not sleeping.'

The definition, however, does not elucidate which semantic structure justifies our assumption. We know that the existential presuppositions resist negation since we understand the sentences. Thus the definition in (6) is only based on an intuitive interpretation but not on a grammatical test. While Propositional Logic treats sentences as negatable statements (cf. (8)),

(8) For every valuation V and for all formulas Φ:
$V(\neg\Phi) = 1$ iff $V(\Phi) = 0$ (cf. GAMUT 1991, p. 44)

natural-language sentences are expressions with a complex internal structure. We achieve an expression ϕ only by obeying the rules of semantic composition. Example (9), for instance, combines a verbal predicate (*sleep*) with its argument (the DP *the child*).

(9) (a) $\exists x[[\mathbf{Child}(x)] \wedge [\mathbf{Sleep}(x)]]$

In simplifying terms, (9a) would be the result of the semantic composition. If we apply the negation of Propositional Logic to the semantic representation of a natural-language sentence, negation operates on the whole expression and thus produces an external negation (cf. (9b)).

(9) (b) $\neg\exists x[[\mathbf{Child}(x)] \wedge [\mathbf{Sleep}(x)]]$

Several investigations in the seventies (e.g. Givón 1978, Fodor 1979, Hajičová 1984), however, argue that the external representation results in incorrect semantic forms. If we paraphrase the external negation as in (9b), we can show clearly that, by expanding the negation domain to the entire sentence, external negation produces inadequate truth conditions.

(10) (a) *Sarah cannot sleep because of her headache.*
(b) *It is not the case that [Sarah can sleep because of her headache].*

Rejecting the solution of Propositional Logic and turning instead to Predicate Logic as the familiar format of semantic representation, we can make use of the fact that natural-language sentences are internally structured expressions. Accordingly, sentences are nested and coordinated functions or function-argument structures. This presumption enables us to determine an internal scopal position for the negation functor. The resulting internal negation corresponds to the negation of the nuclear scope.

(11) $\exists x\ [[\mathbf{Child}(x)] \wedge \neg[\mathbf{Sleep}(x)]]$

We might postulate furthermore that presupposition is the result of an inference triggered by the definite article. This position is supported by many approaches, including recent investigations of discourse structure and text coherence (e.g. Chierchia 1995, Asher/Lascarides 1998a, and others). This cannot be the whole truth though. Even languages without an article system, such as most Slavic languages, generate analogous existential presuppositions, although there is no definite article serving as an alleged trigger of these presuppositions.

(12) (a) *Dítě nespí.* (Czech)
Ø child **neg** sleeps.

(b) Internal negation:
$\exists x\ [[\mathbf{Child}(x)] \wedge \neg[\mathbf{Sleep}(x)]]$

We recognize that the DP is located outside the scope of negation. Therefore, as in the German example before, the DP is not subjected to sentence negation.

The problems addressed so far are still common ground, but internal negation raises further issues: What is the actual descriptive content of the existential presupposition? Is it nothing more than that we assert the unique existence of a child?

(12) (c) Unique existential presupposition:
$\exists!x$ [**Child**(x)]

It seems that (12c) is not really informative. We can derive the same information from every sentence which has *das Kind* as its subject. Thus the presupposition is detached from the state of affairs which the carrier sentence denotes. Seuren's (1991) text-acceptability test for presuppositions (cf. (12d)), however, demonstrates that presuppositions somehow depend on the state of affairs underlying the proposition of the carrier sentence.

(12) (d) [*There is exactly one child*]$_{\text{Presupposition}}$ *and* [*it is sleeping*]$_{\text{Propositional condition}}$

This encourages us to claim that we have to interpret the presupposition with regard to the particular event that the sentence describes. The event predetermines the spatial and temporal domain to which the assertion of the existence of the referent applies, that is, it predetermines the discourse model of which the discourse referent is a part. Thus sentence negation always impacts those qualities which the sentence attributes to the event. But can we conclude on this that sentence negation automatically negates the existential assertion of the event, as represented in (13)?

(13) Negating the existential assertion of the event:
$\exists x\ [[\mathbf{P}(x)] \wedge \neg\exists e\ [\ \dots e \dots x \dots\ ]]$

This solution would lead us straight back to the same problem: negating the event's existence, we would not be able to anchor the referent within an asserted spatio-temporal context and thus we would not be able to link it to the underlying state of affairs. Moreover, we have to consider what the truth-conditions following from the negation of the event's existence would predict for other grammatical phenomena, such as, for instance, anaphoric reference.

(14) *Es regnet nicht.*
'It isn't raining.'

(a) - *Das freut Maria.*
'Mary is pleased about that.'

(b) - *Deshalb geht Maria mit ihren Kindern spazieren.*
'Therefore Mary is going for a walk with her children.'

(c) - *Das erleichtert das Autofahren.*
'This facilitates driving.'

The verb *regnen* involves only one argument which is the event argument. Thus negating the existence of this event excludes the possibility of establishing any discourse referents in the discourse model, raising the question of how we then would be able to establish anaphoric reference in the subsequent sentences ((14a) to (14c)), given that the previous sentence denoted an empty set of discourse referents. It seems that, in equating sentence negation with the negation of the existence of an event, we accept that sentence (14) does not tell us anything about the universe of discourse at all. But obviously, the sentence does express something and, in particular, it does assert the existence of a spatio-temporal entity to which we can refer. Therefore it seems more conclusive to assume that the sentence expresses that it is the case that it is not raining, and the fact that this is the case pleases Mary.

Another point is that, throughout semantic composition, further constituents such as manner adverbials have to access the event argument. Adverbs occur above and below the syntactic position of sentence negation. The two possibilities are associated with different readings.

(15) (a) *weil Gustav nicht auf taktvolle Weise die Wahrheit sagte.*
'since Gustav didn't tell the truth in a tactful manner.'

$\exists x\ [[\mathbf{Gustav}(x)] \wedge \neg\exists e[\ \mathbf{tactful}(e) \wedge [\mathbf{tell\_the\_truth}(x)](e)\ ]]$

(b) *weil Gustav auf taktvolle Weise nicht die Wahrheit sagte.*
'since Gustav, in a tactful manner, didn't tell the truth.'

$\exists x\ [[\mathbf{Gustav}(x)] \wedge \mathbf{tactful}(?) \wedge \neg\exists e[\ [\mathbf{tell\_the\_truth}(x)](e)\ ]]$

The representation using the negation of the event quantification (cf. (15a)) has no serious troubles with modification in the scope of sentence negation - besides the fact that the representation of the complete sentence only asserts the existence of a person named Gustav and, beyond that, does not claim anything else relevant with respect to this referent. Thus the sentence might at least somehow be anchored in the discourse model, but it is questionable how it can be evaluated. In sentence (15b), the modifier has scope over sentence negation. Even if the sentence expresses that Gustav did anything but telling the truth, the modifier belongs to the asserted information, is not canceled by negation, and describes that something that Gustav did was tactfully done. It is unclear, however, how this description of manner can be compositionally linked to the event argument if the event's existence is denied.

The data discussed so far suggests that sentence negation is an operator with a fixed syntactic position. The specific-unspecific dichotomy with respect to DP readings provides further evidence for this hypothesis. (16) compares the unspecific reading (a) of the internal argument DP with its specific reading (b).

(16) (a)	*Der*	*Richter*	*hat*	*[keinen*	*ZEUgen*	*vereidigt]*$_{\text{Focus}}$
	The	judge	has	**[neg+art**$_{\text{indef}}$	witness	sworn_in]
(b)	*Der*	*Richter*	*hat*	*einen Zeugen*	*[nicht*	*verEIDigt]*$_{\text{Focus}}$
	The	judge	has	a witness	**[neg**	sworn_in]

A number of analyses explain the difference by referring to the Tree-Splitting Mapping Hypothesis. According to this well-known methodic framework, the DP in (16a) is regarded as non-presuppositional and is mapped therefore onto the nuclear scope, whereas the presuppositional DP in (16b) is mapped onto the restrictor. This analysis rests on the syntactical precondition of LF-movement.

The Mapping Hypothesis, on the one hand, indeed reflects an empirically correct observation, namely that DPs with different readings show different scopes. On the other hand, the theory regards the actual reading of a DP as the only decisive factor for whether the DP is presuppositional or non-presuppositional. Such an actual reading, however, is produced by our conceptual interpretation and not by semantic composition or the syntax-semantics mapping. Hence the theory suggests that the feature of being (non-) presuppositional is independent of any syntactic constellations before LF. In contrast to this consequence, nonetheless, it is obvious that we can derive the respective reading of the DP *(k-)einen Zeugen* in the examples (16a) and (16b) simply by inspecting the syntactic surface structure.

We conclude that the trigger of presuppositional and specific readings is the DP's position in relation to a possible negation operator – based on the syntactic precondition that sentence negation operates below the existential event quantification.

(17) $\exists x\ [[\mathrm{P}(x)] \wedge \exists e\ [\neg(\ldots e \ldots x \ldots)]]$

The different scope relations in the examples in (16) are a consequence following on the fact that the DP moves out of the sentence focus and thereby also leaves the scope of a possible sentence-negation operator. The division of a sentence in presupposition and assertion, as it has already been proposed by Chomsky (1971) and Jackendoff (1972), proves to be an adequate partition for the truth-functional evaluation of the sentence with regard to information structure. In prosodically unmarked sentences, the division especially clarifies Löbner's (1990) claim that the focus of a sentence signifies which information unit describes the positive and true case or the contrary negative and false case. Only predicates and propositions confront us with such a polar alternative between true and false. Focus marks the part of the sentence on which the polar decision operates. The polar decision determines the conditions obtaining for the presupposition of the sentence (i.e. the presupposed referents), and these conditions are the same regardless of whether the entire sentence is true or false (cf. Löbner 1990: p. 169). Hence the focus is a (complex) function which decides on the truth-functional evaluation of the sentence. The existential assertion of referents denoted by constituents within the background (and thus within the presupposition of the sentence) is true with respect to this function of the focus. According to Roberts (1998), the focus gives a *partial answer*: "A *partial answer* to a question q is a proposition which contextually entails the evaluation – either true or false – of at least one element of Q-alt(q). A *complete answer* is a proposition which contextually entails an evaluation for each element of Q-alt(q)."

3 Truth-making: ontology as a key to referential keying

The structural solution proposed in (17) perfectly satisfies the grammatical requirements listed in section 1. Does it also lead, however, to a logical representation with an ontologically appropriate conceptual interpretation? The problem we meet if we try to place negation below the event quantification is that the expression in the negation scope is, in its own right, a complex structured expression.

(18) $\ldots \exists e\, [\neg[\ldots p(e)\ldots]]$

Thus we still have more than one option for internal negation, as a closer look at the complex propositional condition will show. Reichenbach (1947) assumes that predications may constitute higher-order predications on event arguments. We suppose that the instantiation relation introduced by Bierwisch (1988) or even simple bracketing serve the same purpose in equivalent ways[5].

(19) Structured eventive predications

(a)	Reichenbach's fact function[6]	$\exists e\, [[P(x)]^{*}(e)]$ with $^{*} \in \langle t, \langle e, t\rangle\rangle$
(b)	Bierwisch's instantiation relation	$\exists e\, [e \text{ inst } P(x)]$
(c)	Simple bracketing	$(P(x))(e)$

We will refer to all such descriptions of events as *structured eventive predications*.

[5] The Davidsonean and Neo-Davidsonean variants of Reichenbach's fact function, however, have to be regarded more critically with respect to their logical and semantic behavior. In general, both representation formats disguise the higher-order character of the structured eventive predication:

Davidson $\ldots \exists e\, [P(x, \ldots, e)]$

Neo-Davidson $\ldots \exists e\, [P(e)\ \&\ \ldots(\ldots e)\ \&\ \ldots.]$

In terms of Reichenbach's distinction between expressive and denotative terms (cf. Reichenbach (1947), p. 319-320), the functor-argument relation between the propositional condition and the event argument is represented using both denotative and expressive terms (the bracketing, the asterisk, and the syntax) in the fact function. The Davidsonean and the Neo-Davidsonean strategies, in contrast, hide this relation behind a purely expressive notation (the syntax of the main predication) and thereby make it impossible in advance to place a negation operator within the propositional condition – a possibility, nevertheless, that we will discuss in the following. Furthermore, the two strategies raise further serious problems concerning the compositional computability of a semantic sentence meaning and concerning the ontological adequacy of its conceptual interpretation.

[6] The asterisk marks that 'P of x' is used as a higher-order function.

Starting off with these representational formats, (18) turns out to be syntactically ambiguous. The ambiguity derives from the fact that the enclosed expression is itself a proposition and thus a truth-functional expression to which we can attribute a truth-value. Hence we can interpret (18) in two ways:

(20) $\neg \ldots p(e) \ldots$

$\neg(p(e))$ $\qquad\qquad$ $(\neg p)(e)$

Obviously, the two alternative readings do not receive the same interpretation. For a more transparent comparison, we will also include the negation of the event quantification as a possible solution in the following discussion, although, as shown above, there are some serious arguments against it. Thus, in total, there are three negative expressions in question[7].

(21) Semantic interpretation of sentences: three formats of structured eventive predications

F¬∃. Negative Event Quantification
$[\![\varphi\ [\alpha_{sent\text{-}neg}\ [p]]\ ]\!] = [\![\varphi]\!] \wedge \neg\exists e\ [e\ \text{INST}\ [\![p]\!]\ ]$

F¬INST. Negative Instantiation
$[\![\varphi\ [\alpha_{sent\text{-}neg}\ [p]]\ ]\!] = [\![\varphi]\!] \wedge \exists e\ [\neg[e\ \text{INST}\ [\![p]\!]\ ]]$

F¬φ. Negative Propositional Condition
$[\![\varphi\ [\alpha_{sent\text{-}neg}\ [p]]\ ]\!] = [\![\varphi]\!] \wedge \exists e\ [e\ \text{INST}\ \neg[\![p]\!]\ ]$

For Reichenbach, (F¬∃) and (F¬p) are anyway equivalent. He derives this equivalence from his definition of the fact function.

(22) Reichenbach's equivalence:
$p \equiv \exists e\ [(p)^*(e)]$ therefore $\neg p \equiv \neg\exists e\ [(p)^*(e)] \equiv \exists e\ [(\neg p)^*(e)]$

But is this equivalence actually desirable? What do the three different negative expressions actually denote from the viewpoint of conceptual interpretation?

We assume that every conceptualization - be it a mental image or a formal theory of reality - is grounded on a set of more or less explicit ontological commitments, which we can regard as the minimal consensus about the structure of the world (cf. Quine 1948/61). From an ontological point of view, the instantiation relation can be interpreted as a relation that links entities to a sort. We will not discuss, however, whether the semantic forms representing such sortal knowledge correspond to type concepts or to universals. As previously mentioned, the semantics expressions that denote sorts comprise nominal and propositional descriptions. Physical objects (or *continuants*) that fall under a

---

[7] Double square brackets $[\![\,]\!]$ stand informally for any semantic interpretation function. For better clarity, we use Bierwisch's instantiation function. We furthermore disregard the possibility of placing the negation in the main predication (cf. $\exists e\ [\ e\ \text{INST}\ [\neg P](x)\ ]$), which is completely out from a compositional and extensional view.

certain sort of spatial entity are possible reference-makers for the nominal description which denotes the sort. Analogously, events (or *occurrents*) that fall under a certain sort of spatio-temporal entity are possible truth-makers for the propositional descriptions which denote the sort. Thus to know what a certain segment of the world has to look like if we are able to refer to the segment using a certain description may serve as a clue to the ontological foundation of referential keying and, in particular, to the ontological foundation of truth-making.

On this background, (23) illustrates a first attempt to capture propositional descriptions in terms of events (e), event sorts (p), and an instantiation relation INST holding between the entities of both categories. Then we can compare the three approaches defined in (21) in view of what their logical representations tell us about the truth-making events. Note that, in accordance with the results of section 2 and with the list in (21), p does not stand for complete sentences but only for that part of a natural-language sentence which denotes the polar alternative and thus the non-presupposed event description.

(23) Truth-making based on instantiation

(a) Negative event quantification:
$\neg\exists e[e \text{ INST } p]$

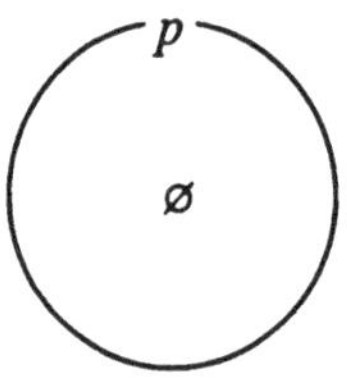

(b) Negative Instantiation:
$\exists e[\neg(e \text{ INST } p)]$

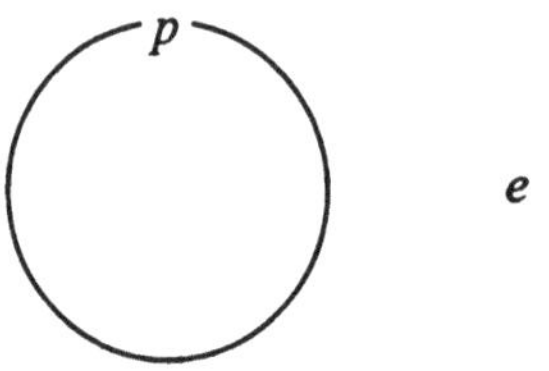

(c) Negative Propositional Condition:
$\exists e[e \text{ INST } \neg p]$

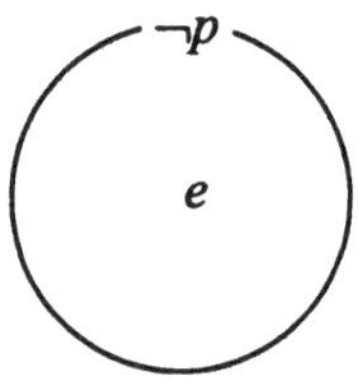

At first glance, these extensional interpretations do not seem informative. Given that (i), p is a grammatically well-formed, non-tautological proposition and that (ii), sufficiently many events are regularly distributed across the universe, we will necessarily always find an event in the universe which is an instance of p and thus proves **negative quantification** false. In contrast, we will necessarily always find events which are not an instance of p and, respectively, which are instances of $\neg p$, such that the **negative instantiation** and the **negative propositional condition** would be true in any context.

The schemas in (23), however, only considered the sortal information of event descriptions but not the referential marker represented by declarative sentence mood. The referential marker indicates that the recipient can only locate the truth-maker if she takes the relevant discourse model into account. The relevant discourse model, in turn, is associated to a referential domain in the world. Accordingly, the discourse domain functions similarly to a grid that is projected onto the spatio-temporal world, while the referential marker functions similarly to an instruction that leads the recipient to looking for the intended truth-maker in one particular grid square. In accord with Löbner (1985), therefore, we claim that we have to restrict the event quantification to a certain spatio-temporal domain.

(24) **Requirement for truth-making (R.I): spatio-temporal restriction (truth-making is always relative to a spatio-temporal domain)**

An instance of a proposition is always only a truth-maker of the proposition with respect to the spatio-temporal domain of evaluation. The domain is defined by the contextual interpretation of the explicit and implicit spatial and temporal information (such as tense, aspectual information, modifying information, etc.) provided by the corresponding sentence, and by supplementing information inferred from the discourse domain.
Let Δ be our spatio-temporal domain, and INST^{Δ} a relation between events and propositional event descriptions, such that $e\ \text{INST}^{\Delta}\ p$ means 'e is a truth-maker for p in Δ'.

But do we thereby reach our goal?

(25) Truth-making seen as instantiation restricted to a spatio-temporal domain

(a) Negative Event Quantification:
$\neg\exists e^{\subseteq\Delta}[\ e\ \text{INST}^{\Delta}\ p\ ]$

As before, **negative quantification** (cf. (25a)) allows many too many models. We only know that the class p is empty. We know nothing else, however, about the rest of the domain. In particular, we do not know whether there is an instance of $\neg p$ or whether there is an event in our domain Δ at all that could serve as an antecedent for linking compositional or discourse contexts.

(25) (b) Negative Instantiation:
$\exists e^{\subseteq\Delta}[\ \neg(e\ \text{INST}^{\Delta}\ p)\ ]$

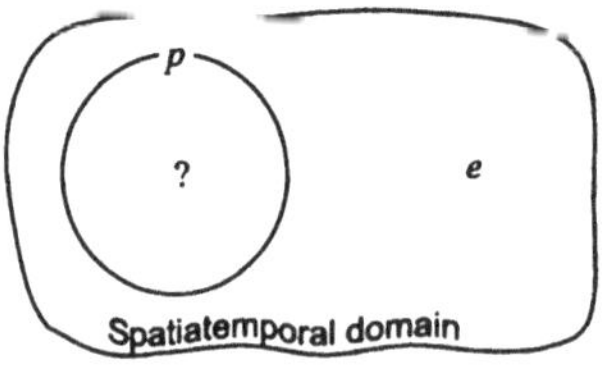

Reichenbach also rules out **negative instantiation** (cf. (25b)). We know that there is an event which is not an element of *p*. But we still do not know whether this event is an element of $\neg p$. And, even worse, it is possible that there are events in this domain which are elements of *p*, although our negative sentence intends exactly this case to be excluded.

(25) (c) Negative Propositional Condition:
$\exists e^{\subseteq\Delta}[\ e\ \text{INST}^{\Delta}\ \neg p\ ]$

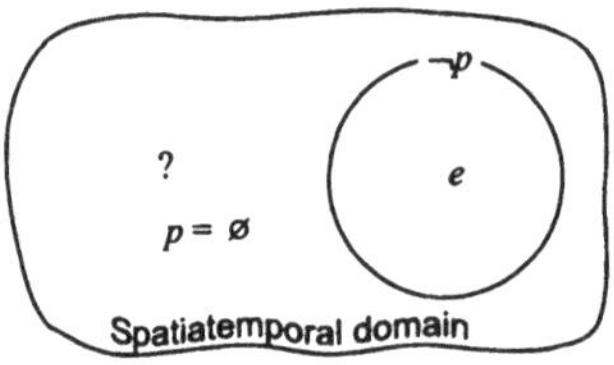

Negative propositional condition (cf. (25c)) does not tell us much about the domain's events outside $\neg p$. Nevertheless (F¬p) specifies an event of a concrete (negative) type - in contrast to (F¬∃) and (F¬INST): (F¬∃) does not speak about existing events and their types at all; (F¬INST) invents an event but only determines that it is not classed with a certain type; this information does not really seem suitable as a sortal criterion for identification since every entity belongs to a particular type or a particular hierarchy of types and thus does not fall under an unrestricted number of further types.

Unfortunately, (F¬p) does not entail that the existence of a truth-maker of *p* is excluded. This is required, however, since negation is contrary, such that there cannot be both a truth-maker for a polar proposition and a truth-maker for its negative counterpart in one and the same spatio-temporal domain. Since we are talking about the correspondence between sentence types and evaluation contexts, we cannot reduce this contrariness to a logical triviality. With regard to the ontological foundation of truth-making, it is a perfectly meaningful question whether all polar sentences and their anti-polars always constitute contrary pairs. Thus we may ask, for instance, if there are any world contexts that allow that a pair of a positive and a negative sentence with one propositional condition holds true in one and the same context. Since we are dealing with sentence types, there could possibly exist some cases in which a domain comprises truth-makers for contrary propositions.

(26) *Es regnet und es regnet nicht.*
'It's raining and it's not raining.'

(27) *Hansi sprach ein Mädchen offensichtlich an und Hansi sprach ein Mädchen offensichtlich nicht an.*
'Hansi has obviously spoken to a girl and Hansi has obviously not spoken to a girl.'

(28) *Frank hat offensichtlich angehalten und Frank hat offensichtlich nicht angehalten.*
'Frank has obviously stopped and Frank has obviously not stopped.'

We observe, however, that all attempts of constructing such sentence pairs result in a division of the spatio-temporal truth-making domain. We will call this phenomenon *contextual branching*. Accordingly, it is obvious that the sentence pair (26), when applied to one and the same domain, splits this domain up into two spatial parts (spatial contextual branching). We are able to imagine contexts where it makes sense to utter (26), but, nevertheless, it seems that all these contexts are composed out of two spatially disjoint (i.e. non-overlapping) spaces, such that it is raining in one of them and is not raining in the other one. The two events described by the pair in (27) could happen simultaneously within one single space, but it is clear that the two girls cannot be identical. Thus the domain is split up into two referential contexts (referential contextual branching). Finally, (28) shows that most of such contrary sentence pairs result in temporal contextual branching of the relevant truth-making domain. The truth-making events for the two sentences cannot take place at the same time, as long as we accept that *Frank* refers to the same person.

We thus conclude that polar sentences generally stand in a contrary opposition to their negated counterparts, and vice versa.

(29) **Requirement for truth-making (R.II): contrariness of negation (negation produces contrary sorts)**

Within one intended spatio-temporal domain of evaluation, the existence of an event instantiating a polar proposition excludes the possibility that there also exists an event instantiating the negated proposition. Let the relation $\text{INST}^{\Delta,+C}$ be such that every requirement holding for INST^{Δ} holds for $\text{INST}^{\Delta,+C}$, too. And furthermore it holds that

(i) $\exists e^{\subseteq\Delta}[\, e \ \text{INST}^{\Delta,+C} \neg p \,] \rightarrow \neg\exists e_i^{\subseteq\Delta}[\, e_i \ \text{INST}^{\Delta,+C} p \,]$

(ii) $\exists e^{\subseteq\Delta}[\, e \ \text{INST}^{\Delta,+C} p \,] \rightarrow \neg\exists e_i^{\subseteq\Delta}[\, e_i \ \text{INST}^{\Delta,+C} \neg p \,]$

If we restrict the instantiation relation such that the contrariness of truth-making holds, the three formats yield the models illustrated in (30).

(30) Truth-making regarded as an instantiation relation, $\text{INST}^{\Delta,+c}$, which satisfies the contrariness of negation[8]

(a) Negative Event Quantification:
$\neg\exists e^{\subseteq\Delta}[\, e\ \text{INST}^{\Delta,+c}\ p\,]$

$\nvdash \exists e_i^{\subseteq\Delta}[\, e_i\ \text{INST}^{\Delta,+c}\ \neg p\,]$

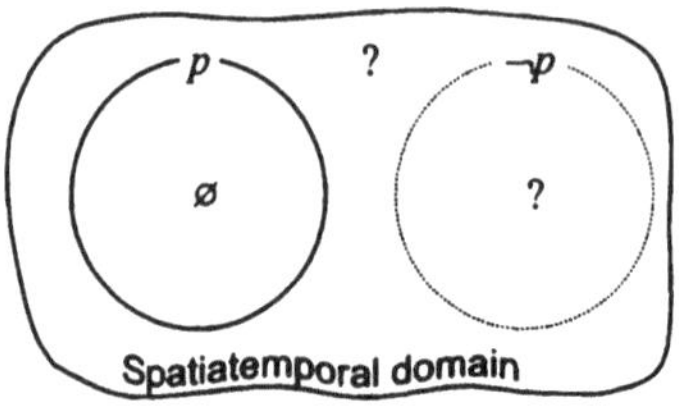

(b) Negative Instantiation:
$\exists e^{\subseteq\Delta}[\, \neg(e\ \text{INST}^{\Delta,+c}\ p)\,]$

$\vdash$?

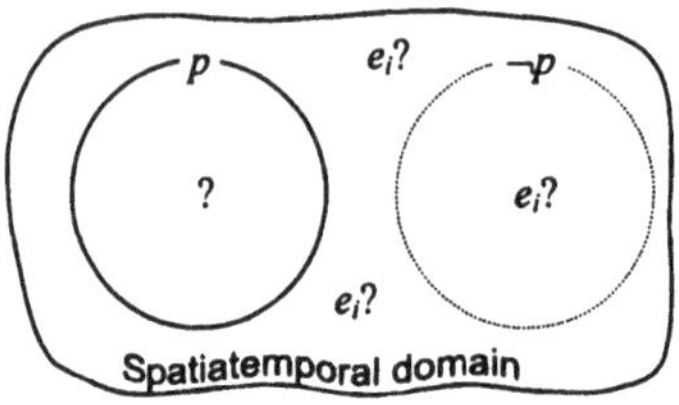

(c) Negative Propositional Condition:
$\exists e^{\subseteq\Delta}[\, e\ \text{INST}^{\Delta,+c}\ \neg p\,]$

$\vdash \neg\exists e_i^{\subseteq\Delta}[\, e_i\ \text{INST}^{\Delta,+c}\ p\,]$

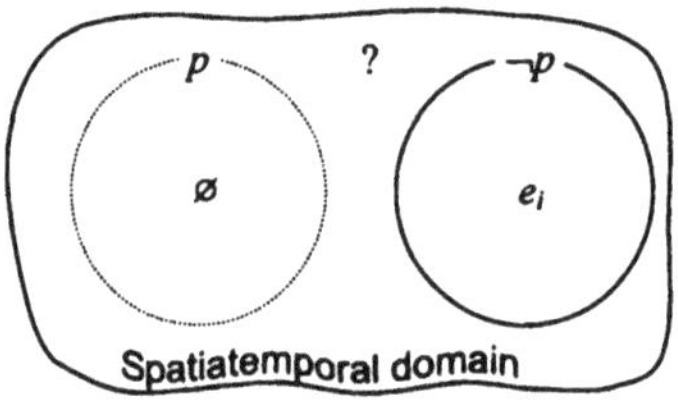

The contrariness of truth-making applies perfectly to (F¬p), since we can restrict the definition simply by adding requirement (R.II) as an axiom. The logical representation of (F¬p) then satisfies the implicans of the axioms. The contrariness of truth-making does not apply to (F¬∃) and (F¬INST) however. Why not? (F¬∃) satisfies the logical format of the implicatum of requirement (R.II), but the contrariness requirement is only a necessary but no sufficient condition for truth-making. Thus we cannot conclude anything from (F¬∃). This observation shows one more time that (F¬∃) is a very weak description for a spatio-temporal domain as it does not indentify any truth-maker.

Our intuition about (F¬INST) is that the exclusion of an event from a certain type is not information enough to characterize the event. The complement of a type does not provide a sufficient characterization of those entities which are not of this type. Thus we cannot conclude from the existence of an event in the complement of a type that the class specified by the type is empty – at least within the given domain. Nor can we conclude that there is an instance of a class specified by the negated proposition. Reichenbach's conception suggests that propositions are **privative** descriptions. The graphs in (30) anticipate the

[8] We use $\vdash$ and $\nvdash$ here as informal abbreviations for 'enables us to infer' and 'does not enable us to infer'.

fact that an entity, which is not an instance of a certain description, is not automatically an instance of a complementary negative description. Imagine that we have two events in one spatio-temporal domain, the first one being Peter's reading the newspaper, the second being Mary's playing the piano.

(31) Events and Privative Descriptions

(a) $\exists e^{\subseteq\Delta}[\, e \text{ INST}^{\Delta,+C}$ **[read(Peter, newspaper)]]**[9]

(b) $\exists e^{\subseteq\Delta}[\, \neg(e \text{ INST}^{\Delta,+C}$ **[read(Peter, newspaper)])]**

Disregarding the linguistic description and thinking of the two pictograms as ontological entities, we then are able to apply both (31a) and (31b) to this context without producing a contradiction since Mary's playing the piano is naturally not an instance of *Peter is reading the newspaper.*[10] Now we can formulate a third requirement as follows.

(32) **Requirement for truth-making (R.III): privativeness of truth-making (sortality is privative)**

Within the intended spatio-temporal domain of evaluation, the existence of an event that does not make a proposition true does not exclude the possibility that there exists a truth-maker of the proposition in the spatio-temporal domain. Nor does it entail the existence of a truth-maker of the negated proposition. Let the relation $\text{INST}^{\Delta,+C,+P}$ be such that every requirement holding for $\text{INST}^{\Delta,+C}$ holds for $\text{INST}^{\Delta,+C,+P}$, too. And furthermore it holds that

(i.a) $\exists e^{\subseteq\Delta}[\, \neg(e \text{ INST}^{\Delta,+C,+P}\, p)\,] \nvdash \neg\exists e_i^{\subseteq\Delta}[\, e_i \text{ INST}^{\Delta,+C,+P}\, p\,]$

(i.b) $\exists e^{\subseteq\Delta}[\, \neg(e \text{ INST}^{\Delta,+C,+P}\, \neg p)\,] \nvdash \neg\exists e_i^{\subseteq\Delta}[\, e_i \text{ INST}^{\Delta,+C,+P}\, \neg p\,]$

(ii.a) $\exists e^{\subseteq\Delta}[\, \neg(e \text{ INST}^{\Delta,+C,+P}\, p)\,] \nvdash \exists e_i^{\subseteq\Delta}[\, e_i \text{ INST}^{\Delta,+C,+P}\, \neg p\,]$

(ii.b) $\exists e^{\subseteq\Delta}[\, \neg(e \text{ INST}^{\Delta,+C,+P}\, \neg p)\,] \nvdash \exists e_i^{\subseteq\Delta}[\, e_i \text{ INST}^{\Delta,+C,+P}\, p\,]$

As a consequence, we have to refine the schemas once more. Now the entailments derived from the respective assumptions (and in particular those derived from negative instantiation) become clear.

---

[9] The treatment of DPs is simplified in this and the following representation.

[10] In particular, we cannot conclude on $\exists e[\neg(e \text{ INST}^{\Delta,+C}\, p)]$ that $\neg\exists e[\, e \text{ INST}^{\Delta,+C}\, p)]$. Beyond the discussion of logical formats, this observation meets a natural intuition we have about descriptions paraphrasing the existence or presence of events and objects in a certain domain.

(i) *There is something in this room which is not a book.* $\nvdash$ *There is no book in this room.*

(ii) *Something is happening right here and now which is my reading a book .* $\nvdash$ *I am not reading a book.*

(33) Truth-making regarded as an instantiation relation, $\text{INST}^{\Delta,+C,+P}$, which satisfies the requirements of contrariness and privativeness

(a) Negative Event Quantification (F¬∃):
$\neg\exists e^{\subseteq\Delta}[\ e\ \text{INST}^{\Delta,+C,+P}\ p\ ]$

$\nvdash \exists e_i^{\subseteq\Delta}[\ e_i\ \text{INST}^{\Delta,+C,+P}\ \neg p\ ]$

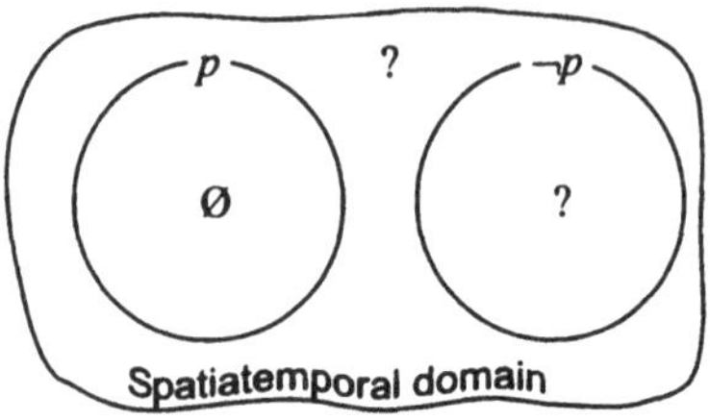

(b) Negative Instantiation (F¬INST):
$\exists e^{\subseteq\Delta}[\ \neg(e\ \text{INST}^{\Delta,+C,+P}\ p)\ ]$

$\nvdash \neg\exists e_i^{\subseteq\Delta}[\ e_i\ \text{INST}^{\Delta,+C,+P}\ \neg p\ ]$
$\nvdash \neg\exists e_j^{\subseteq\Delta}[\ e_j\ \text{INST}^{\Delta,+C,+P}\ p\ ]$

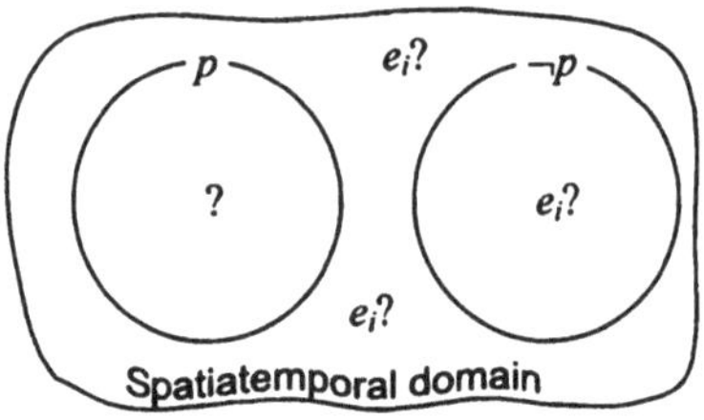

It turns out that the formats (F¬∃) and (F¬ INST) are not restricted enough to capture the notion of truth-making, since (F¬∃) hardly provides a description of the domain and its events, and (F¬INST) does not let us see of which sort e_i actually is. Therefore the two approaches are not able to exclude that Δ or parts of Δ verify an unrestricted number of negative sentences which are definitely not relevant in Δ.

Let p be the polar predication within the sentence *weil Goethe Friederike Brion* [$_p$ *heiratete*], 'since Goethe married Friederike Brion', which is false at any time and at any place in our world (as long as the reference is clear). Let furthermore Δ_1 be any situation in the past before our 'here and now'. Then we will certainly not find any truth-maker for p in our real-world domain Δ_1, since only the event of their marriage itself could be a truth-maker of p. Therefore, according to the inversion of definition (F¬∃), the negation of p would be true in Δ_1. At first glance, it is quite tolerable if we just say that it holds true in Δ_1 that Goethe did not marry Friederike Brion. The point is, however, that obviously neither p nor its negated counterpart (i.e. the polar part $\neg p$ of *weil Goethe Friederike Brion* [$_{\neg p}$ *nicht heiratete*] 'since Goethe did not marry Friederike Brion') are descriptions of Δ_1 or of any event in Δ_1. As evidence for the truth of $\neg p$, we rather consider the lifetime or a part of the lifetime of Goethe as possible candidates, but not Ceasar's assassination, the Storming of the Bastille, or our latest appointment with our dentist. The proposition p is false **during** Δ_1 not because Δ_1 or part of Δ_1 is a truth-maker of $\neg p$, but p is false **during** Δ_1 because Δ_1 belongs to a concrete world with a concrete history, and this history contains an event disjoint from Δ_1 which is a truth-maker of $\neg p$.

The format (F$\neg$INST) also does not provide a way out of this mess, since we naturally find an event in Δ_1 which is not a truth-maker of p, such that this solution, too, erroneously suggests that the negative sentence $\neg p$ was a description of Δ_1.

We conclude that instantiation only be necessary but not sufficient conditions for truth-making. Requirement (R.IV) in (34) formulates the conditional link between truth-making and the instantiation, extended by the previous requirements, as a further partial definition of the truth-making relation.

(34) **Requirement for truth-making (R.IV): instantiation only provides necessary but not sufficient conditions for truth-making**

If an event makes a polar proposition true in a domain Δ, this fact necessarily excludes the possibility of that there is an event in Δ of the anti-polar sort, and, furthermore, this fact necessarily requires that there is at least one event in Δ which does not belong to the anti-polar sort. Thus it holds that

(i.a) $\exists e^{\subseteq\Delta}\,[\, e\,\mathrm{TM}^{\Delta}\, p\,] \rightarrow \neg\exists e_i^{\subseteq\Delta}[\, e_i\,\mathrm{INST}^{\Delta,+C,+P}\,\neg p]$

(i.b) $\exists e^{\subseteq\Delta}\,[\, e\,\mathrm{TM}^{\Delta}\,\neg p\,] \rightarrow \neg\exists e_i^{\subseteq\Delta}[\, e_i\,\mathrm{INST}^{\Delta,+C,+P}\, p]$

(ii.a) $\exists e^{\subseteq\Delta}\,[\, e\,\mathrm{TM}^{\Delta}\, p\,] \rightarrow \exists e_j^{\subseteq\Delta}[\neg(e_i\,\mathrm{INST}^{\Delta,+C,+P}\,\neg p)]$

(ii.b) $\exists e^{\subseteq\Delta}\,[\, e\,\mathrm{TM}^{\Delta}\,\neg p] \rightarrow \exists e_j^{\subseteq\Delta}[\neg(e_i\,\mathrm{INST}^{\Delta,+C,+P}\, p)]$

(iii.a) $\exists e^{\subseteq\Delta}\,[\,(e\,\mathrm{TM}^{\Delta}\, p) \rightarrow (e\,\mathrm{INST}^{\Delta,+C,+P}\, p)\,]$

(iii.b) $\exists e^{\subseteq\Delta}\,[\,(e\,\mathrm{TM}^{\Delta}\,\neg p) \rightarrow (e\,\mathrm{INST}^{\Delta,+C,+P}\,\neg p)\,]$

It seems that format (F$\neg$p) comes close to the intended semantics of the TM-relation, since it can satisfy all requirements for truth-making, (R.I) to (R.IV).

(35) Truth-making in the format of Negative Propositional Condition (F$\neg p$)

$\exists e^{\subseteq\Delta}[\, e\,\mathrm{TM}^{\Delta}\,\neg p\,]$

$\vdash \neg\exists e_i^{\subseteq\Delta}[\, e_i\,\mathrm{TM}^{\Delta}\, p\,]$

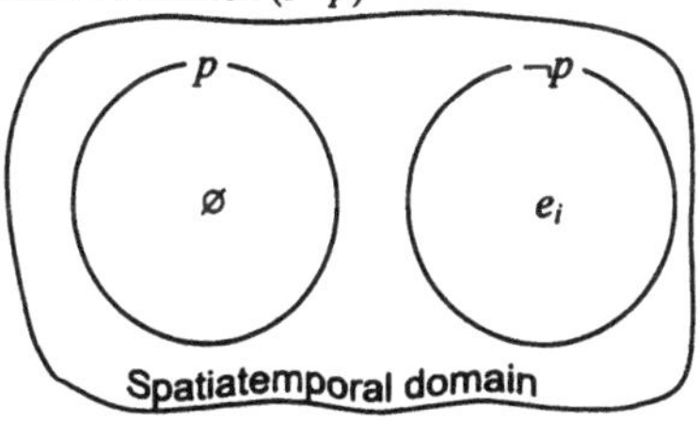

Using negative sorts, however, rests on a strong presumption, namely, that negative propositions are able to cover a world which does not contain any 'negative events'. There are no non-existing objects, events, state of affairs, or universals in the world. Nor are there disjunctions of such entities. It is conceivable, however, that type **concepts,** such as, for instance, the type NON-RED, involve negations, complements, disjunctions, and so forth. We also encode such complementary sorts in language, but there are only few primitive lexicalizations (e.g. *schlafen*, 'sleep' – *wachen*, 'be awake'). Our belief is that there are no non-reds in the world, but that, nonetheless, the NON-RED concept is able to project onto the world and class part of its entities. The meta-conceptual relations that hold between the NON-RED concept and the RED concept enable us to reason about the set of carriers of a property like color, and its complement. Without these meta-conceptual relations, such complementary type concepts would be completely opaque with respect to the entities which they map.

Another interesting point is that the requirements (R.I) to (R.IV) do not really speak about the logical characteristics of sort-instantiation or truth-making. Nor do they explain the characteristics of the two relations, since such an explanation should show how sorts and true/false sentences relate to the world. Rather the requirements speak about **the world** as to describe what it has to be like whenever we are able to produce true or false assertions about it. Accordingly, it is the world and its structure which forbid that both a polar sentence and its negated counterpart can hold true in one and the same spatio-temporal domain, since, otherwise, the domain can always be devided in spatial, temporal, or referential subdomains. This is reflected by requirement (R.V).

(36) **Requirement for truth-making (R.V): approximation of a definition of the truth-making relation**
An event e is a truth-maker of a polar proposition $\neg p$ in a spatio-temporal domain Δ if and only if e is a false-maker of p in Δ, and this is the case if and only if, for ontological reasons, the existence of e in Δ excludes the possibility that there is an e_i in Δ which is a truth-maker of p in Δ. Thus with respect to a knowledge base $\mathcal{K}$ it holds that

(i) $e\,\mathbf{TM}^{\Delta}\,p \leftrightarrow \mathcal{K} \cup [\,e \subseteq \Delta\,] \vdash \neg\exists e_i^{\subseteq\Delta}[\,e_i\,\mathbf{TM}^{\Delta}\,\neg p]$

(ii) $e\,\mathbf{TM}^{\Delta}\,\neg p \leftrightarrow \mathcal{K} \cup [\,e \subseteq \Delta\,] \vdash \neg\exists e_i^{\subseteq\Delta}[\,e_i\,\mathbf{TM}^{\Delta}\,p]$

This is exactly what is going on: the contradictoriness of negation only holds if instances of p and instances $\neg p$ exclude each other for general ontological reasons in one and the same spatio-temporal domain. If we cannot find any other ontological justification for the satisfaction of this condition, the truth-maker of a negative sentence is the complete spatio-temporal domain. A 'general ontological reason' can be any necessary condition which applies to the spatio-temporal constellation in our domain.[11] Hence it is clear that the representation of truth- or false-making has to refer to the entire information in our knowledge base in order to find the ontological reasons. Thus the definition in (36) is, at the same time, a law of inference.

The solution provides correct results for our Goethe example: the event of our latest visit to our dentist is no truth-maker for *weil Goethe Friederike Brion heiratete*. But there also is no e in this domain whose existence excludes for ontological reasons that there is an e' in the domain which makes p true. There could be a marriage of Goethe and Brion taking place in the domain – but, in fact, there is not. There is no false-maker of the sentence' polar predica-

[11] Thus it is not enough to refer only to the fact that the structure of the domain is such as it is actually given in reality.

tion p and thus no truth-maker of $\neg p$. Hence neither p nor $\neg p$ are descriptions of the domain or its parts. The solution also fits our intuition about generic negative sentences such as (37).

(37) *There is no golden sphere with a diameter of 10 miles.*

Since we will not find either a truth-maker nor a false-maker in a spatially and temporally restricted domain, we would have to extend the focus of our discourse model ad infinitum. Obviously, only the whole universe can be the truth- or false-maker of such a generic negative sentence, unless we find a truth-maker for a law of nature that excludes the existence of such objects in the whole universe. Then this truth-maker would be a false-maker for the positive counterpart of (37), *There is a golden sphere with a diameter of 10 miles*, and thus would prove (37) true.

4 Logical representation and compositional feasibility

Another problem with the logical representation of (F¬p) is that there is no real option for the semantic composition above the lexical level.

(38) Compositionally (im)possible sentence-negation operators

(a) S: $\exists e\,[\,p(e)\,]$
NEG₁: $\lambda p\,[\,\neg p\,]$ — Negative existential quantification
$\neg\exists e\,[\,p(e)\,]$

(b) VP: $\ldots\lambda e\,[\,p(e)\,]$ — Negative instantiation
NEG₂: $\lambda Q \ldots \lambda e\,[\,\neg(Q(e))\,]$
$\ldots\lambda e\,[\neg([\,p(e)\,])\,]$

(c) V°: $\ldots\lambda x\,\lambda e\,[\,[P(x, \ldots)](e)\,]$ — Negative propositional condition
NEG₃: ?

There are simple solutions with plain negation operators which enable us to derive negative quantification and negative instantiation but do not derive negated propositional condition. The problematic point is that the propositional condition is bound as an argument such that modifiers or negation cannot access it after lexical insertion. To separate the eventive argument and the instantiation from the core proposition and combine it later on with sentence mood does also not provide a real option since the event argument has to be accessible for temporal operators and any kinds of modifiers during the composition of the sentence. The unfeasibility of a compositional realization of sentence negation as (F–p) is, in our view, not just incidental. Sentence negation is a grammatical phenomenon which, as we have shown, is inseparably linked to the internal organization of information in a sentence. Hence it cannot operate at an lexicon-internal level.[12]

We conclude that we cannot regard the semantic form of negative sentences as a realization of (F$\neg\exists$), since this approach yields a logical representation which is not adequate with respect to information structure and conceptual interpretation. Nor can we regard it as a simple mapping of (F$\neg$INST), since this definition has turned out as too weak to explain truth-making. We also cannot regard sentence negation as a realization of (F$\neg$p), since this approach is ruled out by syntactic and semantic constraints on sentence structure. We need instead an interpretation rule that translates the semantic form into the intended conceptual structure.

(39) Conceptual interpretation of sentence negation

$$[\![\ldots\exists e\,[\ldots\neg[\ldots p(e)\ldots]\ldots\wedge e\subseteq\Delta]\ldots]\!] = \ldots[\ldots[\![e]\!]\,\mathrm{TM}^{\Delta}\,\neg[\![p]\!]\,\ldots]\ldots$$

5 Syntactic preconditions for semantic mapping

The equivalence in (39) only solves half of the compositionality problem though. The crucial presumption of the above discussion is that *p* does not completely represent natural-language sentences but structured eventive predications – which only constitute the core proposition, or propositional condition, of a full sentence. Accordingly, in agreement with Löbner (1990) and Roberts (1996), negation partitions sentences (i) in such segments that contain presupposed information and thus are not subject to evaluation, and (ii) in such segments whose information is decisive for the truth value of the entire sentence. In total, we have to consider two kinds of structuring.

(40) The nested complexity of natural-language sentences

Structured sentence semantics	S: $\ldots\wedge\varphi\wedge\ldots\wedge$ (**neg**)p
	$\updownarrow$
Structured eventive predication	(**neg**)p: $\exists e\,[\ldots\wedge(\mathbf{neg})\varphi(e)\wedge\ldots]$

The previous section only considered the truth-conditions of structured eventive predications, whereas the presupposed information in structured sentences has been left out as irrelevant for referential keying. Nevertheless, we now have to tackle the problem of how to distinguish both kinds of information. The sentence meaning has to have been built compositionally such that the negation operator and the positions of the constituent relative to the negation operator are the trigger for the setup of the discourse model. So let us resume

[12] There are some negation-like compositional operations within the lexicon though. Negative affixes and ad-hoc constructions such as *nicht-rot*, 'non-red', can trigger such operation. However, such phenomena are completely independent of sentence negation.

the discussion of section 2. We have seen that the focus domain and the scope of negation interrelate. Dölling (1988) demonstrated in detail that the scope of negation coincides with the focus domain of the sentence. Contrasting examples (41a) and (41b) (which reiterate (16a) and (16b)) points out that specific presuppositional DPs move outside the negation scope and thereby outside the focus.

(41) (a) *Der Richter hat [keinen ZEUgen vereidigt]*$_{\text{Focus}}$

(b) *Der Richter hat einen Zeugen [nicht verEIDigt]*$_{\text{Focus}}$

In comparison, non-presuppositional DPs remain in situ or, at least, within the focus. They thereby remain within the negatable part of the sentence.

The focus-background structure divides a sentence into anaphoric, i.e. presuppositionally given, constituents on the one hand, and non-anaphoric constituents on the other hand. Anaphoric constituents move out of the negation functor whereas non-anaphoric constituents remain in situ and thus remain part of the focus domain. Speaking with Fodor (1979, p. 211), they are "excused from having to refer in the real world." In this respect, the two sentences in (41) differ in their way of referring to a discourse model.

In (41a), the existence of a witness is under negation and is excused from having to refer to the real world, that is, from having to refer to a given discourse referent. In contrast, sentence (41b) is only true if the existence of a witness is presupposed in the given discourse model. The truth-condition of the two sentences differ exactly in this point. With respect to semantic composition, we assume that, in accord with Haftka (1994), the negation functor is a VP-adjunction, just as the position functor is a VP-adjunction in affirmative sentences. The morphosyntactic feature in negative sentences is specified as [+neg]. The structure tree in (42a) representing sentence (41a) shows that the DP remains in situ and thereby within the negatable sentence part.

(42) (a) Example: *Der Richter$_i$ hat [keinen ZEUGEN t_i VEREIDIGT]*$_{\text{NegScope}}$]$_{\text{Focus}}$

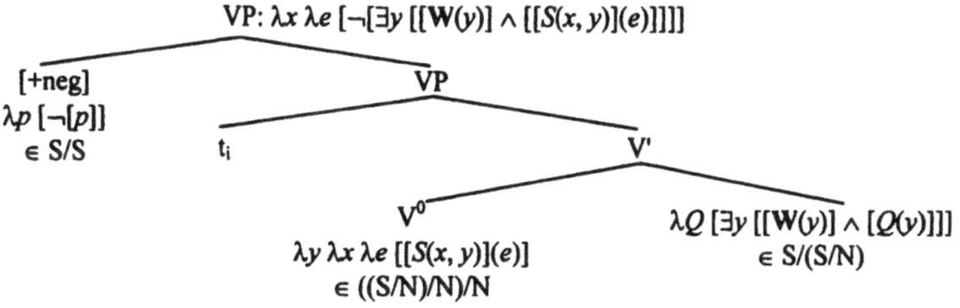

In contrast, we observe in (42b) that the DP in (41b) has been moved outside the sentence focus and thus outside the negatable part of the sentence.

(42) (b) Example: *Der Richter$_i$ hat einen Zeugen$_j$* [[*nicht t_i t_j VEREIDIGT*]$_{NegScope}$]$_{Focus}$

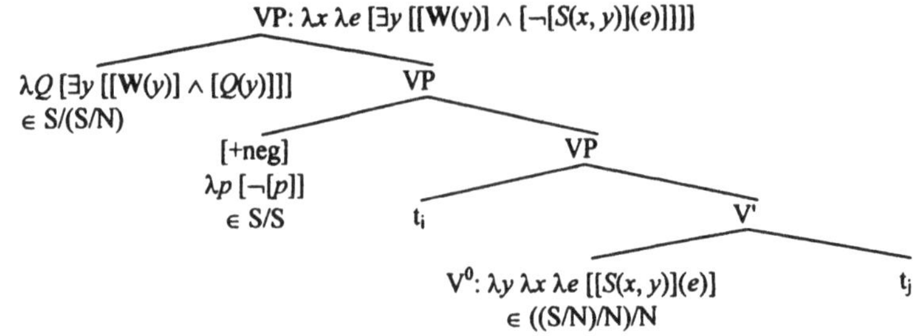

The specific reading is brought about by the syntax-semantics mapping. The DP is located outside the scope of negation such that the negation cannot access the existential assertion of the internal argument DP. The structural preconditions of the resulting syntactic constellation equal those that obtain on individual terms, for individual terms, too, cannot be negated.[13] We finally accomplish the conceptual interpretation of the indefinite DP using an equivalence.

(43) $\underbrace{\exists x\, [[P(x)] \wedge [\neg[Q(x)]]]}_{SF} \equiv \underbrace{\neg Q\, (\varepsilon x\, [P(x)])}_{CS}$

At the level of compositional semantics, we receive a structure constituted by a main functor, i.e. the DP, and a secondary functor, i.e. the propositional condition. In example (41a), in contrast, the DP is part of the complex function that corresponds semantically to the focus domain and hence is part of the negatable function of the sentence. Therefore the DP cannot be a presuppositional one.

During the next steps of semantic composition, the sentence-mood operator binds the event role in the head of CP. The sentence-mood operator introduces the existential assertion of the event. It is a crucial point that the sentence-negation operator does not move up to C^0 (cf. the structure trees in (44)) since otherwise, we would erroneously postulate identical truth-conditions for (41a) and (41b).

---

[13] The matter becomes more complicated when the sentence contains attitudinal adverbials. Such adverbials are positioned above negation. Accordingly, it is possible to extend (41b) to (41c):

(38c) Der Richter hat *wahrscheinlich* [einen Zeugen nicht VEREIDIGT]$_{Focus}$

The answer on the question *Was ist denn mit dem Richter los?* 'What's up with the judge?' shows that *einen Zeugen* 'a witness' in (41b) can be a referential constituent out of the scope of negation but it need not be anaphoric (cf. Haftka (in preparation); Steube/Alter/Späth (this volume)). So it is the attitudinal adverbial which separates background and focus, and it is negation which separates the constituents outside and inside the scope of negation. We only notice that focus and scope of negation do not conflate, however, when both an attitudinal adverbial and sentence negation are present in a sentence.

(44) (a)

CP: $\exists!x[\,[\mathbf{J}(x)] \wedge [\,\exists e[\,\neg[\,\exists y[[\mathbf{W}\,(y)] \wedge [[\mathbf{S}(x, y)](e)]]]]$

$\lambda Q\,[\exists!x\,[[\mathbf{J}(x)] \wedge [Q(x)]]]$ $\in$ S/(S/N)

C': $\lambda x\,[\exists e[\neg[\exists y\,[[\mathbf{W}(y)] \wedge [[\mathbf{S}(x, y)](e)]]]]$

$\lambda Q\,\lambda x\,[\exists e\,[Q(e, x)]]$ $\in$ S/(S/N)

VP

$\lambda x\,\lambda e\,[\neg[\exists y\,[[\mathbf{W}(y)] \wedge [[\mathbf{S}(x, y)]\,(e)]]]]$

(b)

CP: $\exists!x\,[[\mathbf{J}(x)] \wedge [\,\exists e[\,\exists y[\,[\mathbf{W}(y)] \wedge [\,\neg[\mathbf{S}(x, y)](e)]]]]$

$\lambda Q\,[\exists!x\,[[\mathbf{J}(x)] \wedge [Q(x)]]]$ $\in$ S/(S/N)

C': $\lambda x\,[\,\exists e[\,\exists y[[\mathbf{W}(y)] \wedge [\,\neg[\mathbf{S}(x, y)](e)]]]]$

$\lambda Q\,\lambda x\,[\,\exists e[Q(e, x)]]$ $\in$ S/(S/N)

VP

$\lambda x\,\lambda e\,[\,\exists y[[\mathbf{W}(y)] \wedge [\,\neg[\,\mathbf{S}(x, y)](e)]]]]$

The following example provides further justification for excluding a movement of the sentence-negation operator to CP. If the negation in sentence (45) were hosted by the head of CP and took scope over the rest of the sentence, it would be unclear how we are able to interpret the presuppositional object DP outside the scope of negation.

(45) [$_{CP}$ *Der Richter* [$_{C}$ **neg** [... [*hat den Zeugen nicht vereidigt*] ...]]]

Even the assumption that the definite article triggers an existential presupposition does not provide us a way out of this problem: the following example from Czech shows that, under the same syntactic and prosodic conditions, we arrive at a specific or referential reading, although Czech cannot use a definite article.

(46) *Soudce*	*svědka*	*nevzál*	*do*	*přísahy.*	(Czech)
ø judge	ø witness	**neg**-take-pret	to	ø oath.	

Soudce svědka$_i$ [*NEVZÁL do přísahy* t_i]$_{\text{Negation scope}}$

Remaining in situ and thus within the focus domain, the DP would trigger a non-specific reading. Hence the definite article cannot be the only and exclusive trigger of existential presuppositions. Rather it is the case that, in the first place, information structure rules the processes of semantic mapping (i.e. the mapping of the focus function onto the next embedded constituent as its argument, and – in our case – the mapping of the focus function onto the internal argument).

6 Further applications

The division of the semantic forms of sentences into presupposed and non-presupposed information and the mapping of this division in syntax and semantic composition is certainly a strong claim which is followed by serious consequences in all the fields of Formal Semantics that aim at a compositional explanation of the impact of information structure on sentence meaning. Since sentence negation is just an indicator but not the trigger of this division, the effects on the reading of certain constituents should occur independently of whether a sentence is positive or negative. The following two sections present exemplary applications, testing that our hypothesis leads to correct explanations for (i) the scope-dependent interpretation of associative anaphors and (ii) for the scope-dependent interpretation of temporal modifiers.

6.1 A comment on bridging

Both DPs in example (46) are presuppositional. But what triggers these presuppositions? We have seen that the referential semantic status of a DP is relevant for the presuppositions that the DP's noun induces. To know whether a DP is a referential one and whether a DP presupposes the existence of a referent is an essential precondition for reconstructing the coherence of a text. Theoretical frameworks dealing with discourse relations or rhetorical relations such as, for instance, the one proposed by Asher/Lascarides (1998a,1998b) attempt to handle the problems related to text coherence. The following example – taken from Asher/Lascarides (1998a) – elucidates the problem of discourse linking.

(47) (a) *I took my car for a test drive.*
(b) *The engine made a weird noise.*

The sequence in (47) establishes a narrative relation between sentence (a) and sentence (b). In general, text coherence can be generated by inferential processes which we call *bridging*. Asher/Lascarides (1998a) agree with Chierchia (1995) in that the definite article serves as an input for bridging. Within their theoretical framework, the quoted authors treat definite descriptions as anaphoric expressions. If the definite article marked a DP as anaphoric and this semantic information actually were the input for bridging, the question would arise, however, how languages lacking the definite article are able to achieve text coherence. If so, we could expect that determinerless DPs remain semantically underspecified with respect to reference, text coherence, and discourse linking. This, however, is not the case. In example (48), the DP *otec*, 'father', exemplifies the same kind of correspondence we recognize in (47).

(48)	(a)	*Rodina*	*pricestovala*	*vlakom.*	
		ø family	came	by train.	
	(b)	*Otec*	*dal*	*auto*	*[do servisu]*$_{Focus}$
		ø father	gave	ø car	[to garage]$_{Focus}$
	(b')	**Otec*	*dal*	*[AUto*	*do servisu]*$_{Focus}$
		ø father	gave	[ø car	to garage]$_{Focus}$

The sentence-initial position is not the only position which is associated to presuppositional reading. The DP *auto*, 'car', in example (48) also presupposes the existence of a referent. Bearing the focus exponent, however, the DP does not contribute to linking presupposed referents to the discourse. Rather the DP is part of the possible negation scope and – speaking with Fodor (1979: p. 211) again – is "a referring expressions that is within the focus and is excused from having to refer in the real world".

We furthermore achieve similar effects in German. Although all internal DPs in (49) are definite descriptions, the focus structure of the subsequent sentence (b') and (b") blocks bridging. Therefore we fail in establishing an anaphoric reference of the internal DPs.

(49)	(a)	*Die Kinder*	*gehen*	*heute*	*nicht*	*zur*	*Schule.*	
		The children	go-3ps.pl	today	neg	to	school.	
	(b)	*Die Baupolizei*	*hat*		*das*	*Gebäude*	*[GESPERRT]*$_{Focus}$	
		The building inspection	aux-3.ps.sg		the	building	[close-part.perf.]$_{Focus}$	
	(b')	* *Die Baupolizei*$_i$	*hat*	[t$_i$	*das GeBÄUde*	*gesperrt]*$_{Focus}$		
		The building inspection$_i$	has-aux-3.ps.sg	[t$_i$	the building	close-part.perf.]]$_{Focus}$		
	(b")	* *Die Baupolizei*$_i$	*hat*	[t$_i$	*die EINrichtung*	*gesperrt]*$_{Focus}$		
		The building inspection$_i$	has-aux-3.ps.sg	[t$_i$	the institution	close-part.perf.]]$_{Focus}$		

The trigger of the presuppositionality of a DP is evidently not the definite article but the position of the DP relative to a possible negation functor. The functor is mapped onto the subsequently nested constituent. This results in a functor-argument constellation such that the DP *Gebäude* in (49b) serves as an argument for the focus function. According to Löbner (2000), a function is undividedly valid with respect to its argument. The polar decision is made on the focus, which contains the predicate of the state of affairs. In (49b') and (49b"), the DP is itself part of the polar function. The sentence only holds true if the complex state of affairs, paraphrased by *closing exactly one building / institution*, is true with respect to the building inspection.

6.2 A comment on temporal modifiers

Up to now, we have only considered DP readings in dependency on sentence negation. If sentence negation is an adjunct of VP, this also leads to crucial consequences for any expressions above and below the sentence-negation operator that specify temporal and aspectual reference. Sentence negation cancels the privative properties expressed by the propositional condition. The remaining semantic content may be highly unspecific since negated descriptions of event normally do not correspond to an 'opposite' positive description of the same event. What a scenario described by a sentence such as (50a) looks like, for instance, is almost undetermined and even hardly inferable from the context. Beyond this, sentence negation cancels the complete aspectual information of the propositional condition. The default case is that the aspectual classes of negative sentences are non-bounded (cf. (50a) and (50b)) but not necessarily stative (cf. (50b)).

(50) (a) *Eli did not run for an hour / *in an hour.* → ?

(b) *Eli did not stop for an hour / *in an hour.* → Eli moved for (at least) 1 hour

Temporal and aspectual modifiers circumscribe characteristics of an event referent by introducing a further spatio-temporal[14] referent *e'* with the quality χ and setting this spatio-temporal referent into a temporal relation **R** with the event argument of the VP.

(51) Temporal modifier: $\lambda P\, \lambda x_n ... x_i\, \lambda e\, [\, \exists e' [\, P(e, x_n ... x_i) \wedge \chi(e') \wedge \mathbf{R}(e, e')\,]]$

Assuming that (51) is the target structure for representing sentence negation, it is obvious that sentence negation has an impact on whether or not the existence of this spatio-temporal referent introduced by the modifier is presupposed.

(52) (a) *Eli hat zwei Stunden lang [nicht angehalten]*
Eli **aux** for two hours [**neg** stopped]

(b) *Eli hat [nicht zwei Stunden lang angehalten]*
Eli **aux** [**neg** for two hours stopped]

In (52a), we are talking about a certain time period within which an event occurred that is described by the negative propositional condition. This event is temporally non-bounded and thus can be modified by a duration adverbial. In (52b), in contrast, the modifier is part of the propositional condition and thus is interpreted within the scope of negation.[15] Therefore, in analogy to DPs enclosed in the negation scope, the time period's existence is not presupposed

[14] These spatio-temporal referents may be interpreted ontologically either as events or as time periods individuated by some external ontological criterion (such as time measurement).

[15] Note that this structure based on sentence negation has to be kept apart from a constituent negation such as in (i). Constituent negations open sets of alternatives and are subjected to certain rigid prosodic patterns.

(i) *Eli hat [nicht zwei STUNden lang] angehalten(, sondern...)*
Eli **aux** [**neg** for two hours] stopped(, but...)

by the modification operator but might fail to exist. The table in (53) shows how temporal modifiers group around the sentence-negation operator.

(53) The syntactic positions of aspectually relevant modifiers relative to sentence negation

presupposed					**non-presupposed**					
	sentence adverbs	frame-setting modifiers	sequential / habitual modifiers	event-related duration / time-frame modifiers		event-related duration / time-frame modifiers		process-related time-frame modifiers	further process-related modifiers	
weil	*wohl*	*letztes Jahr*	*wieder*	*2 Monate lang*	*nicht*	*3 Stunden*	*ein Pianist*	*in weniger als 60 Sekunden*	*wenig gefühlvoll*	*einen Walzer spielte*
since	pro-bably	last year	again	for 2 months	**neg**	for 3 hours	a pianist	in less than 60 seconds	with little feeling	a waltz play-3.ps-pret
				[+durative]	**DEL**	[+durative]		[+resultative]		[+telic]

In accordance with Frey/Pittner (1998), and Maienborn (2001), we presume that adverbial modifiers are adjuncts of projections of either lexical or functional categories. We disregard furthermore the question of whether adverb-like modifiers of different types are generated in specific basic positions. We assume instead that the hierarchical positions these adjuncts hold in relation to each other are motivated by purely semantic reasons. This view justifies regarding the syntactic linearization of modifiers only as a reflection of the intended scope relations. Accordingly, the syntactic position of sentence negation divides the aspectual and temporal description of the main event into presupposed and non-presupposed information.

Sentence negation cancels the entire aspectual and modifying information within its scope. The remaining information about the event is the verb's semantic presupposition of a pre-existent situation, which, as usual, is negation-resistant. Modifiers above the sentence negation operate on this presupposed information (which normally is quite poor, cf. (50a)).

Following the derivations in (42), a temporal modifier can, in dependence of its referential status, be applied to a VP above or below the sentence-negation operator in a way analogous to our treatment of presupposed and non-presupposed DPs.

(54) (a) *Der Richter$_i$ hat 2 Stunden lang einen Zeugen$_j$* [[*nicht t_i t_j VEREIDIGT*]$_{\text{NegScope}}$]$_{\text{Focus}}$

VP: $\lambda x\, \lambda e\, [\, \exists e' [\, \mathbf{quant}(e') = 2\text{H} \wedge e \subset_T e') \wedge \wedge [\exists y\, [\mathbf{W}(y) \wedge \neg[S(x, y)](e)]]]]$

AdvP: $\lambda p\, [\exists e\, [\mathbf{quant}(e') = 2\text{H} \wedge e \subset_T e') \wedge p]] \in S/S$ VP: $\lambda x\, \lambda e\, [\exists y\, [\mathbf{W}(y) \wedge \neg[S(x, y)](e)]]$

$\lambda Q\, [\exists y\, [[\mathbf{W}(y)] \wedge [Q(y)]]]$ VP

[+**neg**] $\lambda p\, [\neg[p]]$ VP ⋮

In (54a), the modifying operator is applied to the VP resulting from (42b). The existential quantification over time periods is outside the negation scope and is read as specific. In (54b), in contrast, the same temporal modifier is applied to V' and thus is in the negatable part of the sentence, such that we do not know anything about its referential status.

(54) (b) *Der Richter$_i$ hat einen Zeugen$_j$ [[nicht t_i 2 Stunden lang t_j VEREIDIGT]$_{NegScope}$]$_{Focus}$*

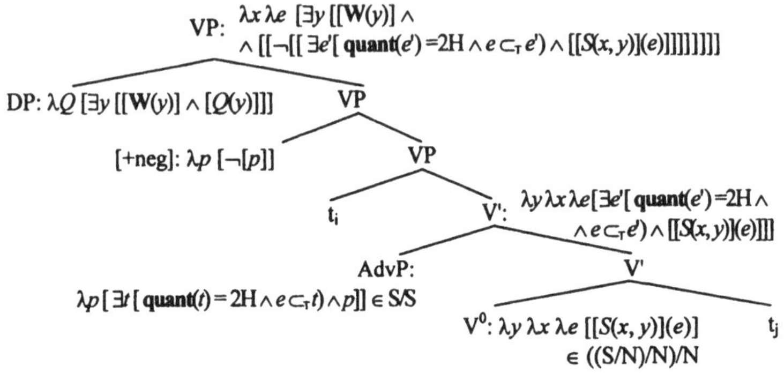

The fact that sentence negation also cancels the aspectual information of the verb and of respective temporal and aspectual modifiers – if there are any – is implicitly presumed in the semantic derivations.[16]

7 Results

We have shown how a formal-semantic theory of sentence negation can be fit into a methodic framework which exceeds the view of 'single-sentence semantics'. Sentences are not bearers of hypothetical truth-conditions, but types of grammatical units that are materialized in concrete token utterances, anchored to coherent models in the discourse domain, and evaluated in concrete token contexts. Information structure is the class-one instrument of language for controlling these processes of uttering, anchoring, and evaluating. Sentence negation has a striking position in dividing and marking the function of the individual information units in a sentence, since it does not affect the complete sentence but only those of its parts whose truth is subject to evaluation. Due to negation's fixed central position above the focus domain, an external negation, as used in Propositional Logic, is not applicable to the conditions of truth and usage of natural-language sentences – at least not as a simple one-to-one trans-

[16] There are attempts to make aspectual information visible within the semantic form (cf. Trautwein (2002)). In this way, we are able to comprehend the interaction of the SF of the verbs, modifiers, and sentence negation with respect to their respective relative syntactic position in the surface structure and the resulting scope of their aspectual information.

lation of sentence negation. Sentences are complex and nested functor-argument or functor-function structures, and the syntactic position of constituents above or below sentence negation solely result from scopal requirements. Constituents outside the negation scope are presuppositional and – among other factors – condition how the sentence can be anchored in a discourse model. Sentences within the negation scope, in contrast belong to prediction which – in declarative sentences – has to be evaluated.

To know how to match the truth-conditions of a predication with the world, however, requires that we know something about how sentences depict the structures of segments of the non-linguistic, spatio-temporal world. Thus every linguistically founded theory of truth and reference needs an ontological theory of truth- and reference-making. We have demonstrated that traditional event semantics following Reichenbach, Davidson, and Bierwisch does a good job as long as it explains the truth of positive sentences. Negative sentences, however, confront us with the problem that, from an ontological view, the application of propositions as secondary functions to event arguments is far too weak – if predicating on event arguments just means classing the denoted events with a certain sort of spatio-temporal entities. The instantiation relation (as a denotive sign for the function-argument relation between structured eventive predications and event arguments) and thus the sortal classification of events is just a necessary but not sufficient criterion for truth-making. Rather we have to consider the ontological necessities that rule the world and its possible spatio-temporal constellations, and involve these necessities in our theory of truth. We have approached these requirements by outlining the formal characteristics of a truth-making relation. This relation can be used as the conceptual interpretation of every event description consisting of a proposition and an event argument.

We give a syntactic explanation for the central position of sentence negation in the sentential structure, and show how the syntax of negative sentences is mapped onto the appropriate semantic form. The sentence-negation operator has a fixed position above VP. Constituents such as DPs or modifiers which are presuppositional and thus do not belong to the evaluable event description have to move above this position. There, outside the negation scope, their referential status cannot be canceled by negation. Over and above all, by choosing this strategy, we are able to explain why the article-less Slavic languages do not differ from German in this point. Since the readings of referring constituents correlates with and only with the constituents' syntactic position in the surface structure relative to sentence negation, Slavic languages do not need a definite article to mark the specifity or unspecifity of DP-referents.

8 References

Asher, N. and A. Lascarides (1998a): Bridging, Journal of Semantics 15(1), 83-113.

Asher, N. and A. Lascarides (1998b): The Semantics and Pragmatics of Presupposition, Journal of Semantics 15, 239-299.

Bierwisch, M. (1988): On the Grammar of Local Prepositions. In: M. Bierwisch, M. Motsch, and I. Zimmermann (eds): Syntax, Semantik und Lexikon, studia grammatica 29, Berlin, 1-65.

Chierchia, G. (1995): Dynamics of Meaning. Anaphora, Presupposition, and the Theory of Grammar, Chicago, London: The University of Chicago Press.

Chomsky, N. (1972): Studies on semantics in generative grammar, The Hague: Mouton.

Dölling, J. (1988): Natürlichsprachliche Negation und Logische Negationsoperatoren. Ein Beitrag zur semantischen Analyse der lexikalischen Einheit 'nicht', Linguistische Studien Reihe A, Arbeitsberichte 182, 1-106.

Fodor, J. D. (1979): In defense of the truth-value gap. In: C. K. Oh and D. A. Dineen (eds): Presuppositions, Syntax and Semantics 11, Academic Press, New York, 199-294.

Frey, W. and K. Pittner (1998): Zur Positionierung der Adverbiale im deutschen Mittelfeld. In: Linguistische Berichte 176, Opladen: Westdeutscher Verlag, 489-534.

Gamut, L. T. F. (1991): Logic, Language, and Meaning, Vol. 1, Introduction to Logic, Chicago: The University Of Chicago Press.

Givón, T. (1978): Negation in Language: Pragmatics, Function, Ontology. In: P. Cole (ed): Syntax and Semantics 9: Pragmatics, New York: Academic Press, 69-112.

Haftka, B. (1994): Wie positioniere ich meine Position? Überlegungen zu funktionalen Phrasen im deutschen Mittelfeld. In B. Haftka (ed): Was determiniert Wortstellungsvariation? Studien zu einem Interaktionsfeld von Grammatik, Pragmatik und Sprachtypologie, Opladen: Westdeutscher Verlag, 139-159.

Hajičová, E. (1984): Presupposition and Allegation Revisited, Journal of Pragmatics 8, 155-167.

Jackendoff, R. (1972): Semantic Interpretation in Generative Grammar, Cambridge (MA): MIT Press.

Löbner, S. (1985): Definites, Journal of Semantics 4, 279-326.

Löbner, S. (1990): Wahr neben Falsch: Duale Operatoren als die Quantoren natürlicher Sprache. Tübingen: Niemeyer.

Maienborn, C. (2001): On the Posititon and Interpretation of Locative Modifiers.In: Natural Language Semantics 9, 191-240.

Quine, W. v. O. (1948/61). On What There Is. In: W. v. O. Quine, From a Logical Point of View: 9 Logico-Philosophical Essays, 2nd edition, Cambridge/Mass.: Harvard University Press 1961, 1-19.

Reichenbach, H. (1947): Elements of Symbolic Logic, London and New York: MacMillan.

Roberts, C. (1998): Information Structure in Discourse: Towards an Integrated Formal Theory of Pragmatics. In: J. H. Yoon and A. Kathol (eds): OSU Working Papers in Linguistics 49: Papers in Semantics, 91-136.

Seuren, P. (1991): Presuppositions. In: A. von Stechow and D. Wunderlich (eds): Semantik: Ein internationales Handbuch der zeitgenössischen Forschung, Handbücher zur Sprach- und Kommunikationswissenschaft 6, Berlin and New York, 286-318.

Seuren, P. A. M., V. Capretta, and H. Geuvers (2001): The logic and mathematics of occasion sentences, Journal of Linguistics and Philosophy 24, 531-595.

Smith, B. and B. Mulligan (2003): A Unified Theory of Truth and Reference. In: Loqique et Analyse 169/170, 49-93.

Späth, A. and M. Trautwein (2003): Events under Negation. In: M. Weisgerber (ed): "sub7 Sinn und Bedeutung". Proceedings of the 7th Annual Meeting of the Gesellschaft für Sematik, Abeitspapiere des Fachbereichs Sprachwissenschaft der Universität Konstanz (Konstanz linguistics working papers), Arbeitspapier 114, 295-309.

Trautwein, M. (2002): The Time Window of Language: The Interaction between Linguistic and Non-Linguistic Knowledge in the Temporal Interpretation of German and English Texts, doctoral thesis, Leipzig: University of Leipzig.

Beáta Gyuris (Budapest)

Two Types of Contrastive Topics?[1]

1 Introduction

The aim of this paper is to present some new data concerning the structure of discourses where contrastive topic DPs are licensed in Hungarian, and to propose an account of these data in the spirit of Büring's (1997) proposals on the presuppositions and implicatures introduced by contrastive topics and Kadmon's (2001) account of the congruence of questions and answers containing such constituents.

It has been proposed by several authors (including von Fintel 1994, Büring 1997, Kadmon 2001, etc.) that sentences containing contrastive topics cannot be uttered 'out of the blue,' but have to be preceded by an appropriate discourse licensing them. In this paper we show some Hungarian data which appear to suggest that contrastive topic DPs differ according to their monotonicity properties as to whether they can be licensed by other DPs in the discourse, or only by an instance of the same one, and as to whether they can occur in certain types of declaratives at all. We will propose that instead of dividing contrastive topic DPs into two categories depending on how freely they are licensed in discourse, the basis for judging whether they are used felicitously is whether they can be seen as contributing at least a partial answer to some general (possibly implicit) question in the discourse.

The next section will list the data under discussion. In section 3, Büring's (1997) approach to the licensing of contrastive topics is summarized and evaluated from the point of view of the data. Section 4 provides an overview of the requirements that congruent question-answer sequences have to satisfy according to Kadmon (2001), and proposes an account of the interpretability and the licensing of sentences with contrastive topics in discourse. In section 5 the results of the study are summarized.

---

[1] Financial support for the research reported here was provided in the form of a János Bolyai Research Scholarship, awarded to the author by the Hungarian Academy of Sciences, and from OTKA-NWO project no. N 37276, which is hereby gratefully acknowledged.

2 The data

The discourse-conditions licensing the use of contrastive topic DPs will be illustrated in two types of contexts. In the first one, the declarative containing a contrastive topic is preceded by a *yes-no* question, and in the second one by a *wh*-question. The first set of exchanges is shown in (1)-(6) below. In the examples, the contrastive topic constituents are enclosed within square brackets, and the place of the *eradicating stress* within this constituent (cf. Kálmán and Nádasdy 1994[2]), which also marks the beginning of the rising intonation characteristic of the contrastive topic, is marked by '′.' Since here we concentrate on the issue of how the semantic properties of determiners influence the felicitous occurrences of DPs in the contrastive topic role, it will be assumed that the eradicating stress within the contrastive topic falls on the determiner.

It has been pointed out in several studies on various other languages that contrastive topics have to be followed in the same sentence by a constituent with a falling pitch accent (cf. Lambrecht 1994, Vallduví & Engdahl 1996, Lee 1999, von Fintel 1994, Büring 1997, Kadmon 2001 etc.), which are usually referred to as a/the *focus*. Similar observations have been made with respect to Hungarian in Kenesei 1989 and Molnár 1998, for example. In view of the fact, however, that in contemporary Hungarian linguistics (following the work of Katalin É. Kiss, e.g., É. Kiss 2002), focused constituents are assumed to occupy a specific syntactic position, which is not always satisfied by constituents of the type which necessarily follow the contrastive topic (and which bear the second eradicating stress in the sentence and a falling tone according to Kálmán and Nádasdy 1994), we will refer to the latter as the *associates of the contrastive topic*. The place of the eradicating stress within the associate is marked by '`' in what follows. Among the declaratives, those which are considered inappropriate answers to the preceding question will be marked by '#,' and those which cannot be uttered felicitously in any context (i.e., which speakers perceive as ungrammatical) will be marked by '*':

(1) Q: Beszéltél öt tanárral?
talked-2SG five teacher-INSTR
'Have you talked to five teachers?'

A_1: [$_{CT}$ ′Öt tanárral] `beszéltem / `nem beszéltem.
five teacher-INSTR talked-1SG / not talked-1SG
'As for five teachers, I did/didn't talk to that many.'

[2] Kálmán and Nádasdy (1994) define *eradicating stress* as a main stress which cannot be followed by another main stress in the sentence, unless the latter is an eradicating stress, too.

A_2: [CT 'Két tanárral] `beszéltem / #`nem beszéltem.
two teacher-INSTR talked-1SG / not talked-1SG
'As for two teachers, I did / #didn't talk to that many.'

(2) Q: Beszéltél sok tanárral?
talked-2SG many teacher-INSTR
'Have you talked to many teachers?'

A_1: [CT 'Sok tanárral] `nem beszéltem.
many teacher-INSTR not talked-1SG
'Many teachers, I didn't talk to.'

A_2: [CT 'Néhány tanárral] `beszéltem.
a few teacher- INSTR talked-1SG
'A few teachers, I did talk to.'

A_3: #[CT 'Legalább két tanárral] beszéltem / `nem beszéltem.
at least two teacher-INSTR talked-1SG / not talked-1SG
'As for at least two teachers, I did / didn't talk to that many.'

A_4: *[CT 'Kevés tanárral] `beszéltem / `nem beszéltem.
few teacher-INSTR talked-1SG / not talked-1SG
*'Few teachers, I did/didn't talk to.'

(3) Q: Beszéltél tanárokkal? / a tanárokkal?
talked-2SG teachers-INSTR the teachers-INSTR
'Have you talked to teachers / the teachers?'

A_1: [CT 'Két / 'néhány tanárral] `beszéltem.
two a few teacher-INSTR talked-1SG
'Two / a few teachers, I did talk to.'

A_2: [CT 'Sok tanárral] `nem beszéltem.
many teacher- INSTR not talked-1SG
'Many teachers, I didn't talk to.'

A_3: #[CT 'Legalább két tanárral] `beszéltem / `nem beszéltem.
at least two teacher- INSTR talked-1SG / not talked-1SG
'At least two teachers, I did/didn't talk to.'

A_4: *[CT 'Pontosan két tanárral] `beszéltem / `nem beszéltem.
exactly two teacher-INSTR talked-1SG / not talked-1SG
'Exactly two teachers, I did/didn't talk to.'

A_5: *[CT 'Kevesebb, mint öt tanárral] `beszéltem / nem beszéltem.
fewer than five teacher-INSTR talked-1SG not talked-1SG
*'Fewer than five teachers, I did talk to.'

(4) Q: Beszéltél legalább öt tanárral?[3]
talked-2SG at least five teacher-INSTR
'Have you talked to at least five teachers?'

A: [CT 'Legalább öt tanárral] `beszéltem / `nem beszéltem.
at least five teacher-INSTR talked-1SG / not talked-1SG
'At least five teachers, I did/didn't talk to.'

(5) Q: Kevesebb, mint öt tanárral beszéltél?[4]
fewer than five teacher-INSTR talked-2SG
'Did you talk to fewer than five teachers?'

A_1: *[CT 'Kevesebb, mint öt tanárral] `beszéltem.
fewer than five teacher-INSTR talked-1SG
*'Fewer than five teachers, I did talk to.'

A_2: *[CT 'Kevesebb, mint öt tanárral] `nem beszéltem.
fewer than five teacher- INSTR not talked-1SG
*'Fewer than five teachers, I didn't talk to.'

(6) Q: Pontosan öt tanárral beszéltél?
Exactly five teacher- INSTR talked-2SG
'Did you talk to exactly five teachers?'

A_1: *[CT 'Pontosan öt tanárral] `beszéltem.
exactly five teacher- INSTR talked-1SG
*' Exactly five teachers, I did talk to.'

A_2: *[CT 'Pontosan öt tanárral] `nem beszéltem.
exactly five teacher-INSTR not talked-1SG
'Exactly five teachers, I didn't talk to.'

The data in (1)-(6) thus illustrate that with respect to the possibility of their felicitous occurrence in declaratives which can be used to answer *yes-no* questions (i.e, which have a *verum focus*, and where the associate of the contrastive topic is a negative particle or the verb itself), contrastive topic DPs appear to fall into two classes. The first one is constituted by DPs with monotone in-

[3] Note that in all the examples considered in this paper, the questions and answers are assumed to describe the situation at a particular reference time, and not intended to express implicit quantification over events occurring within a longer time-span.

[4] Note that this is the only possible way to ask the question 'Did you talk to fewer than five teachers?' in Hungarian, which is probably due to the fact that the DP, as all other DPs with monotone decreasing or non-monotone determiners, has to occupy the immediately preverbal position, cf. example (6) below. (Szabolcsi (1997) claims that such DPs occupy the Predicate Operator position, which is not identical to the Focus position, although these two positions cannot be filled simultaneously. É. Kiss (2002) assumes, however, that these DPs occupy the focus position.)

creasing determiners, which, even in their non-referential uses, can appear in declaratives which can answer *yes-no* questions containing the same DP, as in (1Q-A_1), and (2Q-A_1), a variant of the DP with a different monotone increasing determiner, as in (1Q-A_2), and (2Q-A_2), or only the nominal part of the DP, as in (3Q-A_1), and (3Q-A_2). Contrastive topic DPs with determiners of the *at least n* type are more restricted in their distribution, however, since they are judged felicitous only if they follow a question where the same DP appears, as the contrast between the discourses in (4Q-A) versus (2Q-A_3) and (3Q-A_3) shows. I propose that the reason why the contrastive topic DP does not appear to be licensed in the latter two discourses is that the truth-conditional meanings of sentences with DPs containing the determiner *at least n* and those containing the determiner *n* are identical, and thus there appears to be no reason to use the more complex form. In the case of (4), the use of the *at least n* form is justified, since it is the one which appears in the preceding question as well.

The second group of DPs is constituted by those with monotone decreasing or non-monotonic determiners. As the data in (2Q-A_4), (3Q-A_4), as well as those in (5) and (6) show, members of this group cannot appear as contrastive topics in declaratives intended as answers to *yes-no* questions at all.

The next set of data consists of declaratives with contrastive topic DPs which can answer to *wh*-questions. In these declaratives, the contrastive topics are followed by associates occupying the focus position of the sentence:

(7) Q: Hová utaztak a tanárok?
where travelledthe teachers
'Where did the teachers travel?'

A_1: [$_{CT}$ ´Két tanár / ´néhány tanár] [$_F$ a `hegyekbe] utazott.
two teacher a few teacher the mountains-ILLATIVE travelled
'As for two/a few teachers, that many went to the mountains.'

A_2: #[$_{CT}$´Legalább két tanár] [$_F$ a `tengerhez] utazott.
at least two teacher the sea-ALLATIVE travelled
'As for at least two teachers, that many went to the sea.'

A_3: #[$_{CT}$´Pontosan két tanár] [$_F$ a `tengerhez] utazott.
exactly two teachers the sea-ALLATIVE travelled
'As for exactly two teachers, they went to the sea.'

A_4: #[$_{CT}$ ´Négynél kevesebb tanár] [$_F$ a `hegyekbe] utazott.
four-THAN fewer teacher the mountains-ILLATIVE travelled
'As for fewer than four teachers, that many went to the mountains.'

(8) Q: Hová utazott sok tanár?
Where travelled many teacher
'Where did many teachers travel?'

A_1: [$_{CT}$ ´Sok tanár] [$_F$ a `tengerhez] utazott.
many teacher the sea-ALLATIVE travelled
'As for many teachers, they went to the sea.'

A_2: [$_{CT}$ ´Néhány tanár] [$_F$ a `hegyekbe] utazott.
a few teacher the mountains- ILLATIVE travelled
'As for a few teachers, they went into the mountains.'

A_3: [$_{CT}$ ´Két tanár] [$_F$ a `tengerhez] utazott.
two teacher the sea-ALLATIVE travelled
'As for two teachers, that many went to the sea.'

A_4: #[$_{CT}$´Pontosan két tanár] [$_F$ a `tengerhez] utazott.
exactly two teachers the sea-ALLATIVE travelled
'As for exactly two teachers, that many went to the sea.'

A_5: #[$_{CT}$ ´Négynél kevesebb tanár] [$_F$ a `hegyekbe] utazott.
four-THAN fewer teacher the mountains-ILLATIVE travelled
'As for fewer than four teachers, that many went to the mountains.'

(9) Q: Hová utazott legalább két tanár?
Where travelled at least two teachers
'Where did at least two teachers travel?'

A_1: [$_{CT}$ ´Legalább két tanár] [$_F$ a `tengerhez] utazott.
at least two teachers the sea-ALLATIVE travelled
'As for at least two teachers, that many went to the sea.'

A_2: #[$_{CT}$´Pontosan két tanár] [$_F$ a `tengerhez] utazott.
exactly two teachers the sea-ALLATIVE travelled
'As for exactly two teachers, that many went to the sea.'

(10) Q: Hová utazott pontosan két tanár?
where travelled exactly two teachers
'Where did exactly two teachers travel?'

A: [$_{CT}$ ´Pontosan két tanár] [$_F$ a `tengerhez] utazott.
exactly two teachers the sea-ALLATIVE travelled
'As for exactly two teachers, that many went to the sea.'

(11) Q: Hová utazott négynél kevesebb tanár?
where travelled four-THAN fewer teacher
'Where did fewer than four teachers travel?'

A: [$_{CT}$ ´Négynél kevesebb tanár] [$_F$ a `hegyekbe] utazott.
four-THAN fewer teacher the mountains-ILLATIVE travelled
'As for fewer than four teachers, that many went to the mountains.'

The data in (7) show that DPs with monotone decreasing determiners, with the exception of the *at least n* type, can be licensed in the contrastive topic position of a declarative by the nominal part of the DP itself, but DPs with monotone decreasing and non-monotonic determiners cannot be licensed in the same way. (8) shows that DPs with monotone increasing determiners, excluding those of the type *at least n,* can be licensed if the same DP or a variant of it, which differs from the original one in that its determiner is replaced by a different monotone increasing one, appears in the preceding *wh*-question.

(9)-(11) show that contrastive topic DPs with monotone decreasing and non-monotonic determiners as well as those of the form *at least n* are only felicitous if they are preceded by a question which contains the same DP. Regarding ($9A_1$), similar considerations apply as in the previous set of examples: since the truth-conditions of this sentence are identical to the truth-conditions of the one where the determiner *at least two* is replaced by *two,* its appearance in discourse is only justified if preceded by a question with the same determiner (cf. ($8A_3$)).

In the rest of the paper we will try to find an explanation for the data presented above, concentrating on two phenomena. On the one hand, we will investigate the reasons why the contrastive topic DPs with monotone decreasing and non-monotonic determiners cannot appear in sentences like ($5A_1$-A_2) and ($6A_1$-A_2), and what makes them acceptable in (10A)-(11A). Note that since ($5A_1$-A_2) and ($6A_1$-A_2) cannot be differentiated from a syntactic point of view from the well-formed example in (12) below, the reason for the impossibility of the former must be based on semantic and not syntactic principles.

(12) [$_{CT}$ 'Pontosan	öt	tanárral]	'nem	beszélhettem.
exactly	five	teacher-INSTR	not	talked-POSS-1SG

'Exactly five teachers, I couldn't talk to.'

On the other hand, we will offer an explanation why DPs with monotone decreasing versus non-monotonic and monotone decreasing determiners differ in their ability to be licensed as contrastive topics by DPs with different determiners in discourse, as shown in (7)-(11).

3 Büring's (1997, 1999) theory on interpretability and question-answer congruence, and its applications

3.1 Topic values and implicatures

Büring (1997, 1999) proposes a condition which can help to account for the congruence of questions and answers containing a contrastive topic, and puts forward an explanation why grammatically well-formed sentences with contrastive topics can in certain cases be left without a "coherent" interpretation.

Büring (1997, 1999) argues that sentences which contain a contrastive topic are associated with a specific semantic value, which he refers to as their *topic value*, abbreviated as $\| S \|^t$. The topic value is constituted by a set of sets of propositions which differ from the one expressed by the sentence in that the denotations of the contrastive topic and/or the focus constituents are substituted in them for their type-identical alternatives. Depending on the set of alternatives associated with the denotation of the contrastive topic and the focus constituents in (13A) (in the sense of Rooth 1985), the topic value of the latter sentence would be as shown in (14):

(13) Q: Which book would Fritz buy?
A: Well, [$_{CT}$ I] would buy [$_F$ The Hotel New HAMPshire].

(14) {{I would buy *War and Peace*, I would buy *The Hotel New Hampshire*, I would buy *The World According to Garp*, ...}, {Rufus would buy *War and Peace*, Rufus would buy *The Hotel New Hampshire*, Rufus would buy *The World According to Garp*, ...}, {Fritz would buy *War and Peace*, Fritz would buy *The Hotel New Hampshire*, Fritz would buy *The World According to Garp*, ...}, {Fritz's brother would buy *War and Peace*, Fritz's brother would buy *The Hotel New Hampshire*, Fritz's brother would buy *The World According to Garp*, ...}, ... }

In the spirit of Hamblin (1973), the above set of propositions corresponds to the following set of questions:

(15) {which book would you/I buy, which book would Rufus buy, which book would Fritz buy, which book would Fritz's brother buy, ... }

Büring (1997, 1999) argues that questions and answers containing a contrastive topic are congruent if they satisfy the following condition:

(16) The meaning of the question Q must match one element in the topic value of the answer A. (Formally: $\| Q \|^o \in \| A \|^t$).

Note that the exchange in (13Q-A), which is felt to be congruent by speakers, does meet the above condition, since the denotation of (13Q) is a member of the topic value of (13A).

Büring (1997, 1999) proposes in addition that the contrastive topic introduces the implicature that there is an element Q in the topic value associated with the sentence where the contrastive topic appears which is still under consideration after uttering the sentence. The notion that a question is under consideration means for Büring that the set of propositions corresponding to the question has at least one element which is neither included in the common ground nor is in contradiction with it. This means, practically, that in any of the sets constituting the topic value of a sentence A, there is at least one proposition which is neither entailed nor contradicted by the truth of A.

Büring (1997) shows that the reason why certain grammatically well-formed sentences with a contrastive topic lack one or all[5] of their possible interpretations is that these do not give rise to the above implicature, i.e., there is no element in the topic value associated with the particular reading of the sentence whose truth or falsity does not follow from the intended truth-conditional meaning of the sentence uttered.

For example, although the following sentence is potentially ambiguous in German, it can only have a reading according to which the negation takes wide scope over the universal quantifier, as paraphrased in (17a).

(17)	$[_{CT}$ ALLE]	Politiker	sind	$[_{F}$ NICHT]	korrupt.
	all	politicians	are	not	corrupt

a. 'It is not the case that all politicians are corrupt.'

b. #'All politicians are such that they are not corrupt.'

The reason why reading (17b) is missing is that all propositions in the topic value associated with the sentence on this reading are such that they are either entailed by or contradict the proposition intended to be expressed by the sentence. The formula in (18a) (Büring 1997) is an abstract characterization of the elements of the topic value set, where ALT(**x**) denotes the set of alternatives to **x**, while (18b) lists a set of propositions satisfying the formal requirements in (18a):

(18) a. $\lambda P.\exists Q_{\langle et,\langle et,t\rangle\rangle}[Q \in \mathrm{ALT}(\mathbf{all})\ \&\ P = \lambda p.\exists \pi_{\langle tt\rangle}[\pi \in \mathrm{ALT}(\mathbf{not})\ \&\ p =$
$= Q(\mathrm{politicians})(\lambda x.\pi(\mathrm{corrupt}(x)))]]$

b. $\{\{\mathrm{all}(\mathrm{politicians})(\lambda x.\neg\mathrm{corrupt}(x)), \mathrm{all}(\mathrm{politicians})(\lambda x.\mathrm{corrupt}(x))\},$
$\{\mathrm{most}(\mathrm{politicians})(\lambda x.\neg\mathrm{corrupt}(x)), \mathrm{most}(\mathrm{politicians})(\lambda x.\mathrm{corrupt}(x))\},$
$\{\mathrm{some}(\mathrm{politicians})(\lambda x.\neg\mathrm{corrupt}(x)), \{\mathrm{some}(\mathrm{politicians})(\lambda x.\mathrm{corrupt}(x))\},$
$\{\mathrm{one}(\mathrm{politicians})(\lambda x.\neg\mathrm{corrupt}(x)), \{\mathrm{one}(\mathrm{politicians})(\lambda x.\mathrm{corrupt}(x))\},$
$\{\mathrm{no}(\mathrm{politicians})(\lambda x.\neg\mathrm{corrupt}(x)), \{\mathrm{no}(\mathrm{politicians})(\lambda x.\mathrm{corrupt}(x))\}, ...$

According to (18), the propositions in the set of sets constituting the topic value of (17) on reading (b) state that there is a subset of the set of politicians with the specified number of elements such that its members are corrupt or not corrupt. If the sentence in (17) is assumed to express the proposition that the whole set of politicians is such that it is not corrupt, then, due to the distributivity of the property of being not corrupt, it would have to follow that the same property holds for any subset of the set of politicians, and thus the truth

[5] For example, in case the sentence contains at least two scope-bearing elements (quantifiers, modals or negation), the relative scopes of which can vary across readings.

or falsity of all propositions constituting the topic value associated with this reading would follow.

Having discussed Büring's proposals on the interpretability of sentences with contrastive topics and on question-answer congruence, in the next section we will investigate how they can explain the Hungarian data at hand.

3.2 Investigating interpretability

It was observed above with respect to ($5A_1$-A_2) and ($6A_1$-A_2) that DPs with monotone decreasing and non-monotonic quantifiers cannot serve as contrastive topics in declaratives which are uttered as answers to *yes-no* questions. The relevant data are repeated below:

(5) A_1: *[CT 'Kevesebb, mint öt tanárral] 'beszéltem.
fewer than five teacher-INSTR talked-1SG
*' Fewer than five teachers, I did talk to.'
A_2: *[CT 'Kevesebb, mint öt tanárral] 'nem beszéltem.
fewer than five teacher-INSTR not talked-1SG
*'Fewer than five teachers, I didn't talk to.'

(6) A_1: * [CT 'Pontosan öt tanárral] 'beszéltem.
exactly five teacher- INSTR talked-1SG
*'Exactly five teachers, I did talk to.'
A_2: *[CT 'Pontosan öt tanárral] 'nem beszéltem.
exactly five teacher- INSTR not talked-1SG
*'Exactly five teachers, I didn't talk to.'

Note that in the light of Büring's proposal, the lack of interpretations for ($5A_1$) and ($6A_1$) can be explained. If it is assumed that the proposition which was intended to be expressed by ($5A_1$) is that 'I talked to fewer than five, but not more, teachers,'[6] for any alternative to the determiner which is not fewer than five, the corresponding proposition would be false (and its negation true). The sets constituting the topic value associated with this sentence can be formally characterized as in (19a). If the relevant alternatives to *fewer than five* in the

[6] This proposition is identical to the one expressed by the interpretable sentence where the DP occupies an immediately preverbal position, as shown below:
[F Kevesebb, mint öt tanárral] beszéltem.
fewer than five teacher-INSTR talked-1SG
'I talked to fewer than five teachers.'

context are, among others, *exactly five* and *more than five,* the topic value set associated with the sentence is as shown in (19b):

(19) a. $\lambda P.\exists Q_{<et,<et,t>>}[Q \in$ ALT(**fewer than five**) & $P = \lambda p.\exists \pi_{<tt>} [\pi \in$ ALT(**not**) & $p =$ $= \pi$(I talked to Q(teachers))]]

b. {{(I talked to *fewer than five* teachers),
¬(I talked to *fewer than five* teachers)},
{(I talked to *exactly five* teachers),
¬(I talked to *exactly five* teachers)},
{(I talked to *more than five* teachers),
¬(I talked to *more than five* teachers)}, ...}

Note that the truth of ($5A_2$) (the second member of the first set in (19b)), does not entail the truth or falsity of all the alternative propositions in the topic value set. (If it is not true that I talked to fewer than five teachers, it does not follow that I talked to exactly five or more than five teachers.) Thus, in the spirit of Büring (1997), the latter sentence would give rise to the implicature normally introduced by contrastive topics, and, thus, there would be no reason to consider it uninterpretable.

Similar considerations apply to ($6A_1$-A_2) as well. If the relevant alternatives to *exactly five* are, for example, *fewer than five* or *more than five*, among others[7], then the topic value set associated with these sentences is identical to (19b). It is easy to see that the truth of ($6A_1$), i.e., the truth of the proposition that the number of teachers I talked to is exactly five (the first member of the second set in (19b)) entails the truth or falsity of the rest of the propositions. On the basis of the same principles, the uninterpretability of ($6A_2$) cannot be proved, however, since from the fact that it is not true that I talked to exactly five teachers it does not follow whether I talked to fewer than five or more than five teachers.

Note that German counterparts of ($5A_2$) and ($6A_2$), illustrated in (20a-b), are also uninterpretable (thus felt to be ill-formed by speakers), which shows that the explanation for the above data must be based on some cross-linguistic semantic principles:

(2)	a.	*Höchstens /FÜNF	Politiker	sind	NICHT\	korrupt.	
		at most five	politicians	are	not	corrupt	
	b.	*Genau /FÜNF	Politiker	sind	NICHT\	korrupt.	
		exactly five	politicians	are	not	corrupt	

[7] This is, naturally, not the only option, though.

On the basis of the preceding discussion, it can be established that the mechanism proposed by Büring (1997, 1999) to account for the lack of theoretically possible readings of sentences with contrastive topics does not account for all syntactically possible but uninterpretable sentences. In the next section we investigate whether the condition assumed by him to account for question-answer congruence can be used to predict the licensing data listed above.

3.3 The licensing of contrastive topics in discourse

The second issue we focus on here is why particular DPs, i.e., the majority of those containing monotone increasing determiners, appear to be licensed more freely in the discourse than others, i.e., those containing monotone decreasing and non-monotone determiners, which, as illustrated above, normally appear in a discourse only if they are preceded by a question containing the same DP.

The licensing of contrastive topic DPs with monotone increasing determiners by DPs which differ from the former in that they contain a different, monotone increasing determiner, as illustrated in ($1Q-A_2$), ($2Q-A_2$) and (8), is predicted by Büring's (1997) question-answer condition, shown in (16) above, provided that the denotation of the determiner of the DP in the question is considered an alternative of the determiner of the contrastive topic.[8] On the basis of the above assumptions, the topic value associated with (both the positive and the negative versions of) ($1A_2$) would be the set shown in (21):

(21) {{(I talked to one teacher), ¬(I talked to one teacher))},
{(I talked to two teachers)), ¬(I talked to two teachers)}, ...
{(I talked to five teachers)), ¬(I talked to five teachers))}, ...}

The congruence of (1Q) and the positive version of ($1A_2$) is then predicted, since the denotation of the question (1Q) is a member of the topic value in (23), but so is the congruence of the same question and the negative version of ($1A_2$), which contradicts the relevant data, however.

The reason why ($8Q-A_2$) do form a felicitous exchange is, however, predicted on Büring's theory, provided that the alternatives to the stressed constituent of the contrastive topic in ($8A_2$) are constituted by denotations of other monotone increasing determiners, as in (22), which illustrates some members of the topic value set associated with ($8Q-A_2$):

[8] It is assumed implicitly by Büring, although never stated explicitly, that the alternatives introduced by monotone increasing determiners constitute the set of all other monotone increasing determiners and the determiner *no*.

(22) {{(One teacher went to the sea), (One teacher went to the mountains), (One teacher went to the lakes), ...},
{(A few teachers went to the sea), (A few teachers went to the mountains), (A few teachers went to the lakes), ...},
{(More than three teachers went to the sea), (More than three teachers went to the mountains), (More than three teachers went to the lakes), ...}, ...}

It does not follow from Büring's theory why ($8A_4$-A_5) are not licensed by (8Q) unless it is assumed that the denotations of monotone decreasing or non-monotonic determiners cannot be considered alternatives to monotone decreasing determiners. In view of the fact, however, that Büring himself lists the monotone decreasing determiner *no* among the alternatives of *all*, as (18b) shows, the above assumption does not seem justified. In fact, Büring (1997, 1999) does not discuss contrastive topics with monotone decreasing and non-monotonic determiners at all.

The data in (3Q-A_1, A_2) and (7Q-A_1) can be accounted for by adopting Büring's assumption (1997:68) that the topic value associated with a sentence can also contain questions where the contrastive topic denotation is replaced by the union of its possible alternatives. Accordingly, the topic value set associated with ($3A_1$) could contain, in addition to the members listed in (21) above, the following member, which in fact corresponds to the question in (3Q):

(23) {(I talked to all teachers), ¬(I talked to all teachers)}

Similarly, the topic value of ($7A_1$) could contain the following member as well, which corresponds to the question in (7Q)

(24) {(All teachers went to the sea), (All teachers went to the mountains), (All teachers went to the lakes), ...}

The above approach does not account for the fact, however, that ($3A_4$), ($3A_5$) and ($7A_3$), ($7A_4$) are not licensed in the same manner by the questions in (3Q) and (7Q), respectively.

Having found that the principles proposed by Büring to account for the conditions determining the interpretability of sentences with contrastive topics and the congruence of questions and answers with such constituents do not account for the Hungarian data, we turn to Kadmon's (2001) proposals on the same issues.

4 Contrastive topics in an efficient information exchange

4.1 Kadmon's (2001) theory on discourse congruence

Kadmon (2001) proposes a theory which can predict for particular discourses with contrastive topics whether they count as congruent or incongruent. Kadmon (2001) follows Roberts (1996) in claiming that information is organized in the discourse in relation to questions being addressed (originally due to Carlson (1983)).

Roberts (1996) assumes that the goal of discourse is to discover and share with other interlocutors information about our world. These goals are achieved as a result of asking and answering questions. Naturally, efficient information exchange requires that questions are answered as soon after they are asked as possible. Roberts assumes that Relevance (in the sense of Sperber and Wilson 1986) is an organizing principle of discourses which ensures the achievement of the above goals, i.e., guarantees coherence and facilitates the processing and storage of information.

The principle of Relevance requires that each move (i.e., a question or an answer) be relevant to the preceding discourse, i.e., contribute to the aim of answering the questions under discussion. A declarative is relevant to a question if it constitutes a complete or partial answer to it. (A partial answer contextually entails the evaluation of, i.e., the assignment of the values *true* or *false,* to at least one element in the set of propositions corresponding to the question, whereas a complete answer contextually entails the evaluation of all of them.) A question, however, is relevant to another question if it is part of a strategy to answer it, i.e., constitutes a subquestion of it. Questions which have already been asked but have not yet been answered at a particular point in the discourse constitute the ordered set of Questions Under Discussion (*QUD*). When a question is accepted by the interlocutors, it is placed on top of the *QUD stack.* The strategy for answering the questions under discussion always involves answering the one on the top of the stack. For any move *m*, last(*QUD*(*m*)) represents the last question under discussion at the time *m* is made.

Kadmon (2001) offers a theory on the discourse structure associated with contrastive topics, which is based on the above insights of Roberts' (1996) theory, and her own constraint on the felicitous use of contrastive topics. She assumes that not only declaratives but also questions can have a focus semantic value, which is generated by replacing the focused constituent in the question denotation with a variable, and interpreting the resulting formula with respect to all assignment functions which differ only in the value they assign to this variable. She then proposes that a contrastive topic creates a presupposition regarding the focal structure of the last question under discussion in the following way: an utterance with a contrastive topic presupposes that its topic semantic value is identical to the focus semantic value of its last *QUD*. For an illustration, consider the sentence in (25a), its topic semantic value shown in (25b), which is identical to a set of sets of propositions, some members of which are listed in (25c), which in turn corresponds to a set of questions, listed in (25d) (Kadmon 2001: 391):

(25) a. [$_{CT}$ Larry] kissed [$_{F}$ Nina].
b. {{ $\| kiss(x,y) \|^{g'}$: *g'* is identical to *g* except that it may assign a different value to y}: *g* assignment}
c. {{'Larry kissed Sue,' 'Larry kissed Mary', 'Larry kissed Lisa,' ... },
{'Bill kissed Sue,' 'Bill kissed Mary', 'Bill kissed Lisa,' ... },
{'John kissed Sue,' 'John kissed Mary', 'John kissed Lisa,' ... }, ... }
d. {'Who did Larry kiss?', 'Who did Bill kiss?', 'Who did John kiss?', .. }

The above constraint predicts that (25a) presupposes that the focus semantic value of the last *QUD* for it is identical to (25d), i.e., that the above declarative is preceded in the discourse by a question in the set (25d). Naturally, among the questions in the above set, (25a) appears to be capable of answering the first one only. Kadmon predicts this by adopting the proposal by Roberts (1996) on the presuppositions of focus, which says that utterances (i.e., both questions and declaratives) containing prosodic focus in English presuppose that their *focus alternative set* is identical to the set of propositions corresponding to their last *QUD*. The focus alternative set, as conceived of by Roberts, differs from the focus semantic value of sentences as defined by Rooth (1985, 1992) in that in the former not only the focused expressions but also the *wh*-constituents are replaced by variables, and the result is then interpreted relative to each member of the set of all assigment functions which vary at most in the values they assign to those variables. Thus, the last *QUD* for (25a) is predicted to be the following: 'Who did Larry kiss?'. Due to the fact that the questions under discussion can remain implicit, it does not contradict the theory that (25a) is in fact overtly following the question 'Who did Bill kiss?'. According to Kadmon (2001: 396), the reason why a move from the latter question to the former one is allowed is that their ordinary denotations are both members of the set constituting the topic value of the answer.

In the next section we consider whether the constraints proposed by Kadmon (2001) on the felicitous occurrence of contrastive topics in English can be used to explain the facts concerning the requirements declaratives with contrastive topics impose on the preceding discourse in Hungarian.

4.2 Interpretability and relevant questions

In section 3 we found that although the impossibility of sentences ($5A_1$) and ($6A_1$) can be explained by means of Büring's (1997) proposal on the implicatures associated with contrastive topics, a similar procedure cannot be applied to ($5A_2$) or ($6A_2$), since the truth of these sentences on the intended interpretation does not entail the truth or falsity of all the alternative propositions. I believe, however, that by following Kadmon's (2001) approach to the relation between contrastive topics and the preceding discourse the apparent ill-formedness of these sentences can be handled successfully. Consider again ($6A_2$), repeated below:

(6) A_2: *[$_{CT}$ 'Pontosan öt tanárral] \`nem beszéltem.
exactly five teacher-INSTR not talked-1SG
'Exactly five teachers, I didn't talk to.'

Let us assume for a moment that ($6A_2$) is an acceptable sentence in Hungarian, it expresses the proposition that I talked to exactly five teachers (only) in the relevant situation, and that the verum focus and its negation share the semantic properties of 'ordinary' foci, and they introduce a set of alternatives which consist of the denotations of these constituents. Following Kadmon (2001), ($6A_2$) would then presuppose that its topic value, shown in (26), is identical to the focus semantic value of the last *QUD* for it, i.e., that the set of questions which ($6A_2$) can be uttered as an answer to consists of those exemplified in (27).

(26) $\{\{ \| \pi(\text{talk-to}(j, \text{y teachers})) \|^{g'} : g'$ is identical to g except that it may assign a different value to $\pi\} : g$ assignment$\}$

(27) a. [$_F$ Pontosan öt tanárral] beszéltél?[9, 10]
exactly five teacher-INSTR talked-2SG
'Did you talk to exactly five teachers?'

b. [$_F$ Kevesebb, mint öt tanárral] beszéltél?
fewer than five teacher-INSTR talked-2SG
'Did you talk to fewer than five teachers?'

[9] These are the only possible *yes-no* questions in the language which can be used to ask whether the interlocutor talked to exactly five, fewer than five or more than five teachers, respectively.

[10] Following É. Kiss (2002), I assume that the DP occupies the focus position.

c. [F Több, mint öt tanárral] beszéltél?
more than five teacher- INSTR talked-2SG
'Did you talk to more than five teachers?'

Note that the constraint proposed by Kadmon on the presuppositions of focus would predict that only the first question in (27) could serve as an appropriate last QUD for ($6A_2$). The problem, however, is that a negative answer to (27a) has to have the DP in focus position, as shown in (28):

(28) Nem [F pontosan öt tanárral] beszéltem.
not exactly five teacher- INSTR talked-1SG
'It wasn't exactly five teachers that I talked to.'

The above data thus show that there is no question in the language which ($6A_2$) could be uttered as an answer to, which explains, on the basis of Kadmon's (2001) proposal on the presuppositions of sentences with contrastive topics and foci, why it is an impossible sentence.

4.3 A new look at licensing conditions

The next question to be considered here is why contrastive topic DPs with monotone increasing determiners appear to be licensed in a much wider range of contexts than the monotone decreasing or non-monotonic determiners, as illustrated in (7)-(11) above. In section 3.3 we saw that Büring's theory can account for the act why ($8A_2$) is licensed by a question like (8Q), repeated below:

(8) Q: Hová utazott sok tanár?
where travelledmany teacher
'Where did many teachers travel?'

A_2: [CT ˊNéhány tanár] [F a ˋhegyekbe] utazott.
A few teacher the mountains- ILLATIVE travelled
'As for a few teachers, they went into the mountains.'

According to Kadmon (2001), ($8A_2$) presupposes that its topic value, shown in (29), and the focus semantic value of its last *QUD* are identical. This means that the last *QUD* for ($8A_2$) has to be a member of the set in (30).

(29) {{ ‖ *n* teachers travelled to *x* ‖$^{g'}$: *g'* is identical to *g* except that it may assign a different value to *x*}: *g* assignment}

(30) {'Where did no teacher travel?,' 'Where did one teacher travel?,' 'Where did two teachers travel?,' 'Where did a few teachers travel?,' 'Where did many teachers travel?', ...}

In addition, ($8A_2$) presupposes, due to the focus, that its focus semantic value and the ordinary semantic value of its last *QUD* are identical, which means that the only possible last *QUD* for ($8A_2$) is the one in (31):

(31) Hová utazott néhány tanár?
where travelled a few teacher
'Where did a few teachers travel?'

Although (8Q) is not identical to (31), it could be assumed, following Kadmon's suggestion with respect to (25a) above, that (31) is an implicit question following (8Q), and this implicit move is licensed due to the fact that the ordinary semantic values of these questions are both members of the topic value of ($8A_2$).

It seems to be a problem for the above proposal, however, that ($8A_5$)(=(11Q)), repeated here, cannot follow (8Q) in discourse, although there appears to be no reason why the former could not be preceded by an implicit question like (11Q) as well, since at first sight, (11Q) seems to be as similar to (8Q) as (31).

(8) A_5: [$_{CT}$ ˊNégynél kevesebb tanár] [$_F$ a ˋhegyekbe] utazott.
four-THAN fewer teacher the mountains-ILLATIVE travelled
'As for fewer than four teachers, that many went to the mountains.'

(11) Q: Hová utazott négynél kevesebb tanár?
where travelled four-THAN fewer teacher
'Where did fewer than four teachers travel?'

I would propose that there is one important respect in which (11Q) differs from both (8Q) and (31): (8Q) and (31) are subquestions of the same general question, expressed by (7Q), which asks about the set of all (relevant) teachers where they went.

(7) Q: Hová utaztak a tanárok?
where travelled the teachers
'Where did the teachers travel?'

(11Q), however, cannot be conceived of as a subquestion of (7Q), since it can be answered in such a way which does not tell about any of the teachers where she/he went. For example, ($9A_5$) can be true even if there is no teacher who went to the mountains. I believe that the general question which (11Q) constitutes a subquestion of is something like the following:

(32) 'For each possible/relevant cardinality, where did the subset of teachers with this cardinality go?'

presupposes that for each possible/relevant cardinality, there is one subset of the set of teachers whose members share the property of going to the same place. This presupposition is shared by the corresponding declaratives as well, since ($8A_5$), for example, presupposes that there is only one place where less than four teachers travelled. (This presupposition is due to the semantics of focus in Hungarian.) A complete answer to (32) would specify for each possible cardinality where sets of teachers with that cardinality travelled. Note that since a particular cardinality can be referred to in many ways (a set of teachers with two members can be referred to as *two teachers, at least one teacher, a few teachers, few teachers, less than five teachers,* etc.) it cannot be expected in reality that a complete answer be given to the above question. Instead, an answer which is considered complete in a particular situation would list for each relevant cardinality where subsets with that cardinality went. In determining what count as relevant cardinalities (or, rather, relevant ways of referring to cardinalities), context and discourse have a major role. As regards the examples discussed in (9)-(11) above, which all involve subquestions of the above general question, it could be assumed that subsets of teachers which are considered relevant are identified in the extralinguistic context, i.e., if the interlocutors study a table which shows a set of places and the numbers of teachers who travelled to the particular places, or due to the similarity of the linguistic expressions which are used to characterize one of the subsets. For example, the question in (11Q) could be answered by (33) or (34), which contain contrastive topic DPs characterizing types of sets which differ minimally from the expression characterizing another set type in the question:

(11) Q: Hová utazott négynél kevesebb tanár?
where travelled four-THAN fewer teacher
'Where did fewer than four teachers travel?'

(33) [$_{CT}$ Négynél ˊtöbb tanár] [$_F$ a ˋhegyekbe] utazott.
four-THAN more teacher the mountains-ILLATIVE travelled
'As for more than four teachers, that many went to the mountains.'

(34) [$_{CT}$ ˊÖtnél kevesebb tanár] [$_F$ a ˋhegyekbe] utazott.
five-THAN fewer teacher the mountains-ILLATIVE travelled
'As for fewer than five teachers, that many went to the mountains.'

The superquestions in (7Q) and (32) thus differ from each other in that (7Q) intends to find out some information about a set, the set of teachers, whereas (32) intends to find out some information about a set of sets. A possible strategy for answering (7Q) would be to divide the set asked about into subsets in such a way that the union of these subsets be identical to the original set. So that it can easily be seen that the union of the subsets constitutes the set asked about the subsets have to be identified by specifying the minimal possible number of their elements. Specifying a subset by means of an expression which determines the maximum number of its elements, i.e., by expressions like *fewer than four teachers* (cf. ($7A_4$)), does not enable the listener to find out how many elements he/she still needs to find information about, since expressions like the one below can also identify the empty set, as mentioned already. It was also mentioned that determiners of the type *at least n* make the same contribution to the truth-conditions of a sentence as determiners of the type *n*, and thus to identify a subset of teachers with at least n members the use of the longer form *at least n teachers* does not appear to be justified. The impossibility to answer (7) by ($7A_2$) illustrates this. Similarly, I don't believe it provides additional information about the members of the superset if one of its subsets is said to have exactly *n* members instead of saying that it has *n* members. This is the reason, I believe, that ($7A_3$) is not an appropriate way to give a partial answer to (7Q). Compare ($7A_1$-A_4) also to (35), which cannot be uttered as a legitimate answer to (7Q), either:

(35) $[_{CT}$ ´Ötnél több tanár] $[_{F}$ a \`tengerhez] utazott.
five-THAN more teacher the sea-ALLATIVE travelled
'As for more than five teachers, that many went to the sea.'

I propose that the reason why the above sentence does not sound as a felicitous answer to (7Q) is that although it specifies the minimal cardinality of the relevant set, it gives the same information as the sentence with a contrastive topic DP of the form *six teachers* would do, but in a less economical way. Having said that, we have now accounted for all the examples in (7) and (8) above.

It was argued in the preceding discussion that the licensing of a declarative with a contrastive topic in discourse by a question has at least two requirements: the first one, due to Kadmon (2001) is that the last question under discussion for the declarative and the overt question preceding it must be both members of the topic value associated with the declarative, whereas the second one is that this topic value has to correspond to a 'superquestion' which is relevant in the discourse.

I wish to propose here, however, that there is a third requirement as well. Consider (1Q) and the negative version of ($1A_2$) again:

(1) Q: Beszéltél öt tanárral?
talked-2SG five teacher-INSTR
'Have you talked to five teachers?'
A_2': #[$_{CT}$ 'Két tanárral] `nem beszéltem.
two teacher-INSTR not talked-1SG
'#As for two teachers, I didn't talk to that many.'

Note the following relation between the truth-conditions of ($1A_2$') and the possible answers to (1Q): the truth of the declarative entails a negative answer to (1Q). (36) illustrates a similar example, where the truth of the declarative entails a positive (i.e., complete) answer to the question:

(36) Q: Beszéltél három tanárral?
talked-2SG three teacher-INSTR
'Have you talked to three teachers?'
A: #[$_{CT}$ 'Öt tanárral] `beszéltem.
five teacher-INSTR talked-1SG
'#As for five teachers, I did talk to that many.'

Based on the fact that the answers to (1Q) and (36Q) above do not appear to be licensed by the preceding question, in spite of the fact that the last *QUD*'s for the declaratives and the overt questions are both members of the topic value associated with the declarative and that the two questions can easily be conceived of as being subquestions of the same superquestion, I propose that a third condition for the licensing of a declarative by a question which is not identical to its last *QUD* is that the declarative should not entail a complete answer to the overt question. The three conditions on the relation between declarative sentences with contrastive topics and the questions which can precede them in discourse listed above enable us to account for all the Hungarian examples listed above, and refute the preliminary hypothesis, resulting from superficial observation of the data, according to which monotonicity properties have a central role in determining whether particular occurrences of contrastive topic DPs are felicitous.

5 Conclusions

In this paper it was claimed that there is no evidence to support the binary division within DPs into those which can be licensed by the appearance of the same DP in the preceding discourse only and those which can be licensed by other DPs as well. It was shown that a declarative with a contrastive topic DP has to satisfy three conditions in order to be licensed by a question in a discourse: i) the last question under discussion for the declarative and the question preceding it overtly must be members of the topic value associated with the declarative, ii) the two questions must be capable of acting as subquestions of the same superquestion in the discourse (determined by the topic value of the declarative), and iii) if the overt question is not identical to the last *QUD* for the declarative, the declarative must not entail a complete answer to the overt question.

It was also shown that the idea according to which the aim of discourses is to answer explicit and implicit questions can account for the fact why certain, grammatically well-formed sentences with contrastive topics have no interpretation in Hungarian.

6 References

Bosch, P. and R. van der Sandt (eds) (1999): Focus: Linguistic, Cognitive and Computational Perspectives. Cambridge, New York and Melbourne: Cambridge University Press.

Büring, D. (1997): The Meaning of Topic and Focus. The 59th Street Bridge Accent. London, New York: Routledge.

Büring, D. (1999): Topic. In: P. Bosch and R. van der Sandt (eds), 142–165.

Carlson, L. (1983). Dialogue Games: An Approach to Discourse Analysis. Dordrecht: Reidel.

É. Kiss, K. (2002): The Syntax of Hungarian. Oxford: Oxford University Press.

von Fintel, K. (1994): Restrictions on Quantifier Domains. Doctoral dissertation, University of Masschusetts at Amherst.

Kadmon, N. (2001): Formal Pragmatics. Malden, MA, Oxford: Blackwell.

Kálmán, L. and Á. Nádasdy (1994): A hangsúly [Stress]. In: F. Kiefer (ed) : Strukturális magyar nyelvtan 2. Fonológia. [A Structural Grammar of Hungarian 2: Phonology]. Budapest: Akadémiai Kiadó, 393–467.

Kenesei, I. (1989): Logikus-e a magyar szórend? [Is Hungarian word order logical?] Általános nyelvészeti tanulmányok XVII, 105–152.

Lambrecht, K. (1994): Information Structure and Sentence Form. Cambridge, New York and Melbourne: Cambridge University Press.

Lee, Ch. (1999): Contrastive topic: A locus of interface evidence from Korean and English. In: K. Turner (ed): The Semantics/Pragmatics Interface from Different Points of View. Oxford: Elsevier.

Molnár, V. (1998) Topic in focus: the syntax, phonology, semantics, and pragmatics of the so-called "contrastive topic" in Hungarian and German. Acta Linguistic Hungarica 45, 389-466.

Roberts, C. (1996) Information structure in discourse: towards an integrated formal theory of pragmatics. In. J. Hak Yoon and A. Kathol (eds): Ohio State University Working Papers in Linguistics 49.

Sperber, D. and D. Wilson (1986): Relevance. Cambridge: Basil Blackwell.

Vallduví, E. and E. Engdahl (1996): The linguistic realization of information packaging. Linguistics 34(3), 459–519.

Ingolf Max (Leipzig)

Information Structure – Two-dimensionally Explicated[1]

1 Introduction

In the literature at least four different versions of characterizing the internal information structure IS of sentences S can be found:

1. the **thetic-categorical distinction,**
2. the **focus-background structure (FBS),**
3. the **topic-comment structure (TCS)**, and
4. the **theme-rheme structure (TRS)**.[2]

All these distinctions can be made on the basis of linguistic and extra-linguistic context. Another tendency consists in using the highly controversial notion *presupposition* to clarify the interaction between the mentioned levels (dimensions) of information structure. Presuppositions are often connected with *background* (old/given information part of a sentence) and *topic* (what the sentence is about).

This paper tries to shed some light on these informational categories and their complex interaction. In what follows a formal explication of these notions within a two-dimensional framework is given and the new model is used to explain some prominent cases: congruence of questions and answers regarding their background; scope inversion with respect to hat contour; correction by contrastive focus and by German *nicht–sondern*-constructions. Finally we

---

[1] This paper presents some results of the project "Multi-dimensional Representation of Linguistic and Conceptual Knowledge. Investigations on Presupposition and Negation" which is part of the research group "Linguistic Foundations of Cognitive Science. Linguistic and Conceptual Knowledge" sponsored by the *Deutsche Forschungsgemeinschaft*. We thank our sponsor for making this research possible in a very productive atmosphere. I am very indebted to Johannes Dölling, Nils Kürbis, Ewald Lang, Marko Malink, Martin Schäfer, Andreas Späth, Anita Steube, Carla Umbach, Tatjana Zybatow, and especially Thomas Weskott for inspirations and very fruitful discussions. They are not responsible for the content of this paper.

[2] We shall not deal with this distinction in this paper. Regarding focus see e.g. Bosch & van der Sandt (1999).

show how thetic sentences can be represented in a two-dimensional framework.

We start with the introduction of a notation that makes the levels 1 to 3 and their interaction more transparent. It shows further some difficulties regarding a coherent and formally satisfying formal explication. The basic concepts will be explained.

In the second part we introduce our basic matrix expressions which can be used to give the semantic form SF of any sentence including relevant aspects of its information structure. Such basic expressions consist of two dimensions: (a) Given any simple sentence S the first (upper) dimension expresses the proper meaning (IS-free SF) of S. (b) The additional second dimension copies those parts of the first dimension which are marked as the background of S. The next step consists in characterizing a presupposition-preserving negation as a reduction operator associated with an IS-sensitive reduction rule. Then we can define the notions *presupposition* and *assertion* as characteristic relations between our two-dimensional matrix expressions – negated and unnegated – and specific subparts of them.

Using a background-sensitive reading of German "*alle*" and our IS-sensitive negation hat contours can be described as direct scope inversion. The constituents of the background of S are not within the scope of this negation.

These cases have in common that the second dimension which represents the background of a sentence S remains unchanged. Corrections by contrastive focus can be interpreted as updating the second dimension by existential expressions which introduce a space of alternatives. The main point is that the update is restricted by the already given information. Alternatives to constituents which are already in the background are not allowed. A correction operator produces the appropriate update. Together with the presupposition-preserving negation it gives a model for German *nicht–sondern*-constructions.

2 Information structure

2.1 General framework-notation

Throughout the whole paper we use the following notation and abbreviations:

S/$[_{CP}]$:	Sentence / Clause Phrase
T:	Topic
$\mathfrak{T}_S$:	Set of *possible* topics of a sentence S
C:	Comment
TCS:	Topic-Comment Structure (indicated by superscripts)
B:	Background: B_i is a constituent of the background usually marked by [-F].

F:	**F**ocus: F_i is a constituent of the background usually marked by [+F].
FBS:	**F**ocus-**B**ackground **S**tructure (indicated by subscripts)
CF:	**C**ontrastive **F**ocus
$[]_F$	indicates the scope/domain of **F**
$[]_B$	indicates the scope/domain of **B**
$\{\}^T$	indicates the scope/domain of **T**
$\{\}^C$	indicates the scope/domain of **C**
$[_{CP} S]^{TH}$	marks a sentence as thetic
$[_{CP} S]^{CAT}$	marks a sentence as categorical
P:	**P**resupposition

2.2 Focus-background structure (FBS)[3]

"DPs or PPs expressing background information are anchored in context and situation and express entities which are familiar to the communicative partners. They are characterized by definite articles or possessive pronouns. In the rare cases when indefinite articles characterize background information, they are interpreted generically or specifically. Definite articles in the background part of the sentence may have all the interpretations which are possible: definite, indefinite, generic. But when definite articles are to express focus information, they have to refer not only specifically but uniquely."[4]

"The focus domain begins at the right of the attitudinal adverbials and particles. It coincides with the maximal VP. Usually the pronouns and the defocused DPs, PPs expressing background information are moved to the left of the focus domain and leave a trace behind. To be even more precise: They are moved to the left of the attitudinal adverbials and particles. There is good reason for attitudinal adverbials and particles to form the right border between background and focus in a sentence. Background information is known or at least accessible to all the communicative partners."[5]

The new, not-given, not-inferable information belongs to focus F. Uttering a sentence the speaker introduces this information as new. A sentence can contain either one, several, or only F-constituents. Each F-constituent belongs to the F-domain. The converse does not hold for German. **Categorical sentences**

---

[3] There is a large variety of versions of explicating the notions *focus* and *background* (cf. e.g. Rooth (1985, 1996), Krifka (2001/02)). Here we follow the approach introduced by Steube and others (cf. e.g. Steube (2001a), Steube & Späth (2002)) which forms the basis of some projects within our DFG research group "Linguistic Foundations of Cognitive Science".

[4] Steube (2001b), 225, cf. Steube & Späth (2002), 236, Heusinger (2000a), and Heusinger (2000b).

[5] Steube (2001b), 226. Cf. also Lang (1983).

are characterized by both focus and background. Regarding **thetic sentences** there can be contextual anchored or anaphoric elements in their focus.[6]

General conditions of focus-background structure (FBS):

Form: $[_{CP}\ []_B\ []_F]$

- $F \subseteq S$ & $B \subset S$ (The whole sentence can not be background: $B \neq S$)
- $F \cup B = S$ (even satisfied if F=S: thetic sentences.)
- $F \cap B = \emptyset$ (even satisfied if $B=\emptyset$.)
- $F \neq \emptyset$ (Sentences have to contain at least one F-constituent.)
  The whole sentence can be within the F-domain $([_{CP}\ [\,S\,]_F])$.
  Such fully-focused sentences consist exclusively of F-constituents.
  They can be called **thetic** sentences.[7]
- Question: maximal one B?

Types of F:

(a) F=S: **Full** focus (**thetic** sentences with a maximum of new information)

(1) $[_{CP}$ [Es REGnet $]_F$ $]^{TH}$
It rains (It is raining)[8]

(b) $F \subset S$ & F>B: **Intermediate** focus

(2) Was macht Anton?
What does Anton? (What is Anton doing?)

(3) $[_{CP}$ [Anton $]_B$ [küsst Maša $]_F$. $]^{CAT}$
Anton kisses Maša

(c) $F \subset S$ & F<B: **Minimal** focus

(4) Wen küsst Anton?
Whom kisses Anton?

(5) $[_{CP}$ [Anton küsst $]_B$ [Maša $]_F$ $]^{CAT}$.

---

[6] Steube & Späth (2002), 236.

[7] Regarding the discussion of thetic sentences cf. Brentano (1874/English 1973), Kuroda (1972), Marty (1897, 1918), Milsark (1974), Sasse (1987), Vallduví (1993).

[8] Throughout the paper a word-for-word translation of the German examples is given – occasionally followed by a real English variant in round brackets.

2.3 Topic-comment structure (TCS)

"We characterize topics as the anchored referring constituents which the rest of the sentence (comment) is about. Topics are subsets of background constituents. A sentence with a topic comment division has exactly one topic. The syntactic position of the German main-clause topic is in Spec CP or immediately at the right of C°. The latter position is the position of a topic in a subordinate clause, too. But these positions can be filled with (contrastively) focused constituents, too. Therefore, German topics cannot be defined by positions alone."[9]

"Topics do not have a characteristic intonation contour, although at the beginning of a sentence, frequency has to increase in order for to get modulated later on. Topics or even the larger class of sentence-initial constituents seem to be thematically connected to the so-called topic of the text and help to organize the inner structure of texts and even characterize types of texts."[10]

Topics T have to be constituents that are able to refer and fulfill the pragmatic criterion of "aboutness". That means that the remaining sentence (the comment C) says something *about* the topic.[11] Usually but not necessarily sentences have a topic.

General conditions of topic-comment structure (TCS):

Form: $[_{CP} \{\}^{T} \{\}^{C}]$

- $C \subseteq S$ & $T \subset S$ (The whole sentence can not be topic: $T \neq S$)
- $T \cup C = S$ (even satisfied if $C=S$.)
- $T \cap C = \emptyset$ (even satisfied if $T=\emptyset$.)
- That means: $C=S-T$. Comment can be defined negatively. Sentence minus topic gives us comment.[12]
- T is a set with at most one element.[13]

2.4 Interaction of FBS and TCS

General conditions of the relation between **TCS** and **FBS**:

- $\mathfrak{T}_S \subseteq B$: the set of possible topics consists of B-constituents.
  If $T=B$ there is no difference in writing $\{[]_B\}^T$ or $[\{\}^T]_B$ and writing $\{[]_F\}^C$ or $[\{\}^C]_F$ in our representation schema.
- $F \subseteq C$?

---

[9] Steube (2001b), 227.

[10] Steube (2001b), 227.

[11] Cf. Jacobs (2001) and Steube & Späth (2002), 237.

[12] Steube & Späth (2002), 237. That is why we find very seldom an explicit notation of C. But there is the problem of overlapping brackets in cases $T \neq B/C \neq F$ which becomes simply invisible.

[13] Other authors accept more than one element in T. Cf. Szuszich (2002).

- impossibility of $T \subset B$ & $F=C$ (violates one general TCS-condition: $T \cup C = S$)
- impossibility of $F \subset C$ & $T=B$ (violates one general FBS-condition: $F \cup B = S$)?
- possibility of $F,B \subset S$ & $T=\varnothing$ & $C=S$: $[\{[]_B[]_F\}^C]^{CAT}$: This version of categorical sentences equals thetic sentences in being topic-free.

Here is one example:

(6) Wer kommt?
Who comes? (Who is coming?)

(7) $[_{CP} \{[\{[\text{Es kommt}]_B \ [\text{PEter}]_F \}^C \ ]^{CAT}$
It comes Peter (Peter is coming. / It is Peter who is coming.)

The placeholder "es" and the finite verb "kommt" cannot be topics of this sentence. Therefore: Categorical sentences do not have to contain a topic. This is one of the main reasons why we need both kinds of information structure: FBS *and* TCS. Furthermore, topicality does not run parallel to categoricity.

- Problem: $\{\}^T_B[\ldots[]_{KF}\ldots]^C_F$ as an abbreviation of $[_{CP}[\{\}^T]_B[\{\ldots[]_{CF}\ldots\}^C]_F]^{CAT}$: What do the dots "…" mean? How do they behave with respect to B?
- Analogous problem regarding I-topics which should be computed within the F-domain: $[\{\ldots[t_1]_{KF}\ldots\}^T_B[\ldots t_1\ldots]^C_F]^{CAT}$ as abbreviation of $[[\{\ldots[t_1]_{KF}\ldots\}^T]_B[\{\ldots t_1\ldots\}^C]_F]^{CAT?}$

Examples of truly IS-structured sentences ($T,C,F,B \neq \varnothing$) with **T=B and F=C**:

(8) $[_{CP} [\{\text{Friedrich}\}^T \ ]_B \ [\{\text{ist gestorben}\}^C \ ]_F \ ]^{CAT}$
Friedrich is died

(9) $[_{CP} [\{\text{Der Peter}\}^T \ ]_B \ [\{\text{hat gestern einen SCHWEINSbraten gegessen}\}^C \ ]_F \ ]^{CAT}$ [14]
The Peter has yesterday a joint-of-pork eaten

Examples of truly IS-structured sentences with **T≠B and F≠C**:

(10)(a) Was hat Peter gekauft?
What has Peter bought?
(b) Peter hat $[\text{ein AUto}]_F$ gekauft.
Peter has a car bought

[14] The examples (9), (12), (13), and (14) were used by Weskott in one of his illuminating handouts about information structure. Cf. also the examples (5a) – (5e) in Weskott (this volume).

(c) *Ein Auto hat [PEter]$_F$ gekauft.
A car has Peter bought

(11) Peter hat [ein AUTO gekauft]$_F$
Peter has a car bought
[$_{CP}$ [{ Peter }^{T} { hat]$_B$ [ein AUTO gekauft]$_F$ }^{C}].

If we look at the part "{ hat]$_B$ " it becomes clear that the "strange" bracketing of "hat" tells us something about the overlapping of TCS and FBS. Usually such strange structure is avoided by not explicating the whole IS of that sentence. Usually the comment C is to be understood as the pure complement of T.[15]

(12) [$_{CP}$ [{ Der Peter }^{T}]$_B$ { hat gestern [einen SCHWEINSbraten]$_F$ gegessen }^{C}]^{CAT}
The Peter has yesterday a joint-of-pork eaten

(13) [$_{CP}$ [{ Der Peter }^{T}]$_B$ { hat [GESTERN]$_F$ einen Schweinsbraten gegessen }^{C}]^{CAT}
The peter has yesterday a joint-of-pork eaten

The problem here is: Should "hat gestern" ["hat"] and "gegessen" ["einen Schweinsbraten gegessen"] be considered as two separate B-parts? This would lead to B⊂C. Is this desirable and compatible with the TCS-FBS-preconditions? This would lead to various disconnected B-constituents. E.g.

(14) [$_{CP}$ [{ Der Peter }^{T}]$_{B1}$ [{ hat]$_{B2}$ [GESTERN]$_F$ [einen Schweinsbraten gegessen]$_{B3}$ }^{C}]^{CAT}

Some further questions:

- What is the relation between topic / background on the one hand and presupposition on the other (T=P or H=P)?
- Are full-focused (thetic) sentences constructions without presuppositions?
- [$_{CP}$[{}^{T}]$_B$[{...[]$_{CF}$...}^{C}]$_F$]^{CAT} is our schema for contrastive focus. Does the part "[ ]$_{CF}$ " trigger any new presupposition?
- We are confronted with a similar problem regarding *correction sentences*:

(15) [**PAUL**]$_{CF}$ kommt.
Paul comes

[15] Is this a difficulty connected with auxiliary verbs in general or with perfect constructions in particular? Some authors accept this overlapping (e.g. Späth & Trautwein (this volume)) other authors try to avoid this (e.g. Weskott (this volume)).

Like *thetic* sentences such a construction is without any topic. Contrastive focus marks that constituent prosodically which has been substituted for another constituent of the same type. What do such sentences presuppose? Because of $\mathfrak{T}_S = \varnothing$ (no T) (15) cannot trigger an existence presupposition. Otherwise: The contrastive focus may trigger another type of existence presupposition regarding the alternatives of "Paul". This will be discussed in section 4.

3 The two-dimensional representation of information-structured sentences

"The linearization of the arguments of verbs does not necessarily correspond to the canonical order of the argument structure. Nevertheless, both syntactic linearization and the order of the argument structure are determined by the grammatical system. Within the argument structure of those verbal predicates with two structural arguments, the internal argument precedes the external:

(16) $\lambda y_{\text{internal}}\, \lambda x_{\text{external}}\, \lambda e_{\text{referential}}\ [\ \dots\ e\ \dots\ x\ \dots\ y\ \dots\ ]$"[16]

This can be generalized to

(17) $\lambda x_{n\,(\text{internal})} \dots \lambda x_{2(\text{internal})}\, \lambda x_{1(\text{external})}\ \ [\, x_1\ x_2 \dots x_n\,]$

(18) The child sleeps.

(19) $S(\iota x[C(x)])$ or $\exists y[y = \iota x[C(x)] \wedge S(y)]$ or $\exists! x[C(x) \wedge S(x)]$

For example with respect to $\exists! x[C(x) \wedge S(x)]$ we call $[C(x) \wedge S(x)]$ the **matrix** of $\exists! x[C(x) \wedge S(x)]$. In this paper we are only concerned with operators which can be explicated as predecessors of matrices. Let $\otimes$ be a placeholder that marks the position for negation, correction etc.:

(20) $\otimes[C(x) \wedge S(x)]$ (Matrix of $\lambda x \otimes [C(x) \wedge S(x)]$, $\exists! x \otimes [C(x) \wedge S(x)]$, etc.)

3.1 General two-dimensional form of a sentence S

(21) $\lambda x_n \dots \lambda x_1 \otimes \begin{bmatrix} \alpha \\ \beta \end{bmatrix}$:

[16] Späth (2003), 1. Cf. also Weskott (this volume) formula (2).

- α represents the proper (ordinary) meaning of a sentence. This coincides with the matrix of the semantic form SF given in a language of first-order logic.
- β represents the meaning component induced by the information structure of the sentence which is characterized by the background B. Parts of β are matrix expressions of the Form $F_i^1(x_i)$ which represents DPs. One of these $F_i^1(x_i)$ can be the topic T of S. The fact that "F_i^1" and "x_i" have the same index "i" says that the used x-variable is of "its" DP-type. We assume a Russellian style of representing DPs by using exactly one unary predicate. In cases there the VP of S is part of B the expression of the form $F_j^n(x_1,\ldots,x_n)$ is part of β.
- α and β have a conjunctive form and "X is part of α" / "X is part of β" means that X is a conjunct of α / β.

Specified general form:

$$(22) \qquad \lambda x_n \ldots \lambda x_1 \otimes \begin{bmatrix} F_1^1 x_1 \wedge \ldots \wedge F_n^1 x_n \wedge F_{n+1}^{(n)}(x_1,\cdots,x_n) \\ \beta \end{bmatrix}.$$

The $F_1^1,\ldots,F_n^1$ are the matrix predications expressed by DPs. Expressions of the form F_{n+1}^n represent the VP-predications. The superscript i of F_j^i indicates the number of the arguments of F_j^i. The subscript j acts as a counter which numbers the occurrences of F_j^i in α.
Let α_i be any of the conjuncts of α with $\alpha_i \triangleq F_i^1 x_i$ if $1 \leq i \leq n$ and $\alpha_{n+1} \triangleq F_{n+1}^n(x_1,\ldots,x)$.
Let α_{k_j} be any of the conjuncts of β. Then

(23) $\beta \triangleq \alpha_{k_1} \wedge \ldots \wedge \alpha_{k_m}$, $1 \leq k_j \leq n+1$ and $1 \leq m < n+1$.

- k_j with $1 \leq k_j \leq n+1$ indicates that each constituent (conjunct) of α can be a possible part of β (a possible B-constituent). The whole β represents the **background B** of the sentence. The α_i ($1 \leq i \leq n$) are possible **topics T** of the sentence (usually α_1).
- $k_j \leq n+1$ (i.e. it is possible that $1 \leq k_j = n+1$) tells us that α_i can be $F_{n+1}^n(x_1,\ldots,x_n)$. The VP can be part of the background B.
- $1 \leq m$ says that the sentence S has at least one B-constituent, one part of the background: usually the topic / the external argument in neutral cases. In other words, S is a **categorical sentence**.
- Because m is not allowed to be $n+1$ ($m \neq n+1$) the sentence cannot exclusively consist of B-constituents (B⊂S!).

We get

$$(24)\qquad \lambda x_n \ldots \lambda x_1 \otimes \begin{bmatrix} F_1^1 x_1 \wedge \ldots \wedge F_n^1 x_n \wedge F_{n+1}^{(n)}(x_1,\cdots,x_n) \\ \alpha_{k_1} \wedge \ldots \wedge \alpha_{k_m} \end{bmatrix},$$

or more styled

$$(25)\qquad \lambda x_n \ldots \lambda x_1 \otimes \begin{bmatrix} \alpha_1 \wedge \ldots \wedge \alpha_n \wedge \alpha_{n+1} \\ \alpha_{k_1} \wedge \ldots \wedge \alpha_{k_m} \end{bmatrix}.^{17}$$

Again, ⊗ marks the position of the negation, correction etc.

A simplification: We omit the lambda-operators: $\otimes \begin{bmatrix} \alpha_1 \wedge \ldots \wedge \alpha_n \wedge \alpha_{n+1} \\ \alpha_{k_1} \wedge \ldots \wedge \alpha_{k_m} \end{bmatrix}$.

The information structure is responsible for the second meaning dimension of a sentence S. The first dimension represents the proper meaning of S. From our representation it is very clear, that the second dimension is a proper sub-conjunction of the first one. Therefore, B depends on S.
Let us have a look at one example:

(26) The child sleeps: $\exists! x[child(x) \wedge sleep(x)]$

Who sleeps?

$$\otimes \begin{bmatrix} ?(x) \wedge sleep(x) \\ sleep(x) \end{bmatrix}$$

What does the child do?

$$\otimes \begin{bmatrix} child(x) \wedge ?(x) \\ child(x) \end{bmatrix}$$

$[_{CP}$ {[The CHILD $]_F$ [sleeps $]_B$ $\}^C$ $]^{CAT}$

$$(\exists!)\otimes \begin{bmatrix} child(x) \wedge sleep(x) \\ sleep(x) \end{bmatrix}$$

[{[The child $]_B$ $\}^T$ { [SLEEPS $]_F$ $\}^C$ $]^{CAT}$

$$(\exists!)\otimes \begin{bmatrix} child(x) \wedge sleep(x) \\ child(x) \end{bmatrix}$$

3.2 Necessitation relation ($\gg$)

$$(\gg)\qquad \begin{bmatrix} \alpha \\ \beta \end{bmatrix} \gg \gamma \;=_{df}\; \text{(i) } \vDash \alpha \supset \gamma, \text{ and (ii) } \vDash \beta \supset \gamma.^{18}$$

A sentence S represented as $\begin{bmatrix} \alpha \\ \beta \end{bmatrix}$ necessitates γ if and only if (iff) γ follows
(i) from the proper meaning α of S, and
(ii) from the information-induced meaning b of that sentence S. What is still missing is an appropriate presupposition preserving negation of S with neg-S $\gg \gamma$.

---

[17] The sign "$\wedge$" represents the operator of classical conjunction. Throughout the paper operators within brackets have to be read classically. The details of a two-dimensional system can be found e.g. in Max (1998).

[18] The symbol "$\supset$" represents the operator of material (classical) implication. "$\vDash \alpha$" indicates that α is classically valid, i.e. for each valuation of α we get the output *true*.

The γ which satisfies the necessitation regarding S and neg-S is named a **presupposition**. First we have

(27) $$\begin{bmatrix} \alpha_1 \wedge \ldots \wedge \alpha_n \wedge \alpha_{n+1} \\ \alpha_{k_1} \wedge \ldots \wedge \alpha_{k_m} \end{bmatrix} \gg \alpha_{k_1} \wedge \ldots \wedge \alpha_{k_m}.$$

This holds because $\alpha_{k_1}, \ldots, \alpha_{k_m}$ are also conjuncts of the first dimension.

3.3 Entailment (→)

(→) $$\begin{bmatrix} \alpha \\ \beta \end{bmatrix} \rightarrow \gamma =_{df} \text{ (i) } \vDash \alpha \supset \gamma, \text{ and (ii) } \nvDash \beta \supset \gamma.$$

$\begin{bmatrix} \alpha \\ \beta \end{bmatrix}$ entails γ if and only if α logically implicates γ and β does not logically entail γ.

(28) $$\begin{bmatrix} \alpha_1 \wedge \ldots \wedge \alpha_n \wedge \alpha_{n+1} \\ \alpha_{k_1} \wedge \ldots \wedge \alpha_{k_m} \end{bmatrix} \rightarrow \alpha_{k_{m+1}} \wedge \ldots \wedge \alpha_{k_{n+1}}.$$

The $\alpha_{k_{m+1}}, \ldots, \alpha_{k_{n+1}}$ are the remaining parts of the first dimension. Therefore, they are normally not logically implicated by the second dimension.

(29) $$\begin{bmatrix} C(x) \wedge S(x) \\ S(x) \end{bmatrix} \gg S(x) \qquad \begin{bmatrix} C(x) \wedge S(x) \\ C(x) \end{bmatrix} \gg C(x)$$

(30) $$\text{not: } \begin{bmatrix} C(x) \wedge S(x) \\ S(x) \end{bmatrix} \gg C(x) \qquad \text{not: } \begin{bmatrix} C(x) \wedge S(x) \\ C(x) \end{bmatrix} \gg S(x)$$

(31) $$\begin{bmatrix} C(x) \wedge S(x) \\ S(x) \end{bmatrix} \rightarrow C(x) \qquad \begin{bmatrix} C(x) \wedge S(x) \\ C(x) \end{bmatrix} \rightarrow S(x)$$

(32) $$\text{not: } \begin{bmatrix} C(x) \wedge S(x) \\ S(x) \end{bmatrix} \rightarrow S(x) \qquad \text{not: } \begin{bmatrix} C(x) \wedge S(x) \\ C(x) \end{bmatrix} \rightarrow C(x)$$

3.4 The presupposition-preserving, IS-sensitive negation $\neg_{\wedge}$:

There is a well-known difficulty: How is it possible to put a negation in front of a conjunction and getting only the negation of one of its conjuncts separately?

$*(\alpha \wedge \beta) \Leftrightarrow (\neg\alpha \wedge \beta)$?

$*(\alpha \wedge \beta) \Leftrightarrow (\alpha \wedge \neg\beta)$?

From a (one-dimensional) classical point of view this is not possible if we hope to find a *function* which should yield this result. When do we need this kind of negation? One prominent case is the inner occurrence of a negation regarding Russell's analysis of definite descriptions. The step from "none" to "there is at least one which is not" cannot be reduced to direct scope inversion from "$\neg\exists$" to "$\exists\neg$". $\exists x\neg[\forall y[F(y)\leftrightarrow y=x]\wedge G(x)]$ does not work here: It produces $\exists x[\forall y[F(y)\leftrightarrow y=x]\supset\neg G(x)]$. That's not what we wanted to get. Our target is $\exists x*[\forall y[F(y)\leftrightarrow y=x]\wedge G(x)]\Leftrightarrow\exists x[\forall y[F(y)\leftrightarrow y=x]\wedge$ $\wedge\neg G(x)]$! If we look at such cases we have convincing arguments for looking at $\forall y[F(y)\leftrightarrow y=x]$ as a *presupposition* (background). This part remains invariant under our negation $*$. Therefore a better representation of the matrix would be

$$\begin{bmatrix}\forall y[F(y)\leftrightarrow y=x]\wedge G(x)\\ \forall y[F(y)\leftrightarrow y=x]\end{bmatrix}\text{, i.e. }\begin{bmatrix}\forall y[F(y)\leftrightarrow y=x]\wedge G(x)\\ \forall y[F(y)\leftrightarrow y=x]\end{bmatrix}\gg\forall y[F(y)\leftrightarrow y=x].$$

What we want now is

$$*\begin{bmatrix}\forall y[F(y)\leftrightarrow y=x]\wedge G(x)\\ \forall y[F(y)\leftrightarrow y=x]\end{bmatrix}=\begin{bmatrix}\forall y[F(y)\leftrightarrow y=x]\wedge\neg G(x)\\ \forall y[F(y)\leftrightarrow y=x]\end{bmatrix}.$$

To get this we have to use both dimensions of our matrix expression. But how? Here is our candidate: We introduce a special reduction operator "$\neg_{\wedge}$" associated with the following rule:

$$(\mathbf{R}\neg_{\wedge})\quad \neg_{\wedge}\begin{bmatrix}\alpha\\ \beta\end{bmatrix}\Rightarrow\begin{bmatrix}\beta\wedge\neg\alpha\\ \beta\end{bmatrix}.$$

$\neg_{\wedge}$ is a complex operation which demands the following:

- Copy the IS-induced part of the meaning of S – the background B – to the first dimension.
- Negate the proper meaning of S completely ($\neg\alpha$).
- Create a new conjunction of the products of the first two steps ($\beta\wedge\neg\alpha$)
- Keep the second dimension (the background of S).

Let α be the conjunction $(\beta\wedge\gamma)$. Following our rule $(\mathbf{R}\neg_{\wedge})$ we get

(33) $\neg_{\wedge}\begin{bmatrix}\beta\wedge\gamma\\ \beta\end{bmatrix} \overset{=}{=} \begin{bmatrix}\beta\wedge\neg(\beta\wedge\gamma)\\ \beta\end{bmatrix}$, therefore $\neg_{\wedge}\begin{bmatrix}\beta\wedge\gamma\\ \beta\end{bmatrix} \overset{=}{=} \begin{bmatrix}\beta\wedge\neg\gamma\\ \beta\end{bmatrix}$.[19]

This is exactly what we want! Look at Russell's example:

(34) $$\neg_{\wedge}\begin{bmatrix}\forall y[F(y)\leftrightarrow y=x]\wedge G(x)\\ \forall y[F(y)\leftrightarrow y=x]\end{bmatrix} \overset{=}{=} \begin{bmatrix}\forall y[F(y)\leftrightarrow y=x]\wedge\neg G(x)\\ \forall y[F(y)\leftrightarrow y=x]\end{bmatrix}$$

after $\neg_{\wedge}$ -reduction we get

(35) $$\begin{bmatrix}\forall y[F(y)\leftrightarrow y=x]\wedge\neg(\forall y[F(y)\leftrightarrow y=x]\wedge G(x))\\ \forall y[F(y)\leftrightarrow y=x]\end{bmatrix} \overset{=}{=} \begin{bmatrix}\forall y[F(y)\leftrightarrow y=x]\wedge\neg G(x)\\ \forall y[F(y)\leftrightarrow y=x]\end{bmatrix}$$

We need exactly one negation characterized by our reduction rule **(R$\neg_{\wedge}$)** to get the negation of conjuncts within a conjunction. But its computing depends on the background B of the conjunction. Only one part of the conjunction is new information. The other one is presupposed. The negation $\neg_{\wedge}$ affects only the focused part (the new information):

(36) $$\neg_{\wedge}\begin{bmatrix}\beta\wedge\gamma\\ \beta\end{bmatrix} \overset{=}{=} \begin{bmatrix}\beta\wedge\neg\gamma\\ \beta\end{bmatrix} \qquad \neg_{\wedge}\begin{bmatrix}\beta\wedge\gamma\\ \gamma\end{bmatrix} \overset{=}{=} \begin{bmatrix}\gamma\wedge\neg\beta\\ \gamma\end{bmatrix}.$$

3.5 Presupposition ($\mapsto$)

We are now able to introduce our **presupposition relation** ($\mapsto$) which uses the above defined notion of *necessitation* together with our rule (R$\neg_{\wedge}$) relative to IS-sensitive two-dimensional expressions:

($\mapsto$) $$\begin{bmatrix}\alpha\\ \beta\end{bmatrix}\mapsto\gamma =_{df} \text{(i)} \begin{bmatrix}\alpha\\ \beta\end{bmatrix}\gg\gamma, \text{ and (ii)} \neg_{\wedge}\begin{bmatrix}\alpha\\ \beta\end{bmatrix}\gg\gamma.$$

Regarding the above mentioned cases of negations of exactly one conjunct within a conjunction we get the following:

(37) $$\begin{bmatrix}\beta\wedge\gamma\\ \beta\end{bmatrix}\mapsto\beta \qquad \begin{bmatrix}\beta\wedge\gamma\\ \gamma\end{bmatrix}\mapsto\gamma$$

[19] The symbol "=" indicates that – using the indicated reduction rules – the left ("X") and the right part ("Y") of "X=Y" can be transformed into formulae of the same shape. To get this we furthermore use the familiar logically equivalent transformations within brackets.

In the first case we can call "β" a "**presupposition**" whereas in the second case γ is the presupposition.[20]

3.6 Assertion ($\rhd$)

What is asserted by uttering a sentence S is new information. This information cannot be presupposed. An assertion should be altered under negation. S asserts γ means that S entails γ and $\neg_\wedge$ S does not entail γ:

$$(\rhd) \quad \begin{bmatrix}\alpha\\ \beta\end{bmatrix} \rhd \gamma =_{df} \text{(i)} \begin{bmatrix}\alpha\\ \beta\end{bmatrix} \to \gamma, \text{ and (ii) not: } \neg_\wedge \begin{bmatrix}\alpha\\ \beta\end{bmatrix} \to \gamma.$$

Let us have a further look at our example of a conjunction:

$$(38) \quad \begin{bmatrix}\beta\wedge\gamma\\ \beta\end{bmatrix} \rhd \gamma \qquad \begin{bmatrix}\beta\wedge\gamma\\ \gamma\end{bmatrix} \rhd \beta$$

Here are some examples (representation of the matrix only):

(39) Der Mann hat kein AUTO gekauft.
the man aux neg a CAR bought-participle'

$$\neg_\wedge \begin{bmatrix} man(x) \wedge car(y) \wedge bought(x,y) \\ man(x) \wedge bought(x,y) \end{bmatrix} = \begin{bmatrix} man(x) \wedge bought(x,y) \wedge \neg car(y) \\ man(x) \wedge bought(x,y) \end{bmatrix}$$

$$\neg_\wedge \begin{bmatrix} man(x) \wedge car(y) \wedge bought(x,y) \\ man(x) \wedge bought(x,y) \end{bmatrix} \mapsto man(x) \wedge bought(x,y)$$

$$\neg_\wedge \begin{bmatrix} man(x) \wedge car(y) \wedge bought(x,y) \\ man(x) \wedge bought(x,y) \end{bmatrix} \rhd \neg car(y)$$

(40) Das Auto hat kein MANN gekauft.
the car aux neg a man bought-participle'

$$\neg_\wedge \begin{bmatrix} man(x) \wedge car(y) \wedge bought(x,y) \\ car(y) \wedge bought(x,y) \end{bmatrix} = \begin{bmatrix} car(y) \wedge bought(x,y) \wedge \neg man(x) \\ car(y) \wedge bought(x,y) \end{bmatrix}$$

$$\neg_\wedge \begin{bmatrix} man(x) \wedge car(y) \wedge bought(x,y) \\ car(y) \wedge bought(x,y) \end{bmatrix} \mapsto car(y) \wedge bought(x,y)$$

(and $\rhd \neg man(x)$)

[20] If we take properties of relevance or text coherence into consideration it would be plausible to restrict β resp. γ to the strongest case. E.g., if $\models \beta \supset \delta$ and $\not\models \delta \supset \beta$ then δ is no presupposition.

(41) Der Mann hat das Auto nicht GEKAUFT.
the man aux the car neg bought-participle'

$$\neg_{\wedge}\begin{bmatrix} man(x)\wedge car(y)\wedge bought(x,y) \\ man(x)\wedge car(y) \end{bmatrix} = \begin{bmatrix} man(x)\wedge car(y)\wedge \neg bought(x,y) \\ man(x)\wedge car(y) \end{bmatrix}$$

$$\neg_{\wedge}\begin{bmatrix} man(x)\wedge car(y)\wedge bought(x,y) \\ man(x)\wedge car(y) \end{bmatrix} \mapsto man(x)\wedge car(y)$$

(and $\triangleright \neg bought(x,y)$).

This type of analysis gives an explanation of the fact that focus and background of a given question and its answer have to be congruent:

(42) Peter hat ein Auto gekauft.
Peter has a car bought.

(43) $[_{CP}$ {[Peter $]_B$ $\}^T$ { [hat ein Auto gekauft $]_F$ $\}^C$ $]^{CAT}$: $\begin{bmatrix} peter(x)\wedge car(y)\wedge bought(z) \\ peter(x) \end{bmatrix}$

Peter has a car bought.

(44) Was hat Peter gekauft? $\begin{bmatrix} peter(x)\wedge ?(y)\wedge bought(z) \\ peter(x)\wedge bought(z) \end{bmatrix}$

What has Peter bought?

(45) Peter hat ein [Auto $]_F$ gekauft: $\begin{bmatrix} peter(x)\wedge car(y)\wedge bought(z) \\ peter(x)\wedge bought(z) \end{bmatrix}$

Peter has a car bought

(46) *Ein Auto hat [PETER $]_F$ gekauft: $\begin{bmatrix} peter(x)\wedge car(y)\wedge bought(z) \\ car(y)\wedge bought(z) \end{bmatrix}$

A car has Peter bought

The last sentence is not a good answer to the above question. Why? Look first at (44) and (45):

(47) $$\begin{bmatrix} peter(x)\wedge ?(y)\wedge bought(z) \\ peter(x)\wedge bought(z) \end{bmatrix} \mapsto peter(x)\wedge bought(z)\,.$$

(48) $$\begin{bmatrix} peter(x)\wedge car(y)\wedge bought(z) \\ peter(x)\wedge bought(z) \end{bmatrix} \mapsto peter(x)\wedge bought(z)\,.$$

That is a good answer. It shares the presuppositions (the B-constituents $peter(x)$ and $bought(z)$) with the question. But the next forms no congruent answer:

(49) $$\begin{bmatrix} peter(x)\wedge car(y)\wedge bought(z) \\ car(y)\wedge bought(z) \end{bmatrix} \mapsto car(y)\wedge bought(z)\,.$$

This changes one presupposition ($peter(x)$ to $car(y)$) and makes it an assertion:

(50) $$\begin{bmatrix} peter(x) \wedge car(y) \wedge bought(z) \\ car(y) \wedge bought(z) \end{bmatrix} \rhd peter(x) .$$

This is unlike the good answer which asserts $car(y)$:

(51) $$\begin{bmatrix} peter(x) \wedge car(y) \wedge bought(z) \\ peter(x) \wedge bought(z) \end{bmatrix} \rhd car(y) .$$

4 Two-dimensional representation of a quantifier and hat contour

4.1 Generalization - the standard case

We take as our paradigmatic case the following example:

(52) Alle Politiker sind verrückt.
All politicians are crazy.

The SF of (52) – represented in a classical first order style – is:

(53) $\forall x[politician(x) \supset crazy(x)]$.

Starting with Aristotle sentences of this kind had been interpreted as presupposing the existence of at least one *politician*: $\exists x[politician(x)]$. Therefore, the two-dimensional reading of our sentence (52) is

(54) $$\begin{bmatrix} \forall x[politician(x) \supset crazy(x)] \\ \exists x[politician(x)] \end{bmatrix}$$

The matrix of the sentence (52) is

(55) Politiker sind verrückt: $(politician(x) \wedge crazy(x))$.
Politicians are crazy

The IS-reading with an assertion which takes wide scope is

(56) Politiker [sind verrückt $]_F$: $$\begin{bmatrix} politician(x) \wedge crazy(x) \\ politician(x) \end{bmatrix},$$

i.e. *politician*(x) belongs to the background and is presupposed. We are looking for an operator which is able to produce (53) using our matrix (56). This operator should be characterized by an appropriate reduction rule. Let us try whether the following explication will do:

(R∀∃) $$\forall\exists i\begin{bmatrix}\alpha\\ \beta\end{bmatrix} \Rightarrow \begin{bmatrix}\forall i(\beta \supset \alpha)\\ \exists i\beta\end{bmatrix}.$$ [21]

(57) Alle Politiker [sind verrückt]$_F$: $\forall\exists x\begin{bmatrix}politician(x) \wedge crazy(x)\\ politician(x)\end{bmatrix}$

All politicians are crazy

(58) $$\forall\exists x\begin{bmatrix}politician(x) \wedge crazy(x)\\ politician(x)\end{bmatrix} = \begin{bmatrix}\forall x[politician(x) \supset (politician(x) \wedge crazy(x))]\\ \exists x[politician(x)]\end{bmatrix}$$

(59) $$\forall\exists x\begin{bmatrix}politician(x) \wedge crazy(x)\\ politician(x)\end{bmatrix} = \begin{bmatrix}\forall x[politician(x) \supset crazy(x)]\\ \exists x[politician(x)]\end{bmatrix}.$$

This explication differs from all the above discussed cases in that being in the second dimension (being part of the background B) and being a presupposition does not coincide. *Being a politician* (*politician*(x)) is a presupposition of the matrix expression. But it is not a presupposition of the generalized version despite the fact that its existentially quantified version remains in the background.

4.2 *Hat contour* and scope inversion of generalization and negation

Take our example in a negated version where negation takes scope over the quantifier:

(60) Nicht alle Politiker sind verrückt:
Not all politicians are crazy

The usual classical first-order formulation of its SF gives us

(61) $\neg\forall x[politician(x) \supset crazy(x)]$ this is classically equivalent to

[21] Please keep in mind that " ∀∃ " is *one* symbol indicating that after using the reduction rule we get an " ∀ " in the first and an " ∃ " in the second dimension. The "*i*" represents any individual variable, e.g. "*x*".

(62) $\exists x[\mathit{politician}(x) \wedge \neg \mathit{crazy}(x)]$ (There is at least one politician who is not-crazy.)

Here is the other version in which the quantifier takes scope over negation:

(63) Alle Politiker sind nicht verrückt.
All politicians are not crazy

The desired classical SF-representation is

(64) $\forall x[\mathit{politician}(x) \supset \neg \mathit{crazy}(x)]$.

This type of *scope inversion* of $\forall$ and $\neg$ is not a simple switch of the positions of $\forall$ and $\neg$:

$\forall x \neg[\mathit{politician}(x) \supset \mathit{crazy}(x)]$ leads to $\forall x[\mathit{politician}(x) \wedge \neg \mathit{crazy}(x)]$ which is not equivalent to $\forall x[\mathit{politician}(x) \supset \neg \mathit{crazy}(x)]$. It looks as if we need a special movement rule for $\neg$ over $\supset$. This should yield $\forall x[\mathit{politician}(x) \supset \neg \mathit{crazy}(x)]$ starting with $\forall x \neg[\mathit{politician}(x) \supset \mathit{crazy}(x)]$. But is this the right way of thinking? Take our two-dimensional formalization in which $\neg_{\wedge}$ immediately follows $\forall\exists$:

(65) $$\forall\exists x \neg_{\wedge}\begin{bmatrix}\mathit{politician}(x) \wedge \mathit{crazy}(x) \\ \mathit{politician}(x)\end{bmatrix} = \forall\exists x\begin{bmatrix}\mathit{politician}(x) \wedge \neg(\mathit{politician}(x) \wedge \mathit{crazy}(x)) \\ \mathit{politician}(x)\end{bmatrix}$$

(66) $$\forall\exists x \neg_{\wedge}\begin{bmatrix}\mathit{politician}(x) \wedge \mathit{crazy}(x) \\ \mathit{politician}(x)\end{bmatrix} = \forall\exists x\begin{bmatrix}\mathit{politician}(x) \wedge \neg \mathit{crazy}(x) \\ \mathit{politician}(x)\end{bmatrix}$$

(67) $$\forall\exists x \neg_{\wedge}\begin{bmatrix}\mathit{politician}(x) \wedge \mathit{crazy}(x) \\ \mathit{politician}(x)\end{bmatrix} = \begin{bmatrix}\forall x[\mathit{politician}(x) \supset (\mathit{politician}(x) \wedge \neg \mathit{crazy}(x)] \\ \exists x[\mathit{politician}(x)]\end{bmatrix}$$

(68) $$\forall\exists x \neg_{\wedge}\begin{bmatrix}\mathit{politician}(x) \wedge \mathit{crazy}(x) \\ \mathit{politician}(x)\end{bmatrix} = \begin{bmatrix}\forall x[\mathit{politician}(x) \supset \neg \mathit{crazy}(x)] \\ \exists x[\mathit{politician}(x)]\end{bmatrix}$$

It works very well. The interaction of F-constituents and B- constituents with the reduction operators yields the correct reading. No additional movement of the negation is necessary. If we compare

(69) $$\begin{bmatrix}\forall x[\mathit{politician}(x) \supset \mathit{crazy}(x)] \\ \exists x[\mathit{politician}(x)]\end{bmatrix} \text{ and } \begin{bmatrix}\forall x[\mathit{politician}(x) \supset \neg \mathit{crazy}(x)] \\ \exists x[\mathit{politician}(x)]\end{bmatrix}$$

we observe that both expressions are identical with regard to its B-components. Additionally this part is not affected by the negation $\neg_{\wedge}$.

It is widely accepted that by using a special rise-fall contour we get the phenomenon of scope inversion.[22]

(70) /ALle Politiker $_i$ sind $_j$ [NICHT t_i verrückt t_j]$_F$.
All politicians are not crazy.

In this case „alle“ has scope over “nicht” but the characteristic hat contour leads to a “nicht–alle”-reading: $\neg\forall x[politician(x) \supset crazy(x)]$. What happens if we combine $\forall\exists$ with the negation operator $\neg_\wedge$ which takes scope over $\forall\exists$?

(71) $$\neg_\wedge\forall\exists x\begin{bmatrix} politician(x) \wedge crazy(x) \\ politician(x) \end{bmatrix} = \neg_\wedge\begin{bmatrix} \forall x[politician(x) \supset (politician(x) \wedge crazy(x))] \\ \exists x[politician(x)] \end{bmatrix}$$

(72) $$\neg_\wedge\begin{bmatrix} \forall x[politician(x) \supset (politician(x) \wedge crazy(x))] \\ \exists x[politician(x)] \end{bmatrix} = \neg_\wedge\begin{bmatrix} \forall x[politician(x) \supset crazy(x)] \\ \exists x[politician(x)] \end{bmatrix}$$

(73) $$\neg_\wedge\begin{bmatrix} \forall x[politician(x) \supset crazy(x)] \\ \exists x[politician(x)] \end{bmatrix} = \begin{bmatrix} \exists x[politician(x)] \wedge \neg\forall x[politician(x) \supset crazy(x)] \\ \exists x[politician(x)] \end{bmatrix}$$

and finally

(74) $$\neg_\wedge\forall\exists x\begin{bmatrix} politician(x) \wedge crazy(x) \\ politician(x) \end{bmatrix} = \begin{bmatrix} \exists x[politician(x) \wedge \neg crazy(x)] \\ \exists x[politician(x)] \end{bmatrix}.$$

This formalization shows that our S *asserts* that *some other politicians are not-crazy* ($\exists x[politician(x) \wedge \neg crazy(x)]$).[23] What is important here is that the scope inversion triggered by a hat contour can be formalized by inverting the direct order of $\forall\exists$ and $\neg_\wedge$.

5 Information structure, corrections, negation and presupposition

“Corrections consist of at least two sentences, the corrigendum [cd] and the corrigens [cs]. A German corrigens can be a *nicht – sondern* (‘not – but’) construction or a simple sentence with contrastive focus...

[22] Cf. Krifka (1998), who speaks of “rise-fall contour”. Steube (2001a) uses the term “Hutkontur” (“hat contour”). There are other terms on the market.

[23] We have to consider *other politicians* because the two occurrences of “ $\exists x$ ” allowes us to take different individuals for them into consideration.

A corrigens interrupts the sequential development of a text and offers the contrastively marked entity as a replacement for the corresponding incorrect element in the corrigendum."[24] Let us embed the following example into a question context [ct]:

(75ct) Wer wird denn morgen kommen?
Who will (then) tomorrow come

(76cd) [PEter $]_F$ kommt.
Peter (will) come(s)

(77cs) [PAUL $]_{CF}$ kommt. (Peter ist zurückgetreten.)
Paul (will) come(s) (Peter has cancelled)[25]

The sentence (76d) is a possible answer to the question (75ct). It has a focus F on the left: the constituent "Peter". Therefore there's no topic T. "kommt" belongs to the background B. A more detailed representation of (76cd) is

(78) $[_{CP}\ \{[\text{PEter}\ ]_F\ [\ \text{kommt}\ ]_B\ \}^C\ ]^{CAT}$.

This sentence has the following two-dimensional matrix:

(79) $$\begin{bmatrix} comes(x) \wedge peter(x) \\ comes(x) \end{bmatrix}.$$

(80) $$\begin{bmatrix} comes(x) \wedge peter(x) \\ comes(x) \end{bmatrix} \mapsto comes(x) \quad \begin{bmatrix} comes(x) \wedge peter(x) \\ comes(x) \end{bmatrix} \rhd peter(x)$$

What about (77cs)? Its surface structure looks like that one in (76cd). But additionally it is a reaction to (76cd). This type of correction looks like a *substitution.* We get (77cs) from (76cd) by substituting the expression "Paul" for the expression "Peter". (76cd) does not presuppose the existence of Peter (it is asserted!). But the corrigens (77cs) presupposes the existence of at least one alternative. The first step is adding an existence assumption to the background of (76cd):

(Step1) $$\begin{bmatrix} comes(x) \wedge peter(x) \\ comes(x) \wedge \exists G G(x) \end{bmatrix}, \text{ where } G(x) \text{ is an alternative to } peter(x).$$

[24] Steube (2001b) 215 f.

[25] Cf. Steube (2001b) 216. We do not restrict the context to two persons (one of two brothers). May be it is enough to have a preceding sentence (cd) for getting a contrastive reading.

At any case "$G(x)$" has to be an alternative to $peter(x)$ but also to $comes(x)$. In general, alternatives cannot be predicates which are already present in the background. If "$G(x)$" stood for "$peter(x)$" then the sentence would be without focus. That is impossible. A negation of this construction would be inconsistent in the first dimension:

(81) $$\neg_{\wedge}\begin{bmatrix} comes(x) \wedge peter(x) \\ comes(x) \wedge peter(x) \end{bmatrix} = \begin{bmatrix} (comes(x) \wedge peter(x)) \wedge \neg(comes(x) \wedge peter(x)) \\ comes(x) \wedge peter(x) \end{bmatrix}.$$

The next step uses $\neg_{\wedge}$ for denying the corrigens:

(Step2) $$\neg_{\wedge}\begin{bmatrix} comes(x) \wedge peter(x) \\ comes(x) \wedge \exists G G(x) \end{bmatrix} = \begin{bmatrix} comes(x) \wedge \exists G G(x) \wedge \neg peter(x) \\ comes(x) \wedge \exists G G(x) \end{bmatrix}.$$

We observe that the background is presupposed in the defined sense: This expression (step2) *and* its unnegated version (step1) necessitate $comes(x) \wedge \exists G G(x)$, therefore

(82) $$\begin{bmatrix} comes(x) \wedge peter(x) \\ comes(x) \wedge \exists G G(x) \end{bmatrix} \mapsto comes(x) \wedge \exists G G(x).$$

The last step is adding at least the new information (the assertion) of (76cd) to the result of (step2):

(Step3) $$\begin{bmatrix} comes(x) \wedge \exists G G(x) \wedge \neg peter(x) \\ comes(x) \wedge \exists G G(x) \end{bmatrix} \,\&\, paul(x) = \begin{bmatrix} comes(x) \wedge \neg peter(x) \wedge paul(x) \\ comes(x) \wedge \exists G G(x) \end{bmatrix}.$$

(Step1) uses a kind of correction operator COR which can be understood as a context-sensitive reduction operator. Its schema is

(R COR) $$\mathrm{COR}\begin{bmatrix} \alpha \\ \beta \end{bmatrix} \Rightarrow \begin{bmatrix} \alpha \\ \beta \wedge \gamma_{\beta} \end{bmatrix}.$$

COR adds γ_{β} to the second dimension (=B). γ_{β} depends on β in the following way: Let β again be the sequence $\alpha_{k_1} \wedge \ldots \wedge \alpha_{k_m}$, $1 \le k_j \le n+1$ and $1 \le m < n+1$. Then $F_{k_1}, \ldots, F_{k_m}$ are the predicates occurring in β. The $F_{k_{m+1}}, \ldots, F_{k_{n+1}}$ are the predicates which do not occur in β but which belong to α. The $G_{k_{m+1}}, \ldots, G_{k_{n+1}}$ are predicate variables which represent possible alternatives for $F_{k_{m+1}}, \ldots, F_{k_{n+1}}$ in the above indicated restricted sense. Then γ_{β} has the form $\exists G_{k_{m+1}} \alpha_{k_{m+1}} \wedge \ldots \wedge \exists G_{k_n} \alpha_{k_n}$. In principle, COR creates an alternative space for all these parts of a sentence S, which are not in the background B, i.e.

that are in the focus domain F of S. In other words, we get alternatives to what S was originally asserting.

Let us have a look at our example in form of a *nicht*[cd]–*sondern*[cs]-construction:

(83) Nicht [PEter $]_{CF}$ kommt, sondern [PAUL $]_F$ (kommt).
Not Peter comes but Paul (comes)

The matrix of "[PEter $]_F$ kommt"[26] is

(84) $$\begin{bmatrix} comes(x) \wedge peter(x) \\ comes(x) \end{bmatrix}.$$

The matrix of "[PAUL $]_F$ (kommt)" is

(85) $$\begin{bmatrix} comes(x) \wedge paul(x) \\ comes(x) \end{bmatrix}.$$

The complete two-dimensional translation with respect to the matrix of (78) is

(86) $$\neg_\wedge \mathrm{COR}\begin{bmatrix} comes(x) \wedge peter(x) \\ comes(x) \end{bmatrix} \;\&\; \begin{bmatrix} comes(x) \wedge paul(x) \\ comes(x) \end{bmatrix}.$$

Its schema looks like

(87) $$\neg_\wedge \mathrm{COR}\begin{bmatrix} F_2(x_1) \wedge F_1(x_1) \\ F_2(x_1) \end{bmatrix} \;\&\; \begin{bmatrix} F_2(x_1) \wedge F_3(x_1) \\ F_2(x_1) \end{bmatrix}.$$

[F_3 is an alternative to F_1 which is not a B-constituent.]

The computation runs as follows:

(88) $$\neg_\wedge \mathrm{COR}\begin{bmatrix} F_2(x_1) \wedge F_1(x_1) \\ F_2(x_1) \end{bmatrix} = \neg_\wedge \begin{bmatrix} F_2(x_1) \wedge F_1(x_1) \\ F_2(x_1) \wedge \exists G_1 G_1(x_1) \end{bmatrix} =$$
$$\begin{bmatrix} F_2(x_1) \wedge \exists G_1 G_1(x_1) \wedge \neg(F_2(x_1) \wedge F_1(x_1)) \\ F_2(x_1) \wedge \exists G_1 G_1(x_1) \end{bmatrix} = \begin{bmatrix} F_2(x_1) \wedge \exists G_1 G_1(x_1) \wedge \neg F_1(x_1) \\ F_2(x_1) \wedge \exists G_1 G_1(x_1) \end{bmatrix}$$

(89) $$\begin{bmatrix} F_2(x_1) \wedge \exists G_1 G_1(x_1) \wedge \neg F_1(x_1) \\ F_2(x_1) \wedge \exists G_1 G_1(x_1) \end{bmatrix} \;\&\; \begin{bmatrix} F_2(x_1) \wedge F_3(x_1) \\ F_2(x_1) \end{bmatrix} = \begin{bmatrix} F_2(x_1) \wedge \neg F_1(x_1) \wedge F_3(x_1) \\ F_2(x_1) \wedge \exists G_1 G_1(x_1) \end{bmatrix}.$$

[26] We omit the "C" in "CF" because we consider the focus first and than the contrastive focus of that sentence.

The re-translation gives us

(90) $\begin{bmatrix} comes(x) \wedge \neg peter(x) \wedge paul(x) \\ comes(x) \wedge some\text{-}alternative\text{-}to\text{-}peter(x) \end{bmatrix}$,

(91) $\begin{bmatrix} comes(x) \wedge \neg peter(x) \wedge paul(x) \\ comes(x) \wedge some\text{-}alternative\text{-}to\text{-}peter(x) \end{bmatrix} \mapsto comes(x) \wedge some\text{-}alternative\text{-}to\text{-}peter(x)$,

(92) $\begin{bmatrix} comes(x) \wedge \neg peter(x) \wedge paul(x) \\ comes(x) \wedge some\text{-}alternative\text{-}to\text{-}peter(x) \end{bmatrix} \triangleright \neg peter(x) \wedge paul(x)$.

The result is that the *nicht*[cd]–*sondern*[cs]-sentence *asserts* that the person in question is *Paul* and not *Peter* and *presupposes* that this person is an *alternative-to-peter* and *comes*. Both dimensions together mean that *Paul – the alternative-to-Peter – comes*. One part of this information is given/old/presupposed, the other part is new/asserted. The whole expression is true/false only if *there is some-alternative-to-peter who comes* (the presupposition must be fulfilled).[27]

6 Thetic Sentences, tautological background and external negation

The so-called **fully-focused/thetic** sentences (for example typical opening sentences) are still free of background information. A common ground is not created yet. Such sentences contain only focus information. The DP-constituents are non-anaphoric. In fully-focused sentences there are no topics. The fully-focused sentence gets its focus accent on a pure syntactic-lexical basis.[28]

General conditions of **thetic/fully-focused** sentences of the form $[_{CP}\{[]_F\}^C]^{TH}$:

- C=F=CP=S (fully-focused sentences, no FBS, no TCS)
- T=B=∅ (no *aboutness*, no presuppositions?)

Examples of thetic sentences:

[27] There is no space in this paper to show how this type of analysis can be extended to *n*-placed predicates.

[28] Cf. Steube & Späth (2002), 237f.

(93) $[_{CP}\ \{[\text{Es REGnet}]_F\ \}^C\ ]^{TH}$
It rains (It is raining)

(94) $[_{CP}\ \{\ [\text{Die SONne scheint}]_F\ \}^C\ ]^{TH}$
The sun shines. (The sun is shining)

(95) $[_{CP}\ \{\ [\text{FRIEDrichs ist gestorben}]_F\ \}^C\ ]^{TH}$
Friedrichs is died (Friedrichs died)

(96) $[_{CP}\ \{\ [\text{Der HUND bellt}]_F\ \}^C\ ]^{TH}$
The dog barks (The dog is barking)

Thetic sentences can be understood as presupposition-free constructions. The constituents of a sentence S do not trigger some specific presuppositions (background information). That means that no specific knowledge is available regarding S. It can be assumed that the only knowledge available for speakers and hearers is logical knowledge, i.e. the knowledge of some tautology. Thetic sentences presuppose only tautologies. Hence a possible reconstruction of thetic (full-focused) sentences would be:

(97) $\begin{bmatrix} Taut \wedge \alpha \\ Taut \end{bmatrix}$, i.e. $\begin{bmatrix} \alpha \\ Taut \end{bmatrix}$ (*Taut* can be any tautology).

What happens if we deny such constructions using $\neg_\wedge$?

(98) $$\neg_\wedge \begin{bmatrix} \alpha \\ Taut \end{bmatrix} = \begin{bmatrix} Taut \wedge \neg\alpha \\ Taut \end{bmatrix} = \begin{bmatrix} \neg\alpha \\ Taut \end{bmatrix}.$$

In the first dimension, $\neg_\wedge$ acts like the external (classical) negation. It negates the complete proper meaning of our sentence S.

(99) $$\neg_\wedge\neg_\wedge \begin{bmatrix} \alpha \\ Taut \end{bmatrix} = \neg_\wedge \begin{bmatrix} \neg\alpha \\ Taut \end{bmatrix} = \begin{bmatrix} Taut \wedge \neg\neg\alpha \\ Taut \end{bmatrix} = \begin{bmatrix} \alpha \\ Taut \end{bmatrix}$$

The only possible presupposition is *Taut*:

(100) $\begin{bmatrix} \alpha \\ Taut \end{bmatrix} \mapsto Taut$

((i) $\models (\alpha \supset Taut)$, (ii) $\models (Taut \supset Taut)$, and (iii) $\models (\neg\alpha \supset Taut)$).

There is no β with $\not\models \beta$ and $\models \begin{bmatrix} \alpha \\ Taut \end{bmatrix} \mapsto \beta$

Another strategy would consist in assuming that the reduction goes a step further to get a complete linearization. E.g.

(101) $\neg^{\bullet}_{\wedge}\begin{bmatrix}\alpha\\ \beta\end{bmatrix} \Rightarrow (\beta \wedge \neg\alpha)$. This yields $\neg^{\bullet}_{\wedge}\begin{bmatrix}\alpha\\ Taut\end{bmatrix} = \neg\alpha$.

This strategy makes sense only on the sentence level assuming that we finish our analysis after getting a result for that sentence. From a discursive point of view it seems much more plausible to keep the two dimensions. We gain the possibility of analyzing iterations and more complex forms of context embeddings.

7 Conclusion

Starting with a first order representation of the semantic form [SF] of a sentence [S] and considering only the matrix of such a conjunctively formalized SF we take the information structure [IS] of S into consideration. We accept the SF-relevance of IS. This forces us to postulate a second dimension which can be used for a formal representation of the background [B] of S. If S has a topic [T] it has also to be part of B. Considering categorical sentences the whole B is a proper and non-empty sub-conjunction of the conjunction which represents the original SF of S. Thetic sentences can be incorporated in the two-dimensional framework by looking at (the apparently empty) B as a tautological background.

This type of two-dimensional matrix-expressions is very helpful because it allows the specification of a lot of semantic notions and the creation of models for a series of linguistic phenomena. We introduce a new type of presupposition-preserving negation as a reduction operator which acts in both dimensions: (i) It copies the IS-induced part of the meaning of S to the first dimension. (ii) It negates the proper meaning (first dimension) of S completely. (iii) It creates a new conjunction of the products of the first two steps. And (iv) it keeps the second dimension B (the presupposition of S). Using only *one* negation ($\neg_{\wedge}$) we can differentiate several semantic readings of S with a fixed surface structure. In cooperation with the IS of S it produces plausible variants of SF which differ in the first dimension (proper meaning).

Using the notion *necessitation* and our negation $\neg_{\wedge}$ we can define a non-trivial relation of *semantic presupposition*. Presuppositions have to be present both in the first and the second dimension of S and its negated variant $\neg_{\wedge}$ S. Analogously we get our fruitful notion of *assertion* on the basis of the notion of *entailment* (inferences exclusively from the proper meaning of S, i.e. the first dimension). Assertions have to be in the scope of $\neg_{\wedge}$.

We show how several prominent cases of IS-relevant phenomena can be analyzed within our framework. Generalized sentences can be formalized two-dimensionally by explicating an existence presupposition regarding the universe of discourse in the second dimension. This enables us to represent the meaning change triggered by a hat contour (rise-fall contour) by a simple direct scope inversion of the presupposition-sensitive quantifier and our negation $\neg_{\wedge}$.

Correction sentences contain a characteristic contrastive focus. Our interpretation bases on the assumption that contrastive focus triggers a special kind of existence presupposition regarding alternatives to a given individual. Within the two-dimensional framework a reduction operator COR introduces this presupposition in accordance with the already established background (already triggered presuppositions). Correction sentences can be explicated using the cooperation of our negation $\neg_{\wedge}$ with COR regarding two-dimensional matrix arguments.

Finally, *thetic* – fully focused – sentences can be interpreted within the two-dimensional framework as having tautological presuppositions. This leads us back to a classical-style form of representing sentences. We think that keeping both dimensions after computing the IS-dependent SF is very useful if we take more complex discourse structures into account. But this is a program that deserves further intensive investigation.

8 References

Bosch, P. and R. van der Sandt (eds) (1999): Focus – Linguistic, Cognitive, and Computational Perspectives. CUP.

Brentano, F. (1874/1955, 1874/1924): Psychologie vom empirischen Standpunkt (1874). Mit Einl., Anm. und Reg. von O. Kraus (ed): Hamburg 1955 / [Psychology from an empirical point of view]. Translated by A. C. Rancurello, D. B. Terrell, and L. L. McAlister from Psychologie vom empirischen Standpunkt (1874, 1924). 1973, Sections V-IX.

Heusinger, K. v. (2000a): Anaphora, Antecedents and Accessibility. Theoretical Linguistics 26, 75–93.

Heusinger, K. v. (2000b): Information Structure and Discourse Semantics. The Prague Bulletin of Mathematical Linguistics 73–74, 13–32.

Jacobs, J. (2001): The Dimensions of Topic-Comment. Linguistics 39 (4), 641-681.

Krifka, M. (1998): Scope Inversion under the Rise-Fall Contour in German, Linguistic Inquiry 29, Nr. 1, 75–112.

Krifka, M. (2001/02): Lecture on Topic and Focus. Berlin. http://amor.rz.hu-berlin.de/~h2816i3x/TopikFokus2.pdf etc.

Kuroda, S.-Y. (1972): The categorical and the thetic judgment: evidence from Japanese syntax, Foundations of Language 9, 153–185.

Lang, E. (1983): Einstellungsausdrücke und ausgedrückte Einstellungen. In: R. Růžička and W. Motsch (eds). Untersuchungen zur Semantik (= studia grammatica XXII), Berlin: Akademie-Verlag, 305–341.

Marty, A. (1897): Über die Scheidung von grammatischen, logischen und psychologischem Subjekt resp. Prädikat. Archiv für systematische Philosophie 3, 174–190, 294–333.

Marty, A. (1918): Gesammelte Schriften, 2. Band, 1. Abteilung: Schriften zur deskriptiven Psychologie und Sprachphilosophie. Halle: Niemeyer.

Max, I. (1998): Handling inconsistencies in multi-dimensional logics, Logique and Analyse 161-162-163, 67–93.

Milsark, G. L. (1974): Existential sentences in English, Ph.D. dissertation, MIT.

Rooth, M. (1985): Association with Focus. PhDiss. University of Massachusetts at Amherst.

Rooth, M. (1996): Focus. In: S. Lapin (ed): The Handbook of Contemporary Semantic Theory, chapter 10. Oxford: Blackwell, 271-297.

Sasse, H.-J. (1987): The thetic/categorical distinction revisited Linguistics 25, 511–580.

Späth, A. (2002): On the truth conditional potential of negations. In: G. Katz, S. Reinhard, and P. Reuter (eds): Sinn und Bedeutung VI. Proceedings of the Sixth Annual Meeting of the Gesellschaft für Semantik, University of Osnabrück, 325–341.

Späth, A. (2003): The Linearization of Argument DPs and Its Semantic Reflection. In: H. Härtl and H. Tappe (eds): Mediating between Concepts and Grammar. Trends in Linguistics. Studies and Monographs 152. Mouton de Gruyter: Berlin/New York, 165-195.

Späth, A. and M. Trautwein (this volume): Negative description of events: Some semantic and conceptual aspects of sentence negation.

Steube, A. (2001a): Grammatik und Pragmatik von Hutkonturen. In: Linguistische Arbeitsberichte 77, Leipzig, 215–233.

Steube, A. (2001b): Correction by Contrastive Focus. Theoretical Linguistics 27, 215–249.

Steube, A. and A. Späth (2002): Semantik, Informationsstruktur und grammatische Modularität. In: A. Steube (ed): Sprachtheoretische Grundlagen der Kognitionswissenschaft: Sprachliches und nichtsprachliches Wissen. Linguistische Arbeitsberichte 79, Leipzig, 235–254.

Szucsich, L. (2002): Informationsstruktur in komplexen russischen Sätzen. In: A. Steube (ed): Sprachtheoretische Grundlagen der Kognitionswissenschaft: Sprachliches und nichtsprachliches Wissen, Linguistische Arbeitsberichte 79, Leipzig, 215–233.

Vallduví, E. (1993): Information packaging: A survey. University of Edinburgh. http://www.hcrc.ed.ac.uk/publications/rp-44.ps.gz .

Weskott, T. (this volume): Towards a scalar notion of information structured markedness.

Brigitta Haftka (Potsdam)

Topic Constraints in the German Middlefield[1]

1 Introduction

1.1 The topic concept

Werner Frey (2000) discusses two possibilities to explicate the concept of "(sentence) topic":

(i) Topics are expressions that code given / known information ('familiarity-concept")
(ii) Topics are those expressions that have referents about which the sentence predicates something. Topic is a category of the pragmatic "About which" ("aboutness concept").

I will not discuss here the different topic concepts, but for the description of the German word order we need both:

- an aboutness topic or theme (aboutness concept (ii))
- possibly more than one item that codes given background information that is often called topic also ('given' is non-identical with 'known' or 'familiar' in (i)).

I think that we have to differentiate between given and known information: A referent of an expression is given if it is in the immediate short-term memory of the speaker and the hearer, that is to say, if it is already in the partner's focus of attention – through context or through situation, cf. Haftka (1980).[2] The speaker can therefore refer to it in an anaphoric way – by a personal or a demonstrative pronoun, but also by a definite DP.

---

[1] This paper is based on both a talk given at the GGS-meeting 2000 in Potsdam and a contribution to Dölling & Pechmann (2000) in German language = Haftka (2000). I would like to thank all contributors for helpful discussions at the GGS-meeting and at the birthday workshop for Anita Steube. A word of thanks to Ilse Zimmermann who encouraged me to reformulate my system of filters for the order of unstressed phrases in the so called Wackernagel position in Haftka (1988) and to Anita Steube for the encouragement to publish this paper here.

[2] In Haftka (1980), I chose the German term "Bewusstseinspräsenz".

It follows that not all referents in a large text can be given ones in this sense. But each previously mentioned referent in a text is a known or familiar one for the speech-act partners. The speaker normally has to refer to such referents by definite expressions or proper names. That means that they are background elements, like all individuals and classes of individuals relevant in the speech act[3].

Familiarity with a specific referent (anaphoric or non-anaphoric) is a sufficient condition for using an expression as a topic about which the sentence predicates something in the sense of the aboutness concept (ii), cf. table 1. But familiarity with the referent does not force the expression to move into a topic position; not all expressions with familiar referents are topics. Depending on the planned text, the speaker has to decide about which one of the familiar referents to predicate something. In this paper I will name the corresponding expression moved to the top of the sentence 'proper topic', 'aboutness topic' or 'theme' of the sentence. In this sense, familiarity is a sufficient condition for an aboutness topic.

The given referents are only a part of the known familiar background referents. Givenness of a referent is a sufficient condition for the anaphoricity of an expression. Anaphoric expressions normally are stressless and move from the vP into a higher position of the German sentence. I will name these anaphoric elements anaphoric topics, cf. table 1.

Table 1:

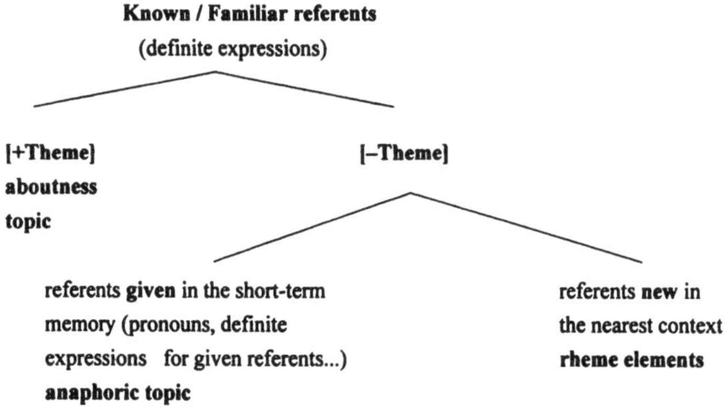

In this sense, familiarity of the referent is a sufficient condition for the one, and only one, aboutness topic, and givenness of a familiar referent is a sufficient condition for anaphoric topics. Non-thematic and non-given familiar referents that are new in the narrow text as rheme elements normally stay in the base position.

[3] Actual information and references about the relation between known and new referents you will find e. g. in Schwarz (2000).

1.2 Anaphoric expressions

Anaphoric DPs refer to such background information that is given in the immediate context or in the immediate speech-act situation. They are stored in the narrow short-term memory of the speaker and probably of the hearer.

Unstressed anaphoric nominal phrases (DPs) can stay in situ - in their basic position (cf. (1b) vs. (1a)) -, but normally they move to the left and precede the elements of the new-information domain of the sentence in a special unstressed position, the so-called Wackernagel position. Prepositional or postpositional phrases (PPs) containing an anaphoric element sometimes, but not always, have to move to the left as well.

The following list contains some typical German anaphoric expressions:

- Personal pronouns: *er* 'he', *sie* 'she', *es* 'it'; *sie* 'they' including the speech-act persons *ich* 'I', *du* 'you', *wir* 'we', *ihr* 'you'$_{pl}$, *Sie* 'you' and their case forms, cf. (1c, d, e)
- *Man* 'you' and its suppletive case forms *einen, einem* (2e) that include the speech-act persons
- Demonstrative pronouns: *der* 'he$_{demonstr}$' , *die* 'she$_{demonstr}$', *das* 'that$_{demonstr}$', *die*$_{pl}$. 'they$_{demonstr}$', *dieser* 'this$_{masc}$', *diese* 'this$_{fem}$', *dieses* 'this$_{neutr}$', *diese*$_{pl}$ 'these' and their case forms, if they do not refer to newly introduced entities
- Definite DPs: e.g. *der Kerl* 'the guy', *der Mann* 'the man', *die(se) Leute* 'these people', *das Ding* 'the thing', *der Wildfang* 'the little devil' (2d) et al., if they do not refer to newly introduced entities
- Prepositional phrases containing an anaphoric DP (*mit ihnen* 'with them', *mit diesen Leuten* 'with these people', *wegen des Computers* 'because of the computer' (2a))
- Postpositional phrases containing a demonstrative background element like *da(r)-* (*darüber* 'over that', *damit* 'with that', *dabei* 'at the same time' (2c)), or *des-* (*deshalb / deswegen* 'therefore' et al.) (2a)
- Adverbials containing elements that refer to the background: *dann* 'after that', *damals* 'at that time', *daher* 'from there', *sonst* 'otherwise', et al. (2d).

If a definite element is in the unstressed Wackernagel position, it will be interpreted as referring to an anaphoric entity, if available (Lenerz 2001: "background determined interpretation"), cf. (1c, d, e):

(1) (*Heute habe ich$_j$ mit* ***unseren KINDERN$_i$*** *gesprochen*
'I talked to our children today')

(a) **Morgen wird [wahrscheinlich unser Opa* ***die JUNGS$_i$*** *besuchen]*[4]
(in situ, stressed, nonanaphoric)

(b) *Morgen wird [wahrscheinlich unser OPA* ***die Jungs$_i$*** *besuchen]*
(in situ, unstressed, anaphoric)
Tomorrow will probably our grandpa$_{nom}$ the boys$_{acc}$ visit
'Our grandpa will probably visit the boys tomorrow'

(c) *Morgen wird* ***die Jungs$_i$ / sie$_i$*** *[wahrscheinlich unser OPA t$_i$ besuchen]*
(moved, unstressed, anaphoric)
Tomorrow will the boys$_{acc}$ / them$_{acc}$ probably our grandpa$_{nom}$ visit
'Our grandpa will probably visit the boys / them tomorrow'

(d) *Morgen werden dich$_k$* ***die Jungs$_i$*** *[wahrscheinlich t$_i$ t$_k$ beSUchen]*
(moved, unstressed, anaphoric)
Tomorrow will you$_{acc}$ the boys$_{nom}$ probably visit
'The boys will probably visit you tomorrow'

(e) *Morgen werde ich$_j$* ***die Jungs$_i$ / sie$_i$*** *[wahrscheinlich t$_j$ t$_i$ beSUchen]*
(moved, unstressed, anaphoric)
Tomorrow will I the boys$_{acc}$ / them$_{acc}$ probably visit
'I will probably visit the boys / them tomorrow'

(2) (Situation: [Problems with the laptop$_n$]$_q$:
Ich$_j$ habe ***meinen Kindern$_i$*** *gesagt,* 'I said to my children')

(a) *dass* ***ich$_j$ sie$_i$ [wegen [des Computers]$_n$]/ deshalb$_q$*** *[sicher* ***t$_q$*** *morgen* ***t$_j$ t$_i$*** *beSUche]$_k$*
that I them$_{acc}$ because of the computer / therefore surely tomorrow visit
'that I would probably visit them because of the computer tomorrow'
(*Sie$_i$ sagten,*'They said')

(b) *dass* ***ihnen$_i$ das$_k$*** *[wirklich* ***t$_i$ t$_k$*** *sehr ANgenehm sei] und*
that them$_{dat}$ that$_{nom}$ really very pleasant is and
'that they were very pleased with that and'

(c) *dass* ***ich$_j$ dabei$_k$*** *[ja auch* ***t$_k$*** *t$_j$ meine ENkelin$_l$ ins Bett bringen könnte]$_m$*
that I at the same time ptc also my granddaughter to bed put could
'that at the same time I could put my granddaughter to bed '

(d) *weil* ***der Wildfang$_l$ ihnen$_i$ sonst$_m$*** *[vermutl.* ***t$_m$ t$_l$ t$_i$*** *den TheAterbesuch verdirbt]*
because the little devil$_{nom}$ them$_{dat}$ otherwise presumably the visit to the theatre spoils
'because otherwise the little devil would presumably spoil their visit to the theatre'

---

[4] Bold-faced parts of sentence examples are in the focus of our examination. Capital letters mark the focus syllable (or if necessary the focus word, like *OPA, UFER et al.*) within the focus exponent or within one of the possible focus exponents of the sentence. Sometimes I use small capitals to mark an I-topic or a stressed theme-constituent. Normally I will only mark the intonation of ungrammatical sentences if this is necessary for comprehension, as here.

(e) *So gewinnt* ***man$_o$*** ***einen$_p$*** *[natürlich t_o am BESten t_p zur Kinderbetreuung t_v]*
like that wins one$_{nom}$ you$_{acc}$ of course best for baby sitting
That is naturally the best way to get a babysitter'

1.3 Syntax and information structure

I assume the following minimal syntactic clause structure given in (3) with a subject including vP, a Tense Phrase (TP), a Negation or Position Phrase (PosP) (cf. Haftka (1994, 1995, 2003)), a Finiteness Phrase (FinP) in the sense of Rizzi (1997)[5], and optionally a sentence adverbial adjoined to the FinP. The topic positions that are relevant here are marked as aboutness topic or theme [+Th], and as Wackernagel position for anaphoric background topics.

(3)

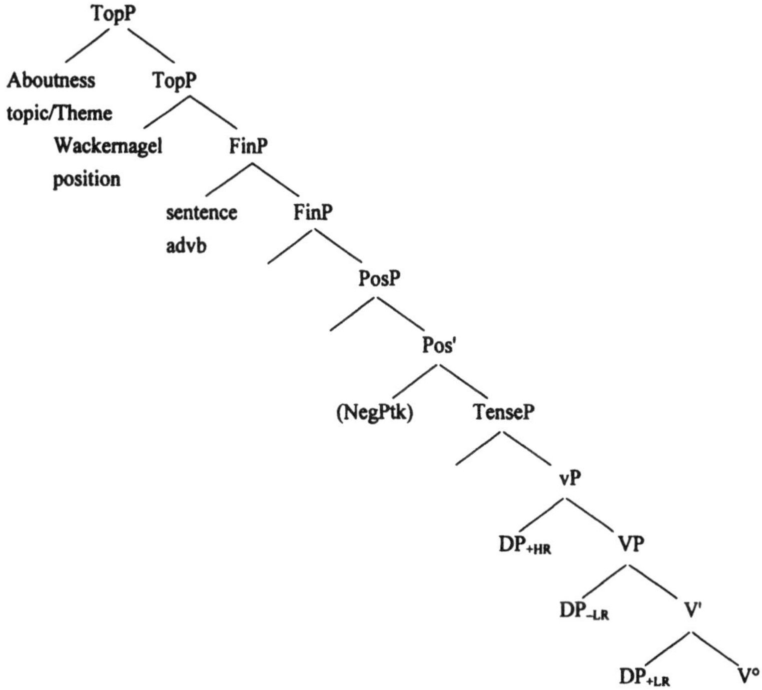

[5] More information about the internal structure of the FinP I assume you will find in Haftka (2003). For this paper it is relevant that both anaphoric topics and the aboutness topic leave the phrase that is able to have a sentence adverbial adjoined to it. Rizzi's (1997) topic positions are to the left of his FinP. Therefore I assume that the sentence adverbial as border between topics and new information is adjoined to FinP. If you assume another grammar, all statements about leftward moved topics have to be related to the phrase that is able to contain the propositional sentence adverbial, cf e.g.:
(i) (XP_{+Th}) (Wackern. position) [$_{TP}$ (sentence advb) [$_{TP}$ [$_{TP}$ [$_{vP}$ DP_{+HR} [$_{VP}$ DP_{-LR} DP_{+LR} V°]]]]]

+HR = + higher role = most V°-distant DP argument
(e. g. agens-SU higher than IO/DO, IO higher than DO)
–HR = – higher role = V°-nearer DP argument
+LR = + lowest role = V°-next DP complement
–LR = – lowest role = complement preceding the V°-next DP complement immediately

Indefinite pronouns and indefinite DPs in a finite or non-finite vP are indicators of the base order of DPs, cf. table 2(a,b): A DP bearing the higher role [+HR] in a construction precedes a DP that doesn't have the higher role [–HR] in the basic linearization. A DP bearing the lowest role [+LR] follows a DP that doesn't bear the lowest role [–LR] (if available)[6]. We will use these relational features for the formulation of our topic linearization constraints in the second part.

Table 3a surveys the relations between the different syntactic and information structural levels relevant for our purposes. Here we will discuss only the linear order in the domain of topicalization (in this table in bold-faced italics) excepting the so-called I-topics[7]. An I-topic opens a rise-fall intonation contour (hat contour) that ends up with the focus exponent. Steube 2001 assumes two I-topic positions: one that can precede the aboutness-topic or theme (in the prefield or in the middlefield) and all anaphoric elements (I-topic 2) and one that possibly follows a sentence adverbial in Rizzi's Finiteness Phrase (I-topic 1), cf. e.g. Haftka (1995, 2003).

[6] Here I speak about DPs having the higher role or the lower role themselves, but not about DPs having the feature: [There is another DP having a higher role] or [There is another DP having the lower role], cf. Wunderlich (1999).

[7] There are many references about I-topics. I will give here only some of them: Haider & Rosengren (1998), Molnár & Rosengren (1996), Steube (2001), Steube & Umbach (eds.) (2001) where you will find some new papers and more references about this theme.

(a)+HR –LR	–HR +LR	VERBAL COMPLEX	+HR –LR	–HR +LR
	jemandem	*helfen* 'to help s.o.'		dat
	etwas	*lernen* 'to learn s.th.'		acc
jemandem	*etwas*	*ins Stammbuch schreiben* 'to write s.o. s.th. in the family register ' (figurative)	dat >	acc
jemandem	*etwas*	*geben* 'to give s.o. s.th.'	dat >	acc
sich$_{dat}$	*jemanden / etwas*	*vorstellen* 'to imagine s.o./s.th.'	dat >	acc
jemandem	*etwas / jemanden*	*entziehen* 'to take s.th./s.o. away from s.o.'	dat >	acc
jemanden /etwas	*jemandes Einfluss*	*entziehen* 'to remove s.o./s.th. from s.o.'s sphere of influence'	acc >	dat
sich$_{acc}$	*jemandem*	*unterordnen* 'to submit to s.o.'	acc >	dat
jemanden	*eines Verhaltens*	*bezichtigen* 'to accuse s.o. of a behaviour'	acc >	gen
sich$_{acc}$	*jemandes/einer Sache*	*erinnern* 'to remember s.o./s.th.'	acc >	gen
dass jemandem	*etwas*$_{nom}$	*gefällt* 'that s.o. is pleased with s.th.'	dat >	nom
dass jemanden	*etwas*$_{nom}$	*interessiert* 'that s.th. interests s.o.'	acc >	nom

(b)	+HR	+HR –LR	–HR +LR	Verbal Complex	[+HR	[+HR –HR]] –LR +LR
dass jemand		*jemanden*	*etwas*	*machen lässt* 'that s.o. makes / allows s.o. to do s.th.'		acc > acc
dass einer		*jemanden*	*etwas*	*lehrt* 'that s.o. teaches s.o. s.th.'		acc > acc
dass einer	*einen*	*jemanden*	*etwas*	*lehren lässt* 'that s.o. makes s.o. teach s.o. s.th. '	acc >	acc > acc

Table 2

3a) middlefield				
domain of topicalization			variation of newly introduced elements	
(I-topic2)	comment of the I-topic 2			
	aboutness topic	***anaphoric background informations***	information that is newly introduced in the text (rheme)	
	specific definite noun or pronoun...	***anaphoric definite pro-nouns and nouns***	normally indefinite nouns and nonanaphoric definite nouns, proper names, prepositional phrases...	
opening a rise-fall contour	***optionally stressed position***	***obligatorily unstressed (Wackernagel) position***	(I-topic 1) opening a rise-fall contour	focus with the focus exponent
$[_{I\text{-}TopP}$	$[_{TopP}$	$[_{TopP}$	$[_{FinP}$	$[_{PosP}[_{TP}\ .[_{vP}.[_{vP}\ V°]]]]]]]]$[8].

3b)	$[_{I\text{-}TopP}$	$[_{TopP}$	$[_{TopP}$	$[_{FinP}$	$[_{PosP}$	$[_{TP}\ .[_{vP}.[_{vP}.$	$V°]]]]]]]]$
dass	unserem CHEF	Hans		sicher	keines falls	jemals ein Auto	leihen würde
Hat		er	dir	etwa	tatsächl.	einen Ausflug	versprochen?
dass		dem Uwe	damals	sicher Bücher	wirklich	BESSER	gefallen hätten
dass			ihr das Kleid	vielleicht	nicht	mehr	PASST
dass			ihm	offenbar ein Hut	wirklich nicht		STEHT
dass			sich		wirklich einer nicht	für Autos	interessiert
dass			sich		nicht	alle für Autos	interessieren
dass				sicher	keineswegs	immer alle Kinder Grieß-brei	mögen

Table 3a and some examples for illustration (**Table 3b**)

[8] More information about these grammatical assumptions you will find in Haftka (2003).

1.4 Variation of the base order of new-information elements in the FinP

Variations of the German base order inside the FinP are triggered by genericity (4b), by specificity (4c), possibly by intonation (FinP intern I-topic) (4b, 4c, 5b), and by the scope of negation (5d) rather than by case checking.

(4) (*Ich denke*, 'I think')

(a) *dass[$_{FinP}$ natürlich [$_{FinP}$ [$_{TP}$ zu Weihnachten* ***eine GANS*** *im Ofen brutzelt]]]*
that of course at Christmas a goose in-the oven sizzles
'that of course a goose sizzles in the oven at Christmas'

(b) *dass [$_{FinP}$ natürl. [$_{FinP}$* ***eine GANS$_{i\ generic}$*** *[$_{TP}$ zu Weihnachten [$_{vP}$ t_i im OFEN brutzelt]]]]*

(c) *dass [$_{FinP}$ natürl. [$_{FinP}$* ***EIne Gans$_{i\ specific}$*** *[$_{TP}$ zu Weihnachten[$_{vP}$ t_i im OFEN brutzelt]]]],*
that of course a goose at Christmas in-the oven sizzles
(nämlich Auguste)

(5) (*Ich denke*, 'I think')

(a) *dass [$_{FinP}$ natürl.[$_{FinP}$ [$_{TP}$ endlich einer* ***dem Chef*** *unsere SituaTION erklären muss]]]*
that of course after all s.o.$_{nom}$ the boss$_{dat}$ our situation$_{acc}$ explain must
'that of course someone has to explain our situation to the boss after all'

(b) *dass[$_{FinP}$ natürl.[$_{FinP}$* ***dem CHEF$_{I\text{-}top\ i}$*** *[$_{TP}$endl. einer t_i unsere SituaTION erklären muss]]]*
that of course the boss$_{dat}$ after all s.o. our sit uation$_{acc}$ explain must
'that of course someone has to explain our situation to the boss after all'

(c) *dass der$_i$ [$_{FinP}$ natürlich[$_{FinP}$ [$_{PosP}$ nicht [$_{TP}$ t_i* ***seinen CHEF$_j$*** *informierte]]]]*
that he$_{dem.}$ of course not his boss$_{dat}$ informed
'that he of course didn't inform his boss'

(d) *dass der$_i$ [$_{FinP}$ natürl.[$_{FinP}$[$_{PosP}$wirkl.[$_{PosP}$* ***seinen Chef$_j$*** *[$_{Pos'}$ nicht[$_{TP}$ t_i t_j inforMIERte]]]]]]*
that he$_{dem.}$ of course really his boss$_{acc}$ not informed
'that he of course didn't inform his boss'

1.5 Anaphoric background elements

Anaphoric background elements normally leave FinP and move into anaphoric topic positions to the left of FinP and to the left of a possible sentence adverbial adjoined to FinP[9], cf. (6):

---

[9] Contrary to the conventional wisdom – but similar to Büring (1994) – I assume that the movement to topic positions is independent of the existence of a sentence adverbial or another element that indicates the border line between given and new elements. That means that two sentences with definite DPs that have one and the same surface order can have different structures depending on the intonation, cf. (i), where the new-information focus is identical with the Finiteness Phrase (stress on the object-DP), with (ii), where the Finiteness Phrase in the surface structure contains only the stressed verb and the argument traces. (see next page)

(6) (Situation: The boss$_j$ doesn't know about the latest problem$_k$. He is arriving at this moment.
A: *Ich denke,* 'I think')

(a) *dass* ***wir$_i$ es$_k$ ihm$_j$ dann$_l$*** *[$_{FinP}$ natürl. [$_{TP}$ t_i gleich [$_{vP}$ t_i t_j t_k erKLÄren müssen]]]*
that we it him then of course immediately explain must
'that we then of course have to explain it to him immediately'

(b) *dass* ***wir$_i$ ihm$_j$ / dem$_j$ das$_k$*** *[$_{FinP}$ natürl. [$_{TP}$ gleich [$_{vP}$ t_i t_j t_k erKLÄren müssen]]]*
that we him / him$_{dem.\ dat.}$ that$_{dem.\ acc}$ of course immediately explain must
'that we of course have to explain that to him immediately'

(c) *dass* ***wir$_i$ dem Chef$_j$ diese Situation$_k$*** *[$_{FinP}$ natürl. [$_{TP}$ gleich [$_{vP}$ t_i t_j t_k erKLÄren müssen]]]*
that we the boss$_{dat.}$ this situation$_{acc}$ of course immediately explain must
'that we of course have to explain this situation to the boss immediately'

(d) *dass* ***wir$_i$ das$_k$ dem Chef$_j$*** *[$_{FinP}$ natürl. [$_{TP}$ gleich [$_{vP}$ t_i t_j t_k erKLÄren müssen]]]*
that we that$_{acc}$ the boss$_{dat}$ of course immediately explain must
'that we of course have to explain this to the boss immediately'

(e) *dass* DEM CHEF$_j$ ***das$_k$*** *[$_{FinP}$ natürl. [$_{TP}$ gleich einer t_j t_k erKLÄren muss]]*
that the boss$_{dat}$ that$_{acc}$ of course immediately someone explain must
'that someone of course has to explain this to the boss immediately'

1.6 Some open questions

The following are open questions that I will not discuss here:

- Are these unstressed elements in the adjunct of FinP/TP or
- are they in SpecTOP phrases, cf. Rizzi (1997), or
- is the proper topic in SpecTopP, and are the anaphoric ones in SpecAgr phrases, cf. Haftka (1994, 1995), or
- is the proper topic in SpecModP, cf. Zimmermann (1999), and where are the anaphoric ones?

2 Surface topic constraints

In the second part I will first give an overview of all constraints that I shall discuss here. Then these constraints will be developed in detail:

(*Ich denke,* 'I think')
(i) *dass [$_{FinP}$* ***die Eltern dem Jungen das MÄDchen*** *zeigen]*
(ii) dass die Eltern$_i$ dem Jungen$_j$ das Mädchen$_k$ [$_{FinP}$ t_i t_j t_k ZEIgen]
that the parents the boy$_{dat}$ the girl$_{acc}$ show
'that the parents show the boy to the girl'

CONSTRAINT NAMES	PRECEDENCE RULES	CONSTRAINTS
1. TOPIC	topicalic phrase > FinP	$*[_{FinP} \ldots XP_{+top} \ldots]]$
2. THEME	theme-XP > anaphor. XPs	$*[XP_{+an,-Th} \ldots XP_{\pm an,+Th}$ FinP]
3. PP–ANAPH	topicalic-DP > anaphor. PP/AdvP	$*[\ [_{PP} P\ [DP_{+an}]] \ldots DP_{+top}$ FinP]
4. PRON	anaphor. pron. > anaphor. def. DP	$*[DP_{+an,-pron} \ldots DP_{+an,+pron}$ FinP]
5. PERS PRON	pers. pron. > dem. pron.	$*[DP_{+an,-ppr} \ldots DP_{+an,+ppr}$ FinP]
6. HIGHER ROLE	higher θR.$^{\delta}$(+HR)>lower θR.$^{\delta}$(–HR)	$*[DP^{\delta}_{+an,-HR} \ldots DP^{\delta}_{+an,+HR}$ FinP]
7. LOWEST ROLE	pers.pron. (+LR) > pers.pron. (–LR)	$*[DP_{+an,+ppr,-nom,-LR}\ DP_{+an,+ppr,-nom,+LR}$ FinP]

Table 4: Overview of all constraints discussed here

2.1 Constraint TOPIC

Precedence-Rule 1: Topic phrase > FinP
Topic constraint 1: $*[_{FinP} \ldots XP_{+top} \ldots]]$
C-command relation: A phrase$_{+top}$ c-commands the whole Finiteness Phrase.

A topic phrase moves out of the FinP to the left. A phrase can have the feature [+top] under the following conditions:

- if the phrase is anaphoric [+an], because its referent is given in the sense discussed above, cf. (1c, d) here repeated as (8a, b):

(8) (a) *Morgen wird* ***die Jungs***$_i$ */* ***sie***$_i$ *[wahrscheinlich [$_{vP}$ unser OPA t_i besuchen]]*
Tomorrow will the boys$_{acc}$ / them$_{acc}$ probably our grandpa$_{nom}$ visit
'Our grandpa will probably visit the boys / them tomorrow'

(b) *Morgen werden dich$_k$* ***die Jungs***$_i$ *[wahrscheinlich [$_{vP}$ t_i t_k beSUchen]]*
Tomorrow will you$_{acc}$ the boys$_{nom}$ probably visit
'The boys will probably visit you tomorrow'

- if the speaker takes the phrase as a proper topic or "theme" [+Th] (independent of anaphoricity) in the sense of "aboutness", cf. (9), (10):

(9) (*Lutz$_i$ sprach mit seinen KINdern und hörte,* 'Lutz phoned to his children and he heard')
(a) *dass* ***[seine$_i$ FRAU]$_{-an,+Th\ j}$*** *[leider t_j erst MORgen t_j zurückkommt]*
that his wife$_{nom}$ unfortunately not until tomorrow back comes
'that his wife unfortunately will not return until tomorrow'
(b) **dass [leider erst morgen* ***[seine$_i$ FRAU]$_{-an,+Th\ j}$*** *zuRÜCKkommt]*
that unfortunately not until tomorrow his wife$_{nom}$ back comes

(10) (*Lutz$_i$ sprach mit seinen Kindern und hörte,* 'Lutz spoke with his children and he heard')

(a) *dass **[seine$_i$ FRAU]$_{-an,+Th\ j}$** [leider t_j heute keiner t_j erREIchen kann]*
that his wife$_{acc}$ unfortunately today nobody$_{nom}$ get hold can
'that unfortunately nobody can get hold of his wife today'

(b) **dass [leider heute keiner **[seine FRAU]$_{-an,+Th}$** erREIchen kann]*
that unfortunately today nobody$_{nom}$ his wife$_{acc}$ get hold can

The syntactic feature [+top] combines anaphoric reference as a contextual semantic feature and the information structural feature aboutness. The feature [+top] triggers movement of a phrase out of the Fin Phrase to the left.
But it is possible that anaphoric constituents often or systematically stay in situ. That means that not all anaphoric expressions get the feature [+top]. Some examples:

- Unstressed anaphoric DPs sometimes are in situ,
  cf. (1b) here repeated as (11):

(11) (*Heute habe ich$_j$ mit **unseren KINdern$_i$** gesprochen. 'I talked to our children today')*
*Morgen wird [wahrscheinlich unser OPA **die Jungs$_{+an\ i}$** besuchen]*
Tomorrow will probably our grandpa$_{nom}$ the boys$_{acc}$ visit
'Our grandpa will probably visit the boys tomorrow'

- Unstressed anaphoric genitive case objects very often are in situ:

(12) *Zwei Männer haben die LAdenkasse gestohlen. Jemand hat den RUdi$_j$ erkannt. Ich denke,*
Two men stole the till. Someone identified Rudi. I think that')
*sie haben den Kerl$_j$ [wohl t_i t_j zu RECHT **dieses Diebstahls$_{+an\ k}$/ dessen$_{+an\ k}$** bezichtigt t_v]*
they have the man$_{acc}$ perhaps rightly this theft$_{gen}$ / that$_{gen}$ accused
'perhaps they have rightly accused the man of doing this theft / that'

- VP- and vP-modifying PPs containing an anaphoric DP and corresponding adverbs sometimes are in situ , cf. (13):

(13) (*[[Der Sohn von Lutz$_i$]$_j$ hat heute einen wichtigen Termin beim NoTAR]$_k$. Ich denke,*
'The son of Lutz has an important appointment with the notary today. I think')

(a) *dass Lutz$_{+Th\ i}$ ihn$_j$ [wohl **[aus diesem Grunde/deshalb]$_{+an,\ k}$** erst Abends $_{vP}$ t_i t_j trifft]*
that Lutz him probably for this reason /therefore not until the evening meets
'that for this reason / therefore Lutz will probably not meet him until the evening'

(b) *dass Lutz$_{+Th\ i}$ ihn$_j$ [sicher am Abend t_i **dort$_{+an,-Th}$** t_j TRIFFT]*
that Lutz him$_{acc}$ surely in the evening there meets
'that Lutz will surely meet him there in the evening'

- Verbs next PPs containing an anaphoric DP often are in situ: A directive prepositional phrase with an unstressed anaphoric DP stays in situ, cf. (14a). Its prepositional head (here *ZU* 'to') or its postpositional head (here *HIN* 'there') can be stressed, because the directivity is the new information. If this directive PP precedes FinP, the sentence is less acceptable in the given context, cf. (14b):

(14) *([Der Sohn von Lutz$_i$]$_j$ hat heute einen wichtigen Termin beim NoTAR$_l$.. Ich denke,*
'The son of Lutz has an important appointment with the notary today. I think')
(a) *dass Lutz$_{+Th\ i}$ [$_{FinP}$ sicher am Abend t$_i$ **[dort-$_{+an}$]$_l$** HIN] / [ZU **[ihm$_{+an}$]$_l$** geht]*
that Lutz surely in-the evening there - there / to him goes
'that Lutz will surely go there / to him in the evening'
(b) ?/**dass Lutz$_{+Th\ i}$ [**[dort-$_{+an}$]$_l$** hin] / [zu **[ihm$_{+an}$]$_l$**] [$_{FinP}$ sicher am Abend t$_i$ t$_{pp}$ geht]*
that Lutz there - there / to him surely in-the evening goes

- A prepositional object with an anaphoric DP normally stays in situ (15a) and – unlike the directive PP – it is unstressed. Therefore, it is able to move to the left of the sentence adverbial, cf. (15b):

(15) *([Der Sohn von Lutz$_i$]$_j$ hat heute [einen wichtigen Termin beim NoTAR]$_l$. Ich denke,*
'The son of Lutz has an important appointment with the notary today. I think')
(a) dass er$_j$ sich$_k$ [wohl noch t$_j$ t$_k$ [auf [**dieses Treffen**]$_{+an\ l}$]/[**dar-**$_{+an\ l}$ auf] VORbereitet]
that he refl. perhaps still for this meeting / that - for prepares
'that perhaps he is still preparing for this meeting / for that'
(b) dass er$_j$ sich$_k$ [auf [**dieses Treffen**]$_{+an}$]$_l$ /[**dar-**$_{+an}$ auf]$_l$ [wohl noch t$_j$ t$_k$ t$_l$ VORbereitet]
that he refl. for this meeting / that - for perhaps still prepares

- Adjectival predicatives in German have three anaphoric forms: the pronouns *es* 'it' and *das* 'that' and the pro-adjective *so*. The two pronouns have to move to the left into an unstressed position (cf. 2.2 (20)); but *so* can not move into the Wackernagel position (16a, c), it has to follow its referential element in situ (16b, d) or it moves into the prefield, cf. (17):

(16) *(A: Soviel ich weiß, hält Hans den Jungen für genial. B: Ich hätte nicht gedacht,*
A: 'As far as I know Hans thinks that the boy is brilliant. B:I didn't think')
(a) **dass er$_i$ **ihn$_j$** **so$_{+an\ k}$** [tatsächlich t$_i$ t$_j$ t$_k$ beurteilt]*
that he him so really judges
(b) *dass er$_i$ **ihn$_j$** [tatsächlich t$_i$ t$_j$ **so$_{+an\ k}$** beURteilt]*
that he him really so judges
'that he really judges him in this way'
(c) **dass er$_i$ **so$_{+an\ j}$** [tatsächlich t$_i$ t$_j$ ist]*
that he so really is

(d) *dass* ***er***$_i$ *[tatSÄCHlich* t_i ***so***$_{+an\ j}$ *ist]*
that he really so is
'that he really is like that'

(17) ***So***$_{+an\ k}$ *beurteilt er*$_i$ ***ihn***$_j$ *[tatSÄCHlich* t_i t_j t_k t_v*]*
so judges he him really
'he judges him really in this way'

The following constraint concerns the information structural difference: thematicity vs. anaphoricity.

2.2 Constraint THEME

Precedence-rule 2: Theme-XP > anaphoric XPs
Topic constraint 2: $*[XP_{+an,\,-Th} \ldots XP_{\pm an,\,+Th}\ [_{FinP} \ldots]]$
C-command relation: A phrase with the feature [+Th(eme)] c-commands all anaphoric topics in the middlefield.

An XP_{+Th} precedes all anaphoric topics: Its place is immediately behind the complementizer in Verb/End clauses or in the first position (prefield) in V/2-clauses. (18a), (18e) and (19a) are normal in the given contexts (18) or (19):

(18) *(Lutz*$_i$ *hat mit* ***seinen SÖHnen***$_j$ *gesprochen. 'Lutz had a talk with his sons')*

(a) ***Die***$_{+Th,\ +an\ j}$ *werden wir*$_k$ *[wahrscheinlich morgen* t_k t_j *TREFfen* t_v *]*
them$_{dem\ acc}$ will we probably tomorrow meet
'We will probably meet them tomorrow'

(b) **Wir*$_k$ *werden* ***die***$_{+Th,\ +an\ j}$ *[wahrscheinlich morgen* t_k t_j *treffen* t_v*]*
we will them$_{dem\ acc}$ probably tomorrow meet

(c) ***Wir***$_{+Th,+an\ k}$ *werden* t_k *sie*$_{-Th,+an\ j}$ *[wahrscheinlich morgen* t_k t_j *TREFfen* t_v*]*
we will them$_{acc}$ probably tomorrow meet
'We will probably meet them tomorrow'

(d) **Es werden* ***wir***$_{+Th,\ +an\ k}$ *sie*$_{-Th,\ +an\ j}$ *[wahrscheinlich morgen* t_k t_j *treffen* t_v*]*
explet. will we them$_{acc}$ probably tomorrow meet

(e) ***[Seine***$_i$ ***FRAU]***$_{+Th,-an\ k}$ *kann ihn*$_i$ *[leider erst MORgen* t_k t_i *besuchen* t_v*]*
His wife$_{nom}$ can him unfortunately not until tomorrow visit
'His wife unfortunately is not able to visit him until tomorrow'

(f) **Es kann ihn*$_i$ ***[seine***$_i$ ***FRAU]***$_{+Th,-an\ k}$ *[leider erst MORgen* t_k t_i *besuchen* t_v*]*
explet. can him$_{acc}$ his wife$_{nom}$ unfortunately not until tomorrow visit

(19) *(Lutz*$_i$ *hat mit seinen ENkeln*$_j$ *gesprochen und gehört,*
'Lutz spoke with his grandchildren and he heard')

(a) *dass [**das EXAmen**]$_{+Th,-an\ k}$ ihnen$_{+an\ j}$ [offenbar jetzt t_j t_k SORgen macht]*
that the exam$_{nom}$ them$_{dat}$ evidently now worries makes
'that evidently the exam now worries them'

(b) **dass ihnen$_{+an\ j}$ [**das EXAmen**]$_{+Th,-an\ k}$ [offenbar jetzt t_j t_k SORgen macht]*
that them$_{dat}$ the exam$_{nom}$ evidently now worries makes

(c) *dass **es** sich [wohl in MalLORca ganz ANgenehm leben lässt]*
that explet. refl. evidently in Majorca quite pleasant live lets
'that life is evidently quite pleasant in Majorca'

(d) **dass sich **es** [wohl in MalLORca ganz ANgenehm leben lässt]*
that refl. explet. evidently in Majorca quite pleasant live lets

(e) *dass in MalLORca **es** sich [wohl ganz ANgenehm leben lässt]*
that in Majorca explet. refl. evidently quite pleasant live lets

(f) *dass **man** sich [wohl in MalLORca gut erHOlen kann]*
that you$_{impers.}$ refl. evidently in Majorca well relax can
'that evidently you can relax well in Majorca'

(18b), (18f) and (19b) are out in the given contexts: (18b) is out, because an anaphoric accusative demonstrative pronoun with the feature [+Th] is in the position of anaphoric DPs. (18f) and (19b) are out, because their subject-DP is in the position of anaphoric DPs, though it is non-anaphoric. But it is situationally known and therefore definite, and it refers specifically. These are the conditions for aboutness. As a theme it has to be in the first position (cf. (18e), (19a)), rather than in a later unstressed position before the sentence adverbial.

(18d) (18f) with an expletive *es* in the prefield are out too, because they have a theme-XP *wir* as a personal pronoun in the nominative case and a non-anaphoric DP in an anaphor position. One of the relevant conditions for an expletive *es*[10] is the absence of a theme-XP in the clause. (19c) demonstrates that the nominative expletive *es* takes the position of the theme. There is no place for it in a later position, cf. (19d). The example (19e), where the expletive *es* follows the PP *in Mallorca*, does not contradict that, because here an I-topic[11] opening an intonational "hat contour" precedes the theme position.

The anaphoric pronominal subject-DP *wir* in (18c) and the non-anaphoric impersonal pronoun *man* in (19f) are prototypical themes.

---

[10] Here are some references about expletives: Cardinaletti (1990), Lenerz (1981), Postal & Pullum (1988), Pütz (1986), Tomaselli (1986), Vikner (1995).

[11] There are many references about I-topics. I will give here only some of them: Molnár, & Rosengren (1996), Steube (2001), Steube & Umbach (eds.) (2001), where you will find some new papers and more references about this theme.

A topicalized predicated nominative DP[12] always precedes the anaphoric predicative pronoun, because the predicated DP is predestined to become the theme of the clause, cf. (20a, c) vs. (20b, d). Therefore we don't need a special constraint for predicatives.

(20) *(A: War dein Nachbar$_i$ schon als Kind ein FEIGling$_j$? B: Ich denke,*
A: 'Was your neighbour a coward already as child? B: I think,')

(a) *dass* ***[er/der /der Mann]$_{+Th, +an\ i}$ es$_j$*** *damals$_k$ [sicher t_k NICHT t_i t_j war]*
that he /he$_{dem}$ / the man$_{nom}$ it$_{nom}$ then surely not was
'that he surely was not a coward then'

(b) **dass* ***es$_j$ [er/der /der Mann]$_{+Th, +an\ i}$*** *damals$_k$ [sicher t_k NICHT t_i t_j war]*
that it$_{nom}$ he /he$_{dem}$ / the man$_{nom}$ then surely not was

(c) *dass* ***[er/der / der Mann]$_{+Th, +an\ i}$ das$_j$*** *damals$_k$ [sicher t_k NICHT t_i t_j war]*
that he /he$_{dem}$ / the man$_{nom}$ that$_{nom}$ then surely not was
'that he/ the man surely was not a coward'

(d) **dass* ***das$_j$ [er/der /der Mann]$_{+Th, +an\ i}$*** *damals$_k$ [sicher t_k NICHT t_i t_j war]*
that that$_{nom}$ he /he$_{dem}$ / the man$_{nom}$ then surely not was

The following constraint concerns the syntactic form of a topicalized prepositional phrase (PP) vs. a topicalized determiner phrase (determiner + nominal phrase) (DP).

2.3 Constraint PP-ANAPH

Precedence-rule 3:	Topic-DP > anaphoric PP / anaphoric adverbial
Topic constraint 3:	*[[$_{PP}$ P [DP$_{+an}$]]$_{top}$ DP$_{top}$ [$_{FinP}$...]]
C-command relation:	A topicalized PP containing an anaphoric DP or an anaphoric adverbial is c-commanded by all other topics and the PP c-commands the whole Finiteness Phrase, but cf. 2.1).

A topicalized prepositional or postpositional phrase containing an anaphoric DP or an anaphoric adverbial that isn't placed in the position of the theme follows all topicalic DPs and immediately precedes the sentence adverbial and all other non-topicalized phrases. This place is independent of its grammatical function as adverbial, cf. (21), or as prepositional object, cf. (22):

---

[12] Accusative DPs are not relevant here, because they will not be predicated by anaphoric predicative pronouns, but only by the pro-adverb *so*:
(i) *Er hat* ***ihn*** *leider* ***so*** *bezeichnet/genannt*
He has him unfortunately like this called
(ii) **Er hat* ***ihn es/das*** *leider bezeichnet/genannt.*
He has him it/that unfortunately called.

(21) *([[Der Sohn von Lutz$_i$]$_j$ hat heute einen wichtigen TerMIN]$_k$. Ich denke,*
'The son of Lutz has an important appointment today. I think')

(a) *dass Lutz$_{+Th\,i}$ ihn$_{+an\,j}$* ***[$_{PP}$ aus[$_{DP}$ diesem Grunde $_{+an}$]$_k$] / deshalb$_{+an\,k}$***
that Lutz$_{nom}$ him$_{acc}$ for this reason / therefore
*[sicher **t$_k$** erst am ABEND t$_i$ t$_j$ trifft]*
surely not until the evening meets
'that Lutz for this reason / therefore will surely not meet him until the evening'

(b) **dass **deshalb$_{+an\,k}$** Lutz$_{+Th\,i}$ ihn$_{+an\,j}$ [sicher **t$_k$** erst am Abend t$_i$ t$_j$ trifft]*
that therefore Lutz him$_{acc}$ surely not until the evening meets

(c) **dass Lutz$_{+Th\,i}$ **deshalb$_{+an\,k}$** ihn$_{+an\,j}$ [sicher **t$_k$** erst am Abend t$_i$ t$_j$ trifft]*
that Lutz therefore him$_{acc}$ surely not until the evening meets

(22) *([[Der Sohn von Lutz$_i$]$_j$ hat heute ein EXAmen.]$_k$ Ich denke,*
The son of Lutz has an exam today. I think')

(a) *dass er$_{+Th\,j}$ dem Vater$_{+an\,i}$* ***[$_{PP}$von [dieser Sache$_{+an}$]$_k$] / davon $_k$*** *[sicher t$_j$*
that he the father$_{dat}$ about this matter / there-about surely
*t$_i$ NICHTS **t$_k$** erzählt hat]*
nothing told has
'that he surely hasn't told anything about this matter / about that to his father'

(b) **dass **davon$_{+an\,k}$** er$_{+an,\,+Th\,j}$ dem Vater$_{+an,-Th\,i}$ [sicher t$_j$ t$_i$ NICHTS **t$_k$** erzählt hat]*
that there-about he the father$_{dat}$ surely nothing told has

(c) *^{K}dass **DAvon$_{+an\,k}$** er$_{+an,\,+Th\,j}$ dem Vater$_{+an,-Th\,i}$ [sicher t$_j$ t$_i$ NICHTS **t$_k$** erzählt hat]*
that there-about he the father$_{dat}$ surely nothing told has

(d) *dass er$_{+an,\,+Th\,j}$ dem Vater$_{+an,-Th\,i}$ **da$_{+an\,k}$** [sicher t$_j$ t$_i$ nichts **[von t$_k$]** erZÄHLT hat]*
that he the father$_{dat}$ there surely nothing about told has

(e) *dass er$_{+an,\,+Th\,j}$ **da$_{+an\,k}$** dem Vater$_{+an,-Th\,i}$ [sicher t$_j$ t$_i$ nichts **[von t$_k$]** erZÄHLT hat]*
that he there the father$_{dat}$ surely nothing about told has

The acceptability of the sentence (22b) improves if the PP is stressed like in (22c), where it as an I-topic opens a hat contour.

Also the anaphoric nominal part of a split PP (*da$_{+an}$* 'there') in (22d)) can move into the anaphoric PP-position. But cf. also (22e), where the anaphoric *da-* takes the place of an unstressed demonstrative pronoun, (cf. 2.5).

The next constraint concerns the internal structure of the topicalized definite DPs determining their order.

2.4 Constraint PRON

Precedence rule 4:	Anaphoric pronoun > anaphoric definite DP
Topic constraint 4:	*[DP$_{+an,\,-pron,}$ DP$_{+an,\,+pron,}$ [$_{FinP}$...]]
C-command relation:	Anaphoric pronominal DPs c-command all non-pronominal anaphoric DPs before FinP.

All topicalized unstressed anaphoric demonstrative pronouns and personal pronouns (neutral and reduced personal pronouns in the sense of Gärtner & Steinbach 2000[13]) precede unstressed anaphoric definite DPs, that are not the theme of the clause[14], cf. (23f, g, h, i):

(23) (A: *Lutz$_i$ brachte gestern Eva$_j$ zu seinen ELtern$_k$*
'A: Lutz brought Eva to his parents yesterday')

(a) *Dann wird **er**$_i$ **sie**$_j$ **den Alten**$_{+an,-Th\ k}$ [ja endlich t_i t_k t_j VORgestellt haben t_v]*
then will he her$_{acc}$ the parents$_{dat}$ ptc finally introduced have
Then he will have finally introduced her to his parents'

(b) **Dann wird **er**$_i$ **den Alten**$_{+an,-Th\ k}$ **sie**$_j$ [ja endlich t_i t_k t_j vorgestellt haben t_v]*[15]
Then will he the parents$_{dat}$ her$_{acc}$ ptc finally introduced have

(c) *Dann wird **er**$_i$ **denen**$_k$ **seine Freundin**$_j$ [ja endlich t_i t_k t_j VORgestellt haben t_v]*
Then will he them$_{dem\ dat}$ his girlfriend$_{acc}$ ptc finally introduced have
'Then he will have finally introduced his girlfriend to them'

(d) **Dann wird **er**$_i$ **seine Freundin**$_{+an,-Th\ j}$ **denen**$_k$ [ja endlich t_i t_k t_j vorgestellt haben t_v]*
Then will he his girlfriend$_{acc}$ them$_{dem\ dat}$ ptc finally introduced have

(e) *Dazu musste **ihn**$_i$ **das Mädchen**$_{+an,-Th\ j}$ [sicher lange t_j t_i überREden t_v]*
There-into must him$_{acc}$ the girl$_{nom}$ certainly a long time persuade
The girl certainly had to talk him into it for a long time'

(f) *wozu **das Mädchen**$_{+an,+Th\ j}$ **ihn**$_i$ [sicher lange t_j t_i überREden musste]*
what-for the girl$_{nom}$ him$_{acc}$ certainly a long time persuade must
'for what the girl certainly had to persuade him for a long time'

(g) *wozu'**n**$_j$ **das Mädchen**$_{+an,\pm Th}$ [sicher lange t_j t_i überREden musste]*
what-for-him$_{cl,\ acc}$ the girl$_{nom}$ certainly a long time persuade must
'for-what the girl certainly had to persuade him for a long time'

(h) *Dann wird sein BRUder$_{-an,+Th\ l}$ **ihm**$_i$ **das Mädchen**$_j$ [sicher t_l t_i t_j AUSspannen t_v]*
then will his brother him$_{dat}$ the girl$_{acc}$ surely take away
'then his brother will surely take the girl away from him'

---

[13] Gärtner & Steinbach (2000) assume the following groups of personal pronouns that I will adopt here:

```
              personal pronouns
             /                 \
      +stress                  –stress
                               /     \
                         neutral    reduced
```

Note that normally reduced pronouns are colloquial.

[14] Cf. the constraint THEME in 2.2

[15] The reader may have problems with such restrictive valuations of the correctness. But my aim is, to find standard German linearization rules. I know that there are many regional variants in the spoken language where the linearization is less restrictive. You will find some material in Gärtner & Steinbach (2000) especially about reduced pronouns that are not in my focus here.

(i) *Dann wird* F*RITZ*$_{-an,+Th}$ ***'m***$_i$ ***das Mädchen***$_j$ *[sicher* t_i t_i t_j *AUSspannen* t_v*]*
then will Fritz$_{nom}$ him$_{cl,\,dat}$ the girl$_{acc}$ surely take away
' then Fritz will surely take the girl away from him'

(j) **Dann wird sein Bruder*$_{-an,+Th\,l}$ ***das Mädchen***$_j$***'m***$_i$ *[sicher* t_i t_i t_j *ausspannen* t_v*]*
then will his brother the girl$_{acc}$ him$_{cl,\,dat}$ surely take away
'then his brother will surely take the girl away from him'

The examples (23b), (23d) and (23j) are out, because a definite object-DP is placed before a pronominal DP without being the theme of the sentence. But the orders with pronouns before object-DP (23a, c, h) vs. pronoun before subject-DP (23e, g) are acceptable.

The order of reduced pronouns will not be discussed here. A reduced pronoun can be clitisized to a relative expression (23g), to a complementizer or to the finite verb, it can precede the theme (23g) or it can follow the theme ((23i), but it can not follow other definite DPs (23j) and (24d).

The following constraint concerns order differences between unstressed personal pronouns and unstressed demonstrative pronouns.

2.5 Constraint PERS PRON

Precedence rule 5:	Personal pronoun > demonstrative pronoun
Topic constraint 5:	*[DP$_{+an,-ppr}$ DP$_{+an,+ppr}$ [$_{FinP}$...]]
C-command relation:	Anaphoric personal pronouns c-command all other anaphoric DPs before FinP.

Anaphoric (neutral or reduced) personal pronouns precede all other anaphoric pronouns and therefore all other anaphoric DPs:

(24) *(A: Lutz*$_i$ *hat seine Freundin*$_j$ *gestern endlich mit zu seinen ELtern*$_k$ *genommen.*
A: 'Lutz finally took his girlfriend with him to his parents yesterday'.)

(a) *Dann hat* ***er***$_i$ ***ihnen***$_k$ ***die***$_j$ *[ja wohl endlich* t_i t_k t_j *VORgestellt* t_v*]*
Then has he them$_{dat}$ her$_{demonstr.acc}$ ptc perhaps finally introduced
'Then perhaps he has finally introduced her to them'

(b) **Dann hat* ***er***$_i$ ***die***$_j$ ***ihnen***$_k$ *[ja wohl endlich* t_i t_k t_j *vorgestellt* t_v*]*
Then has he her$_{demonstr.acc}$ them$_{dat}$ ptc perhaps finally introduced

(B: Ich wusste gar nicht, 'I didn't know')

(c) *dass* ***er***$_i$ ***sie***$_j$ ***/'se***$_j$ ***denen***$_k$ *[tatsächl. bisher* t_i t_k t_j *VORenthalten hat]*
that he her$_{acc}$/her$_{cl.\,acc}$ them$_{demonstr.dat}$ really until now kept has
'that he really kept her from them until now'

(d) **dass* ***er***$_i$ ***denen***$_k$ ***sie***$_j$ ***/'se***$_j$ *[tatsächl. bisher* t_i t_k t_j *vorenthalten hat]*
that he them$_{demonstr.dat}$ her$_{acc}$/her$_{cl.\,acc}$ really until now kept has

Possible exceptions are required by the constraint THEME: only one phrase can precede the personal pronouns as a theme (25a, b) vs. (25c):

(25) *(A: Lutz$_i$ hat gestern endlich seine FREUNdin$_j$ mit zu seinen Eltern$_k$ genommen. Ich denke,*
A: Lutz finally took Eva with him to his parents yesterday. I think')
(a) *' dass* ***der Bengel$_{+Th\,i}$ ihnen$_k$ die$_j$*** *[wohl endlich t_i t_k t_j VORgestellt hat]*
that the guy them$_{dat}$ her$_{demonstr.acc}$ perhaps finally introduced has
' that perhaps the guy has finally introduced her to them'
(b) *dass* ***der$_{+Th\,i}$ sie$_j$ /se$_j$ den Alten$_k$*** *[wohl endlich t_i t_k t_j VORgestellt hat]*
that he$_{demonstr}$ her$_{.acc}$/her$_{cl.\,acc}$ the parents$_{dat}$ perhaps finally introduced has
'that perhaps he has finally introduced her to his parents'
(c) **dass* ***der Bengel$_{+Th\,i}$ den Alten$_k$ sie$_j$ /se$_j$*** *[wohl endlich t_i t_k t_j vorgestellt hat]*
that the guy the parents$_{dat}$ her$_{.acc}$/her$_{cl.acc}$ perhaps finally introduced has
'perhaps the guy has finally introduced her to his parents'

The constraints PRON and PERS PRON result in three groups of anaphoric topicalic DPs with different degrees of determinacy (δ):

- Personal pronoun > demonstrative pronoun > anaphoric definite DP. The degrees of determinacy (δ) reflect the facts to be illustrated by the following text:

(26)(a) ***Tierschützer$_i$*** *haben* ***rund vierzig Walen$_j$*** *das LEben gerettet.*
Animal welfarists$_{nom}$ have about forty whales$_{dat}$ the life$_{acc}$ saved
'Animal welfarists saved the life of about forty whales'
(b) ***Die Wale$_j$ / Die$_j$ / *Sie$_j$*** *waren in einer kleinen Bucht geSTRANdet,*
The whales / They$_{demonstr.}$ / They were in a little bay stranded
'The whales / They were stranded in a little bay,'

(c) *wo* ****die Wale$_j$ / *die$_j$ / sie$_j$*** *zirka 18 Stunden FESTsaßen,*
where the whales / they$_{demonstr.}$ / they about 18 hours were stuck
'where they were stuck about 18 hours'
(d) *bevor* ****die Wale$_j$ / *die$_j$ / sie$_j$*** *entDECKT wurden.*
before the whales / they$_{demonstr.}$ / they found were
'before they were found'
(e) *Mit kleinen Booten versperrten* ***die Retter$_i$ / *die$_i$ / *sie$_i$***
by little boats obstructed the rescuers$_{nom}$ / they$_{demonstr.nom}$ / they$_{nom}$
den Tieren$_j$ / *denen$_j$ / ihnen$_j$ *den Weg zum UFER.*
the animals$_{dat}$ / them$_{demonstr.dat}$ / them$_{dat}$ the way to-the shore$_{acc}$
'the rescuers obstructed the animal's way to the shore/ their way to the shore with little boats'

(f) *Auf diese Weise trieben* **?*die Leute*$_i$ / **die*$_i$ / *sie*$_i$**
in this way drove the people$_{nom}$ / they$_{demonstr.nom}$ / they$_{nom}$
***die Wale*$_j$ / **die*$_j$ / ?*sie*$_j$** *mit der Flut in den OZEAN zurück*
the whales$_{acc}$ / them$_{demonstr.acc}$ them$_{acc}$ with the tide into the ocean back
'in this way the people / they drove the whales back into the ocean when the tide was in'

A personal pronoun can refer only to an unambiguous directly given referent that has the highest degree of determinacy, cf. (26c, d, e), where the whales are the referents of the personal pronouns, and (26f) where the rescuers are their referents. In (26c, d, f) the personal pronoun is the theme of the narrowest text.

A demonstrative pronoun like *der, die, das; die*$_{pl.}$ contains an additional deictic element that can disambiguate possible referents of the pronoun. It is able to refer to the last mentioned possible given referent which is less determined than the referent of the former mentioned one, cf. (26b).

The definite DP is needed for resuming the referent, if the speaker thinks that it is no longer clear which of the given referents is meant, i.e., if the referent has the lowest degree of determinacy in this scale, cf. (26b, f) and (26c).

The internal order within these three groups of DPs is determined by constraints that refer to the close or less close relationship of the DP to the verb, cf. 1.4, where the terms higher vs. lower Theta-role (+HR vs. –HR) and the lowest vs. next-higher Theta-role (+LR vs. –LR) are described.

2.6 Constraint HIGHER ROLE

Precedence rule 6:	Higher Theta-role > lower Theta-role of the same degree of determinacy δ
Topic constraint 6:	$*[DP^{\delta}_{+an,-HR}\ DP^{\delta}_{+an,+HR}\ [_{FINP}\ldots]]$
C-command relation:	An anaphoric DP with a higher Theta role c-commands all anaphoric DPs of the same degree of determinacy δ with a lower Theta-role, where δ is a definite DP, or a demonstrative pronoun or a personal pronoun.

If two or more anaphoric DPs are either personal pronouns or demonstrative pronouns or definite DPs, the DP with a higher Theta role precedes the DP with a lower Theta-role, cf. the "Parallel Movement" of Müller (1998), who, however, does not consider the degrees of determinacy.

Therefore an anaphoric subject-DP that gets the highest Theta-role (e.g. agents) normally precedes anaphoric object-DPs in the middlefield, if all of them are either personal pronouns (27a - c)[16], or demonstrative pronouns (27d - f), or definite DPs cf. (27g - i).

(27) *(A: Lutz$_i$ hat gestern EVA$_j$ mit zu seinen Eltern$_k$ genommen. B:)*
A: 'Lutz took Eva with him to his parents yesterday'. B:
(a) *Dann hat **er$_i$** **sie$_j$** **ihnen$_k$** [ja wohl endlich t_i t_k t_j VORgestellt t_v] (vgl. auch 2.7)*
Then has he$_{nom}$ her$_{acc}$ them$_{dat}$ ptc perhaps finally introduced
'Then perhaps he has perhaps finally introduced her to them'
(b) **Dann hat **sie$_j$** **er$_i$** **ihnen$_k$** [ja wohl endlich t_i t_k t_j vorgestellt t_v]*
Then has her$_{acc}$ he$_{nom}$ them$_{dat}$ ptc perhaps finally introduced
(c) **Dann hat **sie$_j$** **ihnen$_k$** **er$_i$** [ja wohl endlich t_i t_k t_j vorgestellt t_v]*
Then has her$_{acc}$ them$_{dat}$ he$_{nom}$ ptc perhaps finally introduced
(d) *Dann hat **der$_i$** **denen$_k$** **die$_j$** [ja wohl endlich t_i t_k t_j VORgestellt t_v]*
Then has he$_{demonstr..nom}$ them$_{demonstr\ dat}$ her$_{demonstr.acc}$ ptc perhaps finally introduced
(e) **Dann hat **denen$_k$** **der$_i$** **die$_j$** [ja wohl endlich t_i t_k t_j vorgestellt t_v]*
Then has them$_{demonstr.\ dat}$ he$_{demonstr.nom}$ her$_{demonstr.acc}$ ptc perhaps finally introduced
(f) **Dann hat **denen$_k$** **die$_j$** **der$_i$** [ja wohl endlich t_i t_k t_j vorgestellt t_v]*
Then has them$_{demonstr.\ dat}$her$_{demonstr.acc}$ he$_{demonstr.\ .nom}$ ptc perhaps finally introduced
(g) *Dann hat **der Bengel$_i$** **den Alten$_k$** **die Kleine$_j$** [ja wohl endl. t_i t_k t_j VORgestellt t_v]*
The has the guy$_{nom}$ the old people$_{dat}$ the girl$_{acc}$ ptc perhaps finally introduced
'Then perhaps he has finally introduced the girl to the old people'
(h) **Dann hat **den Alten$_k$** **der Bengel$_i$** **die Kleine$_j$** [ja wohl endl. t_i t_k t_j vorgestellt t_v]*
Then has the old people$_{dat}$ the guy$_{nom}$ the girl$_{acc}$ ptc perhaps finally introduced
(i) **Dann hat **den Alten$_k$** **die Kleine$_j$** **der Bengel$_i$** [ja wohl endl. t_i t_k t_j vorgestellt t_v]*
Then has the old people$_{dat}$ the girl$_{acc}$ the guy$_{nom}$ ptc perhaps finally introduced

Also the anaphoric accusative subject of the a.c.I. construction (e.g. infinitive + *lassen* without *zu*) normally precedes the anaphoric accusative object of the a.c.I., if both the accusative subject and the accusative object have the same degree of determinacy, cf. (28):

(28) *(Situation: Der Bruder$_i$ soll sichern, dass seine Schwester$_j$ das Sandmännchen$_k$ sehen kann.*
'Situation: The brother has to ensure that his sister can see the sandman.'
Mutter: *Ich hoffe,* Mother: 'I hope')
(a) *dass der Junge$_i$ **die Kleine$_{acc\ j}$** **den Film$_{acc\ k}$** [wirklich t_i t_j t_k ANsehen lässt]*
that the boy$_{nom}$ the girl$_{acc.SU}$ the movie$_{acc\ O}$ really ptc watch lets
'that the boy really allows the girl to watch the movie'
(b) **dass der Junge$_i$ **den Film$_{acc\ k}$** **die Kleine$_{acc\ j}$** [wirklich t_i t_j t_k ansehen lässt]*
that the boy$_{nom}$ the movie$_{acc\ O}$ the girl$_{acc.SU}$ really ptc watch lets

---

[16] The nominative personal pronoun preceding all other pronouns prototypically takes the theme position.

(c) *dass der Junge$_i$* ***die$_{acc\,j}$*** ***das$_{acc\,k}$*** *[wirklich t_i t_j t_k ANsehen lässt]*[17]
that the boy$_{nom}$ her$_{demonstr.acc.SU}$ that$_{demonstr.acc}$ O really ptc watch lets
'that the boy really allows her to watch that'

(d) **dass der Junge$_i$* ***das$_{acc\,k}$*** ***die$_{acc\,j}$*** *[wirklich t_i t_j t_k ansehen lässt]*
that the boy$_{nom}$ that$_{demonstr.acc}$ O her$_{demonstr.acc.SU.}$ really ptc watch lets

(e) *dass der Junge$_i$* ***sie$_{acc\,j}$*** ***es$_{acc\,k}$*** *[wirklich t_i t_j t_k ANsehen lässt]*
that the boy$_{nom}$ her$_{acc.SU.}$ it$_{acc}$ O really ptc watch lets
'that the boy really allows her to watch it'

(f) **dass der Junge$_i$* ***es$_{acc\,k}$*** ***sie$_{acc\,j}$*** *[wirklich t_i t_j t_k ansehen lässt]*
that the boy$_{nom}$ it$_{acc}$ O her$_{acc.SU}$ really ptc watch lets

If there are two object-DPs with the same degree of determinacy in a clause, the object-DP with the higher Theta-role precedes the object-DP with the lower Theta-role nearer to the verb, cf. (29), (30), (31). In the case of *jdn. jdm.$_{+LR}$ vorstellen* or *jdm. jdn.$_{+LR}$ vorstellen* 'introduce s.o. to s.o.' (29a, b) two orders of the DPs are acceptable[18]:

(29) *(Lutz$_i$ ist mit seiner Freundin$_j$ zu seinen ELtern$_k$ gefahren.*
'Lutz and his girlfriend went to his parents')

(a) *Dann wird er$_i$* ***den Alten$_k$*** ***die Kleine$_j$*** *[ja vielleicht endlich t_i t_k t_j VORstellen t_v.]*
Then will he the old people$_{dat}$ the girl$_{acc}$ ptc perhaps finally introduce
' Then perhaps he will finally introduce the girl to the old people'

(b) *Dann wird er$_i$* ***die Kleine$_j$ den Alten$_k$*** *[ja vielleicht endlich t_i t_k t_j VORstellen t_v.]*
Then will he the girl$_{acc}$ the old people$_{dat}$ ptc perhaps finally introduce

(30) *(Stell dir vor: Herr Meier$_i$ klagte Hans$_j$ wegen Uhrendiebstahls$_k$ an. Ich denke,*
'Imagine: Mister Meier accuses Hans of watch theft. I think')

(a) *dass der Mann$_i$* ***den Bengel$_j$ dieses Diebstahls$_k$*** *[sicher t_i t_j zu RECHT t_k* bezichtigt t_v]
that the man the guy$_{acc}$ this theft$_{gen}$ certainly rightly accuses
'that the man certainly rightly accuses the guy of this theft'

(b) **dass der Mann$_i$* ***des Diebstahls$_k$ den Bengel$_j$*** *[sicher t_i t_j t_k zu Recht bezichtigt t_v]*
that the man the theft$_{gen}$ the guy$_{acc}$ certainly rightly accuses

(c) *dass der Mann$_i$* ***den$_j$*** ***dessen$_k$*** *[sicher t_i t_j t_k zu RECHT bezichtigt t_v]*
that the man him$_{demonstr\ acc}$ that$_{demonstr\ gen}$ certainly rightly accuses
'that the man certainly accuses him of that rightly'

---

[17] There are not grammatical but stylistic doubts as to whether (28c) is acceptable.

[18] The verb *vorstellen* in the sense of 'introduce s.o. to s.o. has two complements with human referents DPdat and DPacc. There are different opinions about the question of which has the lower Theta-role *jdn. jdm.+LR vorstellen* or *jdm. jdn.+LR vorstellen,* cf. e.g. Meinunger (2002, 6) who tests the order of indefinite pronouns by a negative and a positive one:
(i) weil ich auf der Party niemand(en) jemandem vorgestellt habe vs.
*(ii) */??weil ich auf der Party niemandem jemand(en) vorgestellt habe.*

(d) **dass der Mann$_i$* ***dessen$_k$*** ***den$_j$*** *[sicher t_i t_j t_k zu Recht bezichtigt t_v]*
that the man that$_{demonstr\ gen}$ him$_{demonstr\ acc}$ certainly rightly accuses

(31)(Lutz$_i$ hat für die neue Kollegin$_j$ ein BUCH$_k$ gekauft.
'Lutz bought a book for the new colleague)'
(a) *Er$_i$ will* ***der$_j$*** ***das$_k$*** *[sicher t_i t_j t_k zum GeBURTStag schenken t_v]*
He will her$_{demonstr\ dat}$ that$_{demonstr\ acc}$ surely for-the birthday present
'He probably will present it to her for her birthday'
(b) **Er$_i$ will* ***das$_k$*** ***der$_j$*** *[sicher t_i t_j t_k zum Geburtstag schenken t_v]*
He will that$_{demonstr\ acc}$ her$_{demonstr\ dat}$ surely for birthday present

The constraint HIGHER ROLE also applies to so-called psych-verbs, where the nominative DP is the verb-next argument. Therefore it bears the lowest Theta-role. The dative or accusative DP here gets the higher Theta-role, cf. (32):

(32) *(Lutz$_k$ nahm gestern EVA$_j$ mit zu seinen ELtern$_i$. Ich denke,*
'Lutz took Eva with him to his parents yesterday. I think')
(a) *dass* ***den Alten$_i$*** ***die Kleine$_j$*** *[sicher t_i t_j geFALlen wird]*
that the old people$_{dat}$ the girl$_{nom}$ surely please will
'that the old people surely will like the girl'
(b) *dass* ***den Jungen$_k$*** ***das Mädchen$_j$*** *[vielleicht DOCH t_k t_j interessiert]*
that the boy$_{acc}$ the girl$_{nom}$ possibly ptc$_{affirm.}$ interests
'that the girl possibly interests the boy'

In these cases the nominative DP is often but not necessarily the theme. Therefore the definite nominative DP as theme often precedes the dative or accusative DP (33a, b), and the pronominal nominative DP as theme always precedes the other DPs, cf. the acceptance pairs in (33c-j).

If the two arguments of a psych-verb are personal pronouns (33c, d, g, h), the next constraint LOWER ROLE in addition supports the order nominative DP before case object, cf. 2.7:

(33) *(Lutz$_k$ nahm gestern EVA$_j$ mit zu seinen Eltern$_i$. Ich denke,*
'Lutz took Eva with him to his parents yesterday'. I think)
(a) *dass* ***die Kleine$_{+Th\ j}$*** ***den Alten$_i$*** *[sicher t_i t_j geFALlen wird]*
that the girl$_{nom}$ the old people$_{dat}$ surely please will
(b) *dass* ***das Mädchen$_j$*** ***den Jungen$_k$*** *[vielleicht DOCH t_k t_j interessiert]*
that the girl$_{nom}$ the boy$_{acc}$ possibly ptc$_{affirm.}$ interests
(c) *dass* ***sie$_j$*** ***ihnen$_i$*** *[sicher t_j t_i geFALlen wird]*
that she$_{nom}$ them$_{dat}$ surely please will
(d) **dass* ***ihnen$_i$*** ***sie$_j$*** *[sicher t_j t_i gefallen wird]*
that them$_{dat}$ she$_{nom}$ surely please will

(e) *dass* ***die****$_j$* ***denen****$_i$* *[sicher t_j t_i geFALlen wird]*
that she$_{demonstr.nom}$ them$_{demonstr.dat}$ surely please will

(f) **dass* ***denen****$_i$* ***die****$_j$* *[sicher t_j t_i gefallen wird]*
that them$_{demonstr\ dat}$ she$_{demonstr.nom}$ surely please will

(g) *dass* ***sie****$_j$* ***ihn****$_k$* *[vielleicht DOCH t_k t_j interessiert]*
that she$_{nom}$ him$_{acc}$ possibly ptc$_{affirm.}$ interests

(h) **dass* ***ihn****$_k$* ***sie****$_j$* *[vielleicht doch t_k t_j interessiert]*
that him$_{acc}$ she$_{nom}$ possibly ptc$_{affirm.}$ interests

(i) *dass* ***die****$_j$* ***den****$_k$* *[vielleicht DOCH t_k t_j interessiert]*
that she$_{demonstr\ nom}$ him$_{demonstr.acc}$ possibly ptc$_{affirm.}$ interests

(j) **dass* ***den****$_k$* ***die****$_j$* *[vielleicht doch t_k t_j interessiert]*
that him$_{demonstr\ acc}$ she$_{demonstr\ nom}$ possibly ptc$_{affirm.}$ interests

The constraint HIGHER ROLE is also relevant for the reflexive accusative vs. dative or genitive personal pronoun:

- reflexive accusative (+HR) > dative (–HR) (cf.: *sich jdm. anvertrauen* 'to confide (a secret) to s.o.').

(34) *(Wann willst du$_i$ es dem ProFESsor$_j$ erzählen?*
When will you tell it to the professor?)

(a) *Ich$_i$ vertraue* ***mich****$_i$* ***ihm****$_j$* *[wahrscheinlich nach der PRÜfung t_i t_i t_j an t_v]*
I confide refl$_{acc}$ him$_{dat}$ probably after the exam ptc
'I will probably confide my secret to him after the exam'

(b) **Ich$_i$ vertraue* ***ihm****$_j$* ***mich****$_i$* *[wahrscheinlich nach der Prüfung t_k t_i t_i t_j an t_v]*
I confide him$_{dat}$ refl$_{acc}$ probably after the exam ptc

- reflexive accusative (+HR) > genitive (–HR) (cf.: *sich jds. erinnern* 'to remember s.o.', *sich jds. entledigen* 'get rid of s.o.'[19]):

(35) *(A: Kannst du dich noch an Lehrer K. erinnern? B: Kaum noch, aber*
'A: Do you remember the teacher K.? B: With great difficulty, but)

(a) *Eva$_i$ wird* ***sich****$_j$* ***seiner****$_k$* *[bestimmt t_i t_j t_k geNAUer erinnern t_v]*
Eva will refl$_{acc}$ him$_{gen}$ certainly more exactly remember
'Eva definitely will remember him better'

(b) **Eva$_i$ wird* ***seiner****$_k$* ***sich****$_j$* *[bestimmt t_i t_j t_k genauer erinnern t_v]*
Eva will him$_{gen}$ refl$_{acc}$ definitely more exactly remember

---

[19] From a TV movie:
(i) *Sollten Sie dann versagen, werde ich* ***mich Ihrer*** *wohl entledigen müssen.*
should you then fail, will I refl$_{acc}$ you$_{gen}$ possibly get rid must
'If you fail, I might have to get rid of you'

The constraint HIGHER ROLE is systematically violated by combinations of personal pronouns in other cases provided that the reference is unambiguous, cf. e.g. (27a), where against the constraint HIGHER ROLE the accusative object precedes the dative one, and (36b), where the a.c.I.-object precedes the a.c.I.-subject (cf. 2.7):

(36) *(Mutter bat Hans$_j$, das AUto$_k$ durchzusehen. Aber ich glaube nicht,*
'Mother asked Hans to check the car. But I don't believe,')
(a) $^?$*dass sie$_i$* ***ihn$_j$*** ***es$_k$*** *[tatsächlich t_i t_j t_k repaRIEren lässt]*
that she him$_{acc\ SU}$ it$_{acc\ O}$ really repair lets
(b) *dass sie$_i$* ***es$_k$*** ***ihn$_j$*** *[tatsächlich t_i t_j t_k repaRIEren lässt]*
that she it$_{acc\ O}$ him$_{acc\ SU}$ really repair lets
'That she really allows him to repair it'

If the reference is ambiguous, the order higher role before lower role disambiguates the semantic roles, cf. the a.c.I.-constructions in (28e) vs. (28f), in (37b) vs. (37c), and (37d) vs. (37c):

(37) *(Mutter$_i$ und Tochter$_j$ besuchten das KASperle$_k$. Weil das Mädchen$_j$ ÄNGSTlich war,*
'Mother and daughter went to the puppet show. Because the girl was nervous,')
(a) *ließ die Mutter$_i$* ***das Mädchen$_j$*** ***den Kasper$_k$*** *[ja t_i t_j t_k laut RUfen t_v]*
let the mother$_{nom}$ the girl$_{acc\ SU}$ the puppet$_{acc\ O}$ ptc loudly cry out
'the mother let the girl cry out for the puppet loudly'
(b) *ließ sie$_i$ es$_j$* ***ihn$_k$*** *[ja t_i t_j t_k laut RUfen t_v]* (= 'the girl cries out for the puppet')
let she it$_{acc\ SU}$ him$_{acc\ O}$ ptc loudly cry out
'she let her cry out for him loudly'
(c) **ließ sie$_i$* ***ihn$_k$*** *es$_j$ [ja t_i t_j t_k laut rufen t_v]* (= 'the girl cries out for the puppet')
let she him$_{acc\ O}$ it$_{acc\ SU}$ ptc loudly cry
(d) *ließ sie$_i$* ***ihn$_k$*** *es$_j$ [ja t_i t_k t_j laut RUfen t_v]* (= 'the puppet cries out for the girl')
let she him$_{acc\ SU}$ it$_{acc\ O}$ ptc loudly cry out
'she let him to cry out for her loudly'
(e) **ließ sie$_i$ es$_j$* ***ihn$_k$*** *[ja t_i t_k t_j laut rufen t_v]* (= the puppet cries out for the girl)
let she it$_{acc\ O}$ him$_{acc\ SU}$ ptc loudly cry out

The following constraint concerns only the lowest object personal pronouns in dative and accusative case idiosyncratically violating the constraint HIGHER ROLE in German.

2.7 Constraint LOWEST ROLE

Precedence rule 7: Personal pronoun (+LR) > personal pronoun (–LR)
Topic constraint 7: *[DP$_{+an,+ppr,-nom,-LR}$..DP$_{+an,+ppr,-nom,+LR}$ FinP]

C-command relation: If the two lowest object-DPs in a clause are weak non-clitic (neutral) personal pronouns in dative or accusative case, the object-DP with the lowest Theta-role (+LR) c-commands the object-DP with the next-higher one (–LR).

If there are two object-DPs in different cases in a clause that are neutral personal pronouns, the accusative with the lowest Theta-role (+LR) precedes the non-accusative with the next-higher Theta-role (–LR) – independent of animacy, cf. (38), (39). (41c) shows that this constraint obviously concerns only the two lowest case complements with the exception of genitive pronouns, cf. 2.6.

- Accusative (+LR) > dative (–LR) (e.g.: *jdm. etw. geben* 'to give s.th. to s.o.' (38a, b), *jdm. etw. bringen* 'to bring s.th. to s.o.' (39a, b), *jdm. jdn. zeigen* 'to show s.o. to s.o.' (40a, b), *jdn. jdm. etw. beibringen lassen* 'to make s.o. teach s.th. to s.o.' (41a, b)):

(38) (*Eva*$_i$ *suchte vorhin das Telefonbuch*$_j$.
'Eva searched for the phone book a while ago')
(a) *Nun hat* ***es***$_j$ */'s* ***ihr***$_i$ *[sicher schon einer* t_i t_j *geGEben* t_v*]*
Now has it$_{acc}$ /it$_{acc\ cl.}$ her$_{dat}$ surely already someone given
'Now someone already must have given it to her'
(b) **Nun hat* ***ihr***$_i$ ***es***$_j$ *[sicher schon einer* t_i t_j *gegeben* t_v*]*
Now has her$_{dat}$ it$_{acc}$ surely already someone given
(c) *Nun hat* ***ihr***$_i$ *'s*$_{cl\ j}$ *[sicher schon einer* t_i t_j *geGEben* t_v*]*
Now has her$_{dat}$ it$_{acc\ cl}$ surely already someone given

(39) (*Eva*$_i$ *braucht den neuen TOPF*$_j$. 'Eva needs the new pot')
(a) *Lutz*$_i$ *bringt* ***ihn***$_j$ */ 'n* ***ihr***$_k$ *[selbstverständlich soFORT* t_i t_j t_k t_v*]*
Lutz brings him$_{acc}$ / him$_{acc\ cl.}$ her$_{dat}$ of course immediately
'Lutz of course brings it to her immediately'
(b) **Lutz*$_i$ *bringt* ***ihr***$_k$ ***ihn***$_j$ *[selbstverständlich sofort* t_i t_j t_k t_v*]*
Lutz brings her$_{dat}$ him$_{acc}$ of course immediately
(c) *?Lutz*$_i$ *bringt* ***ihr***$_k$ ***'n***$_{cl\ j}$ *[selbstverständlich soFORT* t_i t_j t_k t_v*]*
Lutz brings her$_{dat}$ him$_{cl.\ acc}$ of course immediately

(40) (*Hanna*$_i$ */ Hans*$_i$ *will den ProFESsor*$_j$ *kennenlernen und*
'Hanna / Hans wishes to meet the professor')
(a) *Eva*$_k$ *ZEIGT* ***ihn***$_j$ */ 'n*$_j$ ***ihr***$_i$ */* ***ihm***$_i$ *[natürlich* t_k t_i t_j t_v*]*
Eva shows him$_{acc}$ /him$_{acc\ cl.}$ her$_{dat}$/ him$_{dat}$ of course
'Eva of course shows him to her / to him'
(b) *??Eva*$_k$ *ZEIGT* ***ihr***$_i$ */* ***ihm***$_i$ ***ihn***$_j$ *[natürlich* t_k t_i t_j t_v*]*
Eva shows her$_{dat}$ / him$_{dat}$ him$_{acc}$ of course

(c) *Eva$_k$ ZEIGT $^?$ihr$_l$ 'n$_j$ /* ihm$_l$ 'n [natürlich t_k t_l t_j t_v]*
Eva shows her$_{dat}$ him$_{acc\ cl}$ / him$_{dat}$ him$_{acc\ cl}$ of course

(41) *(Hans$_k$ erzählte uns, dass sein Vater$_i$ eine FRAU$_j$ kennt, die ItaLIEnisch$_l$ spricht, und*
'Hans told us that his father knows a woman, who speaks Italian, and'
(a) *dass der Alte$_i$ sie$_j$ es$_l$ ihm$_k$ [eventuell t_i t_j t_k t_l BEIbringen lassen wird]*
that the old (man) her$_{acc}$ it$_{acc}$ him$_{dat}$ possibly teach let will
'that the old man possibly will make her to teach it him'
(b) **dass der Alte$_i$ sie$_j$ ihm$_k$ es$_l$ [eventuell t_i t_j t_k t_l beibringen lassen wird]*
that the old (man) her$_{acc}$ him$_{dat}$ it$_{acc}$ possibly teach let will
(c) **dass der Alte$_i$ ihm$_k$ sie$_j$ es$_l$ [eventuell t_i t_j t_k t_l beibringen lassen wird]*
that the old (man) him$_{dat}$ her$_{acc}$ it$_{acc}$ possibly teach let will

- Accusative (+LR) > reflexive dative (–LR) (e.g.: *sich jdn. vorstellen* 'to imagine s.o.'), cf. (42a, b):

(42) *(Abends denke ich$_j$ oft an HANS$_k$.* 'In the evening I often think of Hans)
(a) *Ich$_i$ stelle ihn$_k$ mir$_j$ dann$_l$ [natürlich t_i t_l t_j t_k VOR, (wie er mich ANsieht)]*
I imagine him$_{acc}$ refl$_{dat}$ then of course ptc (how he looks at me)
'I of course then imagine him (how he looks at me)'
(b) **Ich$_i$ stelle mir$_j$ ihn$_k$ dann$_l$ [natürlich t_i t_l t_j t_k vor, (wie er mich ansieht)]*
I imagine refl$_{dat}$ him$_{acc}$ then of course ptc (how he looks at me)

Sometimes a reduced accusative object (+LR) follows the neutral dative pronoun, note the different degrees of grammaticality in (38c)/(39c), and (40c). (40c) indicates that this is possibly a problem of phonetic compatibility (*two nasals).

Provided that the reference is unambiguous (cf. 2.6), the constraint LOWEST ROLE also concerns the double-accusative constructions with verbs such as *jdn. etw. lehren* 'to teach s.o. s.th.' in (43), or with so-called a.c.I.-verbs like *jdn. etw. machen lassen* 'to make / allow s.o. to do s.th.' in (44), *jdn. jdn. mitnehmen lassen* 'to allow s.o. to take along s.o. with one' in (45), *jdn. jdn. etw. lehren lassen* 'to make s.o. teach s.o. s.th.' in (46). The order of the object-pronouns corresponding to the Theta-role hierarchy in the b-variants of (43) - (46) is less grammatical than the order +LR > –LR in the a-variants of these clauses. As a correction strategy the lowest role is taken by a demonstrative pronoun always following the personal pronoun in the c-variants of (43) - (46), cf. the constraint PERS PRON in 2.5.

(43) *(Jan$_j$ würde gern JUdo$_k$ lernen.* 'Jan would like to learn judo')
(a) *Eva$_i$ wird es$_k$ ihn$_j$ [sicher t_i t_j t_k LEHren t_v]*
Eva will it$_{acc}$ him$_{acc}$ surely teach
'Eva probably will teach it to him'

(b) ***Eva_i *wird* ***ihn***$_j$ ***es***$_k$ *[sicher* t_i t_j t_k *lehren* t_v*]*
Eva will him$_{acc}$ it$_{acc}$ surely teach
(c) Eva_i *wird* ***ihn***$_j$ ***das***$_k$ *[sicher* t_i t_j t_k *LEHren* t_v*]*
Eva will him$_{acc}$ that$_{demonstr.\ acc}$ surely teach

(44) *(Hans*$_j$ *will gern Evas*$_i$ *AUto*$_k$ *reparieren.* 'Hans would like to repair Eva's car')
(a) Eva_i *wird* ***es***$_k$ ***ihn***$_j$ *[sicher* t_i t_j t_k *MAchen lassen* t_v*]*
Eva will it$_{acc}$ him$_{acc}$ surely make let
'Eva will allow him to do it'
(b) ?Eva_i *wird* ***ihn***$_j$ ***es***$_k$ *[sicher* t_i t_j t_k *MAchen lassen* t_v*]*
Eva will him$_{acc}$ it$_{acc}$ surely make let
(c) Eva_i *wird* ***ihn***$_j$ ***das***$_k$ *[sicher* t_i t_j t_k *MAchen lassen* t_v*]*
Eva will him$_{acc}$ that$_{demonstr.\ acc}$ surely make let

(45) *(Hans*$_j$ *will gern mit seiner Tochter*$_k$ *nach PaRIS fahren.)*
'Hans would like to go to Paris together with his daughter'
(a) Eva_i *wird* ***sie***$_k$ ***ihn***$_j$ *[sicher* t_i t_j t_k *MITnehmen lassen* t_v*]*
Eva will her$_{acc}$ him$_{acc}$ surely take along let
'Eva surely will allow him to take her along with him'
(b) ?Eva_i *wird* ***ihn***$_j$ ***sie***$_k$ *[sicher* t_i t_j t_k *MITnehmen lassen* t_v*]*
Eva will him$_{acc}$ her$_{acc}$ surely take along let
(c) Eva_i *wird* ***ihn***$_j$ ***die***$_k$ *[sicher* t_i t_j t_k *MITnehmen lassen* t_v*]*
Eva will him$_{acc}$ her$_{demonstr.\ acc}$ surely take along let

(46) *(Hans*$_k$ *erzählte uns, dass sein Vater*$_i$ *eine FRAU*$_j$ *kennt, die ItaLIEnisch*$_l$ *spricht, und*
'Hans told us that his father knows a woman, who speaks Italian, and'
(a) *dass der Alte*$_i$ *sie*$_j$ *es*$_l$ ***ihn***$_k$ *[eventuell* t_i t_j t_k t_l *LEHren lassen wird]*
that the old man her$_{acc}$ it$_{acc}$ him$_{acc}$ possibly teach let will
'that the old man will possibly make her to teach him it'
(b) **dass der Alte*$_i$ *sie*$_j$ ***ihn***$_k$ *es*$_l$ *[eventuell* t_i t_j t_k t_l *lehren lassen wird]*
that the old man her$_{acc}$ him$_{acc}$ it$_{acc}$ possibly teach let will
(c) *dass der Alte*$_i$ *sie*$_j$ ***ihn***$_k$ ***das***$_l$ *[eventuell* t_i t_j t_k t_l *LEHren lassen wird]*
that the old man her$_{acc}$ him$_{acc}$ that$_{demonstr.\ acc}$ possibly teach let will

3 Summary

Our surface constraint system concerns only topicalic middlefield elements that are moved into topic positions to the left of FinP, and to the left of a possible sentence adverbial left adjoined to FinP or to the highest clausal XP that is able to contain a sentence adverbial.

The result of the interplay of the presented constraints is the precedence hierarchy in table 5 substantiated by *dass-sentences*.

Our constraint system resulting in this precedence hierarchy for topics is suitable for the valuation of topic orders independent of the syntactic assumptions, cf. e.g.:

- Rizzi (1997) several topics in SpecTopP, cf. (47a):

(47) (*Ich denke,* 'I think')

(a) *dass* [$_{TopP1}$ ***die REStе***$_{+Th\ k}$ [$_{TopP2}$ ***ihr***$_{j}$ [$_{TopP3}$ ***der Mann***$_{i}$ [$_{TopP4}$ ***dann***$_{l}$
that the leftovers$_{acc}$ her$_{dat}$ the man$_{nom}$ then
[$_{FinP}$ *sicher* [$_{TP}$ t_l t_i t_j t_k *per AUTO bringt*]]]]]]
surely by car brings
'I think that the man then probably will bring her the leftovers by car'

- Adjunction of topicalic elements to TenseP, cf. (48b):

(47) (b) *dass* [$_{TP}$ *die REStе*$_{+Th\ k}$ [$_{TP}$ *ihr*$_{j}$ [$_{TP}$ *der Mann*$_{i}$ [$_{TP}$ *dann*$_{l}$ [$_{TP}$ *sicher*
[$_{TP}$ t_l t_i t_j t_k *per AUTO bringt*]]]]]]

For an optimality theoretic approach you find first considerations about a ranking of these constraints in the Appendix. Because these constraints are not universal but only idiosyncratic German, I do not think that they really are constraints in the sense of OT. Nevertheless I will show that they are able to valuate the topic order in this context too.

Neither adjunct positions nor SpecTopP positions are able to determine the linear order of topicalized anaphoric elements. But we have seen that this order is not arbitrary, it is grammaticalized to a great extent. There are many different syntactic, morphologic and phonologic influences that interact to determine this order. Our surface constraint system can help to valuate the various possible orders as grammatical, less acceptable or ungrammatical. It covers the linear order of the aboutness topic and most types of anaphoric phrases in the Wackernagel position, but certainly not all details. Furthermore these constraints have to be related to various other syntactic constraints (Minimal-link condition, G. Müller's (1998) scrambling constraints, Lenerz's (2001) scrambling principles, Wunderlich's (1999) constraint system et al.). But that is a job for the future.

1. topic >											**new inform.**
2. theme>		**anaphoric phrases**									
3.		**anaphoric DPs >**								**ana-phor. PPs**	
4.		**pronominal DPs >**					**non-pronominal DPs**				
5.		**personal pron. >**		**non-personal pron.**							
6.		**higher > lower θ-R.**		**higher > lower θ-R.**			**higher > lower θ-R.**				
7.		**pers pron.$_{+LR}$ > pers pron.$_{-LR}$**									
1.	***der Junge***				***dem***					***deshalb***	*wohl eine ErZÄHlung vorlas*
2.	***das Buch***		***ihm***				***der Bengel***				*sicher entRISsen hat*
3.			***ihr***				***der Junge***			***damit/ deshalb***	*Sicher impoNIERte*
4.			***ihm***	***der***					***das Buch***	***dann***	*lieber VORlas*
5.	***sie***		***ihm***			***das***				***damals***	*wohl verÜbelte*
6a.							***der Chef***	***der Dame***	***den Jungen***		*sicher gleich VORstellte*
6b.				***die***	***dem***	***das***					*natürlich erKLÄRT*
7a.	***sie***	***sich***	***ihr***								*natürlich gern ANvertrauen*
7b.	***ich***	***ihn***	***mir***								*nur VORstellte*
7c.		***es***	***ihn***							***damals***	*sicher keiner LEHRte*

Table 5: Precedence hierarchy

It covers the linear order of the aboutness topic and most types of anaphoric phrases in the Wackernagel position, but certainly not all details. Furthermore these constraints have to be related to various other syntactic constraints (Minimal-link condition, G. Müller's (1998) scrambling constraints, Lenerz's

(2001) scrambling principles, Wunderlich's (1999) constraint system et al.). But that is a job for the future.

4 Appendix

4.1 Arguments for an OT-Ranking of the topic constraints

If the reader prefers an optimality-theoretic grammar I will try to give some first arguments for a ranking of the topic constraints above in the German language.

In the German constraint hierarchy the constraint Topic is ranked higher than the known universal OT-constraint STAY (cf. e.g. Müller (1998)) that prevents S-structure movement, cf. the following constraint conflict:

- TOPIC >> STAY

(1) *Im Supermarkt irrt ein kleiner JUNge$_i$ umher. Ich denke,*
'In-the supermarket a little boy wanders around. I think'
dass dem Kleinen$_i$ [sicher t_i seine Mutter fehlt]
that the boy surely his mother misses
'that the boy surely misses his mother'

Candidates		STAY	TOPIC
C1	dass sicher dem Kleinen$_i$ seine Mutter fehlt		*
=>C2	dass dem Kleinen$_i$ sicher t_i seine Mutter fehlt	*	

C1 without movement of the anaphoric DP violates the constraint TOPIC, C2 with the moved anaphoric DP violates STAY. TOPIC in C2 requires a less marked order than STAY in C1. Therefore is TOPIC in German higher ranked than STAY.

We can assume that all phenomena discussed here meet the requirements of the constraint TOPIC. The constraint THEME is higher ranked than all anaphora-constraints PP-ANAPH, PRON, PERS PRON, HIGHER ROLE, and LOWEST ROLE.

- THEME >> PP-ANAPH

(2) *(Lutz erzählte seinen Enkeln$_i$ [dass er sie beSUchen wird]$_k$. Er sagte uns,*
'Lutz told his grandsons that he would visit them. He said to us')
dass sich$_i$ die Jungs$_{an+Th\,i}$ darauf$_k$ [offenbar $t_i t_i t_k$ FREUen]
that refl the boys about-that evidently are-glad
'that the boys evidently are-glad about-that'

Each of the candidates violates one constraint: C1 violates THEME. C2 violates PP-ANAPH. There is a constraint conflict: THEME in C1 requires a less marked order than PP-ANAPH in C2, therefore THEME is higher ranked than PP-ANAPH.

Candidates		**THEME**	**Anaphora Constraints**				
			PP-ANAPH	**PRON**	**PERS-PRON**	**HIGHER ROLE**	**LOWEST ROLE**
=>C1	dass sich$_i$die Jungs$_{+Th\ i}$ darauf$_k$ offenbar $t_i t_i$ t_k freuen	*					
C2	dass darauf$_k$ sich$_i$ die Jungs$_{+Th\ i}$ offenbar $t_i t_i$ t_k freuen		*				

- THEME >> PERS PRON:

(3) *Lutz$_j$ hat mit seinen Enkeln$_i$ telefoniert und herAUSgehört,*
'Lutz phoned his grandsons and he heard'
dass die$_{an+Th\ i}$ ihn$_{an\ j}$ [offenbar t_i t_j erWARten]
that they him evidently wait
'that they evidently are waiting for him'

Candidates		**THEME**	**Anaphora Constraints**				
			PP-ANAPH	**PRON**	**PERS PRON**	**HIGHER ROLE**	**LOWEST ROLE**
=> C1	dass die$_{an+Th\ i}$ ihn$_{an\ j}$ offenbar t_i t_j erwarten				*		
C2	dass ihn$_{an\ j}$ die$_{an+Th\ i}$ offenbar t_i t_j erwarten	*					

Each of the candidates violates only one constraint: C1 violates PERS PRON. C2 violates THEME. There is a constraint conflict: THEME in C1 requires a less marked order than PERS PRON in C2, therefore THEME is higher ranked than PERS PRON.

- THEME >> PRON

(4) *Lutz$_i$ hat mit seinen Enkeln$_j$ telefoniert, und sein Gesicht zeigte,*
'Lutz phoned his grandsons and you can tell by looking at him

(a) *dass die Jungs*$_{+Th\,j}$ *ihm*$_{an\,i}$ *[offenbar* t_i t_j *FREUde bereiten]*
that the boys him evidently pleasure give
'that the boys evidently give him pleasure'

Candidates		THEME	Anaphora Constraints				
			PP-ANAPH	PRON	PERS PRON	HIGHER ROLE	LOWEST ROLE
=>C1	dass die Jungs$_{+Th\,j}$ ihm$_{an\,i}$ offenbar t_i t_j Freude bereiten			*			
C2	dass ihm$_{an\,i}$ die Jungs$_{+Th\,j}$ offenbar t_i t_j Freude bereiten	*					

Each of the candidates violates one constraint: C1 violates PRON. C2 violates THEME, if the DP *die Jungs* is marked as theme. There is a constraint conflict: THEME in C1 requires a less marked order than PRON in C2, therefore THEME would be higher ranked than PRON.

But there is a problem, because in the context (4) not only the anaphoric DP *die Jungs* can be the theme of this sentence, but also the dative pronoun *ihm*.

(4) (b) *dass ihm*$_{an\,+Th\,i}$ *dieJungs*$_{an\,j}$ *[offenbar* $t_i t_j$ *FREUde bereiten]*
that him the boys evidently pleasure give
'that the boys evidently give him pleasure'

Candidates		THEME	Anaphora Constraints				
			PP-ANAPH	PRON	PERS PRON	HIGHER ROLE	LOWEST ROLE
C1	dass die Jungs$_{an\,j}$ ihm$_{an\,+Th\,i}$ offenbar t_i t_j Freude bereiten	*		*			
=>C2	dass ihm$_{an+Th\,i}$ die Jungs$_{an\,j}$ offenbar t_i t_j Freude bereiten						

In this case we have two violations in C1: THEME and PRON. C2 doesn' t violate any of these constraints. So the ranking between these constraints is dependent on theme marking.

- THEME >> HIGHER ROLE

(5) *Ich habe dem Sven$_i$ den "Harry POTter"$_j$ gekauft und hoffe nun,*
'I bought "Harry Potter" for Sven'. Now I hope,
(a) *dass das Buch$_{an\ Th\ j}$ dem Jungen$_{an\text{-}\ i}$ [wirklich t_i t_j geFÄLLT]*
that the book the boy really pleases
'that the book really will please the boy'

Candidates		THEME	Anaphora Constraints				
			PP-ANAPH	PRON	PERS PRON	HIGHER ROLE	LOWEST ROLE
C1	dass dem Jungen$_i$ das Buch$_{+Th\ j}$ wirklich t_i t_j gefällt	*					
=>C2	dass das Buch$_{+Th\ j}$ dem Jungen$_i$ wirklich t_i t_j gefällt					*	

The ranking between these constraints is also dependent on theme marking. If the lower nominative argument of a psych-verb *das Buch* should be the theme of the sentence we have two violations: C1 violates THEME. C2 violates HIGHER ROLE. Because the theme has to be in the theme position, the constraint HIGHER ROLE in C1 requires a more marked order than THEME in C2. THEME is higher ranked than HIGHER ROLE.

But if the dative DP with the higher Theta role is marked as theme in the same context (5), C1 doesn't violate any constraint, but C2 violates THEME and HIGHER ROLE:

(5) (b) *dass dem Jungen$_{an\ Th\text{-}\ i}$ das Buch$_{an\ j}$ [wirklich t_i t_j geFÄLLT]*
that the boy the book really pleases

Candidates		THEME	Anaphora Constraints				
			PP-ANAPH	’RON	PERS PRON	HIGHER ROLE	LOWEST ROLE
=>C1	dass dem Jungen$_{+Th\ i}$ das Buch$_j$ wirklich t_i · t_j gefällt						
C2	dass das Buch$_j$ dem Jungen$_{+Th\ i}$ wirklich t_i t_j gefällt	*				*	

- *LOWEST ROLE >> HIGHER ROLE*

(6) *Ich habe Maria$_j$ und diesen Sänger$_i$ bei der AUSstellung gesehen. Nun hoffe ich nur,*
'I saw Mary and this singer at the exhibition. Now I hope,'
dass ihn$_{+LR\,i}$ ihr$_{+HR\text{-}j}$ [endlich einer t_j t_i geZEIGT hat]
that him$_{acc}$ her$_{dat}$ finally someone showed has
'that someone showed her him finally'

Candidates		THEME	Anaphora Constraints				
			PP-ANAPH	'RON	PERS PRON	HIGHER ROLE	LOWEST ROLE
=>C1	dass ihn$_i$ ihr$_j$ endlich einer t_j t_i gezeigt hat					*	
C2	dass ihr$_j$ ihn$_i$ endlich einer t_j t_i gezeigt hat						*

Each of the candidates violates only one constraint: C1 violates HIGHER ROLE, C2 violates LOWEST ROLE. There is a constraint conflict: LOWEST ROLE in C1 requires a less marked order than HIGHER ROLE in C2, therefore LOWEST ROLE is higher ranked than HIGHER ROLE.

In a first summary it may be said:

- In German the constraint TOPIC is higher ranked than the universal constraint STAY.
- TOPIC therefore is higher ranked than all other constraints for moved elements.
- THEME is higher ranked than all anaphora constraints.
- I think that there is no internal ranking between the anaphora constraints PP-ANAPH, PRON, PERS PRON, and HIGHER ROLE.
- Only the German idiosyncratic constraint LOWEST ROLE is higher ranked than HIGHER ROLE in the domain of personal pronouns.

5 References

Askedal, J. O. (1999): Nochmals zur kontrastiven Beschreibung von deutsch es und norwegisch det. Ein sprachtypologischer Ansatz. In: H. Wegener (ed) (1999): Deutsch kontrastiv: Typologisch-vergleichende Untersuchungen zur deutschen Grammatik. Tübingen: Stauffenburg, 33-62.

Büring, D. (1994): Mittelfeldreport V. In: B. Haftka (ed) (1994), 79-96.

Cardinaletti, A. (1990): *Es, pro* and Sentential Arguments in German. In: Linguistische Berichte 126, 135-164.

Chomsky, N. (1995): The Minimalist Program. Chapter 4, Cambridge (Mass.) / London: The MIT Press, 219-394.

Dölling, J. and T. Pechmann (ed) (2000): Prosodie – Struktur – Interpretation. Linguistische Arbeitsberichte 74, Leipzig.

Frey, W. (2000): Über die syntaktische Position der Satztopiks im Deutschen. In: ZAS Papers in Linguistics 20, Berlin, 137-172.

Gärtner, H.-M. and M. Steinbach (2000): What do Reduced Pronominals Reveal about the Syntax of Dutch and German? In: H.-M. Gärtner (ed): Two Papers on Clitics. Linguistics in Potsdam 9, 7-62.

Haftka, B. (1980): Bewußtseinspräsenz und aktuelle Gliederung. In: K. E. Heidolph (ed): Untersuchungen zur deutschen Grammatik II. Linguistische Studien 68, Zentralinstitut für Sprachwissenschaft, Berlin, 1-94.

Haftka, B. (1988): Ob vielleicht vielleicht tatsächlich nicht gern reist? Ein Beitrag zur Topologie auch des Satzadverbiales. In: E. Lang (ed): Studien zum Satzmodus I. Linguistische Studien 177, Zentralinstitut für Sprachwissenschaft, Berlin, 25-58.

Haftka, B. (1994) (ed): Was determiniert Wortstellungsvariation? Opladen: Westdeutscher Verlag.

Haftka, B. (1994): Wie positioniere ich meine Position. In: B. Haftka (ed) (1994), 139-160.

Haftka, B. (1995): Syntactic Positions for Topic and Contrastive Focus in the German Middlefield. In: I. Kohlhof, S. Winkler, and H. B. Drubig (eds): Proceedings of the Goettingen Focus Workshop 17. Arbeitspapiere des Sonderforschungs-bereichs 340, vol 69, 137-158.

Haftka, B. (2000): Topik-Constraints im Deutschen: Wie ich die der Anita natürlich auch erklären könnte. In: J. Dölling and T. Pechmann (ed) (2000), 83-109.

Haftka, B. (2003): Möglicherweise tatsächlich nicht immer. Beobachtungen zur Adverbialreihenfolge an der Spitze des Rhemas. In: W. Abraham and L. Molnárfi (ed): Optionality in Syntax and Discourse Structure – Aspects of Word Order Variation in (West) Germanic and other Indo-European Languages. Folia Linguistica Europaea. XXXVII / 1-2, (C) Mouton de Gruyter, Berlin.

Lenerz, J. (1981): Zur Generierung der satzeinleitenden Positionen im Deutschen. In: M. Kohrt and J. Lenerz (ed): Sprache: Formen und Strukturen. Akten des 15. Linguistischen Kolloquiums, Münster 1980 I. Linguistische Arbeiten 98, Tübingen: Niemeyer, 171-182.

Lenerz, J. (2001): Word Order Variation: Competition or Co-operation. In: W. Sternefeld and G. Müller (ed) Competition in Syntax. Berlin etc.: de Gruyter, 249-282.

Meinunger, A. (2002): Argument Ordering in German: Lexical Decomposition of the 'Atomic' Predicate POSS and its Implications for the Hierarchization of Arguments of Ditransitive Verbs. In: D. Hole, P. Law, and N. Zhang (ed): Webfest für Horst Dieter Gasde. (www.zas.gwz-berlin.de) Berlin.

Müller, G. (1998): German Word Order and Optimality Theory. Arbeitspapiere des Sonderforschungsbereichs 340, vol 126, Stuttgart / Tübingen.

Molnár, V. (1991): Das Topik im Deutschen und im Ungarischen. Lunder germanistische Forschungen 58. Stockholm: Almqvist / Wiksell International.

Molnár, V. and I. Rosengren (1996): Zu Jacobs' Explikation der I-Topikalisierung. In: Sprache und Grammatik 41, 49-88.

Postal, P. M. and G. K. Pullum (1988): Expletive Noun Phrases in Subcategorized Positions. In: Linguistic Inquiry 19, 635-670.

Pütz, H. (1986): Über die Syntax der Pronominalform es im modernen Deutsch. Studien zur deutschen Grammatik 3.

Rizzi L. (1997): The Fine Structure of the Left Periphery. In: L. Haegeman (ed): Elements of Grammar: Handbook of Generative Syntax. Dordrecht (1997), 281-338.

Sandberg, B. (1998): Zum ES bei transitiven Verben vor satzförmigem Akkusativobjekt. Tübinger Beiträge zur Linguistik 443. Gunter Narr, Tübingen.

Schwarz, M. (2000): Textuelle Progression durch Anaphern – Aspekte einer prozeduralen Thema-Rhema-Analyse. In: J. Dölling and T. Pechmann (ed) (2000), 111-126.

Steube, A. (2000): Ein kognitionswissenschaftlich basiertes Modell für Informationsstrukturierung (in Anwendung auf das Deutsche). In: J. Bayer and Chr. Römer (ed): Von der Philologie zur Grammatiktheorie: Tübingen: Niemeyer, 213-238.

Steube, A. (2001): Grammatik und Pragmatik von Hutkonturen. In: A. Steube and C. Umbach (ed) (2001), 7-29.

Steube, A. (2002) (ed): Sprachtheoretische Grundlagen der Kognitionswissenschaft: Sprachliches und nichtsprachliches Wissen. Linguistische Arbeitsberichte 79, Leipzig.

Steube, A. and A. Späth (2002): Semantik, Informationsstruktur und grammatische Modularität. In: A. Steube (ed) (2002), 235-254.

Steube, A. and C. Umbach (ed) (2001): Kontrast – lexikalisch, semantisch, intonatorisch. Linguistische Arbeitsberichte 77, Leipzig.

Tomaselli, A. (1986): Das unpersönliche *es* - Eine Analyse im Rahmen der Generativen Grammatik. In: Linguistische Berichte 102, 171-190.

Vikner, S. (1995): Verb Movement and Expletive Subjects in the Germanic Languages. Oxford Studies in Comparative Syntax. New York: Oxford University Press.

Wunderlich, D. (1999): The Force of Lexical Case: German and Icelandic compared In: Theorie des Lexikons. Arbeiten des Sonderforschungsbereich 282, vol 112, 81-102.

Zimmermann, I. (1999): Die Integration topikalischer DPs in die syntaktische und semantische Struktur von Sätzen. In: M. Doherty (ed): Sprachspezifische Aspekte der Informationsverteilung. Studia grammatica 47. Berlin: Akademie Verlag, 41-60.

Rosemarie Lühr (Jena)

Contrastive Word Stress in Vedic Endo- and Exocentric Compounds[1]

> The frequent combination of declinable stems with one another to form compounds which then are treated as if simple, in respect to accent, inflection, and construction, is a conspicuous feature of the [Vedic] language, from its earliest period. (Whitney 1889: 480)

0 Introduction

Though there are in Vedic basic rules for stressing endocentric and exocentric compounds, a lot of counterexamples are found. For instance, determinative compounds with a final member in *–ta-* are stressed on the initial member like *bahuvrīhis*; compare the endocentric types *ghṛtā-vṛ́dh-* \`enjoying the ghee', *ní-hita-* \`laid, placed, deposited' with *sahásra-pad-* \`thousand-footed'. Hitherto the motive for such differences or correspondences is unknown. Because it seems to be obvious that some rule exists which is higher ranked than the functional distinction between compounds, the analysis of contrastive word stress in Vedic compounds developed here is an optimality theory-approach. It will be shown that markedness of vowels in heads of metrical units and a special rhythmical rule are relevant for stress shift. More important however is, that faithfulness and markedness constraints could be overriden by contrastive stress, whereby stress is shifted not only to differentiate "substantive" and "adjective" as parts of speech, but also within a compound. So in the case of prepositional compounds with governed final member and *bahuvrīhis* "compositionell" *–á-* denotes a contrast between the substantive value of the final member and the adjective of the whole compound. Further this contrastive function of the suffix *–á-* is used in *bahuvrīhis* with the negative prefix *a(n)-* to oppose those *bahuvrīhis* to determinative compounds with the corresponding prefix. In stressing endocentric and exocentric compounds with the negative prefix *a(n)-* differently, a semantically determined contrastive word stress is visible.

[1] I owe critical remarks to Sergio Neri.

1 Preliminaries

Greek and Vedic are languages whose accent-system is neither a stress-accent nor that of a tone language, but something in between. In Vedic, for instance, the Indish grammarians do not talk of strength, but of pitch (*udātta* 'high, prominent'). But pitch seems to be accompanied by some strengthening. Just as in English, where the position of stress can be used as a derivational device to signal the syntactic category of a word (engl. *contrást* vs. *cóntrast* with distinctive stress)[2], this kind of stress also fulfils contrastive functions in differentiating parts of speech; compare Vedic *éṣa-* m. 'the act of seeking or going after' vs. *eṣá-* 'gliding, running, hastening'. As Wackernagel (1905: 19) states, barytonesis is generally characteristic of nouns in Vedic. But adjectives, too, often have a contrastive word stress. If they are compounded, endocentric or determinative compounds (*tatpuruṣas*) are in many cases stressed on the final member, while exocentric compounds as *bahuvrīhis*, or certain prepositional or verbal compounds with a governed final member, are stressed on the initial member; compare *ghṛtā-vṛ́dh-* 'enjoying the ghee' vs. *sahásra-pad-* 'thousand-footed', *áty-avi-* 'passing through the wool', *Trasá-dasyu-* male proper name 'before whom the enemies tremble'[3]. This distribution of stress is inherited from Proto-Indo-European, as in the Greek θηρο-σκόπος 'looking out for wild beasts', δρυ-τόμος 'wood-cutter', μελανό-χροος 'black-skinned', μέτ-ωπον 'the space between the eyes', φερέ-πολις 'upholding the city'. Yet there are many counterexamples. For instance, determinative compounds with a final member in *-ta-* are stressed on the initial member like *bahuvrīhis*; as is RV *ní-hita-* 'laid, placed, deposited'. This stress rule is also a Proto-Indo-European inheritance; compare Greek ἀνδρό-κμητος 'wrought by men's hands'. According to Wackernagel (215), the motive for the stress difference to the endocentric type *ghṛtā-vṛ́dh-* is unknown. But there obviously exists some rule which is higher ranked than the functional distinction between *bahuvrīhis* and determinative compounds. Consequently the analysis of contrastive word stress in Vedic compounds developed here is an optimality theory-approach. Firstly, we account for the initial-element-stress normally occuring in Vedic *bahuvrīhis*, some prepositional, and most verbal compounds with a governed final member as opposed to determinative compounds. Secondly, we consider the counterexamples to the general stress rules in Vedic compounds. After that the OT rankings follow.

---

[2] Spencer 1991: 16; van Coetsem 1996: 62.

[3] We leave out *dvandvas*, for they are stressed on both members in older time (Wackernagel 1905: 150).

2 General stress rules in Vedic and Greek endo- and exocentric compounds and their motivation

In Vedic and Greek, compounds are [stem + stem], [stem + word] or [word + stem] compounds. It has been proposed that [stem + stem] compounds are mapped onto one phonological word whereas [stem + word] compounds vary as to whether they are mapped onto one or two phonological words. According to the Minimal Word Principle "In the mapping of compounds onto phonological words, choose the lowest X^{0}" (Nespor 1999: 139), stems must be destressed; note also Burzio's (1994) stress preservation principle, which states that words, as opposed to stems, enter composition with stress since they have already been mapped onto a phonological word. But in Greek and Vedic both principles do not apply as a rule; compare μελάν-ιππος ‘with a black horse’, (ἵππος), φερέ-οικος ‘carry the house’ (οἶκος) vs. *ádhi-gartya-* ‘being in the driver's seat’ (*ádhi*). On the contrary, these languages are lexical stress languages, in which the rule for primary stress location is sensitive to lexical marks. Here, location of stress must be marked lexically per morpheme on some arbitrary syllable (i.e., is free); but when morphemes are strung together to form words, a rule will decide which of the lexically marked syllables will receive the primary (i.e. word) stress. Accordingly, this kind of accentuation is associated with so called dominant or cyclic stresses (van der Hulst 1999: 17, 21)[4]. For Vedic Kiparsky (1982) first drew attention to the fact that from the viewpoint of stress assignment the suffixes must be divided into two classes: recessive and dominant. In words containing dominant suffixes, the last dominant suffix determines the surface stress. In particular, if the last dominant suffix is underlyingly stressed, the surface stress is located on this suffix. Hence, morphemes may or may not be stressed in their underlying representations. In addition, van der Hulst (50, 52f., 73) mentions another feature of lexical stress systems: They may be unbounded, meaning that the location of primary stress is not foot-based. Whereas in bounded systems the location of primary stress is bound to a three- or two-syllable window (with the extra option of extrametricality) – for instance, in Greek the output stress falls under the rightward "three-syllable window" -[5], in unbounded systems the domain for primary stress is the prosodic word (also with the extrametricality option). Vedic seems to be such a language. As Kiparsky has shown, given the lexical stresses, word stress is located on the leftmost (first) stressed syllable or on the first syllable if there are no stresses. Thus, in this analysis Vedic is a FIRST/FIRST system[6].

---

[4] Compare Hock 1993: 200f. note 25 for the genesis of dominant morphemes.

[5] Drachman and Malikouti-Drachman 1999: 897ff.

[6] Russian and Lithuanian, too, are FIRST/FIRST systems (van der Hulst, Hendriks, and Weijer 1999: 437f.).

2.1 bahuvrīhis

Scholars agree in deriving *bahuvrīhis* like Vedic *sahásra-pad-* `thousand-footed', Greek μελάν-ιππος `with a black horse' from a nominal sentence μέλας ἵππος `the horse is black' which - in the sense of `his horse is black' - is used for characterizing a person: `person who owns a black horse'; `ῥοδο-δάκτυλος ᾿Εώς `Eos (like) roses (are) (her) fingers' (Meier-Brügger 2000: 272). Therefore, to understand the stressing of this compound type one has to consider stress and word order in the Vedic and Greek nominal sentences. In those sentences the predicative noun, being emphatic, precedes the subject; in Vedic *mártya ha vā́ ágre devā́saḥ* `the gods were originally mortals' (ŚB). In German, *Schwárz sind die Pferde*, too, the main stress lies on the initial member, the predicative. When the two words *sahásraḥ páds* `thousandfold are (his) feet' are joined to form a compound or only one phonological word, a greater prominence is given to the main stress than to the stress of the rest; or the following strength hierarchy rule is valid: "The left stress is stronger than the right one" (Haraguchi 1991: 156); compare Engl. *bláckbird* vs. *bláck bírd* (Marchand 1969: 113). In any case, only stress on the initial member survives, whereby the position of the stress in the single word is retained. Greek *bahuvrīhis* like ποικιλό-φωνος `with varied tones' or ποικιλό-θριξ `with various plumes', πολω-άνθραξ in contrast to ποικίλος, πολύς are compatible with this rule, for in Greek stress does not recede beyond the penult if the final syllable ends in a consonant cluster (Steriade 1988: 274). Starting from sentences containing the word order "predicative with main stress – subject" this stressing must have been generalized, for it appears in *bahuvrīhis* with quite different semantic relations, too (see Lühr 2003).

According to the suggested analysis, *bahuvrīhi* in Proto-Indo-European was a frequent syntactical juxtaposition[7] retaining the main stress of this phrase.

2.2 Verbal compounds with a governed final member

In the type *Trasá-dasyu-*, stress is almost always placed on the second syllable of the initial member; note in particular the type in *–át/d-*: *kṣayád-vīra-* `ruling men'. Since in those compounds a relation with an internal argument is established, the verbal element assigns the case-relation object to the final member. Therefore, it seems obvious that stressed *-át/d-* is a verbal ending. Besides present stems of the I. class with an unstressed *–a*-present, stems of the VI. class with a stressed *-á-* (type *tudáti*) and present stems in *–áyati*

[7] Note "syntactic compounds" like Vedic *ahaṃ-pūrvá-* `eager to be first' (from *aháṃ pūrváḥ* `I should be first', *kiṃ-tvá* `asking garrulously' (from *kíṃ tvám* `what are you doing?'), *yād-rādhyàm* `as quickly as possible' (literally `in so far as attainable').

appear as an initial member. Among those compounds with *dhārayát-* are Indo-Iranian; compare Vedic *dhārayát-kavi-*, *-kṣiti-* 'supporting sages resp. bearing creatures' with Old Avestian *Dāraiiat̰-ratha-* male proper name (literally 'supporting carriages'), Old Persian *Dāraya-vauš* (Wackernagel 1905: 318f.). One can assume that at one time a third Singular Injunctive Present of the *áya*-class constituted the initial verbal member, whereby the Injunctive is used in a general sense (compare Hoffmann 1967: 114 to this function of the Injunctive Present): Old Persian *Dāraya-vauš*, originally 'he always maintains the good'. Though in Vedic the subject usually begins the sentence, a stressed verb can move to the beginning if it is strongly emphasized, as it is documented in the prose of the Brāhmaṇas. But after being joined to a compound, stress must for rhythmical reasons be shifted to the heavy ultimate of the first member (with coda in front of an initial consonant), and this stress then extended to other present stems. According to the above-mentioned strength hierarchy rule, stress of the original object was deleted. As an aside, the type *Trasá-dasyu-* may have contained an element *–át/d-*, too[8], if one assumes that in a preform **trasád-dasyu-* 'he always makes frightened the enemies' the first *–d-* is dissimilated. Yet in the case of an original Injunctive Present in this type, Greek φερέ-οικος 'carry the house!', Μενέ-λαος 'one who stops men, abiding-men' must be separated, whereby Greek shows stressing on the first member, too. There is no objection to the older opinion that an Imperative is the initial member; compare German *Fürchtegott, Springinsfeld*, Vedic *sthā́-raśman-* (1) 'loosen the reins', Early Avestian *barō-zaoθra-* 'sacrifice to god!', Old Persian *Xšayā-aršan-* male proper name, literally 'rule the men', Vedic *śíkṣā-nará-* 'help the men', *radā-vasu-* 'dispense wealth' (with lengthened *-ā-* because of a former laryngeal) - in Greek φιλό-ξεινος 'love the guest!' original –ε- is altered to –ο- after the model of the joint vowel –ο- elsewhere. Hence, at least verbal compounds with a governed final member and the element *–át/d-* originally were "syntactic compounds" whose stress reflects the main stressed verb preceding the object.

2.3 Prepositional compounds with governed final member

Prepositional compounds with a governed final member have temporal or local meaning: often they show a formative *-a-*, *-i-*, *-ya-* or -ιο-, respectively: *úpa-māsya-* 'occurring every month', *ánu-patha-* 'following the road', *ántas-patha-* 'being on the way', *antár-goṣṭha-* 'being inside the stable', *api-prāṇa-* 'uttered with every breath', *ápi-vrata-* 'sharing in the same religious acts', *abhí-dyu-* 'directed to heaven', *ā́-pathi-* 'travelling hither or near', *ā́-deva-* 'turning towards the gods', *upári-budhna-* 'raised above the ground', ἀντί-

[8] But see Gotō 1987: 234 note 508: imperative.

θεος 'equal to the gods', ἐγ-κέφαλος 'within the head, brain', ἔμ-πεδος 'in the ground, firm-set', ἐν-άλιος 'in the sea', ἐπι-χώριος 'native, indigenous', παρα-θαλάττιος 'beside the sea', παρα-ποτάμιος 'beside or near a river', παρά-δοξος 'contrary to expectation, incredible' (substantivized μέτ-ωπον 'the space between the eyes'). Also, adjectives or adverbs occur as initial member: homer. πάν-νυχιος 'all night long', homer. παν-ημέριος 'the whole day', gr. μεσο-νύκτιος 'at midnight', Vedic *adhas-pad-á-* 'placed under the feet'. In Vedic, those compounds show a twofold accentuation. Either the preposition is stressed, and that in the same way as in the single word (compare *ádhi-gartya-* 'being on the driver's seat') or the second member (see below). For compounds with stress on the initial member one has to consider the position of adverbs and prepositions in Vedic prose. When used with substantives, genuine prepositions as a rule follow their case, while prepositional adverbs precede it. According to Macdonell (1966: 285) the reason of this is that the former supplement the sense of the case, while the latter modify the sense much more emphatically. But prepositions, too, can precede the governed noun: *ádhi ráthe* 'on the carriage' (Wackernagel 1905: 310). Since this phrase contains two stresses one has to be deleted when the two words are compounded. Stress on the initial member in prepositional compounds[9] can be accounted for by the mentioned strength hierarchy rule [10].

2.4 Verbal compounds with a governed initial member

Verbal compounds with a governed initial member are stressed on the verbal element and function as agent-nouns: *havir-ád-* 'eating the oblation', *sam-ídh-* 'flaming, burning', *jyotiṣ-kṛ́t-* 'creating light', (oxytonic) *abhayaṃ-kará-* 'causing safety', *abhimāti-ṣāhá-* 'conquering enemies', *amitra-khādá-* 'devouring his enemies', *grāva-grābhá-* 'one who handles the Soma stones', *jana-bhakṣá-* 'devouring men', *tad-vaśá-* 'longing for that', *deva-vandá-* 'praising the gods', *puraṃ-dará-* 'destroyer of strongholds', *bhuvana-cyavá-* 'shaking the world'[11], *iṣu-dhí-* 'a quiver', *utsa-dhí-* 'the receptacle of a spring', *uda-dhí-* 'holding water, the ocean', *garbhadhí-* 'nest', *śeva-dhí-* 'wealth, treasure' (literally 'containing dear things'), *uktha-śaṁsín-* 'uttering the

[9] In some cases in English, too, the prefix shows a growing tendency to receive the main stress while the heavy stress of the basis is shifted to a full middle stress: súbwày (Marchand 1969: 138f.).

[10] Prepositions in prepositional compounds may have become dominant prefixes which are inherently main stressed. According to Halle and Vergnaug (1987: 86 note 6), here the element which loses its stress is the stem.

[11] Because of stress of the initial member *bahuvrīhis* seem to be *abhrá-varṣa-* 'dripping or raining from the clouds', *marúd-vṛdha-* 'rejoicing in the Maruts', *dharúṇa-hvara-* 'trembling in its foundations', *dhī́-raṇa-* 'delighting in devotion', *rátha-kṣaya-* 'sitting in a chariot'. A locative *suté* is to be found in *suté-kara-* 'performing (recitation of certain texts) at the preparation of the Soma', *suté-raṇa-* 'delighting in Soma'.

Ukthas', *surūpa-kṛtnú-* 'able to create beautiful things', *vanar-gú-* 'moving about in woods', (paroxytonic) *kratu-prā́van-* 'granting a desire or power' (with stress on a heavy syllable; see below). In Vedic and Greek, other types of polysyllabic agent-nouns are also often stressed on the final part of the word: Greek ψευδής 'lying, false' (ψεῦδος 'falsehood'), Vedic *apás-* 'active' (*ápas-* 'work'), *vīrayú-* 'heroic', *karaṇá-* 'skilfull' (substantivized AV *káraṇa-* 'a helper, companion'), *krośaná-* 'crying', *reśaná-* 'injuring', *dāmán-* 'giver', *darmáṇ-* 'demolisher' (Wackernagel-Debrunner 1954: 181, 231, 760f., 843[12]) and the more nominal type of the two agent-nouns in *–tar-*, *dātár-* 'giver' (Lühr 2002: 8ff.). Therefore, it is possible that the frequent stress on the suffix reflects an old stress distribution caused by the the above-mentioned contrast to the stressing of verbal nouns. This pattern then must have spread to determinative compounds in the function of agent-nouns.[13]

2.5 Determinative compounds

The subtype with a substantive both as initial and final member is either stressed on both members (*gnā́s-páti-* 'husband of a divine wife'), or on one. In the case of one stress, the initial member regularly is stressed: *gṛhá-pati-* 'householder' (22 compounds in *–pati-*, 10 in *–patnī* in the RV), *devá-kṣatra-* 'domain of the gods'. The same rule applies to determinative compounds with an adjective as initial member: RV I-IX *candrá-mās-* 'moon', *bāhv-òjasā* 'with strength of arm', *pūrṇá-māsa-* 'full moon', *úlūka-yātu-* 'a demon in the shape of an owl', *páḍ-bīśa-* 'fetter', *madhyáṃ-dina-* 'midday', *viśvá-mānuṣa-* 'every mortal', RV X,89,12 *drógha-mitra-* 'a mischievous friend', *nítya-hotar-* 'a offerer who is always sacrificing', *vācā́-stena-* 'one who makes mischief by his words', *viśvá-deva-* 'all-divine', *vṛṣā́-kapi-* 'man-ape', *sóma-gopā-* 'keeper of Soma'. Also, some determinative compounds with a prefix or preposition occur: *sú-hotar-* 'a good offerer', *prá-pad-a-* 'the point of the foot', *prá-uga-* 'the forepart of the shafts of a chariot'; note the Greek πρό-δομος 'before the house', προ-άγων 'preliminary contest'. If stress on the initial member is the usual stressing in RV, phrasal stress, too, is imitated, whereby the left stress prevails. But after the RV, more and more the final member gets stressed; compare RV *hiraṇya-piṇḍá-* 'a lump of gold' (Wackernagel 1905: 265ff.). It can be supposed that this stress shift is due to the effort to distinguish *bahuvrīhis* and determinative compounds.

---

[12] The type *cákri-* 'doing, effecting' is stressed on the reduplicative syllable in accordance with the present stems *tíṣṭha-* 'stand', *piba-* 'drink'. Agent-nouns in *–van-*, too, (for example Vedic *kṛ́tvan-* 'causing, effecting') are stressed on the first element (Wackernagel and Debrunner 1954: 291f., 894f.). Some of these compounds as Vedic *tákvan-* 'robber' are substantives.

[13] Stress on a second member in such compounds can be considered as a kind of dominant suffix. For generalization of stress patterns see Drachman and Malikouti-Drachman 1999: 903.

Another type of determinative compound normally stressed on the initial member are compounds with a verbal adjective on *–ta-* or *–na-* or verbal nouns on *–ti-*: Vedic *agní-mūḍha-* `made insane by Agni', *ádri-ṣuta-* `prepared with stones', *índra-jūta-* `promoted by Indra', *índra-prasūta-* `caused by Indra', *índra-jūta-* `promoted by Indra', *tvā́-datta-* `given by thee', *devá-kṛta-* `made by the gods', *devá-hita-* `arranged by the gods', *devé-ṣita-* `sent by the gods', *bāhú-cyuta-* `fallen from the arm', *bháge-'vita-* `satisfied with good fortune', *yajñá-vṛddha-* `exalted with sacrifice', *sóma-śita-* `sharpened by Soma', *dáṁsu-jūta-* `wonderfully quick', *náva-jāta-* `fresh, new', *puró-hita-* `placed in front, appointed', *canó-hita-* `made favourable', *sána-śruta-* `famous of old', *ní-hita-* `placed', *dúr-dhita-* `badly arranged', *sú-kṛta-*`well done', *sú-jāta-* `well born', *sú-dhita-* `well placed', *sú-śruta-* `very famous', *sú-samiddha-* `well kindled', *ví-binna-* `split', *úd-iti-* `ascending', *hásta-cyuti-* `quick motion of the hands', *arká-sāti-* `poetical inspiration', *dyumná-hūti-* `inspired invocation', *náma-ukti-* `homage', *nṛ́-pīti-* `protection of men', *bráhma-kṛti-* `prayer', *vā́ja-sāti-* `the winning of a prize', *havyá-dāti-* `conveying oblations'. Like other stressings, this stressing is undoubtedly inherited from Proto-Indo-European: see Greek ἀπό-βλητος `to be thrown away or aside', ἀνδρό-κμητος `wrought by men's hands', ἀνά-βλησις `putting off, delay' (Wackernagel 1905: 214). Though here phrasal stress may be the starting point, as well, there is a further possibility for explaining stress on the initial member: Since as single words adjectives on Proto-Indo-European **–tó-* or **–nó-* and verbal nouns on **–tí-* are stressed on this suffix, some kind of rhythmical rule could have applied in the compound comparable to the well known example Engl.

w	w	s		s	w	s
three	red	shirts	→	three	red	shirts

Here, a string of two or more adjacent weak and equally prominent elements forms a lapse which is resolved by strengthening one of these elements, the first (i.e. three) (Visch 1999: 162f.).

w	w	s	→	s	w	s	
**ni*	*d^{h}ə*	*tós*		**ní*	*d^{h}ə*	*tòs*	(Proto-Indo-European)
ni	*hi*	*táḥ*		*ní*	*hi*	*tàḥ*	(Vedic)

w	w	s	→	s	w	s
**u.di*		*tís*		**ú.di*		*tìs*

In Vedic, compounds with a prefix as the initial member could permanently be referred to the simplicia, for simplex verbal adjectives on stressed *-tá-*, *-ná-* and simplex verbal nouns on *-tí-* were a productive word pattern throughout the whole Vedic period. And *bahuvrīhis* show that there is reason to believe that some rhythmical rule is of importance in the case of the determinative compounds: In *bahuvrīhis,* the final member cannot regularly be referred to a single word with stress on the last syllable; therefore stress is often shifted from a prosodic weak element in the initial member. If the compared rhythmical pattern is the correct explanation for retaining stress on the first syllable of determinative compounds on *-ta-*, *-na-* and *-ti-*, this stressing must then be generalized by using words other than prepositions as initial members as well: *índra-jūta-* 'promoted by Indra', *dáṁsu-jūta-* 'wonderfully quick', *hásta-cyuti-* 'quick motion of the hand'.

In particular, the fact that stress is mostly retained in determinative compounds with a verbal adjective on *–ta-* and a negative prefix *á(n)-* as the initial member can be explained by this rhythmical rule: *á-kṛta-* 'undone', *á-kṣita-* 'undecayed', *á-cyuta-* 'not fallen', *á-jāta-* 'unborn', *á-jñāta-* 'unknown', *á-tūrta-* 'not outdone, unhurt', *á-dabhda-* 'not deceived', *á-dughda-* 'not milked out', *á-dṛpta-* 'not infatuated', *á-dhṛṣṭa-* 'not bold', *án-āpta-* 'unattained', *á-mita-* 'unmeasured', *á-mṛkta-* 'unhurt', *á-riṣṭa-* 'unhurt', *á-vṛta-* 'unchecked', *á-stuta-* 'not praised'; compare further *á-kṣiti-* 'imperishable'. Supposing that Proto-Indo-European **ń̥-* 'un-' was originally stressed (Knauer 1885: 67), for it denotes a negation or contrast to something, and that this stressing continued into Vedic and Greek, the compound-type *á-kṛta-* is almost always stressed on the negative prefix, because it was always possible to refer that compound to the simplex *kṛtá-* rhythmically[14].

Summary: Our analysis of the normal position of stress in Vedic endo- and exocentric compounds has proven that this phenomenon has different motivations: In *bahuvrīhis* and in determinative compounds with stress on the initial member, this position imitates phrasal accent: In nominal sentences like *Schwárz (sind) die Pferde* the emphasized predicative precedes the subject and has the main stress. To delete stress on the final member, either stress on the adjective is enforced or the general strength hierarchy rule applies: "The left stress is stronger than the right one". Verbal compounds with a governed final member, too, come from a phrase, in Vedic primarily a conjunction of a third Singular Present Injunctive of a verb in *-áya-* and a governed object, whereby the general Injunctive is used. Stress was shifted to the heavy ultimate *–át/d-* (consonant -) of the first member and then generalized; stress on the final member is deleted according to the aforementioned strength hierarchy rule. Original phrasal stressing also determines the stress of prepositional compounds with a governed final member. On the other hand, verbal compounds with a governed final member are stressed on the final member, possibly in analogy to the mainly suffix-stressed derivational agent-nouns.

[14] In other adjectives with negative prefix *á(n)-* stress on this element is not preserved as well; compare *á-vihvarant-* 'undeviating', *á-kṣiyant-* 'not inhabiting, unsettled', *á-khanant-* 'not digging', *á-krīḍant-* 'not playing', *á-riṣaṇya-* 'not failing' vs. *a-codánt-* 'not driving or impelling' (Wackernagel 1905: 216ff.).

Determinative compounds with a verbal adjective in *–ta-*, *-na-* or verbal noun in *–ti-* and stress on the initial member can also imitate phrasal stress. Additionally, a rhythmical rule applies here: Stress on the initial member, especially the prefix, is retained, for reference to simplicia with stress on the final syllable always was at hand. Therefore, unlike in *bahuvrīhis*, stress was rarely shifted from the first member. This rule also relates to the negative prefix *á(n)-* in determinative compounds, which is supposed to be stressed in Proto-Indo-European.

3 Counterexamples to the general stress rules in Vedic compounds

3.1 bahuvrīhis

Many *bahuvrīhis* are stressed on the final member, especially on "compositionell" *–á-*. For this formative, probably an adjectivizing element (see Proto-Indo-European **udr-ó-* 'watery') which became productive to some extent in Vedic and Greek, inheritance from Proto-Indo-European is stated; compare Greek νεο-χμ-óς 'having new' and Vedic *bhūry-akṣ-á-* 'many-eyed' (*ákṣ-*), *deva-karm-á-* 'master of sacred work' (literally 'being engaged in sacred work'), *ardha-garbhá-* 'being inside the womb' (*gárbha-*). As the formative attracts stress, it overrides language specific rules for the stressing of compounds (Wackernagel 1905: 120). But why is this suffix stressed? Stressed "compositionell" *–á-* within a *bahuvrīhi* serves to contrast the adjectival value of the whole compound with the substantive in the final member. Consequently, stress on "compositionell" *–á-* in Vedic originally was a contrastive stress, whose function was the distinction between substantives and adjectives just as in the mentioned pair *éṣa-* m. 'the act of seeking or going after' vs. *eṣá-* 'gliding, running, hastening' (Wackernagel & Debrunner 1954: 139).

The final member can also be stressed, if it contains a heavy syllable: – *pā́na-*: *indra-pā́na-* 'being worthy to be Indra's drink', *jana-pā́na-* 'being a beverage for men', *deva-pā́na-* 'serving the gods for a beverage', *nṛ-pā́ṇa-* 'giving drink to men', *vṛṣa-pā́ṇa-* 'being drunk by men'. Further cases of paroxytonized final members are to be mentioned: *puru-vā́ja-* 'having power', *puru-vā́ra-* 'being rich in gifts', *puru-śā́ka-* 'being helpful', *dvi-dhā́ra-* 'forming two streams (from water)', *dvi-jā́ni-* 'having two wives', *tri-nā́bhi-* 'having three naves (a wheel)', *su-dā́nu-* 'pouring out', *dur-ṇā́man-* name of a disease demon (literally 'having bad names'), *raghu-yā́man-* 'going quickly', *tri-dhā́tu-* 'consisting of three parts', *su-dā́tu-* 'being easy to divide', *su-dī́diti-* 'flaming brightly', *puru-rū́pa-* 'having a multiformity', *dur-éva-* 'being ill-disposed', *su-kṣétra-* 'having an excellent field', *puru-péśa-* 'having multiformed shapes', *puru-médha-* 'being endowed with wisdom', *āśu-héman-* 'running on quickly' (literally 'having a quick drive'), *sa-jóṣa-* 'being associated together', *su-jyótis-* 'shining very brightly'. Cases of stress retraction also occur: *puru-vīra-* 'being in possession of many men or male offspring', *su-vīra-* 'being very manly, heroic' (*vīrá-* 'man, hero'), *tuvi-grīva-* 'having a powerful neck' (*grīvá-* 'neck'). Add stems in *–as-*: *kṣetra-sā́dhas-* 'one, who divides the fields, fixes the landmarks', *abhibhūty-ójas-* 'having superior power', *nṛ-péśas-* 'being formed by or consisting of men', *nṛ-vā́has-* 'conveying men' (*vā́has-* 'conveying'), *nṛ-mánas-* 'having the mind of heroes, heroic') vs. *agní-bhrājas-* 'possessing fiery splendour', *áśva-peśas-* 'being decorated with horses', *ukthá-vāhas-* 'offering verses'; compare also the below mentioned compounds *tuvi-rā́dhas-* 'giving much', *sa-bā́dhas-* 'being urgent', *dur-vā́sas-* 'being poorly clad', *puru-péśas-* 'being multiformed', *puru-bhójas-* 'containing many means of enjoyments', *āśu-héṣas-* 'having quick missiles', *vīḍu-dvéṣas-* 'hating the strong or hating strongly', *a-śéṣas-* 'having no descendants', *su-cétas-* 'having great intelligence' (Garbe 1877: 504). But note that stress on the first syllable of an *s*-stem in the final member does not occur in the case of negative prefix *a(n)-*: *a-cetás-* 'being imprudent' (**cétas-*), *a-codás-* 'being free from compulsion' (**códas-*), *a-javás-* 'being not quick, inactive' (*jávas-* 'quickness'), *an-enás-* 'being blameless, sinless' (*énas-* 'mischief, crime'), *an-ehás-* 'having no rival' (*éhas-* 'rivalry'), *a-peśás-* 'being without a shape' (*péśas-* 'shape'), *a-repás-* 'having no spot' (*répas-* 'spot').

The just given deviations from the normal stressing concern the prosodic structure of the final member: "compositionell" *–á-*, and often heavy syllables, attract stress. Far more differences are caused by the prosody of the initial member. So, contrary to the above given rule, that the initial member retains stress in the same way as in the single word, an initial disyllabic member becomes an oxytone if the first vowel is an originally stressed *í*: Vedic *viśvá-karma-* 'accomplishing everything', *viśvá-bhānu-* 'all illumining', *viśvá-kṛṣṭi-* 'dwelling among all men', *viśvá-sarṣani-* 'having reference to the whole of mankind', *viśvá-janya-* 'containing all men, existing everywhere', *viśvá-tūrti-* 'being all-surpassing', *viśvá-deva-* '(being supported) by all gods', *śvá-dhāyas-* 'all-sustaining', *viśvá-dhena-* 'being all-feeding', *viśvá-peśas-* 'containing all adornment', *viśvá-psu-* 'having all forms', *viśvá-bharas-* 'all-supporting', *viśvá-bheṣaja-* 'containing all remedies', *viśvá-bhojas-* 'all-nourishing', *viśvá-manas-* 'perceiving everything', *viśvá-manus-* 'dwelling among all men', *viśvá-mahas-* 'being all-powerful or all-pleasant', *viśvá-rūpa-* 'being many-coloured', *viśvá-vāra-* 'containing all good things', *viśvá-vedas-* 'all-possessing', *viśvá-vyacas-* 'embracing or absorbing all things', *viśvá-śambhū-* 'being beneficial to all', *viśvá-śardhas-* 'being in a complete troop', *viśvá-ścandra-* 'being all-glittering', *viśvá-śruṣṭi-* 'being compliant to all', *viśvá-saubhaga-* 'bringing all prosperity', *viśvā́-nara-* 'relating to or existing among', *viśvā́-mitra-* 'being friend of all', *viśvā́-vasu-* 'being beneficent to all'.

But stress is retracted in *catúr-*: *cátur-aṅga-* 'having four limbs', *cátur-anīka-* 'having four faces (Varuṇa)', *cátur-aśri-* 'quadrangular', *cátur-bhṛṣṭi-* 'four-cornered, quadrangular', *cátur-yuga-* 'drawn by four (horses)', *cátur-vaya-* 'fourfold', *cátuḥ-śṛṅga-* 'four-horned', *cátuṣ-kaparda-* 'having four tufts', *cátuṣ-pad-* 'having four feet', *cátuḥ-samudra-* 'having four seas'. Only *catur-akṣ-á-* 'four-eyed' is stressed on the final member, due to "compositionell"*-á-*.

The final member is stressed, too, if the initial member is *śiti-*: *śiti-pád-* 'white-footed', *śiti-pṛṣṭhá-* 'white-backed'. Contrary to *visvá-*, stress does not get shifted to the second syllable, for it contains an *i*. But *híri-* shows vacillation: *híri-śmaśru-* 'golden-bearded' vs. *hiri-śiprá-* 'golden-cheeked' (with originally not oxytonized final member *śiprā-* 'the cheeks').

Once is found *hari-śrī-* 'beautifully yellow, goldcoloured' vs. *hári-dhāyas-* 'having or giving yellowish streams', *hári-yoga-* 'having a yoke of bay horses', *hári-varpas-* 'having a yellowish or greenish appearance', *hári-vrata-* 'one who has a yellow sphere or yellow surroundings', *hári-śipra-* 'having yellow (golden) cheek-guards on one's helmet', *hári-śmaśru-* 'having a ruddy or yellow beard'. This member is stressed in other compounds on *-śrī-*, too, probably because of the heavy syllable. In any case, those compounds are lexicalized.

Further examples for stress shifting are the *bahuvrīhis* with the initial member in *tṛṣú-* 'greedy', *kṛdhú-* 'mutilated', *svādú-* 'sweet', *bahú-* 'much', *purú-* 'many': *tṛṣu-cyávas-* 'moving greedily' (literally 'having greedy movement'), *kṛdhu-kárṇa-* 'having short ears', *svādu-ṣaṃsád-* 'sitting round dainties', *bahú-prajā-* 'being blessed with a large offspring'; and oxytonized *bahv-anná-* 'having rich food' (*ánna-* 'food'); *puru-kṣú-* 'being rich in cattle', *puru-tmán-* 'existing variously', *puru-dáṃsa-* 'abounding in mighty or wonderful deeds', *puru-dáṃsas-* id., *puru-drapsá-* 'abounding in drops of water', *puru-nṛmṇá-* 'displaying great valour', *puru-pánthā-* proper name (literally 'having many paths'), *puru-péśa(s)-* 'having many forms', *puru-bhójas-* 'containing many means of enjoyments', *puru-mántu-* 'being full of wisdom', *puru-māyá-* 'possessing various arts or virtues', *puru-mīḍhá-* proper name (literally 'having many prizes'), *puru-médha-* 'endowed with wisdom', *puru-rátha-* 'having many chariots', *puru-rū́pa-* 'having many shapes', *puru-várpas-* id., *puru-vā́ja-* 'being powerful', *puru-vā́ra-* 'having an ample tail or mane; being rich in gifts', *puru-vratá-* 'having many ordinances', *puru-śā́ka-* 'being helpful' (one times vocative *purú-nāman* 'having many names'); with stress retraction *puru-vīra-* 'having a lot of men or male offspring' (*vīrá-* 'man, hero'). Note that if *purú-* is enlarged by a suffix, stress on the initial member is retained: *purudhá-pratīka-* 'appearing variously'.

Other adjectives show vacillation on *-ú-*: *āśú-* 'fast, quick': *āśv-àpas-* 'acting quickly' (*ápas-* 'work'), *āśv-àśva-* 'possessing quick horses' vs. *āśu-*

héṣas- 'having quick missiles', *āśú-héman-* 'running on quickly', *āśú-pátvan-* 'flying quickly';

urú-: *urú-gavyūti-* 'having a wide domain or territory', *urú-dhāra-* 'giving a broad stream, streaming abundantly', *urú-yuga-* 'having a broad yoke', *urú-loka-* 'being visible to a distance' vs. *uru-kṣáya-* 'occupying spacious dwellings', *uru-cakrá-* 'having wide wheels', *uru-cákṣas-* 'far-seeing', *uru-jráyas-* 'moving in a wide course', *uru-vyácas-* 'occupying wide space'; and oxytonesis by changing "theme": *urū-ṇas-á-* 'broad-nosed';

tuví- 'much': *tuví-deṣṇa-* 'giving much', *tuví-brahman-* 'very devoted' (*bráhman-* 'swelling of the spirit'), *tuví-magha-* 'giving much', *tuví-vāja-* 'abounding in food' vs. *tuvi-rā́dhas-* 'giving much' etc. (and with stress retraction from the last syllable *tuvi-grī́va-* 'powerful-necked': *grīvá-* 'neck');

pṛthú- 'broad, wide': *pṛthú-pāṇi-* 'broad-handed', *pṛthú-pragāṇa-* 'having a wide approach or access', *pṛthú-pragāman-* 'wide-striding', *pṛthú-budhna-* 'broad-based' vs. *pṛthu-gmán-* 'broad-pathed', *pṛthu-jráya-* 'widely extended', *pṛthu-pákṣas-* 'broad-flanked', *pṛthu-párśu-* 'armed with large sickles', *pṛthu-pā́jas-* 'far-shining', *pṛthu-budhná-* 'broad-based', *pṛthu-śrávas-* 'far-famed, of wide renown';

raghú- 'hastening, rapid': *raghú-vartani-* 'lightly rolling or turning' vs. *raghu-yā́man-* 'going quickly', *raghu-pátman-* 'flying or moving quickly', *raghu-pátvan-* id.;

vibhú- 'being everywhere': *vibhū́-vasu-* 'possessing mighty treasures or wealth' (with stress on the lengthened *-ú-* caused by a former laryngeal) vs. *vibhu-krátu-* 'strong, heroic';

vīḍú- 'strong, firm': *vīḍú-jambha-* 'strong-jawed', *vīḍú-pāṇi-* 'strong-handed', *vīḍú-haras-* 'seizing firmly', *vīḍv-àṅga-* 'strong-limbed, firm in body' vs. *vīḍu-pāṇí-* 'strong-handed', *vīḍu-dvéṣas-* 'hating the strong or hating strongly', *vīḍu-pátman-* 'flying strongly or incessantly'[15].

Substantives as the initial member in *-í* can also show stress shift: *agni-jihvā́-* 'having Agni for tongue', *agni-tápas-* 'hot as fire', *agni-śrī́-* 'having the brightness of Agni' vs. *agní-dūta-* 'having Agni for a messenger', *agní-bhrājas-* 'possessing fiery splendour', *agní-rūpa-* 'fire-shaped', *agní-hotar-* 'having Agni for a priest'; *maṇi-grīvá-* 'jewel-necked' (Garbe 1877: 507).

Stress shift from *-í* in a disyllabic initial member is also valid for prepositions: *abhi-ṣená-* 'directing arrows against' vs. *abhí-vīra-* 'surrounded by heroes'. But stress from a sequence *á – i* in the initial member can be shifted also: *pari-manyú-* 'being wrathful, angry' (possibly with adjustment to the derivatives in *-yú-*). Yet, word initial stress is much more frequent in this type: *áty-urmi-* 'overflowing', *práti-veśa-* 'neighbour', literally 'living in the neighbourhood', *práti-rūpa-* 'being the counterpart of any realform', *ánty-ūti-* 'being at hand with help', *ádhi-nirṇij-* 'covered over', *ádhi-rukma-* 'wearing

[15] Hapax legomena are cases like *ahiśuṣma-sátvan-* 'whose attendants (*sátvan-*) hiss like serpents'.

gold', *ádhi-vastra-* 'clothed', *ádhy-akṣa-* 'inspector' (literally 'having his eyes above all') (*ákṣ-*).

Accent shift also occurs if the initial member is trisyllabic and the last syllable is stressed: *darśata-śrī-* 'being of conspicuous splendour' (*darśatá-* 'visible, striking the eye').

Further stress in the monosyllables *dví-*, *trí-* as initial members is shifted: *dvi-jánman-* 'having a double birth', *dvi-jā́ni-* 'having two wives', *dvi-dhā́ra-* 'forming two streams', *dvi-pád-* 'two-footed', *dvi-bándhu-* proper name (literally 'having double relationship', *dvi-bárhas-* 'doubly close or thick or strong', *dvi-vartaní-* 'walking on two paths' (literally 'having two paths') vs. *dví-śavas-* 'having or granting twofold strength'; *tri-kakúbh-* 'three-pointed', *tri-cakrá-* 'having three wheels', *tri-tántu-* 'being thrice woven', *tri-dhā́tu-* 'consisting of three parts', *tri-nā́bhi-* 'three-naved (a wheel)', *tri-pád-* 'three-footed', *tri-pājasyá-* 'having three flanks', *tri-pṛṣṭhá-* 'having three backs or surfaces', *tri-mántu-* 'offering threefold advice', *tri-várūtha-* 'protecting in three ways' etc. vs. *try-àmbaka-* 'three-eyed', *try-àruṇa-* proper name (literally 'having three brown things'), *try-àruṣa-* 'marked red in three places', *trý-āśir-* 'mixed with three products of milk'.

Add some compounds with *sa-* 'with' as the initial member, whose final member is a *s*-stem: *sa-cánas-* 'being in harmony with', *sa-jóṣas-* 'being associated together', *sa-práthas-* 'being extensive, wide', *sa-bā́dhas-* 'being eagerly' (see above), or a stem on *–yú-*: *sa-manyú-* 'having the same mind' (compare stress in *pari-manyú-* 'wrathful, angry'); besides *sa-jóṣa-* 'associated together', *sa-dṛ́ś-* 'fit, proper', *sa-dṛ́śa-* 'like, resembling' vs. *sá-keta-* 'having the same intention', *sá-ratha-* 'together with the chariot', *sá-gaṇa-* 'having troops or flocks', *sá-canas-* 'being in harmony with', *sá-nābhi-* 'having the same navel; connected by the same navel or womb', *sá-nāman-* 'having the same name', *sá-nīḍa-*'having the same nest', *sá-nemi-* 'having a felly', *sá-manyu-* 'having the same mind', *sá-rūpa-* ' having the same shape'.

Among the compounds with a negative prefix *a(n)-* only a few are stressed on the prefix: *á-kaniṣṭha-* 'of whom none is the youngest', *á-kravihasta-* 'not having bloody hands', *á-joṣa-* 'being not gratified', *á-pūrvya-* 'unpreceded, first' (literally 'one who has no first person'), *á-bhaya-* 'being not dangerous', *á-śrama-* 'being indefatigable', *á-sama-* 'being unequalled' with underlying *a-* stem, *á-kūpāra-* 'being unbounded', *á-praja-* 'without progeny, childless' (*prajā́* 'children, descendants') with underlying *ā*-stem, *á-kṣiti-* 'being imperishable', *á-gu-* 'having no cows', *á-gopā-* 'without a cowherd', *á-tathā-* 'not saying *tathā* (yes)', *á-diti-* 'not tied', *á-dyu-* 'not burning', *á-dhenu-* 'yielding no milk', *án-āgas-* 'sinless, blameless', *án-āpi-* 'having no friends', *án-ūrmi-* 'not waving or fluctuating', *á-psu-* 'without food', *á-brahman-* 'without devotion', *á-mṛtyu-* 'non-death', *á-śiśu-* 'childless', *á-samāti-* 'having no equal', *á-havis-* 'not offering oblations', *á-giraukas-* 'not to be kept back by hymns' (*ókas-* 'house, home') with underlying not *a-*, *ā*-stem, *á-rāya-* 'not liberal, stingy' with suffix. On the contrary, stress on the final member shows: *a-ketú-* 'shapeless, unrecognizable', *a-gadá-* 'having no disease, healthy' (classical *gada-* 'sickness'), *a-cakrá-* 'having no wheels', *an-akṣá-* 'being blind', *an-avadyá-* 'irreproachable', *an-āśú-* 'not quick, slow', *an-idhmá-* 'having or requiring no fuel', *an-ukthá-*'hymnless', *an-ṛ́c-* 'not containing a verse from the Ṛgveda', *a-pád-* 'footless', *a-bhāgá-* 'having no share', *a-budhná-* 'bottomless', *a-yajñiyá-* 'not fit for sacrifice', *a-reṇú-* 'not dusty', *a-viṣá-* 'not poisonous', *a-vratá-* 'lawless', *a-śipadá-* 'not causing, i.e. averting the sickness called Śipada', *a-śīrṣán-* 'headless'.Whereas oxytonesis also appears in the simplex in the cases with a disyllabic basis, in the following compounds the final member is not originally oxytonized: *a-kalpá-* 'not subject to rules' (*kálpa-* 'sacred ordinance'), *a-kratú-* 'destitute of energy or power' (*krátu-* 'plan'), *a-gavyūtí-* 'without good pasturage for cattle' (*gávyūti-* 'a pasture, piece of pasture land'), *a-cetás-* 'being imprudent' (**cétas-*), *a-codás-* 'being free from compulsion or external stimulus' (**códas-*), *a-javás-* 'being not quick, inactive' (*jávas-* 'quickness'), *a-dakṣiná-* 'being not dexterous' (*dákṣiṇā* 'on the right'), *a-dāmán-* 'unbounded; not liberal' (*dā́man-* 'string, cord; 'gift'), *a-ducchuná-* 'being free from evil' (*ducchúnā-* 'misfortune'), *an-antá-* 'endless, boundless' (*ánta-* 'end, boundary'), *an-apnás-* 'destitute of means' (*ápnas-* 'possession, property'), *an-abhīśú-* 'without bridles' (*abhīśu-* 'rein, bridle'), *an-amīvá-* 'free from disease' (*ámīvā-* 'distress'), *an-aśrú-* 'tearless' (*áśru-* 'tear'), *an-aśvá-* 'having no horse' (*áśva-* 'horse'), *an-āyudhá-* 'weaponless' (*ā́yudha-* 'weapon'), *an-indrá-* 'dispensing with or disregarding Indra' (*índra-*), *an-ūdhás-* 'being udderless' (*ū́dhas-* 'breast, bosom'), *an-ená-* 'having no stags' (*énī-* 'rushing'), *an-enás-* 'blameless' (*énas-* 'mischief'), *an-ehás-* 'having no rival' (*éhas-* 'rivalry'), *a-pūruṣá-* 'being lifeless' (*púruṣa-* 'human being'), *a-peśás-* 'shapeless' (*péśas-* 'shape, form'), *a-pratí-* 'being without opponents' (*práti-* 'in opposition to'), *a-pratimāná-* 'incomporable' (*pratimā́na-* 'well-matched opponent', *a-phalá-* 'having no fruit' (*phála-* 'fruit'), *a-bandhaná-* 'without fetters' (*bándhana-* 'binding, fettering'), *a-bandhú-* 'without kindred' (*bándhu-* 'connection'), *a-balá-* 'having no power' (*bála-* 'power, strength'), *a-bhrātṛvyá-* 'having no rival' (*bhrā́tṛvya-* 'a father's brother's son'), *a-mantú-* 'being silly, ignorant' (*mántu-* 'advice, counsel'), *a-marmán-* 'having no vital part' (*márman-* 'mortal spot'), *a-mená-* 'having no wife' (*ménā-* 'woman'), *a-yakṣmá-* 'being not consumptive' (*yákṣma-* 'sickness'), *a-rakṣás-* 'being harmless, honest' (*rákṣas-* 'guarding'), *a-rajjú-* 'not having or consisting of cords' (*rájju-* 'rope, cord'), *a-rathá-* 'having no car' (*rátha-*'chariot, car'), *a-rapás-* 'not hurting, beneficial' (*rápas-* 'defect, injury'), *a-rasá-* 'being without taste' (*rása-* 'sap, juice'), *a-repás-* 'being spotless' (*répas-* 'spot, stain'), *a-vayuná-* 'being indistinguishable' (*vayúna-* 'moving, active'), *a-vātá-* 'being without wind' (*vā́ta-* 'wind'), *a-śatrú-* 'having no adversary' (*śátru-* 'enemy, rival'), *a-śimidá-* 'being not destructive like a Śimidā' (*śímidā-* name of a female demon), *a-śramá-* 'being indefatigable' (*śráma-* 'fatigue, weariness'), *a-sapatná-* 'being without a rival' (*sapátna-* 'rival, adversary', *sapátnī-* 'female rival'), *a-samaná-* 'not remaining united' (*sámana-* 'meeting'), *a-sūryá-* 'being sunless' (*sū́rya-* 'sun'), *a-hastá-* 'being handless' (*hásta-* 'hand'). Therefore, the rule is: Combine destressed prefix *a(n)-* with oxytonesis. The only exception is *a-śéṣas-* 'without descendants' vs. *śéṣas-* 'offspring' (Wackernagel 1905: 120).

To explain why the negative prefix *a(n)-* is mostly unstressed in *bahuvrīhis*, though its preform **ń̥-* was stressed in Proto-Indo-European (see above) and destressed *a(n)-* deviates from the usual stress of this composition type, one has to consider, on the one hand, that *á* in the outcome *á(n)-* is the most unmarked vowel in stressed syllables; much more marked is *i/u*:

Markedness of vowels in heads of metrical units:

NOHEAD/*ə* >> NOHEAD/*i,u* >> NOHEAD/*a*
(Kenstowicz 1994; Löhken 1997; 38).

On the other hand, determinative compounds show expected stress on this prefix, apart from a few exceptions like the paroxytones *a-kṣára-* 'imperishable', *a-jára-* 'ever young', *a-dábha-* 'not injuring' and the oxytones *a-tṛpá-* 'not satisfied', *a-vadhá-* 'not hurting', *a-vṛdhá-* 'not rendering prosperous' (Wackernagel 1905: 215). It is apparent that stress in *bahuvrīhis* and determinative compounds like *a-kalpá-* 'not subject to rules' or *á-kṛta-* 'undone' respectively has a contrastive function. For the hearer, the last member in Vedic *bahuvrīhis* with *a(n)-* is stressed in order to distinguish this type of compound from determinative compounds with the corresponding prefix: Stress in the oxytone *a-kalpá-* is exactly opposed to the type *á-kṛta-* with stress on the initial syllable. But why is stress shifted in *bahuvrīhis* and not in determinative compounds with *á(n)-*? Firstly, in determinative compounds, the aforementioned rhythmical rule applies which prevents stress from getting shifted, so that stress in these compounds is fixed on the negative prefix *á(n)-*. Secondly, stressed "compositionell" *–á-* within a *bahuvrīhi* is a contrastive stress opposing the "adjective" of the whole compound to the substantive in the final member, whereas in *bahuvrīhis* with *a(n)-* the stressed suffix contrasts with the unstressed prefix both containing the same vowel *-a-*. Therefore, in *bahuvrīhis* with *a(n)-* , a fixed stress pattern arose, and from "compositionell" *–á-* oxytonesis generalized to other stems.

In *bahuvrīhis* with *duṣ-*, stress is shifted, too, whereby original stress on the final member is retained: *dur-ā́dhī-* 'meditating evil', *dur-éva-* 'being ill-disposed', *dur-dṛ́śīka-* 'looking bad', *dur-dhúr-* 'badly yoked or harnessed', *dur-máda-* 'being drunken, mad', *dur-mánman-* 'evil-minded', *dur-māyú-* 'using bad arts', *dur-mitrá-* 'being unfriendly', *dur-vā́sas-* 'badly clad, naked' (literally 'having bad clothes'), *dur-vidátra-* 'ill-disposed' (only one exception:

dúr-āśir- 'badly mixed'). This points less at a contrastive stressing like in *bahuvrīhis* with *a(n)-* than at a stress shift caused by the avoidance of stressed *ú*.

The same is true of most compounds with *su-*, though more oxytones are documented: *su-kárman-* 'performing good works', *su-kiṃśuká-* 'well made of Kiṃśuka wood', *su-kīrtí-* 'having a good praise', *su-ketú-* 'being very bright', *su-krátu-* 'being skilful', *su-kṣatrá-* 'having a good dominion', *su-kṣétra-* 'having an excellent field', *su-khādí-* 'wearing beautiful bracelets or rings', *su-gándhi-* 'sweet-smelling, fragrant', *su-gábhasti-* 'having skilful hands', *su-gādhá-* 'easily fordable', *su-gú-* 'having fine cows', *su-gopā́-* 'being well protected', *su-cakrá-* 'having beatiful wheels', *su-cákṣas-* 'having good eyes', *su-cétas-* 'having great intelligence', *su-cchardís-* 'affording good shelter', *su-jániman-* 'producing or creating fair things', *su-jánman-* 'of noble birth', *su-jámbha-* 'having good jaws or strong teeth', *su-jihvá-* 'being bright-tongued, sweet-voiced', *su-jūrní-* 'blazing or glowing brightly', *su-jyótis-* 'shining very brightly', *su-trātrá-* 'guarding or protecting well', *su-dáṃsas-* 'accomplishing mighty or splendid actions', *su-dákṣa-* 'being very capable or clever', *su-dákṣina-* 'having an excellent right hand', *su-dátra-* 'granting good gifts', *su-dā́tu-* 'easily divisible', *su-dā́nu-* 'pouring out or bestowing abundantly', *su-dína* 'being clear, bright', *su-dītí-* 'flaming, shining', *su-díditi-* 'flaming brightly', *su-dṛ́śīka-* 'looking beautiful', *su-devá-* 'having well-meaning gods', *su-dyumná-* 'shining beautifully', *su-dhána-* 'being very rich', *su-dhánvan-* 'having an excellent bow', *su-dhā́tu-* 'being well-founded, secure', *su-dhī́-* 'having a good understanding' etc. But add some compounds with paroxytonesis: *su-gáva-* 'having fine cows' (*gó-* 'cow'), *su-vī́ra-* 'having good heroes' (*vīrá-* 'man, hero'), *su-dhúr-a-* 'going well under the yoke' (*dhúr-* 'yoke'), *su-pátha-* 'well passable'. Also, secondary oxytones exist: *su-dhārá-* 'streaming beautifully' (*dhā́rā-* 'flood, gush'), *su-pīvás-* 'very fat' (literally 'having much fat') (*pī́vas-* 'fat'), *su-prayás-* 'well regaled' (*práyas-* 'pleasure, enjoyment'), *su-medhá-* 'very nourishing' (*médha-* 'nourishment'), *su-śiprá-* 'having beautiful cheeks or jaws' (*śíprā-* 'the cheeks'), *su-saṃkāśá-* 'of beautiful appearance' (*sáṃkāśa-* 'look, appearance'), *su-hiraṇyá-* 'having beautiful gold' (*híraṇya-* 'gold'), *sū-pasthá-* 'forming a good place of rest' (*upástha-* 'secure place'), *su-aṅguri-* 'handsome-fingered' (*aṅgúri-* 'a finger'), *su-apatyá-* 'having good offspring' (*ápatya-* 'offspring'), *su-gārhapatyá-* 'having a wealthy household' (*gā́rhapatya-* 'household'), *su-abhiṣṭí-* 'being helpful, favourable' (*abhíṣṭi-* 'assistant, protector'), *su-abhīśú-* 'wellbridled' (*abhī́śu-* 'rein, bridle'), *su-aritrá-* 'having good oars' (*arítra-* 'propelling, driving'), *su-āyudhá-* 'having good weapons' (*ā́yudha-* 'a weapon'), *su-iṣú-* 'having good or swift arrows' (*íṣu-* 'arrow'). And two times *su-* is stressed: *sú-gabhasti-* 'having skilful hands', *sú-nīti-* 'guiding well' (besides *su-gábhasti-* id., *su-nītí-* id.).

Finally, as mentioned above, a distinction of parts of speech can be observed by stress shift. If *bahuvrīhis* are substantivized, a stressed "compositionell" suffix *–á-* is added or the stem vowel *–a-* of the final member is stressed; note the so called Dvigus AV *sahasrāhn-yá-* 'a thousand day's journey', *tri-yugá-* 'three generations'. Exceptions are seldom; see RV *á-bhaya-* 'unfearful, secure' (Wackernagel 1905: 304ff.).

Summary: Vedic *bahuvrīhis* inherited distribution of stress from Proto-Indo-European. Usually they are stressed on the initial member: [$STRESS_{In}$].

(i) If stress is retained on this member, a faithfulness constraint [MAX(word formation F)] applies: This means that every stress which is assigned by word formation type in the input has a correspondent in the output.

(ii) If stress distribution corresponds to the stress of the single word either as the initial or as the final member, a further faithfulness constraint [MAX(word F)] applies: [$MAX(w)_{In}$] and [$MAX(w)_{Fin}$]. The stressed negative prefix *á(n)-* belongs to this faithfulness constraint, as well, namely to [$MAX(w)_{In}$].

(iii) Since a lexically marked suffix *–á-*, "compositionell" *–á-* (this can be an additional suffix or a secondary stressed stem vowel *–a-*), attracts stress, a constraint [MAX(*á*)] has to be assumed, which usually is equally ranked with LEX. [MAX(*á*)] forces selection of the candidates generated by a *á*-suffix. In *bahuvrīhis* with a negative prefix oxytonesis is obligatory. This obligation is enforced by constraint [CONTR(AST)] (see (vi)). Further choice of [-*á*-] automatically violates both [$MAX(w)_{In}$] and [MAX(wf)] if the compound is inherently stressed on the initial member.

(iv) Paroxytonesis [PAR] seldom occurs apart from [WSP_{Fin}](viii) and [$MAX(w)_{Fin}$] (ii). This stressing is lexically marked, too.

(v) The constraint [UNIQ(UNESS)] serves to avoid ambiguity (Wunderlich 2001: 8). If stress is shifted to distinguish substantives from adjectives, this kind of contrastive stress shift applies. Here, too, obligation of *–á-* is enforced.

(vi) If stress is shifted from the negative prefix *á(n)-* in *bahuvrīhis* to the last syllable so that an oxytone results, a constraint [CONT(RAST)] is valid, which distinguishes these compounds from determinative compounds with stress on *á(n)-*[16].

(vii) Constraint *[+F] is a markedness constraint: Avoid [F] in the output. Generally, this phenomenon concerns the exclusion of stressed *í* or *ú* in initial members of compounds.

(viii) The relation between syllable weight and prominence is expressed by the quantity-sensitivity enforcing constraint "Weight-to-Stress-Principle" [WSP_{Fin}]

[16] Since in *bahuvrīhis* with a negative prefix *a(n-)* oxytonesis is almost always attested, whereas in other types of compounds this stress pattern is not regular, some kind of positional faithfulness occurs (see Kager's 1999: 407ff.): Positional faithfulness constraints cannot be violated if the output segment fails to occupy the relevant position. If one replaces the notion "position" by "context", since oxytonesis has to occur in the "context" unstressed *a(n)-*,a constraint [C(ontext)-MAX(ox)] could result. But the above given solution seems simplier.

(Kager 1999: 157). While there is a tendency towards this stressing, it does not occur regularly.

Often two rankings and two corresponding "winners" seem to be documented, as pairs like the *bahuvrīhis su-gábhasti-*, *su-nīthí-* vs. *sú-gabhasti-*, *sú-nīthi-* and the determinative compounds *a-praśastá-* vs. *á-praśasta-* (see below) demonstrate. In this case two or more constraints could be tied, i.e. equally ranked, in one speech level (Müller 2000a: 152). Indeed, the optimality theory allows more than one optimal candidate (Löhken 1997: 76ff.; Müller 2000b: 26f.; 2001).

	constraint 1	constraint 2	constraint 3	constraint 4
candidate A	*!			
→ candidate B		*		
→ candidate C			*	

But in Vedic one stress pattern occurs much more frequently than its counterpart. Therefore, a constraint [LEX] is assumed; a default ranking is overridden by a feature value assigned lexically (see Wunderlich's 2001: 7f. definition of MAX(lexF)). Only in the case of real doublets like *su-nīthí-* and *sú-nīthi-*, for the variant, which is from a synchronic view unregularly stressed, is strict lexicalisation assumed. This form then is excluded from competition (here *sú-nīthi-*).

Now the rankings found in *bahuvrīhis* are given – in the input the initial and final member as single words and the usual stress type of the compound are listed:

(i) The initial member is disyllabic:

(a) In a sequence stressed *í* – unstressed *a* in an initial member stress moves to *a*. The constraint [**í* – *a*] is higher ranked than [$\text{MAX(w)}_{\text{In}}$]. But MAX(wf) is observed just as in the normal type *sahásra-pad-* (√ is only used in the case of the top constraints)

Input: *víśva-*, *sahásra-*; *bhānú-*, *pád-*; $\text{STRESS}_{\text{IN}}$	**í* – *a*	$\text{MAX(w)}_{\text{In}}$	MAX(wf)
→ *viśvá-bhānu-*	√	*	
víśva-bhānu-	*!		
→ *sahásra-pad-*			
sahasra-pád-		*	*!

(b) In a sequence unstressed *a* – stressed *ú-* in an initial member stress moves to *a*: [**a* – *ú*]$_{\text{In}}$. In one compound with "compositionell" *–á-* oxytonesis occurs, wherefore lexicalisation is assumed. With the exception of the *bahuvrīhis* with *a(n)-* (see above) constraints which refer to stress on the final member generally are not relevant for the evaluation of the candidates. For if the initial member is stressed, MAX(w)$_{Fin}$ is violated in every case. But if the final member is stressed, either original stress can be retained or it deviates from the stressing as single word. For instance, stress can be shifted from the ultimate to the penultimate in order to observe the constraint [WSP$_{Fin}$].

Input: *catúr-*; *(áśri-)*[17], *kákṣa-*; STRESS$_{In}$	LEX	**a – ú*	*-á-*	MAX(w)$_{In}$	MAX(wf)	MAX(w)$_{Fin}$	WSP$_{Fin}$
→ *cátur-aśri-*		√		*		*	
catúr-aśri-		*!				*	
→ *catur-kakṣá-*	√	√	√	*	*	*	

(c) In a sequence stressed *í-* unstressed *i-* in an initial member, stress can move to the final member either to the place where stress is located as single word [MAX(w)$_{Fin}$] or the compound becomes an oxytone [*-á-*]. Whereas compounds with *śíti-* are always stressed on the final member:

Input: *śíti-*; *pṛṣṭhá-*; STRESS$_{In}$	**í – i*	*-á-*	MAX(w)$_{In}$	MAX(wf)	MAX(w)$_{Fin}$	WSP$_{Fin}$
→ *śiti-pṛṣṭhá-*	√	√	*	*		
śíti-pṛṣṭha-	*!	*			*	

compounds with *híri-* have vacillating stress. Once *híri-* is documented:

Input: *híri-*, *síti-*; *śiprá-*, *śmáśru-*, *pṛṣṭhá-*; STRESS$_{In}$	LEX	**í – i*	*-á-*	MAX(w)$_{In}$	MAX(wf)	MAX(w)$_{Fin}$	WSP$_{Fin}$
→ *hiri-śiprá-*		√	√	*	*	*	
→ *híri-śmaśru-*	√	*				*	
→ *śiti-pṛṣṭhá-*		√	√	*	*		
śíti-pṛṣṭha-	*!	*	*			*	

(d) In a sequence stressed *á-* unstressed *i-* in an initial member, stress is usually retained and [MAX(wf)] regularly observed. The compounds with a sequence *a – i* are lexicalized. *[*a – í*] is excluded.

[17] Round brackets mean that this word is not documented in the RV.

Input: *hári-*, *pári-*, *práti-*; *śrī́-*, *yóga-*, *manyú-*, *veśá-*; $STRESS_{In}$	LEX	**a* - *í*	$MAX(w)_{IN}$	MAX(wf)	$MAX(w)_{Fin}$	WSP_{Fin}
→ *hari-śrī́-*	√		*	*		
→ *hári-yoga-*					*	*
harí-yoga-	*!	*	*		*	*
→ *pari-manyú-*	√		*	*		
→ *práti-veśa-*					*	*

(e) If the initial member ends in stressed *-í* or *-ú*, stress is usually shifted to the final member - either to the place where stress is located as single word or the compound becomes an oxytone. Besides, in a final member, stress can be retracted to a heavy syllable [WSP_{Fin}]:

Input: *kṛdhú-*, *bahú-*, *urú-*, *tuví-*, *agní-*, *abhí-*; *kárṇa-*, *ánna-*, *loká-*, *vā́ja-*, *bráhman-*, *grīvā́-*, *jihvā́-*, *-dūtá-*, *sénā-*, *vīrá-*; $STRESS_{In}$	LEX	*-*í/ú*	*-á-*	$Max(w)_{In}$	MAX(wf)	$MAX(w)_{Fin}$	WSP_{Fin}
→ *kṛdhu-kárṇa-*		√	*	*	*		
→ *bahv-anná-*		√	√	*	*	*	
bahv-ànna-[18]	*!	*	*			*	
→ *urú-loka-*	√	*	*			*	*
→ *puru-vā́ja-*		√	*	*	*		
→ *puru-vī́ra-*		√	*	*	*	*	
→ *tuví-brahman-*	√	*				*	
→ *tuvi-grī́va-*		√	*	*	*	*	
→ *agni-jihvā́-*		√		*	*		
→ *agní-dūta-*	√	*	*			*	*
→ *abhi-sená-*		√	√	*	*	*	*
→ *abhí-vīra-*	√	*	*			*	*

(ii) The initial member is trisyllabic:

Stress is shifted from a final syllable on *-á* of an initial member to the final member *-śrī́*. As mentioned above, compounds with stress on *-śrī́* are lexicalized:

[18] The svarita is preceded by a *y* or *v* representing an originally stressed *i-* or *u*-vowel.

Input: darśatá-; śrī́-; STRESS$_{In}$	LEX	MAX(w)$_{In}$	MAX(wf)	MAX(w)$_{Fin}$	WSP$_{Fin}$
→ *darśata-śrī́-*	√	*	*		

(iii) The initial member is a monosyllable, a prefix:

(a) *dvi-* and *tri-* are almost always unstressed: But *sá-* has priority:

Input: (*dví-*, *trí-*, *sá-*); *jánman-*, *śávas-*, *kakúbh-*, (*ambaka-*), *cánas-*, *rūpá-*; STRESS$_{In}$	LEX	**dví-*, **trí-*	*-á-*	MAX(w)$_{In}$	MAX(wf)	MAX(w)$_{Fin}$	WSP$_{Fin}$
→ *dvi-jánman-*		√		*	*		
dví-janman-	*!	*				*	
→ *dví-śavas-*	√	*				*	
→ *tri-kakúbh-*		√		*	*		
→ *try-àmbaka-*[19]	√	*	*			*	
→ *sa-cánas-*(see below)	√			*	*		
→ *sá-rūpa-*			*			*	*

Therefore, compounds with *sá-* do not violate constraint [MAX(wf)].

(b) As mentioned above, contrary to the supposed stressing of the negative prefix **n̥-* in Proto-Indo-European, in Vedic *bahuvrīhis* stress is usually shifted to the final member; all but one compound are oxytones. Here the supposed constraint [CONTR] applies, enforcing stress shift to the final syllable:

Stress on the penultimate in *a-śéṣas-* is due to the heavy syllable.

[19] Compare note 18.

Input: (*á-*); *dhenú-*, *cakrá-*, *kálpa-*, *śéṣas-*; $STRESS_{In}$	LEX	CONTR	-*á*-	$MAX(w)_{In}$	MAX(wf)	$MAX(w)_{Fin}$	WSP_{Fin}
→ *á-dhenu-*	√	*				*	*
→ *a-cakrá-*		√	√	*	*		
a-cákra-	*!	*	*	*	*	*	
→ *a-kalpá-*		√	√	*	*	*	
→ *a-śéṣas-*	√	*		*	*		

(c) Stress in compounds with *su-* or *duṣ-* as an initial member is shifted almost always, as well. But the final member is mostly stressed on the same syllable as the corresponding single word:

Input: (*dúṣ-*), (*sú-*); *éva-*, *āśír-*, (*nītí-*), *dhā́ra-*, *vīrá-*, *gó-*; $STRESS_{In}$	LEX	**sú-*, **dúṣ-*	-*á*-	PAR	$MAX(w)_{In}$	MAX(wf)	$MAX(w)_{Fin}$	WSP_{Fin}
→ *dur-éva-*		√	*	√	*	*		
dúr-eva-	*!	*	*				*	*
→ *dúr-āśir-*	√	*					*	*
→ *su-nītí-*		√			*	*		*
→ *su-dhārá-*		√	√	*	*	*	*	*
→ *su-vī́ra-*		√	*	√	*	*	*	
→ *su-gáva-*		√	*	√	*	*		

(iv) If the final member is stressed and if this element is an *s*-stem, the root syllable is stressed. But stress on the initial member is also documented. The heavy syllable of *–pā́na-* is always stressed. In all of these cases lexicalisation has to be assumed:

Input: *kṣétra-*, (*sá-*), *agní-*, *tuví-*, *índra-*; *sádha-*, *cánas-*, *bhrā́jas-*, *rā́dhas-*, (*pā́na-*); $STRESS_{In}$	LEX	$MAX(w)_{In}$	MAX(wf)	$MAX(w)_{Fin}$	WSP_{Fin}
→ *kṣetra-sā́dhas-*	√	*	*		
kṣetra-sādhás-	*!	*	*	*	*
→ *sa-cánas-*	√	*	*		
→ *agní-bhrājas-*	√			*	*
→ *tuvi-rā́dhas-*	√	*	*		
→ *indra-pā́na-*	√	*	*		

(v) Dvigus regularly show stress shift to the final *–á-*. Here, the assumed constraint [UNIQUENESS] requiring a stressed suffix *–á-* is valid:

Input: (*trí-*), (*á-*); *yugá-*, *bhayá-*; $STRESS_{In}$	LEX	UNIQ	$MAX(w)_{In}$	MAX(wf)	$MAX(w)_{Fin}$	WSP_{Fin}
→ *tri-yugá-*		√	*	*		
trí-yuga-	*!	*			*	
→ *á-bhaya-*	√	*			*	

3.2 Prepositional compounds with a governed final member

Prepositional compounds with a governed final member which are normally stressed on the initial member become oxytonese only in the case of a stem vowel *–a-* or "compositionell" *-á-*. Like in *bahuvrīhis,* this suffix has a contrastive function: The substantive in the final member is opposed to the adjectival value of the compound: *adho-akṣá-* 'being below the axle' (*ákṣa-* 'axle'), *upa-kakṣá-* 'reaching to the shoulder' (*kákṣa-* 'armpit'), *adhas-pad-á-* 'placed under the feet' (*pád-* 'foot'), *up-ānas-á-* 'being on a carriage' (*ánas-* 'cart'), *ati-rātr-á-* 'performed over-night' (*rā́trī-* 'night'), *áty-avi-* 'passing over or through the strainer' (literally 'passing over sheep's wool') (*ávi-* 'sheep'), *ádhi-ratha-* 'being upon or over a car', *ádhi-gartya-* 'being on the driver's seat' (*gárta-* 'driver's seat'), *upári-budhna-* 'raised above the ground' (*budhná-* 'ground, bottom'), *upári-martya-* 'being more than human' (*mártya-* 'human being') (Wackernagel 1905: 308f.). Consequently, in this type [*-á-*] and [MAX(wf)] are equally ranked. But since in every case where constraint [*-á-*] is dominant, [MAX(wf)] and [$MAX(w)_{In}$] have identical values, the order [$MAX(w)_{In}$] > [MAX(wf)] can be kept:

Input: *adhás*, *purás*, *úpa-*, *áti*, *ádhi*, *upári*; *ákṣá-*, *kákṣa-*, *pád-*, *ánas-*, *rā́trī-*, *vā́sas-*, *ávi-*, *mártya-*, *budhná-*; $STRESS_{In}$	-á-	$MAX(w)_{In}$	MAX(wf)	$MAX(w)_{Fin}$	WSP_{Fin}
→ *adho-akṣá-*	√	*	*		
→ *upa-kakṣá-*	√	*	*	*	
→ *adhas-pad-á-*	√	*	*	*	
adhas-pád-a-	*!	*	*		
→ *up-ānas-á-*	√	*	*	*	*
→ *ati-rātr-á-*	√	*	*	*	*
→ *adhī-vās-á-*	√	*	*	*	*
→ *áti-avi-*		√	√	*	
→ *upári-martya-*	*	√	√	*	
→ *upári-budhna-*	*	√	√	*	

3.3 Determinative compounds

(i) In determinative compounds with suffix *–ta-* or *–ti-*, stress is retained on the initial member, especially on *á(n)-*, because of the above mentioned rhythmical rule [RHYTHM]. As (ii) shows, this rule particularly concerns monosyllables as initial members.

(ii) The rhythmical rule prevents stress from getting shifted in monosyllabic *sú-*, *dúṣ-*; note *sú-dhita-* 'well placed'. Only in *su-baddhá-* 'bound fast', *su-jātá-* vs. *sú-jāta-* both 'well born, nobly born' the final member is stressed (Wackernagel 1905: 226). Therefore, the variants with unstressed *su-* are considered as lexicalized, and [RHYTHM] is equally ranked with [**sú-*, **dúṣ-*].

(iii) But in the initial member *víśva-*, stress is shifted from *i* to *a* like in *bahuvrīhis*: *viśvá-gūrta-* 'approved by everybody', *viśvá-dṛṣṭa-* 'seen by all'.

(iv) Just as in *bahuvrīhis* stress is shifted from *agní-* or *purú-* to the final member, too: *agni-taptá-* 'fire-heated, glowing', *agni-dagdhá-* 'burnt on a funeral pile', *agni-ṣvāttá-* 'tasted by the funeral fire' vs. *agní-mūḍha-* 'made insane by Agni', *puru-jātá-* 'variously manifested or appearing', *puru-gūrtá-* 'welcome to many', *puru-ṣṭutá-* 'praised by many', *puru-hūtá-* 'invoked by many'; compare further *kavi-śastá-* 'pronounced by wise men', *kavi-praśastá-* 'praised by sages'[20].

(v) Sometimes stress is shifted, if another prefix follows the negative prefix *a(n)-*, and oxytones arise: *an-āmṛṇá-* 'having no enemy that can injure', *an-āśastá-* 'not praised', *a-praśastá-* 'not praised, fameless' vs. *án-apacyuta-* 'not

[20] Possibly *ṛ* was a „NOHEAD"-vowel in compounds, too; compare *pitṛ-vittá-* 'acquired by ancestors'.

falling off, holding fast (a yoke)', *án-abhiśasta-* 'blameless, faultless', *án-ādhṛṣṭa-* 'unchecked', *án-ānata-* 'unbent, not humbled', *án-upakṣita-* 'uninjured, undecaying', *á-nibaddha-* 'not tied down, not bound', *á-nibhṛṣṭa-* 'unabated', *á-nivṛta-* 'unchecked', *á-niṣkṛta-* 'unfinished, not settled', *á-niṣṭṛta-* 'unhurt, unchecked', *á-parivīta-* 'not covered', *á-parājita-* 'unconquered', *á-prayuta-* 'attentive', *á-pratiṣkuta-* 'not to be kept off'; compare further the pair *a-praśastá-* 'not praised, fameless' vs. *á-praśasta-* 'not praised, blamable'. Stress on the first *á(n)-* prevails[21].

(vi) Compounds like *puru-prajātá-* 'variously propagated', *puru-praśastá-* 'praised by many' follow constraint (iv) and (v).

(vii) Compounds with another formative than *–ta-* show much more vacillating stress: gerundives on *–ya-* like *á-gohya-* 'not to be concealed or covered' vs. *a-paśyá-* 'not seeing', *a-dayá-* 'merciless, unkind', *an-ādhṛṣyá-* 'not to be meddled with' (Wackernagel 1905: 216ff.). But oxytones are compounds with a root noun as a final member: *a-júr-* 'not subject to old age', *a-cít-* 'foolish', *a-drúh-* 'not harming', *a-bhúj-* 'one who has not experienced or enjoyed', *a-rúk-* 'lightless', *a-sū́-* 'not bringing forth' vs. *á-kharva-* 'not shortened or mutilated', *á-kra-* 'inactive'[22].

(viii) Among the determinative compounds on *–ta-* there also are paroxytones. Since they have a special meaning, they are lexicalisations: *a-mṛ́ta-* 'immortal', Pl. 'the immortals' (*mṛtá-* 'dead'), *a-tū́rta-* 'not outrun, unhurt', 'illimited space' (vs. *á-tūrta-* 'one who does not anticipate someone'), *a-yúta-* 'a myriad', literally 'unbounded', *a-dṛ́ṣṭa-* 'unseen', *a-sū́rta-* 'unilluminated, enveloped in darkness' with stress on the heavy syllable (*sū́rta-* 'bright, illuminated'); but compare further *a-cítta-* 'unnoticed, unexpected' (*cittá-* 'noticed') and some lexicalized compounds with formative *–a-* like *a-kṣára-* 'imperishable' (see above).

(ix) Contrastive word stress to distinguish parts of speech, i.e. the constraint [UNIQUENESS], caused stress shift in *dur-itá-* 'difficulty, danger, evil', *dur-uktá-* 'bad or harsh word', *duṣ-kṛtá-* 'misdeed, sin'; or in the pair *sú-kṛta-* 'well done, well arranged' vs. *su-kṛtá-* 'good deed, moral merit'; just as in *indro-tá-* 'promoted by Indra'; this word is used as a male proper name[23]; sometimes stress shift is documented both in the substantive and in the adjective: *sū-ktá-* 'good recitation, wise saying, song of praise' and 'well or properly said'[24].

---

[21] Just as in án-avahvara- 'not crooked, straightforward', án-apasphura-, án-apasphur- 'not withdrawing', án-abhidruh- 'not malicious', án-abhu- 'disobliging, neglectful', á-prabhu- 'unable, incompetent', á-prahan- 'not hurting' vs. an-av4t- 'not returning'.

[22] Compare further compounds like á-kava- 'not contemptible', á-kavi- 'unwise', á-kumara- 'not a boy' (kumará- 'child, boy, youth') and more complex compounds like á-k1etravid- 'not finding out the way', á-kamakarsana- 'not disappointing desires'.

[23] Lexicalisations seem to be a-daghná- 'reaching up to the mouth (ás-)', ari-1Tutá- (for Indra) 'praised with zeal' with an unclear first element.

[24] Compare further *drupadá-* 'wooden pillar'.

By adding the constraint [RHYTHM] the following ranking results:

Input: (*sú-*), *viśvá-*, *agní-*, *purú-*, (*á-*); *jātá-*, *gūrtá-*, *taptá-*, (*prájāta-*), (*niṣṭṛta-*), (*gohyá-*), *paśyá-*, *mṛtá-*, *kṛtá-*; STRESS$_{In}$	LEX	RHYTHM	UNIQ	**sú-*	**í - a* **- í/ú*	*-á-*	PAR	MAX (w)$_{In}$	MAX (wf)	MAX (w)$_{Fin}$	WPS $_{Fin}$
→ *sú-jāta -*		√		*		*				*	*
→ *viśvá-gūrta-*					√	*		*		*	*
→ *agni-taptá-*					√	√		*	*		
agní-tapta-	*!				*	*				*	
→ *puru-jātá-*					√	√		*	*		*
→ *puru-prajātá-*					√	√		*	*	*	*
→ *á-niṣṭṛta-*		√				*				*	
→ *á-gohya-*		√				*				*	*
→ *a-paśyá-*	√	*				√		*	*		
→ *a-mṛta-*	√	*				*	√	*	*	*	
→ *sú-kṛta-*		√		*		*				*	
→ *su-kṛtá-*		*	√	√		√		*	*		

3.4 Verbal compounds with a governed final member

Verbal compounds with governed final member of the type *dhārayát-kavi-*, *-kṣiti-* 'supporting sages resp. bearing creatures' retain their stress on the last syllable of the first member. The constraint is [STRESS$_{InFinal}$]. The only exception is *śikṣā-nará-* 'help the men'.

Input: *dhāráyat*, *sikṣka*, *trása*; *kaví-*, *kṣití-*, *nár-*, *dásyu-*	LEX	*-á-*	[STRESS$_{InFinal}$]	MAX(w)$_{In}$	MAX(wf)	MAX(w)$_{Fin}$
→ *dhārayát-kavi-*			√	*	√	*
→ *dhārayát-kṣiti-*			√	*	√	*
→ *sikṣā-nará-*	√	√	*	*	*	*
→ *Trasá-dasyu-*			√	*	√	*
Trása-dasyu-			* !	√	*	*

3.5 Verbal compounds with a governed initial member

The stressed final member of verbal compounds with a governed initial member consists mainly of root nouns, which are eventually enlarged by the formative *–t-* (Vedic *ab-jít-* 'conquering waters', *deva-stút-* 'praising the gods', *vṛtra-hán-* 'killing Vṛtra'), or of oxytonic verbal stems like in *aśva-hayá-* 'driving horses', *ratha-kārá-* 'chariot-maker', *madhu-doghá-* 'milking sweetness', *ap-savá-* 'giving water', and with the accusative as the initial member *abhayaṃ-kará-* 'causing safety', *agnim-indhá-* 'kindling the fire', *viśvam-ejayá-* 'all-exciting'; to the contrary, compounds with suffixes occurring otherwise in abstract nouns are lexicalized; note *havir-ádvan-* 'eating the oblation', *soma-pā́van-* (besides *soma-pā́-*) 'drinking Soma', *māṃs-pácana-* 'used for cooking meat', *puṣṭi-várdhana-* 'increasing prosperity or welfare', *abhiśasti-cā́tana-* 'keeping off imprecation', *indra-mā́dana-* 'delighting Indra'.

The ranking differs from that of the compounds with regular stress on the initial member. MAX(w)$_{Fin}$ is higher ranked than MAX(w)$_{In}$:

Input: *devá-*; *vṛtrá-*, *rátha-*, *havís-*, *puṣṭí-*; *stút-*, *hán-*, (*kārá-*), (*ádvan-*), *várdhana-*; STRESS$_{Fin}$	LEX	*-á-*	MAX(w)$_{Fin}$	MAX(wf)	MAX(w)$_{In}$
→ *deva-stút-*			√		*
devá-stut-			*!	*	
→ *vṛtra-hán-*			√		*
→ *ratha-kārá-*		√	√		*
→ *havir-ádvan-*	√		√		*
→ *puṣṭi-várdhana-*	√		√		*

4 General ranking

By comparing the rankings for the different kinds of composition types:
(a) *bahuvrīhis* and determinative compounds

LEX	CONTR	RHYTHM	UNIQ	**sú-*, **dúṣ-*	**í – a* **a – ú* **í – i* *- í/ú **dví-*, **trí-*	*-á-*	PAR	MAX (w)$_{In}$	MAX (wf)	MAX (w)$_{Fin}$	WSP $_{Fin}$

(b) verbal compounds with governed final member

LEX	*-á-*	[STRESS$_{InFinal}$]	MAX(w)$_{In}$	MAX(wf)	MAX(w)$_{Fin}$

(c) prepositional compounds with governed final member

-á-	MAX(w)$_{In}$	MAX(wf)	MAX(w)$_{Fin}$

(d) verbal compounds with governed initial member

LEX	*-á-*	MAX(w)$_{Fin}$	MAX(wf)	MAX(w)$_{In}$

it can be stated that compounds, which normally have stress on the initial member, the exocentric type "*bahuvrīhi*, the verbal compound with a governed final member, the prepositional compound with a governed final member" and the endocentric type "determinative compound", show the same ranking, if one adds the constraint [$\text{STRESS}_{\text{InFinal}}$] and if one considers that constraint [*-á-*] automatically enforces violation both of [$\text{MAX(w)}_{\text{In}}$] and [MAX(wf)]. Consequently, as concerns stress there is no clear distinction between endocentric and exocentric compounds so far.

Only verbal compounds with a governed initial member, a subtype of the endocentric type, are different in ranking: According to stress on the final member, constraint [$\text{MAX(w)}_{\text{Fin}}$] is dominating [$\text{MAX(w)}_{\text{In}}$]. Depending on the Input [$\text{STRESS}_{\text{In}}$] or [$\text{STRESS}_{\text{Fin}}$], the constraint order alternates - the markedness constraints ***sú-*, **dúṣ-*, **í – a*, **a – ú*, **í – i*, **- í/ú*, **dví-*, **trí-*** could function under a cover constraint NOHEAD/*i,u*, for [RHYTHM] concerns stress shift only from monosyllables:

Input: $\text{STRESS}_{\text{Initial member}}$

LEX	CONTR	RHYTHM	UNIQ	**sú-,* **dúṣ-*	**í – a* **a – ú* **í – i* **- í/ú* **dví-* **trí-*	*-á-*	PAR	STRESS InFinal	MAX (w)_{In}	MAX (wf)	MAX (w)_{Fin}	WSP Fin

Input: $\text{STRESS}_{\text{Final member}}$

LEX	CONTR	RHYTHM	UNIQ	**sú-,* **dúṣ-*	**í – a* **a – ú* **í – i* **- í/ú* **dví-* **trí-*	*-á-*	PAR	STRESS InFinal	MAX (w)_{Fin}	MAX (wf)	MAX (w)_{In}	WSP Fin

5 Summary

Since there is nearly one ranking for all the Vedic composition types in spite of different underlying stress patterns, it is not surprising that previous scholars attempted a uniform explanation for Vedic compositionell stress:

> Die lage des accents wird ohne rücksicht auf das vorderglied nur durch die gestaltung des schlussgliedes bedingt und der accent ruht bei den bildungen auf *–ta –ti –tu* und den comparativen und superlativen auf dem vorderglied, bei sämmtlichen übrigen bildungen aber auf der tonsilbe des schlussgliedes (Reuter 1882: 612f.).

But the combination of prosodic constraints with faithfulness constraints concerning the underlying stress of the compound as a whole [MAX(wf)] and of the members as single words [MAX(w)$_{In}$; MAX(w)$_{Fin}$] was not recognized. Nor was the importance of prosodic constraints understood. Admittedly, there are a lot of lexicalisations, but the following constraint is absolutely clear: The more a vowel which functions as the nucleus is unmarked, the more unmarked it is as the nucleus in stressed syllables, too (Löhken 1997: 38). As demonstrated, in compounds this constraint concerns the avoidance of stressed *í* and *ú*. Yet, there are further prosodic constraints: The constraint [RHYTHM] for determinative compounds with suffix *–ta-*, *-na-*, *-ti-* prevents stress from getting shifted, for the rhythm

w w s → s w s
ni hi táḫ *ní hi tàḫ*

could permanently be referred to the corresponding simplex *hitáḫ*. In particular, this constraint is valid for determinative compounds with the negative prefix *á(n)-* `un-´, the outcome of Proto-Indo-Europan stressed **ń̥-*, and suffix *–ta-*. Here, stress on the prefix is almost without exception preserved. But more importantly, prosodic determinated stressing and those stresses which fulfil faithfulness constraints could be overriden by contrastive stress. Firstly, the well known stress shift to differentiate parts of speech must be mentioned; compare the adjective *sú-kr̥ta-* vs. the substantive *su-kr̥tá-*. But contrastive word stress appears within a compound as well. In the case of prepositional compounds with a governed final member and *bahuvrīhis,* "compositionell" *–á-* denotes a contrast between the substantive value of the final member of the compound and the "adjective" of the whole. Further, this contrastive function of the suffix *–á-* is used in *bahuvrīhis* with the negative prefix *a(n)-* to oppose those *bahuvrīhis* to determinative compounds with the corresponding prefix. But whereas in determinative compounds the inherited stress of the prefix is retained by reason of the rhythmical rule "w w s → s w s", in *bahuvrīhis,* stress is shifted to the apparently "stronger" (or dominant) suffix *–á-*; so *bahuvrīhis* of this type are regularly oxytones. In stressing endocentric and exocentric compounds with the negative prefix *a(n)-* differently, a semantically determined contrastive word stress is visible[25].

[25] See Ladd 1996: 160 to the meaning of contrastive stress.

6 References

Burzio, L. (1994): Principles of English Stress. Cambridge: Cambridge University Press.

van Coetsem, F. (1996): Towards a Typology of Lexical Accent. `Stress Accent' and `Pitch Accent' in a Renewed Perspective. Heidelberg: Winter (Monographien zur Sprachwissenschaft 18).

Drachman, G. and A. Malikouti-Drachman (1999): In: H. van der Hulst (1999): 897-945

Garbe, R. (1877): Das accentuationssystem des altindischen nominalcompositums. Zeitschrift für vergleichende Sprachforschung 23, 470-519

Gotō, T. (1987): Die „I. Präsensklasse" im Vedischen. Untersuchungen zu den vollstufigen thematischen Wurzelpräsentia. (Österreichische Akademie der Wissenschaften: Philosophisch-historische Klasse, Sitzungsberichte 489)

Halle, M. and K. P. Mohanan (1985): Segmental Phonology of Modern English, Linguistic Inquiry 16, 57-116

Halle, M. and J.-R. Vergnaud (1987): An Essay on Stress, MIT. Cambridge, MA

Haragouchi, S. (1991): A Theory of Stress and Accent. Dordrecht: Foris Publications.

Hock, W. (1993 [1994]): Der urindogermanische Flexionsakzent und die morphologische Akzentologiekonzeption, Münchener Studien zur Sprachwissenschaft 54, 177-203

Hoffmann, K. (1967): Der Injunktiv im Veda. Heidelberg: Winter.

van der Hulst, H. (ed) (1999): Word Prosodic Systems in the Languages of Europe. Empirical Approaches to Language Typology. Eurotyp 20-4. Berlin/New York: Mouton/de Gruyter.

van der Hulst, H. (1999a): Word accent. In: van der Hulst (1999): 3-115

van der Hulst, H., B. Hendriks, and J. van de Weijer (1999): A survey of word prosodic systems of European languages. In: van der Hulst (1999): 425-475

Kager, R. (1999): Optimality Theory. Cambridge: University Press.

Kenstowicz, M. (1994): Sonority-driven stress. Ms., Rutgers Optimality Archive 33.

Kiparsky P. (1982): The Lexical Phonology of Vedic Accent. Ms., Department of Linguistics, MIT. Cambridge, MA

Knauer, F. (1885): Ueber die betonung der composita mit a privativum im sanskrit, Zeitschrift für vergleichende Sprachforschung 27, 1-69

Ladd, R. D. (1996): Intonational phonology. Cambridge: University Press (Cambridge studies in linguistics 79)

Löhken, S. C. (1997): Deutsche Wortprosodie. Abschwächungs- und Tilgungsvorgänge. (Studien zur deutschen Grammatik 56). Tübingen: Stauffenberg

Lühr, R. (2002): Konzeptionierungen des Prädikativums in der Indogermania. Zeitschrift für Sprachwissenschaft 21, 4-24

Lühr, R. (2003): Die Nominalkomposition im Altindischen und Altgriechischen. In: E. Nowak and R. Lühr (eds): Inkorporation und Komposition. Berlin

Macdonell, A. A. (1916): A Vedic grammar for students. Oxford (1966)

Marchand, H. (1969): The Categories and Types of Present-Day English Word-Formation. A Synchronic-Diachronic Approach. München: Beck'sche Verlagsbuchhandlung.

Meier-Brügger, M. (2000): Indogermanische Sprachwissenschaft. 7. völlig neubearb. Aufl. unter Mitarbeit von M. Fritz und M. Mayrhofer. Berlin/New York: de Gruyter.

Müller, G. (2000a): Das Pronominaladverb als Reparaturphänomen. Linguistische Berichte 181, 135-178.

Müller, G. (2000b): Elemente der optimalitätstheoretischen Syntax. Tübingen: Niemeyer.

Müller, G. (2001): Syntaktisch determinierter Kasuswegfall in der deutschen NP. Ms., Mannheim.

Nespor, M. (1999): Stress domains. In: van der Hulst (1999): 117-159.

Reuter, J. N. (1882): Die altindischen nominalcomposita, ihrer betonung nach untersucht. Zeitschrift für vergleichende Sprachforschung 31, 156-233; 485-613.

Spencer, A. (1991): Morphological Theory. An Introduction to Word Structure in Generative Grammar. Oxford: Blackwell Publishers.

Steriade, D. (1988): Greek Accent: A Case for Preserving Structure. Linguistic Inquiry 19, 271-314.

Visch, E. (1999): The rhythmic organization of compounds and phrase. In: van der Hulst (1999): 161-231.

Wackernagel, J. (1905): Altindische Grammatik II, 1: Einleitung zur Wortlehre. Nominalkomposition. Neudruck der 2. unveränderten Auflage: Göttingen: Vandenhoeck & Ruprecht (1957).

Wackernagel, J. and A. Debrunner (1954): Altindische Grammatik II, 2: Die Nominalsuffixe. Vandenhoeck & Ruprecht: Göttingen.

Whitney, W. D. (1889): Sanskrit Grammar. 2nd ed. Cambridge, Mass.

Wunderlich, D. (2001): Optimal case patterns: German and Icelandic compared. Ms., Düsseldorf.

Thomas Weskott (Leipzig)

Towards a Scalar Notion of Information Structural Markedness*

1 Introduction

The relative variability of German word order allows to linearise a sentence in a flexible way. For example, a declarative matrix sentence with a transitive verb can be encoded by the order subject-verb-object (SVO), or object-verb-subject (OVS). While the former is judged as perfectly normal, the latter will be perceived as marked, or as deviating from the default order. This perceived markedness is mirrored by a huge number of experimental data showing that these marked structures are processed with less ease than their canonical counterparts. This raises the question why German should have developed into a language allowing for such orders in the first place. The answer I will propose here is that marked sentences are not that difficult to process if their contextual requirements are fulfilled by the context they appear in. Following Höhle (1982) and Schwarzschild (1999), I will propose to build a scalar notion of Information Structural markedness on contextual restriction. I will argue that the latter lies at the heart of the problem, and that it not only allows for a better understanding of the relation between IS, context and markedness, but that it also generates empirical hypotheses to which experimental studies conducted in the field can directly pertain.

The paper is organised as follows: section 2 analyses the notion of Information Structural ("IS" hereafter) markedness by building on some basic assumptions about German syntax and accent placement, from which a measure of IS complexity will be developed. This will in turn be interpreted in terms of the contextual requirement of a sentence as represented by dynamic semantic theories.

Based on this formal apparatus, a scale of IS markedness will be formulated in section 3. Section 4 considers the empirical predictions originating from the

* This paper is built on the second chapter of my PhD thesis which was written while I was a member of the Graduiertenkolleg "Universalität und Diversität: Sprachliche Strukturen und Prozesse" at Leipzig University, funded by the Deutsche Forschungsgemeinschaft. I want to express my gratitude for helpful comments and discussion to my thesis supervisors Anita Steube, Thomas Pechmann, and Nicholas Asher, as well as to Martin Schäfer, Andreas Späth, Britta Stolterfoht, and especially Ingolf Max. The usual disclaimer holds.

scale of IS markedness, and discusses two experimental studies that address the issue in exemplary fashion. Section 5 concludes the paper and points to some problems and prospects for further research.

Before starting, a few disclaimers are in place: firstly, I consider German V2 declaratives with transitive verbs only; for a typological account of IS, see e.g. Kruijff (2002). For topicalisation in German ergative constructions, see Muckel (2001). Also, nothing will be said about Scrambling, for a discussion of which the reader is referred to Haider & Rosengren (1998), and Stolterfoht et al. (this volume). Finally, a terminological remark has to be made: since I will propose a configurational definition of Topics, I will use the terms "Vorfeld element" and "Topic" interchangeably; which also means that I will have nothing to say on the issue of the so-called "Mittelfeld Topics" identified by Frey (2000).

2 Information structural markedness

The notion of *markedness* will be understood here in a naïve Jakobsonian way, as it is expressed in the following quote: "The general meaning of a marked category states the presence of a certain (whether positive or negative) property *A*; the general meaning of the corresponding unmarked category states nothing about the presence of *A* (...)" (Jakobson (1971), p. 131). To utilise this grammatical notion of markedness for the present purpose, we will need an explication for the markedness of a construction *relative to a context* it appears in. An attempt at formulating such an explication will be given in the next section.

2.1 Markedness, information structure complexity, and contextual restriction

Intuitively, the information structural variants of a sentence are interrelated. That is, one perceives them as being the offspring from some common underlying structure. For example, sentences (1.b) and (1.c) can be derived from (1.a) by a movement operation.[1]

[1] More specifically, I conceive of topicalisation as A'-movement targeting the specifier position of CP and leaving behind a trace in the base position, following Haider (1993), Frey (2000), and Steube & Späth (2002), among others. However, most of the assumptions to be formulated in the subsequent sections do not depend on this particular syntactic analysis. SMALL CAPS indicate main stress.

(1) (a) dassder Kellner den Gast beleidigte.
that the$_{NOM}$ waiter the$_{ACC}$ guest insulted.
'that the waiter insulted the guest.'

(b) Der Kellner beleidigte den GAST.
The$_{NOM}$ waiter insulted the$_{ACC}$ guest.
'The waiter insulted the guest.'

(c) Den Gast beleidigte der KELLNER.
The$_{ACC}$ guest insulted the$_{NOM}$ waiter.
'The guest was insulted by the waiter.'

Sentences like (1.c) are judged as more marked by German native speakers. This is obviously due to the fact that the sentence-initial position (the so-called "Vorfeld") does not host the subject (which it does in the prototypical German V2 sentence containing a transitive verb), but the direct object. The perceived markedness then is due to the deviation from the canonical order SVO. Following Haider (1993), I assume that this basic order is determined by the properties of the verbal head as specified in the lexicon. That is, for the transitive verb "beleidigen" *(to insult)*, the canonical linearisation of the arguments is dependent on the order of the λ-prefixes in the lexical representation.

(2) $\lambda y \lambda x[V_{tr}(x, y)] \Rightarrow [_{CP}\ XP \ldots [_{VP \ldots}\ YP\ \ V\ ]]$

The canonical linearisation of arguments in a German V2 sentence then will look as follows:

(3) $[_{CP}\ XP_j\ [_{C'}\ V_i\ [_{VP}\ t_j\ [_{V'}\ YP\ \ t_i\ ]]]]$

The structure corresponding to the deviating topicalised structure as exemplified by (1.b) is given in (4):

(4) $[_{CP}\ YP_j\ [_{C'}\ V_i\ [_{VP}\ XP\ [_{V'}\ t_j\ \ t_i\ ]]]]$

The structures in (3) and (4) do not differ with respect to their syntactic complexity—both involve the movement of a DP to the specifier of CP, leaving behind a trace in the core VP. Hence, in order to account for the markedness difference between subject-before-object (hereafter: SVO) and object-before-subject (OVS) structures, they must be differing in some other property. One possibility of accounting for the difference would be to assume that whereas the movement of the subject *XP* to the Vorfeld in (3) takes place to fulfill morphosyntactic needs, in (4), the object moves to that position for Information Structural reasons. But this would necessitate the adoption of IS-features driving syntactic derivation in the same manner as "proper" morphosyntactic ones (s. Rizzi (1997); and, for German, Haftka (2000)). Instead, I propose to capture the markedness difference not by invoking syntactic IS features, but rather by a complexity measure that is defined over Information Structural categories.

In order to make such a notion of complexity work, three basic assumptions constraining the Information Structural realisation of a sentence will have to be made.

The basic order of arguments is determined by the order of the λ-prefixes as specified by the lexical entry of the verbal head.
A rule that assigns accent to phrasal syntactic strings has to be assumed. This will be done in accordance with Cinque (1993) and Reinhart (1996).
A two-dimensional labelling of syntactic constructions with Information Structural categories is proposed, in terms of which IS-complexity is defined.

Since assumption (I) was already worked out above, I will concentrate on the last two.

Following Cinque's (1993) "Null Theory", I will assume that phrasal stress is assigned to the most deeply embedded constituent by a default rule. Given the syntactic structure of German, this position will be at the right periphery of the sentence; that is, it will be hosted by the verb in an intrasitive construction (5.a), by the direct object in a V2 sentence with canonical order (5.b), and the subject in a V2 sentence with a topicalised direct object (5.c), respectively; (5.d) and (5.e) constitute cases of deviation from the default accent assignment, since the constituent that receives stress is not the most deeply embedded one. As witnessed by the approximate English translation, the Vorfeld constituent in (5.d) and (5.e) is used contrastively; s. Steube (2001b).

(5) (a) Der Kellner SCHLÄFT.
The$_{NOM}$ waiter is sleeping.

(b) Der Kellner beleidigte den GAST.
The$_{NOM}$ waiter insulted the$_{ACC}$ guest.

(c) Den Gast beleidigte der KELLNER.
The$_{ACC}$ guest insulted the$_{NOM}$ waiter.
'The guest was insulted by the waiter.'

(d) Der KELLNER beleidigte den Gast.
The$_{NOM}$ waiter insulted the$_{ACC}$ guest
'It was the waiter who insulted the guest.'

(e) Den GAST beleidigte der Kellner.
The$_{ACC}$ guest insulted the$_{NOM}$ waiter.
'It was the guest who the waiter insulted.

To account for the difference in markedness between (5.d) and (e), we have to recur to the first assumption concerning the basic order of arguments; thus, (5.e) is more marked because it deviates from that canonical order. The first assumption then takes care of the default linearisation as defined by the relation between lexical representation and syntax, whereas the second determines the default assignment of main accent to a constituent at the syntax-phonology interface.[2] But so far, these assumptions do not give us any independent basis of judging a construction as marked. As pointed out by Reinhart (1996), this fact makes the theory unfalsifiable: "If it is just as easy to construct examples with 'marked' stress, as with neutral stress, and there is no obvious way to distinguish them, we run into the danger of vacuity—having a theory which excludes nothing. The facts that follow from its rules are labelled 'neutral', and everything else—'marked'. (This type of theory is always true, regardless of what its rules are)." (*ibd.*, p. 165). It seems that there is something missing from the picture drawn so far which gives some sense to the notion of markedness.

This is where the third assumption comes in: I propose to give an explication of the markedness of an IS variant of a sentence in terms of the relative IS complexity, which is related to the notion of contextual restriction.[3] The relative complexity of an IS variant of a sentence is defined over the two dimensions of Information Structure, i.e. Topic-Comment-Structure (TCS), and Focus-Background-Structure (FBS). In order to give this structural relations an interpretive basis, Background information will be treated as anaphoric. How does this work?

Partly following Schwarzschild (1999) in the conception of the constraining relations between a sentence and a context, I will assume that Givenness is the most important relation. That is, the constituents that are part of the Background partition are the ones that restrict the possible contexts in which a variant may appear. I will adopt a dynamic interpretive procedure here according to which interpretation of the respective IS domains procedes from left to right in an incremental fashion.[4] Firstly, the presuppositional operator '∂' will be applied to the Background; if the latter coincides with the Topic, it will be conjoined with the focal part by dynamic conjunction in order to account for

[2] Note that these two assumptions function independently of each other, but that the markedness effect resulting from a simultaneous violation of both of them is additive. I presume that the distinction between the two assumptions in terms of their different interface status can be taken to be supported by the empirical results in Stolterfoht et al. (this volume), although it should be noted that they make a further distinction between accent placement and focus assignment—an issue I shall ignore here.

[3] Here I depart from Reinhart's (1996) treatment of markedness, although I suppose that her explanans, interface economy, is compatible with the explication given here.

[4] The question whether this approach will remain tenable once more complex IS-variants like bridge accents/Hutkonturen (involving scope inversion phenomena) have to be accounted for goes beyond the limits of the present paper. S. Steube (2003).

the property of *informational separation* (cf. Jacobs (2001)). If there is a Topic that does not coincide with the Background, the '∂'-operator will also be applied to it, and the Topic will be dynamically conjoined with the Comment. Then, the Background/Focus division is repeated for the Comment part of the sentence. This guarantees that Topics, as all other Background constituents, will be interpreted as anaphoric; that is, they trigger the presupposition that there exists an antecedent of the right type in previous discourse to which they can bind; otherwise they have to be accommodated (cf. van der Sandt (1992)). That is, an utterance *A* of the form: [5]

$[\{\alpha\}T \{\beta\}C]$
is interpreted as
$\partial\|\alpha\| \wedge \|\beta\|$,
where $\alpha \wedge \beta$ is itself defined relative to a context c as
$\|\alpha \wedge \beta\|(c) = \|\beta\|(\|\alpha\|(c))$.

The interpretation of the Comment depends on whether it does or does not coincide with the Focus. In the first case, the update function '↓' is applied to the Comment/Focus as a whole. [6] In the latter case, where the Focus is properly contained in the Comment, a partition into Background and Focus information like e.g.

$\{\beta[\gamma]_F\}^C$
will be interpreted as
$\partial\|\beta\| \triangle \downarrow\|\gamma\|$.

That is, the Background information has to be related to context first before the update with the focal information can take place.[7]

For an illustration of how IS complexity and contextual restriction tie in with the semantics of Background, consider the following case, which is the simplest possible and hence least IS-complex one:

[5] TCS is indicated by superscripted curly brackets where $\{\ ...\ \}^T$ and $\{\ ...\ \}^C$ stand for Topic and Comment, respectively. FBS is indexed by subscripted square brackets.

[6] For the semantics of the presuppositional operator, as well as that of dynamic conjunction, s. Weskott (2002), chp. 2; there, also an example of the left-to right compositional interpretation is given in the Appendix.

[7] A problem arises if we have to account for discontinuous Background constituents (originating from e.g. a non-peripheral narrow focus on an element inside a larger Background domain); it was brought to my attention by Ingolf Max. For reasons of space, I cannot deal with it here; but I suppose that it can be solved by adopting a mechanism similar to Schwarzschild's (1999) Existential Type Shift, which would have to replace the focal element with a variable and existentially closing the result, yielding a representation for the Background only.

(6) *Die SONNE scheint.* ('The sun is shining.')

FBS: [ ]$_F$

TCS: { }^{C}

This sentence is said to express a *thetic* judgment, i.e. the speaker is presenting some state of affairs in a holistic fashion, as a whole. That is, such sentences do not exhibit the property of *informational separation* (to use Jacobs' (2001) term): they cannot be separated into an object and a property like their counterparts, the sentences that express *categorical* sentences (s. Eckardt (1996) for a discussion). Thetic sentences are said to be all-Focus. This is reflected in their property to be utterable "out of the blue", i.e. without making any background assumptions that go beyond mere Relevance; that is, the restriction such sentences impose on their context of utterance is nil. They also do not exhibit a separation into Topic and Comment, which is witnessed by their failure to pass the "as for X"-test for Topics: the sentence "*As for the sun, it's shining.*" is odd, if not unacceptable. Accordingly, the interpretation of a sentence like (6) above does not require applying the presuppositional operator, since there is no Background information; thus, it can be rendered as follows:

(6') ↓|| the sun is shining ||

That is, the unrestricted context of utterance *c* is mapped onto the context *c'* by adding the focal information in one interpretive step.

Let us continue with the least complex case of a categoric sentence, an intransitive construction:

(7) *Der Kellner SCHLÄFT.* ('The waiter is sleeping.')

FBS: [ ]$_B$ [ ]$_F$

TCS: { }^{T}{ }^{C}

As is evident from the FBS/TCS-bracketings, (7) exhibits a more complex Information Structure than (6)—it represents a case of informational separation as defined by Jacobs (2001). Also note that (7) is not utterable out-of-the-blue, i.e. it requires a specific kind of context in which to be felicitously uttered. Here, a further comment on the relation between FBS and TCS has to be made: as can be seen in (7), the Topic coincides with the Background, and they both precede Focus and Comment, which also coincide. Following a frequently made assumption (e.g. Schwarzschild (1999); Kruijff (2002)), I will suppose that this ordering of IS domains—given before new information—is the natural and hence less complex one. Given what was said so far, this is totally independent from the canonicality assumptions (I) and (II). This is also mirrored in the interpretive left-to-right procedure which will assign the following interpretation to (7):

(7') ∂|| the waiter|| △ ↓|| is sleeping ||

This means that, firstly, the context *c* has to be restricted with the Background information that there has to be a unique waiter in all contexts where (7) is uttered, be it explicitly represented or merely inferable. The resulting context *c′* then will be mapped onto the context *c″* by updating *c′* with the Focal information.

A more complex case of IS in a categorical sentence is constituted by transitive constructions like (5.b) above, repeated here as (8); here, the two dimensions of IS bracketing may or may not coincide:

(8)	(a)		Der Kellner	beleidigte	den GAST.
		FBS:	[ ]$_B$	[	]$_F$
		TCS:	{ }^{T}	{	}^{C}
	(b)		Der Kellner	beleidigte	den GAST.
		FBS:	[	]$_B$[	]$_F$
		TCS:	{ }^{T}{		}^{C}

Depending on how much information is taken to for granted by the speaker, the focus will be wide (8.a), comprising the verb, or it will be narrow (8.b), containing the direct object only. Since in the latter case, the brackets on the two dimensions do not coincide, i.e. the Focus is a proper subpart of the Comment, this case is more complex—it involves a more fine-grained subdivision of IS domains than (8.a). This is in accordance with the frequently made observation that sentences with wide focus can be uttered in reply to out-of-the-blue *questions* like e.g. 'What's happened?', whereas sentences containing a narrow focus do not.[8] In the example above, the question to which the narrow focus sentences gives the answer would be something like 'Who did the waiter insult?'. This is just another way of saying that the contextual restriction exerted by (8.b) exceeds that of (8.a), which is also reflected in the respective interpretations: in (8.a), the presuppositional operator will be applied to the Topic phrase "der Kellner" only, whereas it will also be applied to the Background information supplied by the verb, which is part of the Comment in (8.b).

So far, we have only looked at categorical sentences that comply to assumptions (I) and (II) above, i.e. they did not exhibit deviations from canonical order, nor from default accent placement. This also means that the IS bracketings respected a certain ordering; the focal part of the sentence was always preceded by the Background, and the Topic preceded the Comment. Whereas

---

[8] This, by the way, distinguishes categorical wide Focus sentences from thetic ones. Whereas the latter can be uttered out-of-the-blue, i.e. in a null context, the former are restricted to contexts where a (possibly out-of-the-blue) question precedes them.

the latter ordering never is reversed, the former can be; cf. the following example (= (5.d) above):

(9)		Der KELLNER	beleidigte den Gast.	
	FBS: [	$]_F$ [		$]_B$
	TCS: {	$\}^T$ {		$\}^C$

Here, Focus obviously *precedes* Background. Is this construction more marked than the one in (8.b), where the two bracketings did not coincide? Although it may seem purely stipulative, the answer is in the positive. This is due to the fact that not only the order of Background and Focus is reversed, but also that assumption (II) about the default accent is violated: the Focus is not placed in its canonical position. Further support for this comes from the fact that (9) imposes more constraints on its context of utterance than (8), as witnessed by the number of interpretive steps. Firstly, the context of utterance *c* will have to be updated by binding or accommodating the presupposition supplied by the Topic. But since the latter contains focal information, the resulting context *c'* will also have to be updated with the function '$\downarrow$', yielding a contrastive interpretation of the Topic, i.e. it was the waiter who did something, and not someone else.[9] The information about what it was that the waiter did (and not someone else) is then supplied by updating that context with the information given in the Comment part, which will filter out all alternative referents who did something apart from those who insulted the guest, which then serve as the alternative set for the contrastive Topic *der Kellner*.

In more intuitive terms, (9) requires the situation and/or preceding discourse not only to contain a waiter (as (8) does), but also someone else who was supposedly insulting the guest.

Given the observations made so far, a case where all three assumptions are violated should be even more marked than (9); such a case is constituted by a topicalised direct object bearing the pitch accent, like (5.e) above, repeated here for convenience.

(10)		Den GAST	beleidigte der Kellner.	
	FBS: [	$]_F$ [		$]_B$
	TCS: {	$\}^T$ {		$\}^C$

[9] The exact details of the interpretation of contrastive Topics in a dynamic setting remain to be spelled out. Still, if we assume that both the presuppositional operator '∂' and the update function '$\downarrow$' are sensitive to discourse relations, something along these lines will come out. For example, updating a context with $\partial\|\alpha\|$ (via the rhetorical relation *Background*) and then with $\downarrow\|\alpha\|$ should result in the establishment of the discourse relation *Contrast;* s. Asher (1993); Asher & Lascarides (1998 a, b). The issue of sensitivity of the operators to discourse relations will be picked up in section 4.

This sentence deviates, first of all, from the basic order of arguments as given in assumption (I); secondly, it violates the default accent rule as defined by Cinque's (1993) Null Theory; and finally, it does not comply to the given-before-new law because the Focus precedes the Background. Since it violates a condition which (9) does not violate, (10) is more marked than the former. This is reflected in its stronger contextual restriction: it presupposes a context with a uniquely identifiable guest, and one with an alternative set to the guest for the elements of which it holds that they were insulted by the waiter, a set of "insultees".

As the discussion of the examples has shown, the degree of markedness indeed can be reduced to the amount of information that a given IS-variant of a sentence requires its context of utterance to provide, and that the dynamic treatment of Topic and Background as anaphoric, i.e. presupposed information, provides an adequate formal rendering of that contextual restriction.

Of course, cases are conceivable that are much more complex, like the extensively studied bridge accent or Hutkontur (s. Büring (1995) and Steube (2003b)). But I will refrain here from analysing these cases. Instead, I will try to cast the observations regarding the gradual markedness of IS variants of German V2 transitive sentences made so far into a more formal frame.

3 Defining the scale of IS markedness

As stated above, a sentence expressing a thetic judgement imposes no requirement on its context of utterance whatsoever; since such a sentence consists of Focus and Comment only and the two coincide, its IS complexity will be lesser than that of a sentence expressing a categorical sentence which is partitioned into Topic-Comment and Background-Focus. From this, we may formulate the following hypothesis:

(H1) If $\Sigma = \{S_1, ..., S_n\}$ is the set of Information Structurally annotated variants of an intransitive sentence of type S, and if

(i) $S_1 \in \Sigma$ is a token of S with IS bracketing such that $F=C\neq 0$ and $T=B=0$, and

(ii) $S_2 \in \Sigma$ is a token of S with IS bracketing such that $F=C\neq 0$ and $T=B=0$,

then $S_1 <_R S_2$, where $<_R$ is a total ordering on Σ, meaning "is contextually less restrictive than".

This simply means that a thetic sentence *qua* being less IS-complex, puts less restriction on its context than a categorical one. Hence, according to our definition, it is Information Structurally less marked.

To account for a markedness scale for transitive structures, we will have to take assumption (I) into account; this is done by explicitly referring to the syntactic form the sentence tokens have.

(H2) If $\Sigma = \{S_1, ..., S_n\}$ is the set of Information Structurally annotated variants of a transitive sentence type S, and if
(i) $S_1 \in \Sigma$ is a token of S of the form $[_{CP}\, XP_{i/nom}\, [_{C'}\, V_j\, [_{VP}\, t_i\, [_{V'}\, YP_{acc}\, t_j\,]]]]$ and with an IS bracketing such that $F=C\neq 0$ and $T=B\neq 0$,
(ii) $S_2 \in \Sigma$ is a token of S of the form $[_{CP}\, XP_{i/nom}\, [_{C'}\, V_j\, [_{VP}\, t_i\, [_{V'}\, YP_{acc}\, t_j\,]]]]$ and with an IS bracketing such that $F \subset C$ and $T \subset B$,
(iii) $S_3 \in \Sigma$ is a token of S of the form $[_{CP}\, YP_{i/acc}\, [_{C'}\, V_j\, [_{VP} XP_{nom}\, [_{V'}\, t_i\ \ t_j\,]]]]$ and with an IS bracketing such that $F=C$ and $T=B$,
(iv) $S_4 \in \Sigma$ is a token of S of the form $[_{CP}\, XP_{i/nom}\, [_{C'}\, V_j\, [_{VP}\, t_i\, [_{V'}\, YP_{acc}\, t_j\,]]]]$ and with an IS bracketing such that $B=C$ and $T=F$, and
(v) $S_5 \in \Sigma$ is a token of S of the form $[_{CP}\, YP_{i/acc}\, [_{C'}\, V_j\, [_{VP} XP_{nom}\, [_{V'}\, t_i\ \ t_j\,]]]]$ and with an IS bracketing such that $B=C$ and $T=F$,
then $S_1 <_R S_2 <_R S_3 <_R S_4 <_R S_5$.

The syntactic constructions referred to in the conditions (i) to (v) of (H2) are just those in examples (5.a – e). That is, the construction in (i) is a categorical V2-sentence with a transitive verb which respects the basic order, i.e. the subject inhabits the Vorfeld position, and the verb is part of the (wide) focus. The sentence type in (ii) differs from (i) only in that it has narrow focus on the *in situ* direct object. In tokens of the type described in (iii), the direct object is topicalised but not focussed; the markedness of this structure then results from the deviation from the basic order assumption. Type (iv) is a construction respecting basic order but deviating from the order of IS domains in that it has a focal subject in the Vorfeld. Finally, construction type (v) violates both the basic order assumption by having a topicalised direct object, and the ordering of IS domains by having the Focus in the Vorfeld.

To sum up: based on a formal notion of contextual requirement of a sentence, the scale formulated in (H2) seems to comply with intuition. Moreover, its reference to the complexity of two-dimensional IS-bracketings not only captures the constructions discussed so far, but may be extended to more complex ones like contrastive Topic or Hutkontur, where more fine-grained IS partitions like e.g. $F \subset T$ and $F \subset C$ for Büring's cases like e.g. "{The [/FEMALE]$_F$ popstars}^{T} {wore [\CAFTANS]$_F$}^{C}." can be held responsible for the the strong contextual restriction and hence the strongly marked character of these constructions.

4 Some empirical evidence

The scale of markedness (H2) should not be considered merely as a descriptive generalisation of intuitive judgements about the contextual fit of a sentence, or of its formal rendering in terms of dynamic interpretation. It also serves as a basis for predicting processing difficulties of an IS-variant of a sentence relative to a given context. The psycholinguistic literature on word order variation in German is abundant with evidence for processing difficulties that are associated to sentences with deviating arguments order, or non-default accent assignment, or both (s. Bader et al.(1999) for an overview). Most of these studies, however, did not take into account inter-sentential context. It may be hypothesized on the basis of (H2) that the reported processing difficulties may at least partly be attributed to the lack of satisfaction of the contextual requirements of the experimental sentences by the null context they were presented in. In other words, given what was said above, it is quite reasonable to assume that satisfaction of these requirements will reduce the processing difficulties. This hypothesis is supported by the results of two recent experimental studies, which shall be given a short discussion.

The first experiment is an ERP-study by Bornkessel et al. (2003), in which subjects had to read a context sentence containing an embedded question, to which the target sentence provided an answer. The target sentences were either SOV or OSV. The context sentences varied with respect to 3 dimensions: *givenness* (which should affect the processing of the 1st DP), *contextual prediction* (which should affect the processing of Foci), and the *nature of the contextual prediction* (which should affect the case vs. lexical requirements imposed by the question). The authors basically found two effects: an effect of contextual prediction, and an effect of givenness. The former consisted in a positivity in the ERP-track which is interpreted as the fulfillment of a prediction generated by the context. That is, if an element is explicitly required by a context question, it may be integrated into the current interpretation more easily even if the construction it is part of deviates from canonical order.[10] The second effect, however, was a negativity occurring for the processing of object-first sentences even when the object was given by the context. This is interpreted as saying that contextual licensing in terms of givenness does not suffice to alleviate the local mismatch induced by the deviation from SOV order. Their results clearly showing effects of context on early processing, Bornkessel et al. conclude that being queried does license marked word order, whereas being given does not.

[10] To give an example of such a context-target pair: "Klaus fragt sich, wen der Lehrer am Sonntag besucht hat. — Dann erfuhr er, dass den Gärtner der Lehrer besucht hat." ('Klaus asks himself, who$_{ACC}$ [the$_{NOM}$ teacher] visited has. — Then heard he that [the$_{ACC}$ gardener] [the$_{NOM}$ teacher] visited has.').

This is a point onto which the second study may shed some light. In a series of self-paced reading experiments, I presented participants with target sentences which were embedded into short texts (s. Weskott (2002) , chp. 5, for the methodological and statistical details). The contexts varied with respect to certain pragmatic factors related to the sentence-initial element of the target sentence (Exp. 1: being vs. not being inferable from context; Exp. 3: being vs. not being given in the context).[11] The target sentences in all three experiments varied with respect to word order (canonical (SVO) vs. deviating (OVS)). The prediction was that an interaction between the pragmatic factors and the word order factor should occur if the topicalisation of the direct object was licensed by the presence of the factors in the context. For example, if inferability would license topicalisation, OVS structures should not take significantly more time to read if the object is inferable than SVO, whereas an OVS structure with a non-inferable object should result in a significantly higher reading time the respective SVO. However, Experiment 1 showed no such significant interaction. That is, inferability of the Topic itself is not sufficient to modulate the processing difficulty associated to the deviant OVS order.

Experiment 2 induced the factor parallelity, which consisted in a structurally parallel vs. non-parallel sentence preceding the target sentence (i.e. SVO-SVO and OVS-OVS vs. SVO-OVS and OVS-SVO). Although this factor is known to have a strong influence on processing (cf. Frazier et al. (1984, 2000)), it did not interact with the word order factor. Even when preceded by a structurally parallel sentence, OVS structures were still processed slower than SVO structures.

In Experiment 3, the texts exhibited an elaborative discourse structure. That is, the context provided two discourse referents which were then picked up as sentence initial elements of the two parallel elaborating sentences. This givenness factor was hypothesized to interact with the word order manipulation, i.e. elaborating on given referents with OVS-OVS structures should not be significantly worse than SVO-SVO, whereas an elaboration on non-given referents should show an increase in reading time. This prediction was borne out by the data: the interaction of word order × givenness turned out to be significant in the region towards the end of the second elaborating sentence. This result shows that givenness indeed *can* affect the processing of marked word orders like OVS, as long as the discourse structure is explicit enough to support such an interpretation. That is, perhaps mere givenness of a referent may not suffice

---

[11] An example of such a text: [*Context*: Ein Saboteur hatte sich in den kleinen Zirkus eingeschlichen. Als die schlechte Nachricht (*zum Direktor und zum Dompteur*) durchgesickert war, wurden alle sehr misstrauisch ('A saboteur had crept into the little circus. When the bad news had leaked out (*to the director and the tamer*), everybody got very suspicious.')] *Critical sentence(s)*: Der/den Direktor beschattete den/der Akrobat(en), und der/den Dompteur belauerte den/der Clown argwöhnisch. ('The$_{NOM/ACC}$ director shadowed the$_{ACC/NOM}$ acrobat, and the$_{NOM/ACC}$ tamer eyed the$_{ACC/NOM}$ clown distrustfully.')

to license deviation from canonicality. We may speculate that it has to be backed up by discourse relations like *Elaboration, Contrast*, which strengthen the link between the Topic and its antecedent in the context.

5 Concluding remarks

To sum up: the results presented in the last section seem to be in accordance with the predictions made by (H2): as long as the context provides a rich enough structure, marked constructions like German OVS or OSV structures are not significantly harder to process than canonical ones like SVO or SOV. This can be viewed as a first piece of empirical evidence in favour of the scalar notion of Information Structural markedness put forward in section 2. Further experiments will show whether (H2) can be maintained in the form presented here, or whether some revisions or refinements have to be made. This built-in falsifiability of the approach presented here, together with its formal perspicuity, facilitate further investigations into Information Structural markedness in context.

6 References

Asher, N. (1993): Reference to Abstract Objects in Discourse. Dordrecht: Kluwer.

Asher, N. and A. Lascarides (1998a): Bridging. Journal of Semantics, 15, 83-113.

Asher, N. and A. Lascarides (1998b): The Semantics and Pragmatics of Presupposition. Journal of Semantics, 15, 239-299.

Bader, M. and M. Meng (1999): Subject-Object Ambiguities in German Embedded Clauses: An Across-the-Board Comparison. Journal of Psycholinguistic Research, 28(2), 121-143.Blutner, R. (1999): Some Aspects of Optimality in Natural language Interpretation. In: H. de Hoop and H. de Swart (eds): Papers on Optimality Theoretic Semantics. Utrecht Institute of Linguistics OTS, 1-21

Bornkessel, I., M. Schlesewsky, and A. D. Friederici (2003): Contextual Information Modulates Initial Processes of Syntactic Integration: The Role of Inter- vs. Intra-Sentential Predictions. Journal of Experimental Psychology: Learning, Memory, and Cognition. 29 (5), 971-882.

Büring, D. (1995): The 59th Street Bridge Accent. PhD Dissertation, Tübingen: Eberhard-Karls-Universität.

Cinque, G. (1993): A Null Theory of Phrase and Compound Stress. Linguistic Inquiry, 24 (2) 239-298.

Eckardt, R. (1996): Intonation and Predication.Technical report, Stuttgart University, Arbeitspapiere des SFB 340, 77.

Frazier, L., L. Taft, T. Roeper, Ch. Clifton, Jr., and K. Ehrlich (1984): Parallel Structure as a Source of Facilitation in Sentence Comprehension. Memory and Cognition, 12(5), 421-430.

Frazier, L., A. Munn, and Ch. Clifton, Jr. (2000): Processing Coordinate Structures. Journal of Psycholinguistic Research, 29(4), 343-370.

Frey, W. (2000): Zur syntaktischen Position der Satztopiks im Deutschen. In: ZAS Papers in Linguistics, 20: Issues on Topics. Berlin, Zentrum für Allgemeine Sprachwissenschaft, 137-172.

Haftka, B. (2000): Topik-Constraints im Deutschen: wie ich die der Anita natürlich auch erklären könnte. Linguistische Arbeitsberichte, 74, Leipzig University, 83-109

Haider, H. (1993): Deutsche Syntax—generativ. Tübingen: Narr.

Haider, H. and I. Rosengren (1998): Scrambling. Lund: Sprache und Pragmatik, 49.

Höhle, T. (1982): Explikation für "normale Betonung" und "normale Wortstellung". In: W. Abraham (ed): Satzglieder im Deutschen. Tübingen: Narr, 75-153.

Jacobs, J. (2001): The Dimensions of Topic-Comment. Linguistics, 39.4, 641-681.

Jakobson, R. (1957/1971): Shifters, Verbal Categories, and the Russian Verb. In: Selected Writings II. The Hague: Mouton, 130-147.

Jäger, G. (1996): Topics in Dynamic Semantics. PhD dissertation, Humboldt University Berlin.

Jäger, G. (2000): Some Notes on the Formal Properties of Bidirectional Optimality Theory. Journal of Logic, Language and Information, 11(4), 427-451.

Kruijff, G.-J. (2002): Formulating a Category of Informativity. In: H. Hasselgård, Stig Johansson, B. Behrens, and C. Fabricius-Hansen (eds): Information Structure in a Cross-Linguistic Perspective. Amsterdam, New York: Rodopi, 129-145.

Kruijff-Korbayová, I. (1998): The Dynamic Potential of Topic and Focus. PhD Dissertation, Charles University Prague.

Muckel, S. (2002): Wortstellungseffekte beim Satzverstehen: Zur Rolle syntaktischer, verbspezifischer und prosodischer Information. Wiesbaden: DUV.

Reinhart, T. (1996): Interface Economy: Focus and Markedness. In: Chris Wilder, Hans-Martin Gärtner, and Manfred Bierwisch (eds.): The Role of Economy Principles in Linguistic Theory. (= studia grammtica, vol. 40). Berlin: Akademie Verlag , 146-169.

van Rooy, R. (2001): Presupposition: An (un)common attitude? Ms., University of Amsterdam.

van der Sandt, R. A. (1992): Presupposition Projection as Anaphora Resolution. Journal of Semantics, 9, 333-377.

Schwarzschild, R. (1999): GIVENness, Avoid F and other Constraints on the Placement of Focus. Natural Language Semantics, 7(2), 141-177.

Steube, A. (2003a): Correction by Contrastive Focus. Theoretical Linguistics, 27, 215-249.

Steube, A. (2003b): Grammatik und Pragmatik von Hutkonturen. In: W. Abraham and L. Molnárfi (eds): Folia Linguistica 37/1-2, 163-190.

Stolterfoht, B., A. Hahne, A. D. Friederici, and M. Bader (this volume): Focus Structure and the Processing of Word Order Variations in German..
Weskott, T. (2002): Information Structure as a Processing Guide: The Left Periphery of German Verb-Second Sentences and Its Interpretation in Context. PhD dissertation, Leipzig University.

Claudia Hruska and Kai Alter (Leipzig)

Prosody in Dialogues and Single Sentences: How Prosody can influence Speech Perception

1 Introduction

In communication settings, human beings use prosody to structure information. Prosody is an intrinsic determinant of spoken language (Cutler, Dahan & van Donselaar, 1997), and prosodic cues are used on all levels of speech processing. As compared to written language, these prosodic features provide additional information about both the underlying syntactic structure and the information structure of the utterance (Beckman, 1996; Hirschberg, 2002; Nespor & Vogel, 1986; Selkirk, 1994). Two aspects of prosodic markers were examined in several studies, mostly in single sentence comprehension: the distribution of intonational phrase (IPh) boundaries and the position and type of accents. It has been shown that the placement of IPh boundaries strongly relies on the underlying syntactic structure and that prosodic cues of IPh boundaries can be used for the disambiguation between syntactically homophonous sentences (e.g. Pynte & Prieur, 1996).

Moreover, accentuation patterns can influence the perceptual processes. Two kinds of rule-based accent distributions are so far well established in prosodic research. The first concerns the default accent placements in so called neutral sentences, e.g. sentences produced and perceived in isolation without any contextual information. Here we follow the assumption that accents (and IPh boundaries) reflect the syntactic structure in a single sentence. German, as an SOV-language, typically assigns the main sentence accent to the most embedded constituent (Cinque, 1993; among others).

The picture radically changes when sentences are part of larger informational units such as dialogues. In a hypothetical dialogue situation, the preceding wh-question of speaker A indicates that speaker B has conveyed the information status of speaker A in answering. In this special situation, speaker B will highlight the new information by means of prosodic patterns. This can be realized by moving the main accent position to the constituent considered to be new in a sentence. The speaker's focus producing the answer is therefore related to the constituent previously asked for.

Focus reflects the status of the information structure. The ongoing research on information structure (IS) has described different theoretical definitions (Lambrecht, 1996, Liedtke, 2001; Price, 1981; Steube, 2000). The main description of IS relies on the given/new status. The focus of a sentence is semantically/pragmatically the most salient information and it has been pointed out that these aspects are emphasized as opposed to given or presupposed information (e.g. Halliday, 1967). In intonational languages such as German, Dutch and English, focused information is emphasized by pitch accents in speech. It has been shown that focus-driven accent patterns have a crucial influence on the interpretation of sentences (Schafer, Carlson, Clifton & Frazier, 2000; Warren, Grabe & Nolan, 1995) and appropriate accent patterns due to preceding information facilitate the comprehension of sentences (Bock & Mazzella, 1983; Terken & Nooteboom, 1987).

Nevertheless, most of these studies have been used as behavioral designs to evaluate the influence of prosodic information in spoken language comprehension. Empirical evidence for the usage of prosodic cues in early speech perception from a brain response technique (electroencephalogram) was first reported by Steinhauer, Alter & Friederici (1999). In these studies the difference in prosodic structure was shown for two conditions with sentences providing an identical word order, but differing in the underlying syntactic structure (intransitive vs. transitive verbs). Steinhauer and colleagues measured event-related brain potentials (ERPs) to evaluate the online processing of IPh boundaries while subjects listened to sentences. A specific ERP correlate for the processing of IPh boundaries was consistently revealed, which was termed the Closure Positive Shift (CPS). The ERP-technique is of particular advantage in the on-line study of speech perception. It has a very high time resolution, and ERP components reflect systematic brain activity related to both perception of physical input and higher cognitive processes without requiring the interruption of the speech signal for data collection.

1.1 Open questions/hypotheses

One important issue concerns the employment of prosodic information in daily conversation. In dialogues, it can sometimes be observed that speakers, even aware of the actual situation or of general world knowledge, do not appropriately realize the crucial prosodic speech parameters, resulting in severe misunderstanding. This might be the case in special communicative situations such as in interviews (concerning foreigners or politicians).

In the studies presented here, we investigated the role of focus accents in dialogue situations, namely question-answer pairs, and, in addition, in single sentences. In terms of IS, question focus leads to a specific emphasized accent pattern on new information in the answer. Perceptual processes can be evaluated using both behavioral responses and the high time resolution of ERPs. We investigated speech perception elicited by the focus of preceding context information and aspects of the appropriateness of the accentuation patterns of the following sentences. How focus accents are interpreted in isolated sentences will be shown in a second attempt.

2 Speech production

The German sentence material based on the one described in Steinhauer et al. (1999) and Hruska, Steinhauer & Alter (2001) always contained the same linear word order [NP1][VP1][DP1][VP2][CP]. The material was first produced without any context information (1) and then as the answer to questions establishing narrow focus on either the determiner phrase (the DP1; 2b) or on the verb and following constituents (VP+; 2a). Special context questions were created for material exemplified in 2a/b.

(1) neutral focus
[Peter verspricht Anna zu arbeiten]$_{IPh}$ und das Büro zu putzen
(Peter promises Anna to work and to clean the office)

(2) (a) broad[1] focus on the verb phrase
Q: Was verspricht Peter Anna zu tun?
(What does Peter promise Anna to do ?)
A: Peter verspricht Anna (zu ARBEITEN und das BÜRO zu putzen)F.

(2) (b) narrow focus on the second noun
Q: Wem verspricht Peter zu arbeiten und das Büro zu putzen?
(Whom does Peter promise to work and to clean the office?)
A: Peter verspricht (ANNA)F zu arbeiten und das Büro zu putzen.

2.1 Speech recordings

The sentence material was spoken by a female speaker in either a neutral focus condition or with preceding context questions establishing narrow focus on the second noun or broad focus on the verb phrase. Each condition included forty-eight sentences which always had the identical word order as described above. The material was recorded in an acoustically shielded room and was digitised at 44.1 kHz and 16 bit sampling rate. Each sentence was normalized in loudness in order to avoid specific responses on general loudness differences.

[1] This term is according to the notation of Ladd (1996).

2.2 Acoustic analyzes

The two main parameters of acoustic features - the duration and the F0-contour of constituents at the critical points of DP1 and VP2 - were analyzed in detail. The duration of the DP1 showed significant effects on focus (see Fig.1). The constituent was significantly lengthened in comparison to the other conditions. For the constituent VP2, a shorter duration was measurable for the narrow focused condition while the broad focused condition led to longer durations of this constituent. In sum, constituents related to focus are consistently lengthened in comparison to unfocused fragments.

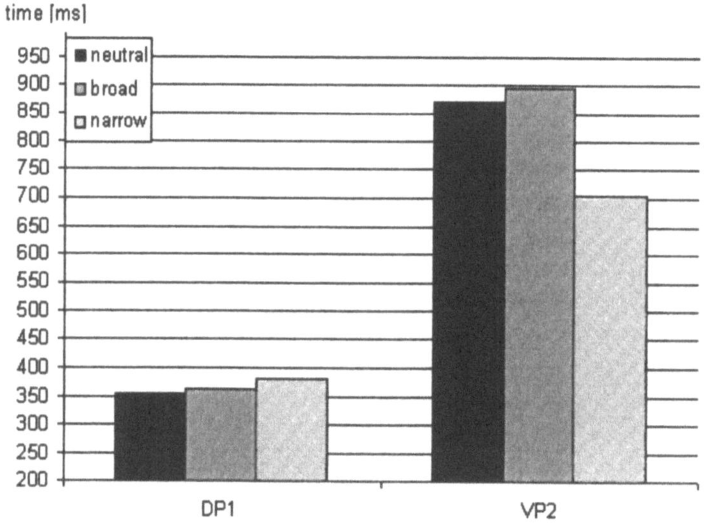

Figure 1: The length of critical constituents demonstrate the effect on IS in lengthening of the focused constituents in direct comparison to neutral intonated sentences.

Further acoustic analyzes of the speech data showed that focused constituents always carry the main pitch accent in the contextually embedded sentences (see Fig. 2). Measurements of F0-value-maxima of the three conditions clearly demonstrated pitch accents for constituents in focus. Under narrow focus on the DP1, the main pitch accent was measurable at this position. The other constituents, especially the following constituents, were clearly de-accented. The accent positions in neutrally and broad focused (VP+) sentences did not differ, but the broad focused condition showed higher F0-values at accent positions than those of neutrally intonated sentences.

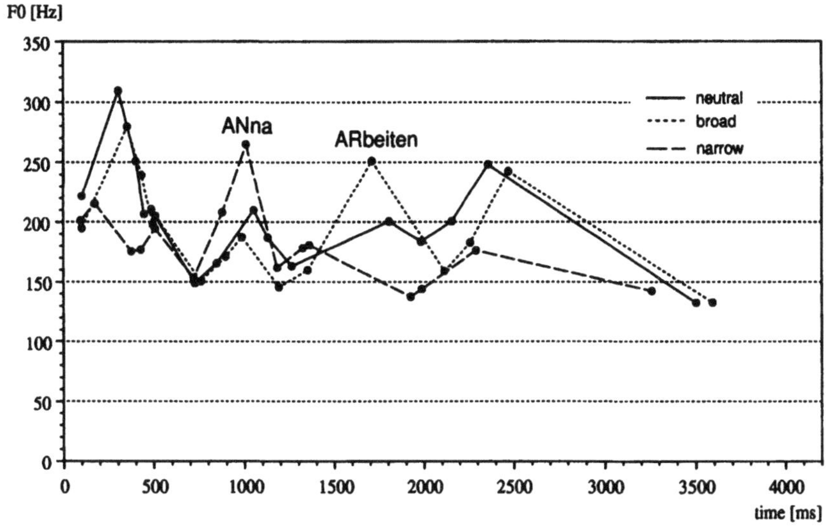

Figure 2: The comparison of prototypical F0-contours of all three conditions. The pitch accent moves from DP1 in the narrow focus condition to the infinitive in broad focused condition. Both differ from neutral intonated sentences in the relative high of the F0-values.

Both acoustic parameters demonstrate the highlighting of focused aspects in spoken sentences according to the information structure. New information was marked by high pitch accents. Without any preceding context information, the accent position depends on the underlying syntactic structure.

To summarize, we found the following prosodic differences between the conditions 1 vs. 2a/b). Capitals mark accents, and brackets indicate IPh-phrasing (see also Fig. 2):

(1) Peter verspricht anna zu ARbeiten]$_{IPh}$ und das büRO zu putzen
(Peter promises Anna to work and to clean the office)

(2) (a) Peter verspricht anna zu ARbeiten]$_{IPh}$ und das büRO zu putzen

(2) (b) Peter verspricht ANna zu arbeiten]$_{IPh}$ und das Büro zu putzen

This simplified prosodic description reveals the major confounds and differences between the three conditions in our experiments. Condition (1) is similar to condition (2b) in pitch accent placements, but differs in prominence. However, both conditions differ with respect to the main accent position in the narrow focused condition (2b).

As shown in Table 1, not all possible combinations are covered by the three experiments discussed here. We focused mainly on the comparison between default accentuation and accentuation triggered by context information. These comparisons among others are necessary to examine the impact of context information on prosodic accent realizations during auditory dialogue perception.

	± isolated presentation	appropriate due to context question	inappropriate due to context question
neutral	Exp 2 / 3		
broad VP+	Exp 2	Exp 1	Exp 1
narrow DP1	Exp 3	Exp 1	Exp 1

Table 1: Comparisons realized in the series of studies presented for the processing of single sentences and sentences embedded in contexts. The term VP+ is related to the realization of the broad focused condition (2a) projecting the focus on the infinitive and the conjunction and term DP1 to narrow focusing conditions (2b).

In the next section, the procedure and the data of the first series of experiments dealing with the comparison between the contextually matching and mismatching conditions are presented. This experiment deals with the crucial point discussed also in Toepel & Alter (in this volume) concerning the appropriateness of prosodic parameters during spoken language processing.

3 Perception of dialogues

3.1 Design

In the first experiment, dialogue sequences were presented containing wh-questions eliciting either broad (VP+; 2a) or narrow (DP1; 2b) focus. In addition to these appropriate dialogue sequences, 'incorrect' dialogues were created, in which the questions were presented in combination with answer sentences which conveyed the inappropriate accent pattern (Tab. 2).

	appropriate accent due to context question	inappropriate accent due to context question
broad VP+	Peter verspricht anna zu ARbeiten]$_{IPh}$ und das bÜRO zu putzen	Peter verspricht ANna zu arbeiten]$_{IPh}$ und das Büro zu putzen
narrow DP1	Peter verspricht ANna zu arbeiten]$_{IPh}$ und das Büro zu putzen	Peter verspricht anna zu ARbeiten]$_{IPh}$ und das bÜRO zu putzen

Table 2: Examples of experimental conditions of the dialogue experiment. Each type of context question was combined with the appropriate prosodic pattern and the inappropriate pattern conducting two kinds of mismatch conditions.

Participants were invited to listen carefully to the presented sequences and to judge the appropriateness of the sentence pattern subsequent to the end of each answer sentence. Behavioral data and electrophysiological recordings were measured.

3.2 General procedure

In all three experiments, the sentences/dialogues were presented via loudspeaker in an acoustically and electro-magnetically shielded chamber. Only right handed subjects with neither known hearing impairments nor psychiatric and neurological disorders participated in the experiments.

In addition to behavioral measurements, the electroencephalogram (EEG) was continuously recorded from 25 Ag-AgCl cap-mounted electrodes referenced against the left mastoid while participants listened to the material and judged the appropriateness of the sentence prosody. ERPs were averaged over artefact-free trials per condition and subject according to sentence onsets. All ERPs were mathematically re-referenced against the linked mastoids to avoid reference induced lateralisation effects. All presented ERPs show the grand average of the whole group of participants.

3.3 Results

Twenty-one subjects (mean age = 23) listened to question-answer pairs which were presented in prosodically appropriate and inappropriate pairs. The judgment performance (prosodic task) was about 98 %. Listeners were very good at identifying appropriate as well as inappropriate prosodic patterns in answer sentences due to question focus.

The ERP data of appropriate conditions are demonstrated in Figure 3. Main effects of *question focus* are reflected in different components. In early time windows, a negative wave for the narrow focus condition was measurable at frontal electrodes right on the position of the DP1. For the broad focused sentences, the negativity was elicited in a later time window and thus shaping is smaller than the negativity for narrow focused sentences. This effect might reflect an orientation to the sentence position where listeners expected the new 'focused' information (expectancy negativity [EN]). Moreover, in later time windows, the effect of *focus* showed a clear posterior dominance for a narrow focused condition when the new information has already been received. This effect did not appear in broad focused sentences until the second verb was presented. In both conditions, this later effect was reflected by a large positive shift in the ERP, resembling the Closure Positive Shift in single sentences (CPS; see Steinhauer et al., 1999).

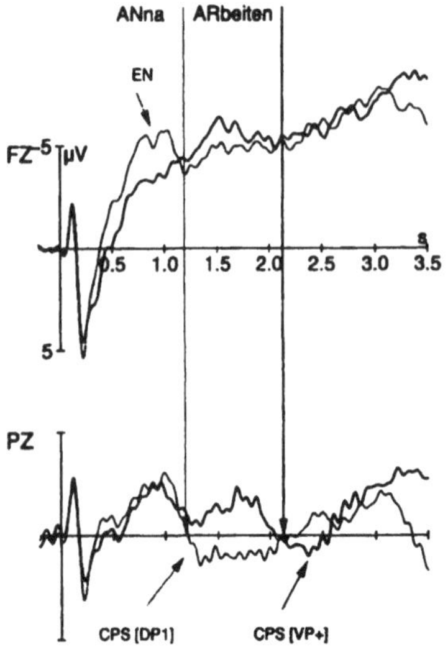

Figure 3: Two referen-tial electrodes demon-strate the perceptional process of the different focused answer sen-tences. Black lines repre-sent the response to a broad focused condition, grey lines of a narrow focused condition, and both in the appropriate manner.

Both observed ERP patterns seem to reflect the strongly context-guided comprehension process in dialogues. Large positive shifts (CPS) only occur after the constituent in focus while this component is considerably diminished at potential IPh-boundary positions. The results of the listener's processing in mismatch conditions show how strongly the perception is influenced by context vs. prosodic cues.

Unexpected accents due to question focus elicited a mismatch effect (Fig. 4 and 5). The effect is most prominent in violation of the narrow focused questions (Fig. 4). The preceding 'Whom ...? ' question requires focus on the DP1, but the verb actually carries the focus accent. In this case, a large negativity (N400) over the focused position is followed by a large positivity (P600), both eliciting with a centro-posterior maximum. The comparison on frontal electrodes showed an earlier negativity for the mismatch condition where the DP1 is in focus. This underlines the interpretation of expectancy orientation given above for appropriate conditions. The distinct mismatch pattern is not shown in the opposite mismatch condition. In the case of violation due to the preceding 'What ...?' question, a superfluous accent on the noun occurs before listeners perceive the focus information. Again, a missing accent on the new information (infinitive) elicited in a negative going waveform (N400; see Fig. 5). Therefore the prominent focus accent on the DP1 leads to a positive shift (CPS) at the offset of this constituent.

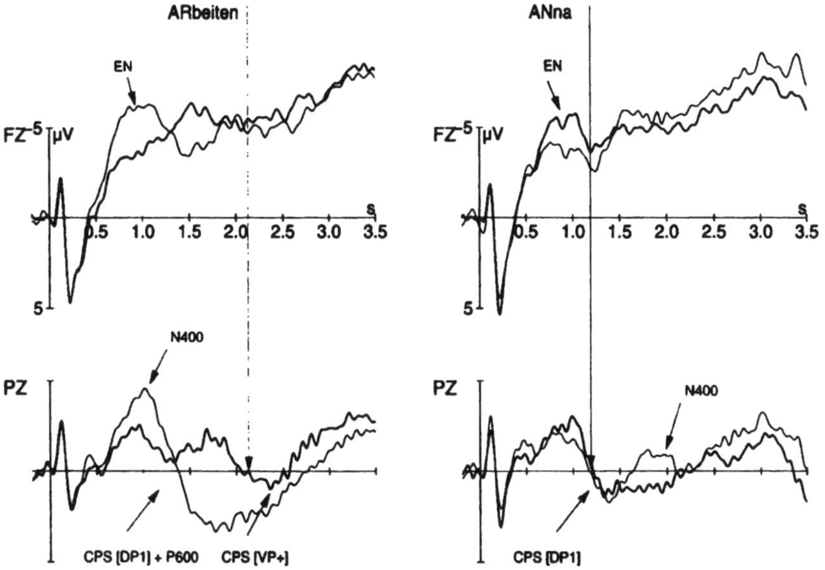

Figure 4/5: Mismatch detections due to the violation of the preceding context question are reflected in the ERPs[2]. In both illustrations appropriate conditions are labelled by black lines and inappropriate conditions by grey lines. The left panel shows the violation of the entire narrow focus question where a broad accented sentence is followed in comparison to appropriate broad focused sentences. The missing accent on this early constituent leads to a strong mismatch effect (N400/P600). The opposite kind of violation responses (preceding VP+ focus question followed by the sentences with DP1 focus accent; right panel) leads to smaller effects and the pitch accent on "Anna" seems to guide an interpretation as new information. The CPS occurred after the DP1 and the N400 appeared on the infinitive where the expected new information is de-accented.

Thus, in terms of prosodic phrasing, information structure seems to override syntactically driven IPh-boundaries. Listeners keep their attention mainly on constituents carrying focused new information in answer sentences (EN) due to the preceding questions. After perceiving new aspects, a positive going waveform (CPS) is measurable at posterior sides reflecting the integration of focused information in already given context information. Inappropriate prosodic patterns, especially missing accents on new aspects, aggravate the integration of new information (N400). The mismatch effect is much stronger when new information is de-accented in early positions in answer sentences (violation of DP1 focus), whereas a superfluous focus accent at an early constituent, before the expected new information is perceived, leads to an interpretation as salient, new information.

[2] Note that the ERPs are based on the same acoustic input, only differing in its appropriateness to the preceding context question.

4 Single sentences

Parts of the dialogue material were used in a further experiment. To evaluate the effect of a superfluous focus accent on the single sentence level, focused sentences without the preceding context question and neutrally intonated sentences were presented in a similar experimental setting. Each experiment combined the neutral focused condition with one of the focused conditions respectively (see Tab. 3).

	neutrally intonated	**focused without preceding context question**
experiment 2	Peter verspricht Anna zu ARbeiten]$_{IPh}$ und das bÜRO zu putzen	Peter verspricht anna zu ARbeiten)$_F$]$_{IPh}$ und das bÜRO zu putzen
experiment 3	Peter verspricht Anna zu ARbeiten]$_{IPh}$ und das bÜRO zu putzen	Peter verspricht ANna)$_F$ zu arbeiten]$_{IPh}$ und das Büro zu putzen

Table 3: Examples of experimental conditions of the first and second single sentence experiment. In each experiment neutral intonated sentences carrying the default accent pattern were presented in comparison to one of the focused sentences without the preceding context question.

4.1 Experiment 2

Neutrally intonated and broad focused sentences (1/2a) were presented in a pseudo-randomised order to elaborate the effect of prosodically highlighted information without a preceding focus question.

Sixteen participants (mean age = 23.7) took part in this experiment and were instructed to judge the appropriateness of sentence prosody. The behavioral data showed a higher acceptance rate for neutrally intonated sentences (82%) then for focused conditions (73%).

The ERP-data reflects that the perception of single sentences is principally based on the underlying syntactic structure (Fig. 6). In neutrally intonated and also in focused sentences, a large positive shift at posterior electrodes (CPS) occurs whenever an IPh boundary is measurable. Nevertheless, frontal effects described above for expected new information in dialogues were not observed on the single sentence level. This lack of any frontal effects underlines the interpretation of an expectancy effect on new aspects in sentences due to preceding context questions. In the focused condition, a prolonged positive shift at posterior sides is measurable where the superfluous focus accent occurred.

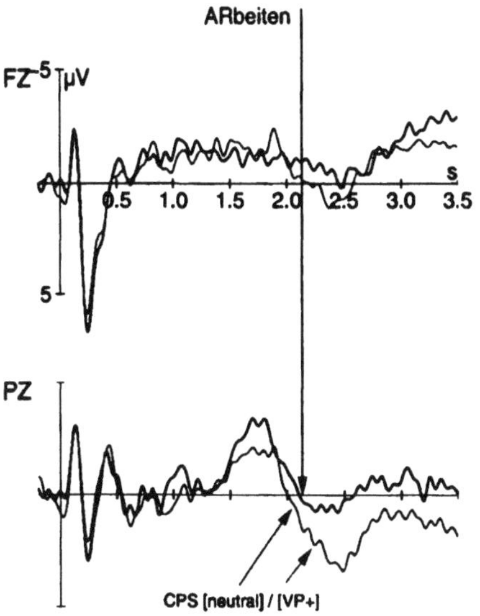

Figure 6: ERPs due to neutral intonated sentences (black lines) and broad intonated sentences (VP+; grey lines) represent that listeners keep their attention to perception of the under-lying syntactic structure. The CPS occurred for both conditions at IPh boundaries. Nevertheless a sustained positivity prior the end of the focus-accented con-stituent was shown for the focused condition.

4.2 Experiment 3

In the third experiment, single sentences were again presented to listeners. The condition with narrow focus on the DP1 (2b) was presented without the preceding context question in direct comparison to neutrally intonated sentences (1; see Tab. 3). As shown in Figure 2, the accentuation pattern differs in position of the main pitch accent, and the relative height from each other and the prosodic structure is influenced by the preceding focus question.

Sixteen participants (mean age = 23.8) took part in this study and listened to the sentences which were again presented in a pseudo-randomised order. Focused sentences were much lower in acceptance. The acceptance rate for narrow focused condition was only 8%, whereas neutrally intonated sentences were highly accepted (94%).

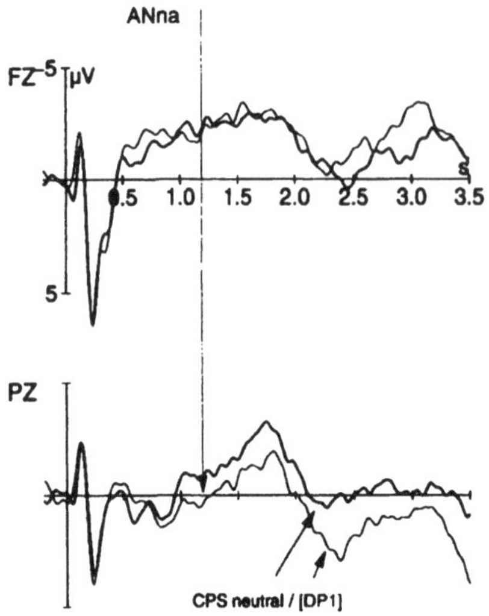

Figure 7: ERPs of the second single sentence experiment. Black lines represent the perception of neutral intonated sentences and grey lines those of narrow focused sentences (DP1) present-ed without any context question. As in the previous single sentence experiment, the CPS occurred at the IPh-boundaries in both conditions. However, the perception of the superfluous focus accent on "ANna" is reflected in a sustained positive shift in the ERP.

The ERP results for sentences carrying narrow focus on the DP1 presented in isolation suggest a syntactically-driven perception (see Fig. 7). The CPS as indicator of phrase boundary perception on the single sentence level occurs whenever an IPh boundary was measurable in the speech signal. Moreover, an additionally prolonged positive effect at posterior electrodes is elicited at the position where the focus accent occurs.

In both single sentence experiments, the focused condition presented without the preceding context question was identified as such. The acceptance of focused sentences was lower than for neutrally intonated sentences with a default accent pattern. Moreover, according to the acoustic data, broad focused sentences and neutrally intonated sentences are much more similar in the accent pattern than the narrow focused condition. The very low acceptance rate of the later condition seems to result from an IS driven interpretation, which is not compatible to an 'out-of-the-blue' perception. As listeners reported in a post-experimental questionnaire, these narrow focus sentences (DP1) strongly guided a focus interpretation. In the ERP-data, no frontal effect was shown and the CPS always occurred at IPh boundaries. Moreover, a prolonged/sustained positive effect occurred at focus-accent positions in both focused conditions in comparison to the neutrally intonated condition.

6 Discussion

The realization of accent pattern relies strongly on the contextual embedding of sentences. In neutral focus, the sentence accent is placed on the position of the most embedded constituent (Ladd, 1996; Cutler & Isard, 1980). In dialogues, exemplified here with context questions preceding the answer, prosodic patterns reflect more the information structure than the underlying syntactic structure. Pitch accents are moved from syntax-driven positions to the respective focus domain. Focused constituents are lengthened and the fundamental frequency at those positions is increased. The pitch variation provides the strongest cue of accentuation and may override other cues (see also in Nooteboom & Kruyt, 1987).

The prosodic judgment in all experiments underline that inappropriate prosodic pattern in dialogues (missing focus accent at new information) and on single sentence level (superfluous focus accents) were clearly identified by listeners. This suggests shared beliefs in the usage of prosodic cues such as accents in dialogues and single sentences.

It has been suggested in previous ERP-studies that context can influence sentence processing. As shown in an ERP-study by van Berkum, Hagoort & Brown (1999) the N400, which reflects the difficulties in semantic/lexical integration, was elicited by sentences that were semantically inappropriate to the preceding context information.

In our studies, we examined the processing of prosodic features related to given context information or non-existing context. The online recordings (ERP) indicate that listeners focus their attention in dialogues to constituents where new information is expected. Frontal negativities reflect the orientation towards these positions without regards to a actual prosodic input. As reported in several studies (visual presented e.g. Fiebach, 2001; King & Kutas, 1995; Kluender & Kutas, 1993) sustained frontal negativities are related to the storage in working memory of the wh-fillers in intra-sentential context. The ERP-data of the dialogue experiment suggests that given information on the context question must be maintained in the working memory until later (new) information is embedded. Moreover, the frontal effect was not shown at single sentence level. Without any preceding information, the listeners analyze each sentence as completely new and no information has to be embedded in an already given context.

The process of embedding the expected new information in dialogues is reflected by the Closure Positive Shift (CPS). The CPS occurs when new information is perceived. In single sentences, the CPS moves to positions where the prosodic cues of IPh boundaries clarify the underlying syntactic structure. Nevertheless, early focus accents can also guide the interpretation of information as new. The CPS occurs whenever prosodic cues are useful to facilitate the perception and might resemble segmentation process of the speech input.

How essential are appropriate accent patterns in dialogues and how do superfluous accent patterns influence perception? The three conducted experiments present answers to these questions. In dialogues, a missing focus accent on new information aggravates the integration of this information. A large negativity (N400) represents the difficulty of integration of new information in an already given context. This effect suggests that the system needs additional resources for embedding new information in the already given informational context. The effect of missing focus accent is much stronger at early positions (violation of the IS in narrow focus). In addition to the N400 on the position of de-accented new information, a P600 component is elicited. This effect might reflect the reanalysis of the violated information structure on the base of the context question before other information is available. Moreover, ERP-data of the dialogue experiment suggests that superfluous focus accents can be ignored at later positions. But a strong focus accent in early positions (narrow focus on the DP1) leads to an interpretation of salient new information. In single sentence presentation, focus accent patterns were not interpreted as such. Nonetheless, the inappropriate accent pattern was identified by listeners. In addition to an unexpected accent placement and further de-accentuation patterns, the sentence meaning was interpreted as implying narrow focus on DP1. As was shown in behavioral studies, given information is verified faster when this information was unaccented, whereas new information must be accented (Terken & Nooteboom, 1987). Additionally, an appropriate prosodic pattern due to focusing questions facilitates the perceptual processes (Bock & Mazzella, 1993).

The usage of prosodic cues is very complex. The accent type, position and prominence determines the mismatch perception. Moreover, appropriate prosodic patterns facilitate the perceptual process at single sentence and dialogue level.

7 Conclusion

Based on these findings, we propose a model of auditory sentence processing which acknowledges IS-constraints in addition to prosody-syntax-mapping. According to the theory of IS, new information is prosodically triggered by pitch accents on focused constituents. The experiments have shown that the appropriate accent pattern plays a crucial role in IS of dialogues but it is less important with regard to the perception of single sentences. As reflected by frontal effects, listeners pay more attention to the position of expected new information in dialogues. New information has to be integrated into already given context information maintained in working memory. Inappropriate accentuation in dialogues leads to disturbed comprehension and, in particular, missing focus accents on new information aggravate the embedding of new information in an already given context.

Our claim is that in single sentence comprehension, the system preferentially uses the prosodic cues of intonational phrase boundaries for an efficient evaluation of the underlying syntactic structure. However, if prior context information is available, the system additionally utilizes this information and is able to predict the position of new information from focus accents. A CPS in dialogues reflects the embedding of new information and is elicited after focused constituents. On single sentence level, this component occurs due to intonational phrase boundaries and resemble the segmentation of the speech input in sense units (Selkirk, 1994). This indicate an underlying integration process in speech perception reflected by this component. In sum, listeners are efficient at using specific information from the multi-cued prosodic structure in dependence of the contextual environment.

8 References

Beckman, M. E. (1996): The parsing of prosody. Language and Cognitive Processes 1, 17-67.

Bock, J. and J. Mazella (1983): Intonational marking of given and new information. Some consequences for comprehension. Memory and Cognition 11, 64-76.

Bolinger, D. (1989): Intonation and its parts. Melody in spoken English. Stanford University Press. Palo Alto.

Cinque (1993): A null-theory of phrase and compound stress. Linguistic Inquiry 24, 239-298.

Cutler, A., D. Dahan, and W. van Donselaar (1997): Prosody in the comprehension of spoken language: A literature review. Language and Speech 40 (2), 141-201.

Cutler, A and S. D. Isard (1980). Production of prosody. In: B. Butterworth (ed): Language production 1 : Speech and talk. New York: Academic Press.

Fiebach, C. J. (2001): Syntax and working memory during sentence processing. A neurocognitive investigation using event-related brain potentials and functional magnetic resonance imaging. No. 23. MPI press.

Halliday, M. A. K. (1967): Notes on transitivity and theme in English, part 2. Journal of Linguistics 3, 199-244.

Hirschberg, J. (2002): Communication and prosody: Functional aspects of prosody. Speech and Communication 36, 31-43.

Hruska, C., K. Steinhauer, and K. Alter (2001): Misleading dialogues: Human's brain reaction to prosodic information. Paper presented at the ORAGE-conference, Aix-en-Provence, 425-430.

King, J. W. and M. Kutas (1995). Who did what to when? Using word- and clause-level ERPs to monitor working memory usage in reading. Journal of Cognitive Neuroscience 7(3), 376-395.

Kluender, R. and M. Kutas (1993): Bridging the Gap: Evidence from ERPs on the processing of unbounded dependencies. Journal of Cognitive Neuroscience, 5(2), 196-214.

Ladd, R. D. (1996): Intonational Phonology. Cambridge: Cambridge University Press.

Lambrecht, K. (1996): Information structure and sentence form: topic, focus, and the mental representations of discourse referents. Cambridge University Press.

Liedtke, F. (2001): Informationsstruktur, Text und Diskurs. In F. Liedtke and F. Hundsnurscher (eds): Pragmatische Syntax. Niemeyer: Tübingen, 73-95.

Nespor, M. and I. Vogel (1986): Prosodic Phonology. Foris: Dortrecht.

Nooteboom, S. G. and J. G. Kruyt (1987): Accents, focus description, and the perceived distribution of given and new information: An experiment. Journal of the Acoustic Society of America 82 (5), 1512-1524.

Prince, E. F. (1981): Taxonomy on the given and new status. In: P. Cole (ed): Radical pragmatics. The Academic Press: New York, 223-255

Pynte J. and B. Prieur (1996): Prosodic brakes and attachment decisions in sentence processing. Language and Cognitive Processes 11, 165-191.

Schafer, A., K. Carlson, C. Jr. Clifton, and L. Frazier (2000): Focus and the interpretation of pitch accent: Disambiguation embedding questions. Language and Speech 43 (1), 75-105.

Selkirk, E. (1994): Sentence prosody: Intonation, stress, and phrasing. In: J. Goldsmith (ed) Handbook of phonological theory. Blackwell: New York, 550-569.

Steinhauer, K., K. Alter, and A. D. Friederici (1999): Brain potentials indicate immediate use of prosodic cues in natural speech processing. Nature Neuroscience 2, 191-196.

Steube, A. (2000): Ein kognitionswissenschaftlich basiertes Modell für Informationsstrukturierung. In: Ch. Römer and J. Bayer (eds): Von der Philologie zur Grammatiktheorie. P. Suchsland zum 65. Geburtstag. Tübingen: Niemeyer, 213-238.

Terken, J. and S. G. Nooteboom (1987): Opposite effects of accentuation and deaccentuation on verification latencies for given and new information Language and Cognitive Processes 2 (3/4), 145-163.

van Berkum, J. J. A., P. Hagoort, and C. M. Brown (1999): Semantic integration in sentences and discourse: Evidence from the N400. Journal of Cognitive Neuroscience 11(6), 657-671.

Warren, P., E. Grabe, and F. Nolan (1995): Prosody, phonology, and parsing in closure ambiguities. Language and Cognitive Processes 10, 457-486.

Ulrike Toepel and Kai Alter (Leipzig)

On the Independence of Information Structural Processing from Prosody

1 Introduction

Prosodic focus can be described as the intonational highlighting of discourse-relevant, i.e., new, information by the speaker. Depending on the preceding discourse structure, this new information can either be confined to discrete constituents or extend to a larger domain of a sentence or to the whole utterance. Following the notation of Ladd (1996) this dichotomy will be expressed as narrow vs. broad focus in this paper.

The concept adopted here furthermore divides narrow foci into those containing new information vs. those conveying contrastive information. Arguments in favour of this tripartition between broad, narrow new information, and contrastive focus can be based on their complementary occurrence in contextually embedded utterances, on their (partly) differing discourse functions and associated accent phenomena. As German is an intonation language, new or relevant information is often expressed by accentual means. Our main goal is the realization and perception of (narrow) focus accents in information structure (IS). Information structure is seen here as a pragmatically determined hierarchy describing the communicative weight of sentence elements embedded in a larger context (Junghanns & Zybatow, 1997). For clarification of the assumed focus tripartition, a short excursion might be useful at this point.

A full-focus or broad focus sentence must either be uttered as an out-of-the-blue statement or as an answer to a preceding "What happened?"- question. To evoke a narrow focus interpretation (which is not contrastive), an interrogative with a wh-element asking for a certain constituent in the following statement (e.g. "Who?" or "What?") is needed. For a contrastive focus interpretation, a discourse set has to be established first (CORRIGENDUM) which can then be corrected (CORRIGENS). Regarding discourse functions, new information in focus (broad or narrow) presents an extension of the topic in an ongoing discourse as soon as it is uttered, while this is not the case for contrastive information. Here, a certain part of the topic of a discourse is not being augmented, only being corrected. Jackendoff (1972) and Rooth (1985) noted that contrast is always associated with explicit alternatives in a certain discourse. This view holds for narrow focus (new and contrastive), since both single out one referent from a potential set. However, only contrastive focus exhaustively excludes all other interpretation possibilities from the discourse.

With regard to accent placement, the expression of broad focus follows the rules of default or neutral accentuation in sentences (Ladd, 1996). The pitch accent falls onto the same position as the nuclear accent, namely, on the constituent that is the rightmost or most embedded in the sentence. Both narrow focus accents, on the other hand, are freely distributable in an utterance and depend only on previous discourse information. It is a matter of debate, however, whether the narrow focus accents are distinguishable by acoustic means, that is, one being more prominent than the other or by differing accent types. By analyzing acoustic data, Pierrehumbert & Hirschberg (1990) report a monotonal pitch peak (H*) as reflecting new information whereas a bitonal accent pattern (L+H*) is seen as indicating contrastive information (in English). The results of Bartels & Kingston (1994) lack this pattern but show more prominent peaks of the fundamental frequency (F0) over contrastive than over new information (Brown, Currie & Kenworthy, 1980; Ladd, 1983; but see Bolinger, 1986). Here, it seems notable that at least in the utterances that Bolinger chose, the corrected constituent can also carry the default sentence accent which might have rendered the overall salience of the pitch accent. But, Krahmer & Swerts (2001) were also unable to find consistent differences in the realization of the focus accents, no matter if they were distributed to default accent positions or not. For German, Alter et al. (2001) report less prominent F0-peaks for new information focus (in their case ambiguous between a broad vs. narrow reading) than for contrastive focus in positions of the actual default sentence accents. The accent types also differ in these data. New information accents are analyzed as embedded into the global intonation contour of the sentence and downstepped (!H*L), and contrastive accents as earlier peaking L+H* that are not influenced by declination within a sentence[1]. The timing of the pitch peaks, together with pre- and/ or post-focal de-accentuation phenomena then seems to be another indicator for the disambiguation of focus accents. Couper-Kuhlen (1984) and Chafe (1974) report a pitch drop (post-focal de-accentuation) after contrastive accents but not after non-contrastive ones. With English spoken materials, Ladd (1996) showed that a nuclear weak-strong prominence pattern (which is the neutral one) is ambiguous between a broad and narrow interpretation whereas a strong-weak pattern is always interpreted as narrow (i.e. new or contrastive). Féry (1993) confirmed these findings and added that the latter pattern also involves pre-nuclear de-accentuation in German.

[1] We don't summarize findings about durational aspects and intensity of the acoustic signals here since Wells (1986) and many others showed convincingly that F0 seems to be the best indicator for focus accents.

To summarize, a tripartion of focus into broad, narrow new, and contrastive is useful to capture the interactions of semantic-pragmatic, phonological and phonetic aspects of focus in discourse.

2 Previous experimental data

Nooteboom & Kruyt (1987) were among the first to present experimental evidence for perceptual consequences of inappropriate focus accents with regard to discourse requirements. They showed that subjects rated Dutch sentences as acceptable when they contained either a focus-marked (new) or a non-focus-marked (given) constituent which is accented (correct and over-specified accents). If, instead, a focus-marked (new) element was not accented (under-specification of accents), the sentences were rated unacceptable. Birch & Clifton (1995) reported similar results for English.

Based on these findings, Hruska, Alter, Steinhauer & Friederici (2001) used event-related potentials (ERPs) to investigate the real-time perception of correctly and incorrectly placed broad and narrow (new information) accents in German. Here, context questions were presented auditorily, followed by answering sentences which either comprised appropriate or inappropriate focus accents. Behavioral results showed that participants were very good at detecting whether the accent distribution in the answers matched the focus structure established by the context. The electrophysiological data revealed a robust positive waveform reflecting the online detection of the elements in focus. Additionally, the presentation of sentences with broad focus in a context that established narrow focus evoked a strong negative waveform in the ERPs for *expected but missing accents*. Notably, there was no effect for the presentation of narrow focus accents that followed broad focus questions *(superfluous accents)*. The positive peak in this study very much resembled the Closure Positive Shift (CPS) that was established by Steinhauer, Alter & Friederici (1999) as a marker of intonational structuring. This component was interpreted as being related to information structural processing.

Recent behavioral results of Alter et al (2001), Mleinek, Rohe, Steube & Umbach (2001) for German, and Krahmer & Swerts (2001) for Dutch provide further evidence for diverging perception of new information vs. contrastive accents in context. Krahmer & Swerts found evidence for a prominence hierarchy of focus accents in a rating study. Single contrastive accents were rated most prominent, new information as weaker, and accentuation of given elements as least prominent. However, this result could not be replicated when the accented words were presented in isolation. This supports the view that the disambiguation of focus accents in intonation languages does not exclusively rely on the prosodic parameters of the focused word itself. Intonational aspects surrounding the element in focus (e.g. pre- and post-focal de-accentuation) indeed seem to play a role in interpretation.

Alter et al. employed explicit prosodic judgments regarding the appropriateness of a focus accent pattern to a preceding story-like discourse. For adequate prosodic realizations (new information accent in a context eliciting new information focus & contrastive accent in a context eliciting contrastive focus) the acceptance rates were 83 %. The study also reports higher ratings for sentences with contrastive accents in contexts eliciting narrow focus, hence for the over-specification of prosodic parameters (55%) in a context. On the other hand, new information accents in contexts eliciting a contrastive interpretation were refused (82%). Under-specified focus accents thus seem to lead to interpretation difficulties.

The present study examines the described perceptual consequences of mis-specified focus accents in discourse using an online electrophysiological measure, namely by ERPs, to enhance our understanding of cerebral mechanisms supporting the interpretation of Information Structure (IS) and focus accents. The study also addresses the question whether the presentation of new information or contrastive accents in appropriate or inappropriate focus environments is reflected in event-related components, as observed in the study by Hruska et al. (2001).

3 Materials

Forty-four dialogues without word-order variations were created per condition establishing either narrow new focus (NEW) or contrastive focus (CON). They were produced by two female native speakers of Standard German (one for the declaratives, and one for the interrogatives) in a dialogue setting, and recorded in a soundproof room. Examples are given in Table 1.

The sentences were then digitized at a sampling rate of 44.1 kHz/ 16bit/ Mono and normalized in loudness. Durations of constituents and pauses as well as the course of the F0 were computed for the critical third sentence of each condition.

Incorrect accentuation patterns for both experiments were designed by combining the first two sentences of one condition with the critical accent-conveying sentence of the other condition. A context establishing new information focus (N) was then followed by a contrastive accent (C) and vice versa.

NN	1) Am Samstag hat Peter mir etwas versprochen. 2) Was hat er dir denn versprochen? 3) Er hat mir versprochen, [Anna zu entlasten und die Küche zu putzen.]$_{NEW}$
	Peter promised me something on Saturday. What then did he promise you? He promised me to support Anna and to clean the kitchen. (literal translation)
CC	1) Am Samstag hat Peter mir etwas versprochen. 2) Hat er dir versprochen, FRAUKE zu entlasten? 3) Er hat mir versprochen, [ANNA]$_{CON}$ [zu entlasten und die Küche zu putzen.]$_{NEW}$
	Peter promised me something on Saturday. Did he promise you to support Frauke? He promised me to support Anna and to clean the kitchen. (literal translation)
NC	1) Am Samstag hat Peter mir etwas versprochen. 2) Was hat er dir denn versprochen? 3) Er hat mir versprochen, [ANNA]$_{CON}$ [zu entlasten und die Küche zu putzen.]$_{NEW}$
CN	1) Am Samstag hat Peter mir etwas versprochen. 2) Hat er dir versprochen, FRAUKE zu entlasten? 3) Er hat mir versprochen, [Anna zu entlasten und die Küche zu putzen.]$_{NEW}$

Table 1: Examples for correct dialogues conveying either new information accents (NN) or a contrastive accent (CC) and incorrect dialogues combining contexts eliciting narrow focus with contrastive accents (NC) and vice versa (CN).

4 Speech production data

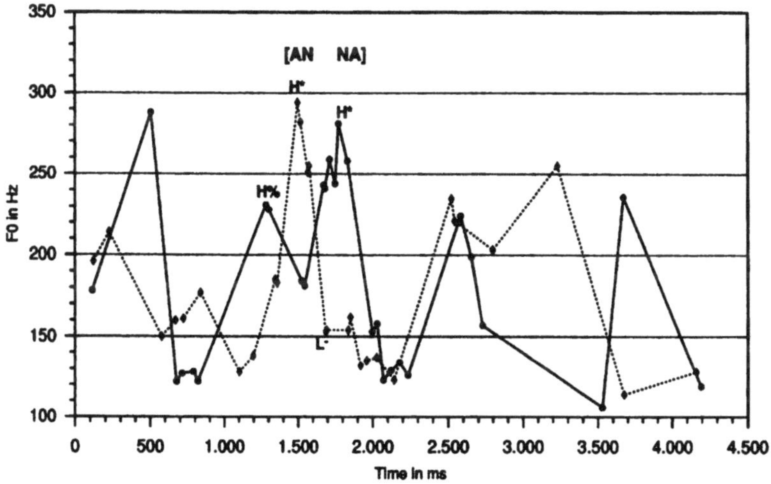

Figure 1: Stylized course of F0 for condition NN (solid black) and CC (dotted).

In intonation languages like German, the fundamental frequency (F0) provides the main prosodic cues for the interpretation of utterances (Wells, 1986). We therefore expected this prosodic parameter to differ between condition NN and CC. For the analysis of the overall intonation contour we therefore computed discrete F0-values. Of main interest to us were the pre-focal accent pattern and the focus positions before the conjunction phrase (the proper name in both conditions, and the following verb only in condition NN). In figure 1, stylized intonation contours for each condition are displayed (averaged per time point over 44 sentences per condition).

Comparing the two conditions NN and CC, the clause before the focused proper name in condition CC is de-accented as compared to the same time range in condition NN. The F0-excursion for NN (170 Hz) is much stronger than for CC (95 Hz). NN also displays a high early pitch peak at about 500 ms after sentence onset whereas CC does not. Also, the tone on the last syllable of the pre-focal clause is realized as a high boundary tone H % (Grice & Baumann, 2002) in condition NN, but rather as a phrase accent L- for CC (in accordance with durational differences between conditions).

In the position of the focused name ('Anna'), CC exhibits a slightly higher F0-peak than condition NN (290 vs. 280 Hz). The pitch for CC peaks during the articulation of the first syllable, which bears the lexically determined stress for all proper names used in the present experiment. For NN, the pitch peak shifts to the second syllable of the proper name. Additionally, only in condition CC does the F0 drop within the accentuation unit of the name. According to these data, we conclude that the accent pattern on new information is bitonal (L+H*) whereas it is more marked (L+H*L-) for contrastive/correction focus.

5 Method and procedure

Based on the same speech materials, two EEG-experiments were conducted. Twenty healthy right-handed students (Oldfield, 1971) took part in each study (mean age 23). Participants were always instructed to listen to the 4 x 44 dialogues which were presented in a pseudo-randomized order and divided into four blocks. The only varying factor between the experiments was the task requirement.

In Experiment 1, participants were asked a content question ('Did Peter promise something on Friday?') in 25 % of the trials and had to answer it by button press. In Experiment 2, participants were instructed to always judge the prosodic appropriateness of the critical sentence to the preceding context (prosodic judgment task).

The electroencephalogram (EEG) was continuously recorded from 25 scalp electrodes while the subjects were placed in an electro-magnetically shielded chamber and while they listened to the dialogues. To avoid eye movements, a fixation point was presented on a screen in front of the participants during sentence presentation. Eye-movements were registered by electrodes that were placed horizontally and vertically to the eyes.

After data acquisition, all trials containing eye blinks or movement artefacts were rejected. Event-related potentials were computed (with the EEP software 3.2) by time-locking the EEG to the beginning of the critical third sentence. For each of the four conditions, averages for every single participant were computed. Only the data of participants with more than 60% analyzable trials per condition were used to compute a group average and entered the statistical analyses.

6 Results

6.1 Behavioral data

In Experiment 1 (content question task), the percentage of false answers was 10,7 %. For Experiment 2 (prosodic judgment task), the error rates for the trials with correct accentuation according to the given context were lower (NN=15.9 %; CC=12.0 %) than for the trials with incorrect accentuation. In judging the prosodic appropriateness of new information accents to contexts eliciting a contrastive interpretation (CN), the error rates were only slightly higher (19,4 %). However, the error rate increased significantly (42,9 %) when participants were asked for the prosodic congruency between contexts which establish a narrow new focus in the answer, although the accent signals contrastive information. This is very much congruent to the results of Alter et al. (2001).

Figure 2 and 3 display the group average ERPs of Experiment 1 (n=20) and Figure 4 and 5 the group average for Experiment 2 (n=20). Note that the ERPs are always based on the same acoustic input, only differing in its appropriateness to the preceding context. Additionally, the plots are low-pass (7 Hz) for depiction. Only statistically significant effects (for the CPS in time windows of 300 ms, for the negative peaks in windows of 200 ms) are being reported in the following section.

6.2 ERP data

6.2.1 Experiment 1: Content question task

In Figure 2, the waveform for the appropriate association of context and focus accents (CC) exhibits a large positive shift in the position of the expected contrastive information ('Anna'). This positive waveform corresponds to the Closure Positive Shift (CPS) found by Hruska et al. (2001). It again appears for those sentence constituents that are expected to be in focus due to the context. Within the new information context, this is true for the proper name and the verb while only the proper name can be expected to be contrastively focused in the contrastive information context (see Materials section). Also for the inappropriate association of new information context with the contrastive accent (NC), two CPS occur analogous to the information foci established by the preceding context.

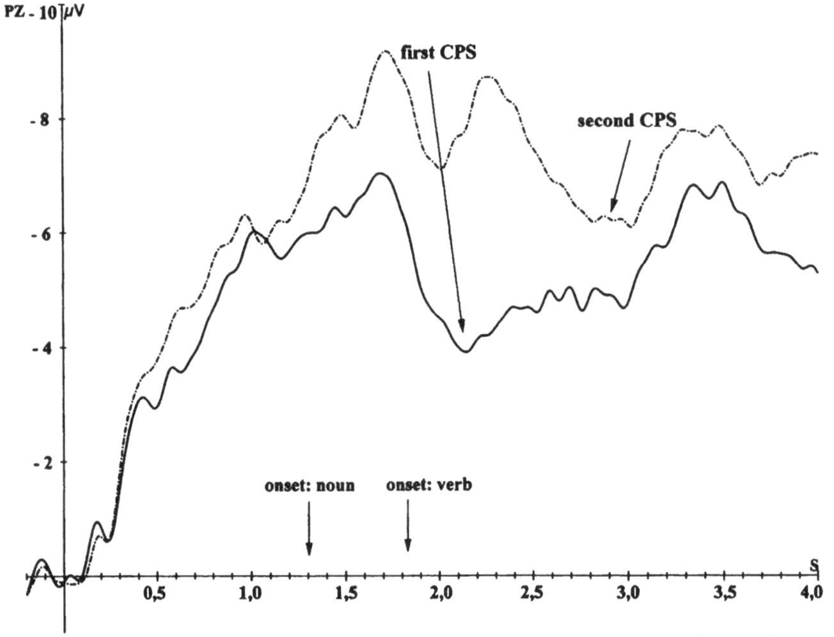

Figure 2: ERPs illustrated at the parieto-central electrode (PZ). The solid line depicts the contrastive accent in appropriate contrastive context (CC) and the dotted line shows the same accent but in new information context (NC).

Furthermore, two negative peaks can be distinguished in the ERPs to the incorrect condition (NC). The first one occurs in the site of the name when a new information accent is expected but a contrastive accent is presented. A second negative shift appears in the locus of the following verb when a new information accent is again being assumed but the preceding adjacent contrastive accent causes the accentuation on the verb to be perceived as not prominent enough to fit the expected accent pattern (Ladd, Verhoeven & Jacobs, 1994).

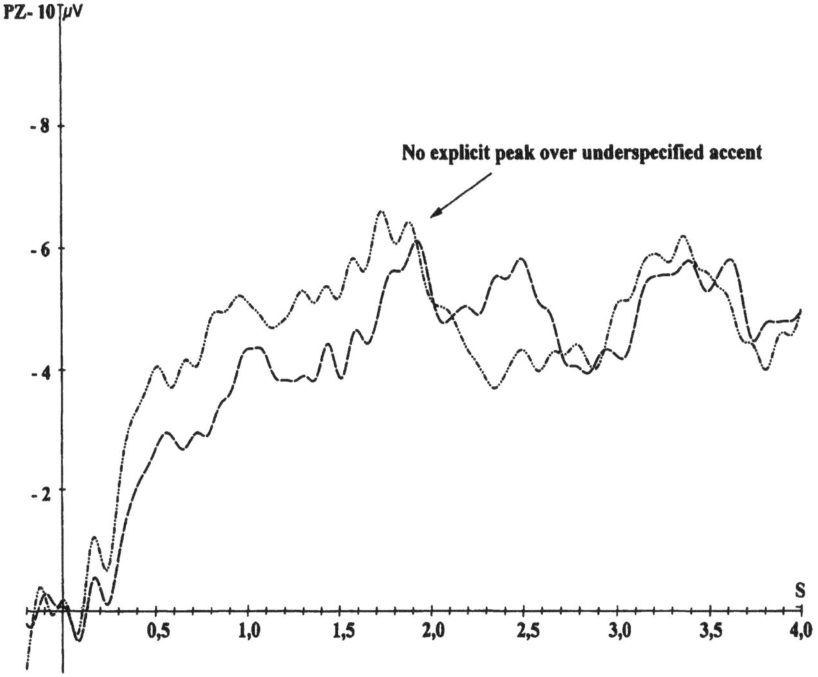

Figure 3: ERPs illustrated at the PZ-electrode. The dark dashed line shows ERPs to the new information accent in its appropriate context (NN) and the light dashed-dotted line shows the same accent but in contrastive context (CN).

Figure 3 illustrates that information structural processing is again resembled by the occurrence of the CPS. However, no significant negative peak is exhibited in comparison of the condition with the appropriate new information accent (NN) and the inadequately accented new information accent in the contrastive focus environment. Thus, the under-specified focus accent pattern does not lead to processing difficulties.

6.2.2 Experiment 2: Prosodic judgment task

The effect of information structural processing, as indicated by the Closure Positive Shift (CPS), is replicated by this experiment (Figure 4). The condition with congruency between the given context and the accent pattern (CC) apparently exhibits just a CPS for the proper name. Due to the IS-requirements, two CPS occur (in the locus of the name and the verb) when context implies a new information interpretation although the accent pattern only signals the name ('Anna') as carrier of the contrastive information (NC).

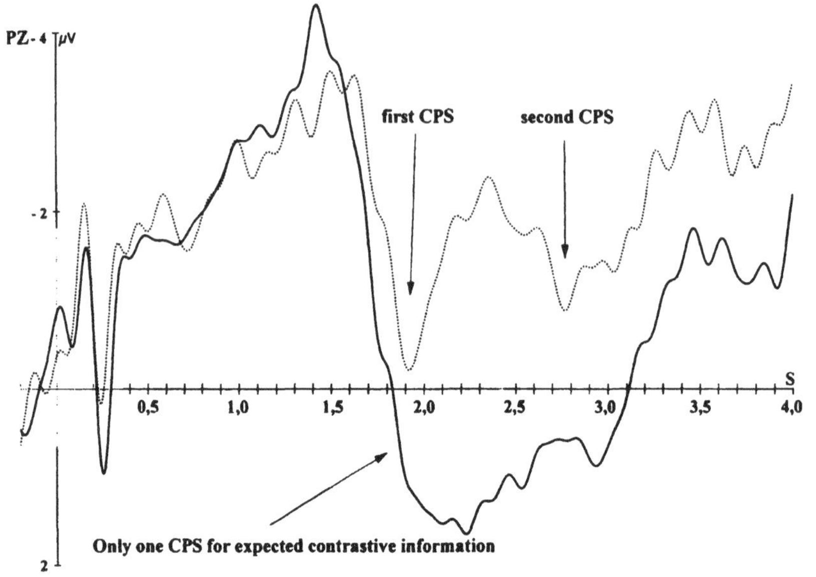

Figure 4: The CPS illustrated at the PZ-electrode. The solid black line depicts ERPs to contrastive information in the appropriate context (CC), the dotted line shows the reactions to the perception of contrastive information in the context actually eliciting a new information focus (NC).

A comparison of the ERP-responses to new information accents in a matching vs. non-matching context shows a negative peak in the incongruent condition (CN). Again, it appears in the position of the proper name where a contrastive focus accent is expected but `only` a new information accent realized (under-specified accent).

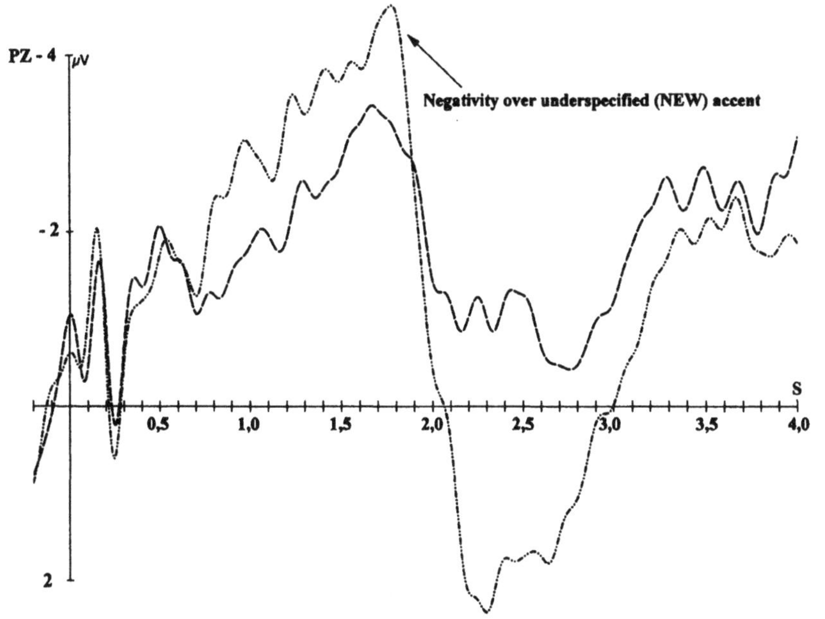

Figure 5: Electrophysiological responses at the PZ-electrode to the perception of the appropriate new information accent in new information context (NN) as depicted by the dark dashed line. Processing of new information accents in contexts eliciting contrastive focus (CN) is depicted by the bright dashed-dotted line.

7 Discussion and Conclusion

The results show that a differentiation of the concept of narrow focus into narrow new information focus and contrastive focus is useful in accounting for the alterations between these two subtypes of focus with regard to acoustic phenomena and their perception in context. New information accents and contrastive accents differ with respect to their acoustic properties, hence in prominence and accent type. The acoustic analyses show that new information is accented with a bitonal L+H* pattern. For contrastive information, this pattern is more faceted (L+H*L-). The slightly differing peak heights might play a role in the interpretation of the focus accents as well (Rietveld & Gussenhoven, 1985) since only in the contrastive condition are there no pre-focal accents. Hence, the prominence of the contrastive accent is further enhanced by the surrounding prosodic pattern.

The behavioral and electrophysiological data present evidence for the human brain`s ability to detect these focus accents whenever they occur in an inadequate focus environment. This detection mechanism is reflected by negative peaks in the ERPs in the positions of mis-specified accents. As indicated by the differing occurrence of these negative peaks in Experiment 1

& 2, the *detection of the prosodic mismatch* between the given context and the actually presented focus accent strongly relies on task requirements. For the content question task in Experiment 1, subjects actually did not explicitly have to consider prosody nor information structure to give a correct answer. Nonetheless, an over-specified focus accent (contrastive accent in new information context) evoked a negative peak in the ERPs. On the other hand, in Experiment 2, the task required an explicit analysis of the prosodic and information structural properties of the discourse. Here, the under-specification of the accent pattern (new information accent in contrastive context) leads to an electrophysiological reaction when this inadequate accent pattern is encountered. Again, a negative peak appears.

Despite these task effects, the *processing of the information structure*, as reflected by the Closure Positive Shift (CPS), is similar in both experiments. All information that is expected to be *new* or *contrastive* due to the context evokes a CPS in the corresponding focus positions of the answer sentences. So, in a context establishing the proper name ('Anna') and the verb as focus positions (new information context), consistently two CPS are evoked while the focus-conveying answer sentences are processed. Accordingly, only one CPS appears when the (contrastive) context implies the existence of only one (contrastive) focus position ('Anna') in the following sentence. Moreover, this effect seems to be independent of the task and underlying accent pattern. The effect is equivalent in the correctly accented conditions (NN & CC) and in the incorrectly accented conditions (NC & CN), and furthermore, under differing task requirements.

Since information structural processing was found to be task-independent, differences in the ERP results between Experiment 1 & 2 can only be evoked by the deviating processing of the prosodic structure due to task requirements.

In Experiment 1, these prosodic mismatch effects occur when a context establishing new information focus is presented with a contrastively accented sentence (NC) as compared to an appropriate new information accent. The resulting two negative peaks can consequently be interpreted as reflecting the brain's detection mechanism for the mis specification of prosodic parameters in discourse. For the first peak, the position of the proper name, the contrastive accent is acoustically too specified to be integrated into the new information discourse. On the other hand, the second peak in verb position appears due to a perceptual prominence phenomenon as described by Ladd et al. (1994). Although the speech production data shows equivalent accent types and pitch peak heights in verb position for the conditions with the new information accent and the contrastive accent, their perception may differ. Ladd et al. showed that an accent immediately following 'emphatically' stressed elements lowers the perceived prominence of that second accent (the position of the proper name in the present experiment). The negative peak on the verb is then interpretable as the detection of a virtually under-specified accent in the context where a new information accent is expected.

The negative peaks in the results of Experiment 2 *only* occur for acoustically under-specified focus accents, hence in the case of new information accents in contexts establishing contrastive focus (CN). It seems that under an explicit structural analysis of the prosodic pattern, as required in the judgment task, acoustically over-specified information can be suppressed or `overheard`.

The ERP data are consistent with our behavioral results and the ones of Alter et al. (2001). Only the error rate for the condition with a contrastive accent in a context establishing new information focus (NC) was significantly higher than for the other conditions. Thus, an over-specification of prosodic parameters in context is much harder for the participants to detect, although the task explicitly relies on the analysis of the prosodic pattern.

To conclude, our behavioral and electrophysiological results confirm the behavioral results of earlier studies (Nooteboom, 1987; Alter, 2001), and the ERP results of Hruska et al. (2001).

It could be shown that not only the dichotomy of given vs. new information, and broad vs. narrow focus is reflected in electrophysiological data (Hruska et al.), but also the more subtle difference between new and contrastive information. Prosodically under-specified (focus) accents in discourse generally lead to processing difficulties, whereas over-specified accents do so only under certain task requirements.

8 References

Alter, K., I. Mleinek, T. Rohe, A. Steube, and C. Umbach (2001): Kontrastprosodie in Sprachproduktion und -perzeption. Linguistische Arbeitsberichte 77, Leipzig, 59-79.

Bartels, C. and J. Kingston (1994): Salient pitch cues in the perception of contrastive focus. In: P. Bosch and R. van der Sandt (eds): Focus and Natural Language Processing. Proceedings of the Journal of Semantics Conference on Focus, IBM Working Papers, TR-80-94-006.

Birch, S. and C. Clifton (1995): Focus, Accent, and Argument Structure: Effects on Language Comprehension. Language and Speech 38 (4), 365-391.

Bolinger, D. (1986): Intonation and its Parts. London: Edward Arnold.

Brown, G., K. Currie, and J. Kenworthy (1980): Questions of Intonation. London: Croom Helm.

Chafe, W. (1974): Language and consciousness. Language 50, 111-133.

Couper-Kuhlen, E. (1984): A new look at contrastive intonation. In: R. Watts and U. Weidman (eds): Modes of Interpretation. Tübingen: Gunter Narr, 137-158.

Fery, C. (1993): German Intonational Patterns. Tübingen: Niemeyer.

Frota, S. (2000): Prosody and Focus in European Portuguese. New York: Garland Publishing.

Grice, M. and S. Baumann (2002): Deutsche Intonation und GtoBI. Linguistische Berichte 191, 267-298.

Hruska, C., K. Alter, K. Steinhauer, and A. Friederici (2001): Misleading dialogues: Human's brain reaction to prosodic information. Proceedings of the ORAGE-conference. Aix-en-Provence, 425-430.

Jackendoff, R. (1972): Semantic Interpretation in Generative Grammar. Cambridge, Ma: MIT Press.

Junghanns, U. and G. Zybatow (1997): Syntax and Information Structure of Russian Clauses. In: E. W. Browne et al. (eds): Formal Approaches to Slavic Linguistics 4: The Cornell Meeting 1995, Ann Arbor: Michigan Slavic Publications.

Krahmer, E. and M. Swerts (2001): On the alleged existence of contrastive accents. Speech and Communication 34, 391-405.

Ladd, D. R. (1996): Intonational Phonology. Cambridge: University Press, 160-163.

Ladd, D. R. (1983): Phonological Features of Intonational Peaks. Language 59, 721-759.

Ladd, D. R., J. Verhoeven, and K. Jacobs (1994): Influence of adjacent pitch accents on each other's perceived prominence. Journal of Phonetics 22, 87-99.

Nooteboom, S. G. and J. G. Kruyt (1987): Accents, focus distribution, and the perceived distribution of given and new information: An experiment. Journal of the Acoustical Society of America 82 (5), 1512-1524.

Oldfield, R. (1971): The Assessment analysis of handedness: The Edinburgh Inventory. Neuropsychologia 9, 97-113.

Pierrehumbert, J. and J. Hirschberg (1990): The meaning of intonational contours in the interpretation of discourse. In: P. Cohan, J. Morgan, and M. Pollack (eds): Intentions in Communication. Cambridge, MA: MIT Press.

Rietveld, A. and C. Gussenhoven (1985): On the relation between pitch excursion size and prominence. Journal of Phonetics 13, 299-308.

Rooth, M. (1985): Association with Focus. Ph.D. thesis. University of Massachusetts, Amherst.

Steinhauer, K., K. Alter, and A. Friederici (1999): Brain potentials indicate immediate use of prosodic cues in natural speech processing. Nature Neuroscience 2, 191-196.

Wells, W. (1986): An Experimental Approach to the Interpretation of Focus in Spoken English. In: C. Johns-Lewis (ed): Intonation in Discourse. London: Croom Helm, 53-75.

Grit Mehlhorn (Leipzig)

The Prosodic Pattern of Contrastive Accent in Russian

1 Introduction

How are contradictions or misunderstandings which occur in discourse corrected by the speakers? Which linguistic means do speakers use in order to mark contrasts as such? How do hearers notice that they are corrected?

It is widely assumed that intonation plays an important role for encoding corrections. Words marked with "special sentence stress" receive "a kind of augmented meaning" which entails the actualisation of certain presuppositions (cf. Svetozarova 1998: 266).[1]

Word order and prosody are linguistic correlates of Information Structure (IS). The constituents marked with the feature [Foc] (focus) occupy a certain position in the clause and their prosodic characteristics include a special pitch accent, movement of fundamental frequency (F0), and time structure.

A contrastive accent goes along with emotional involvement. The prominence of the contrastive accent has an important function in the discourse: to make the intended correction audible and perceivable. Steube (2001) therefore calls the contrastive accent a "linguistic sign".

If the speaker corrects with the help of contrastive accent, all non-contrasted, i.e. de-accented, elements in this utterance are taken for granted as indisputable background information. The contrastive accent emphasizes the valid alternative from the speaker's point of view. At the same time, the false alternative is implicitly rejected. This mechanism helps the hearer to find the right link between the correction and the original utterance.

The aim of the present paper is to investigate prosodic parameters of the so called "contrastive accent". In particular, we are interested in the acoustic and perceptual realization of contrastive focus in Russian declarative sentences. To that end, we conducted experiments that dealt with different types of focus within appropriate contexts.[2]

---

1 For similar observations see Nikolaeva (1982).

2 In this paper, we are dealing only with cases of contrastive focus. For cases of verum focus and contrastive topics cf. Mehlhorn (2002).

This article is organized as follows. Section 2 introduces different types of foci in Russian. In Section 3 we describe a production experiment and present acoustic data that reveal the tonal and durational behaviour of different foci in Russian declarative sentences. Section 4 shows evidence for the existence of a contrastive accent from perception experiments. A summary and a short discussion conclude the paper (Section 5).

2 Different focus types in russian: neutral vs. contrastive focus

Contrast is a discourse phenomenon which does not exist without context. It will be described in the framework of Information Structure (cf. Junghanns and Zybatow 1995, 1997, Junghanns 2002, Molnár 1998, Steube 2000). Information Structure (IS) is a pragmatically determined principle of ordering depending on the communicative situation. In Russian, means of expressing IS include word order, placement and type of pitch accents, and lexical items (cf. Junghanns and Zybatow 1995, 1997, Junghanns 2002).

The association of syntactic constituents with IS features[3] has an effect on word order, phonological properties, and the interpretation of the sentence. The influence on word order is based on the fact that IS features can force the movement of a constituent or disallow it. With regard to phonology, IS features determine placement and types of pitch accents. In a sentence that is well-formed with regard to its context, the IS features are assigned to those constituents which reflect the intentions of the speaker, i.e., his assumptions about the knowledge of the hearer according to discourse function. Therefore, we speak about the adaptation of the sentence to the context. This adaptation is achieved according to several discourse functions. Following Rosengren (1993), Junghanns and Zybatow (1995), (1997), Junghanns (2002), Molnár (1998) and Steube (2000), we proceed from the assumption that there are at least four different discourse functions which determine binary distinctions of IS: on the one hand, Focus-Background Structure and, on the other hand, Topic-Comment Structure. Focus is the most important information from the speaker's perspective in a given context.

2.1 Neutral focus

The function of focus is to emphasize important information in the given context. Various types of focus have different acoustic parameters.

[3] Space does not allow more than a cursory description. For a comprehensive discussion see Junghanns and Zybatow (1995), (1997) and Junghanns (2002).

Neutral focus, or new information focus (NF), is realized at the right periphery of a sentence (cf. Junghanns and Zybatow 1995, Junghanns 2002) and is characterized by a falling pitch accent (cf. Alter 1997). As we indicate below, NF can be maximal (1a), intermediate (1b) or minimal (1c).

(1) (a) A: V čëm delo?
in what matter
'What happened?'
B: [$_{CP:Foc}$ Miroslava uexala v JALtu]
Miroslava left for Jalta
'Miroslava left for Jalta.'
(b) A: Čto s Miroslavoj?
what with Miroslava
'What about Miroslava?'
B: Miroslava [$_{VP:Foc}$ uexala v JALtu]
(c) A: Kuda uexala Miroslava?
where left Miroslava
'Where did Miroslava leave for?'
B: Miroslava uexala [$_{PP:Foc}$ v JALtu]

In example (1a), the whole sentence is a possible answer to the question *V čëm delo? Čto slučilos'?* 'What happened?' and we have maximal focus. In sentence (1b), the neutral focus is assigned to the VP. The focus is non-maximal, and *Miroslava* is a background constituent. As neutral focus in (1b) is also non-minimal, the two constituents remain in the VP. Example (1c) illustrates a minimal (or narrow) focus, where we have a question about the argument-PP of *uexat'*: 'Where did Miroslava leave for?'. However, in all three cases, the focus exponent[4] is the same, namely the syllable JAL- in the word *Jaltu.* We find focus ambiguity in the sentence *Miroslava uexala v Jaltu* which can be disambiguated with the help of the context. A neutral word order is potentially ambiguous with respect to the focus domain.

2.2 Contrastive focus

It is difficult to find a clear definition of contrast in the linguistic literature. Where most linguists agree is that contrast has to do with alternatives (cf. Culicover and Rochemont 1983, Bannert 1985, Dietrich 1990, Hoepelman, Machate and Schnitzer 1991, Junghanns and Zybatow 1995, 1997, É. Kiss

[4] The focus exponent – indicated by capitals – is the syllable carrying the main stress (sentence accent). The findings in our experiments refer to what happens on the accented syllable of the focussed constituent.

1995, King 1995, Rudolph 1996, Drubig 1998, Molnár 1998, Steube 2000 and others). This is a relatively vague definition. Therefore, it is very difficult to find rules that apply to all cases where contrast is involved. In this paper, we are only talking about correction which is a rather narrow definition:

(2) Contrastive focus always entails the correction of an explicit utterance or of a presupposition of the situational context. The speakers correct false information because otherwise the hearers would take this information for granted as the true and valid background for the sentence. The contrast relates to a "false" alternative which was explicitly mentioned in the previous context or which was inferred from the speaker from the situation.

The speakers correct their utterances either if the given sentence involves values that can be misinterpreted by the hearer or if they assume that the hearer has got the wrong background information (cf. Mehlhorn 2002).

Contrastive focus (CF) differs from NF with regard to acoustic realization, freedom of placement and discourse function. With respect to its acoustic realization, we assume that CF starts off higher than the non-contrastive accent and therefore has a greater excursion of the pitch accent.

In contrast to NF, CF does not correspond to a fixed position. In Russian, CF can be assigned to any constituent *in situ* or after movement. Consequently, CF can be realized on the left (3a) or right periphery of the clause (3c) or in between (3b).

(3) (a) A: Ljuda uže uexala v Jaltu?
'Has Ljuda already left for Jalta ?'
B: [$_{DP:FocC}$ **MiroSLAva**] uexala v Jaltu.[5]
Miroslava left for Jalta
'It's MIROSLAVA who left for Jalta.'
Ljuda tak zanjata, čto daže ob ètom i ne mečtaet.
'Ljuda is so busy that she doesn't even dream of going there.'
(b) V Jaltu [$_{DP:FocC}$ **MiroSLAva**] uexala.
for Jalta Miroslava left
'It's MIROSLAVA who left for Jalta.'
(c) V Jaltu uexala [$_{DP:FocC}$ **MiroSLAva**].
for Jalta left Miroslava
'It's MIROSLAVA who left for Jalta.'

[5] The contrastive accent – indicated by bold faced capitals – is the focus exponent (sentence accent) in contrastive utterances. Contrastive accents are assumed to be more prominent than focus exponents of neutral utterances.

Due to the contrastive accent, i.e. a special pitch accent associated with the CF, it is unnecessary to anchor the contrastively focussed constituent to any fixed position within the clause.

2.3 Prosody and information Structure

In speech production, speakers make use of intonation in order to signal the relevant discourse function in the sentence. In speech processing, the hearer uses intonation in order to interpret the speaker's intentions in the right way. Intonation gives the sentence the appropriate communicative interpretation relative to the situational context and the speaker's intentions. In this function intonation is a means of realizing the IS of the clause and, in connection with this, a means of realizing accentuation.

The physical correlate of pitch is the fundamental frequency F0 of the voiced parts of the speech signal. The F0 reflects the progress in time of the periodic closing of the vibrating vocal cords. For oral communication, the form of the tonal pattern in relation to the frequency range of the speaker is much more important than the absolute tonal height.

Prosody can be described by means of accents. On the one hand, 'accent' refers to lexical or word stress, i.e., the stressing of a certain syllable. On the other hand, there is sentence accent, i.e. the most prominent syllable in the sentence which is normally characterized by different prosodic parameters. Stress usually changes the F0, the loudness of sound and the duration of the syllable.

3 Contrastive focus in production: An experimental study

This experiment was designed to investigate two specific questions. First of all, we wanted to find out in what way a typical contrastive accent is prosodically realized in Russian. Secondly, the aim was to find possible differences in the prosodic realization of the different focus types. In particular, we expected a higher vertical excursion on the focus exponent and a greater lengthening of the accented syllable of CF as compared to NF. The prosodic parameters we were interested in are intonation contours as well as the type, location and duration of pitch accents.

3.1 Method

The present experiment was a controlled production study, i.e., the subjects read experimental sentences within their contexts[6] from a list. All texts were recorded.

Material and Design. We tested sentences with NF domains of different sizes as well as CF on different constituents and in different positions in the sentence. All experimental items were embedded in appropriate contexts to form colloquial dialogues. The context was necessary to guarantee a coherent and controllable IS and to ensure that the discourse functions which were to be investigated could be recognized in the text. The length of the texts varied from 2 to 5 sentences. The subjects did not know which items were experimental and which were context. In order to obtain simple intonation contours, the experimental items were short and contained the minimal number of constituents. No such restrictions were imposed on the contexts.

The following parameters were varied systematically in the experiment:

(4) (a) the focus type (NF vs. CF),
(b) the pitch accent position (clause-initial, clause-final, non-peripheral) and
(c) the type of accented constituents (subjects, direct objects, indirect objects, verb complements in the instrumental case, adverbs, and adjectives).

Procedure. Eight female native Russian speakers were recorded. They were given the sentences in written form. The subjects were orally instructed to read all the texts first in order to familiarize themselves with the content. Then they read each individual text silently and were supposed to imagine themselves in the roles of the speakers. Only then did they read the text aloud. All 100 sentences were recorded by all subjects.

Data Treatment. The texts were recorded using a DAT recorder. The speech signals were digitized and the experimental items were extracted from their contexts. From these the intonation contours were drawn by pitch tracking. WinPitch was used to analyze the extracted intonation contours. In this program, the following measurements were taken: At three points of each syllable F0 values were extracted – (a) onset (the first one at the beginning of the syllable), (b) peak (the highest from the F0-peak) and (c) offset (the final one at

[6] Whereas in traditional Russian studies on the subject only isolated sentences without context were recorded and interpreted (cf. Bryzgunova 1980: 100), the sentences in our experiment have a predictable and controllable IS which allows us to describe intonations contours that match the communicative intention of the speaker.

the end of the syllable). There were two important values per measuring point: the fundamental frequency F0 in Hz and the time in msec. On the focus exponent more points were measured in order to be able to describe as exactly as possible what happens on the accented syllable of the focused constituent. The data were transferred to an Excel table and a median value from the data of the eight subjects for each measuring point was calculated. From these values an intonation contour averaged from all subjects was produced for each sentence.

3.2 Results and discussion

Neutral focus. We compared sentences with different focus domains. In the case of maximally focussed sentences, e.g. *[Miroslava uexala v JALtu]*, there is a single intonation phrase which was pronounced without breaks. Both the sentences with intermediate focus of the type *Miroslava [uexala v JALtu]* and maximally focused sentences exhibit a sequence of accents which descend in a stepwise fashion. This so called downstepping begins with the topic constituent, continues with the first lexical stress of the intermediate focus – in this case the verb – and ends with a pitch accent on the focus exponent[7] which is again pronounced as a fall (cf. figure 1).

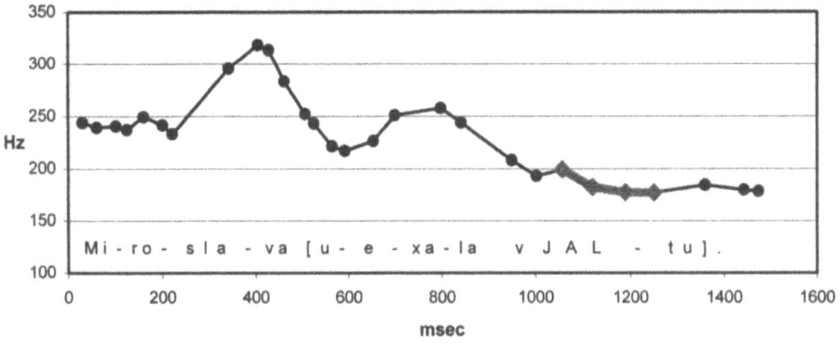

Figure 1: Intermediate NF[8]

In sentences with a minimal NF, e.g. *Miroslava uexala [v JALtu]* (cf. figure 1), there is a somewhat stronger fall on the F0 on the focus exponent than in the cases of maximal and intermediate foci.[9]

For all sentences with a NF, the focus exponent is pronounced with a greater lengthening than any other syllable in the sentence (cf. figure 2).

[7] The focus exponent is marked by the diamonds on the intonation contour.

[8] In each case the curves indicate the median value across all subjects.

[9] These observations correspond with the findings of Alter (1997). A minimal focussed constituent builds it's own prosodic domain (cf. Alter 1997: 408).

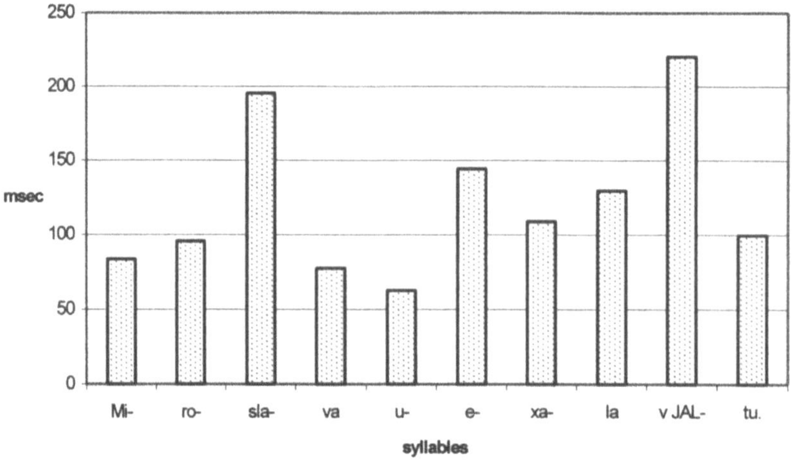

Figure 2: Duration of the syllables in a sentence with NF

Contrastive Focus. In the case of sentence-initial CF, e.g. *[MiroSLAva] uexala v Jaltu*[10], there is a strong rise of the F0 on the focus exponent. Still on the same syllable, the pitch movement is reversed in a beginning descent which is continued on the following unaccented syllables until the end of the sentence. The remaining contour of the sentence is flat; there are no other pitch accents (cf. figure 3).

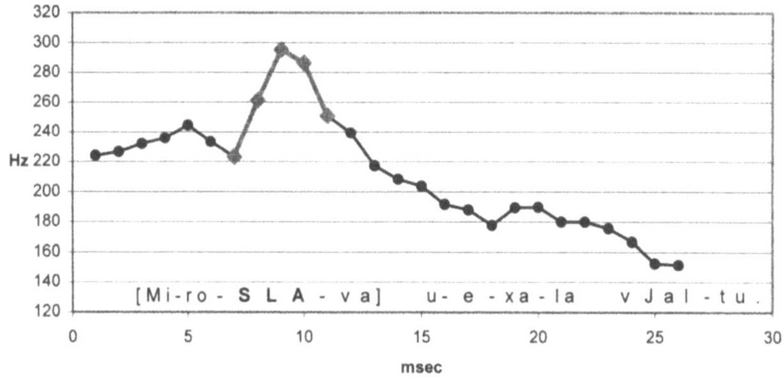

Figure 3: CF on the left periphery of the sentence

The form of a CF on the second syntactic constituent in the sentence, as in *V Jaltu [MiroSLAva] uexala* (cf. figure 4), resembles the sentence-initial CF. Again, a rise and a fall on the accented syllable is observed and the fall of the F0 is continued to the end of the sentence. However, in contrast to a sentence-initial CF, there is a kind of topic accent, albeit one which does not reach such

[10] A low tone precedes the accent, i.e., the pitch falls until the position of the accented syllable.

a large vertical excursion as in sentences with NF. The pitch range on the focus exponent is bigger than we would find in such a sentence with NF. The deviation from the falling F0 declination signals additional information. A late peak which shows the same height as an earlier peak is more prominent in the declination line (cf. Batliner 1988: 270).

If the contrastive pitch accent is assigned to the last syntactic phrase in the sentence, as is the case in *V Jaltu uexala [MiroSLAva]* (cf. figure 5), the focus exponent is realized with a strong fall of the F0 which is preceded by a small rise on the same syllable which intensifies the vertical excursion of the fall. Again, the pitch range of the focus exponent is extended. Generally, the vertical excursion of the CF will be higher the closer it is to the beginning of the sentence.

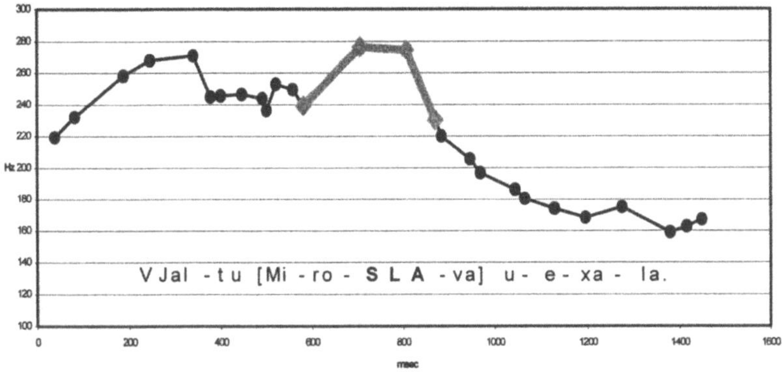

Figure 4: Non-Peripheral CF

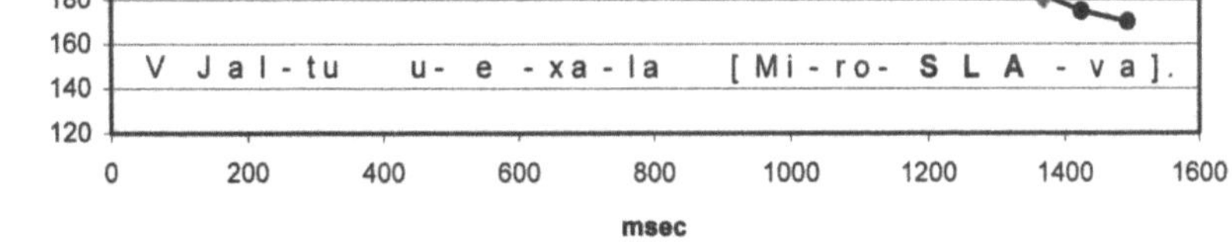

Figure 5: CF on the right periphery of the sentence

In all sentences with CF, the syllable bearing the focus accent is characterized by a very strong lengthening which is even larger than the one on the nuclear accent of a NF (compare figures 2 and 6). This salient lengthening on the accented syllable in sentences with CF seems to be an additional contribution to the perception of contrast.

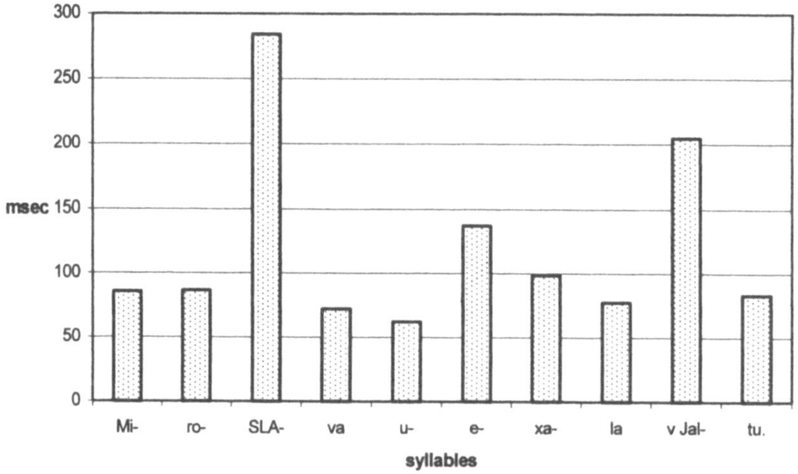

Figure 6: Duration of the syllables in a sentence with CF

The production experiment reported above provides empirical evidence for focus structure in Russian as reflected in placement and prosodic characteristics of pitch accents. The subjects placed the sentence accents at the expected position in the sentence, i.e., on the focus. The context and the IS of the sentence in question forced this intonation.

The focus exponent of the NF is usually located on the last lexical accent in the sentence and is produced by a fall of the F0. Sentences with NF are, in terms of intonation, relatively independent from the lexical stressed syllables preceding the sentence accent. They can be rhythmically subdivided.

The sentence accent in contrastive contexts exhibits somewhat more distinctive parameters in the speech signal: the vertical height on the accented syllable is essentially higher than that on the NF, and the duration of the nuclear accent is clearly increased. The local tonal pattern, a combination of a rise and a fall of the F0, dominates the whole utterance. The contour of the remaining declination is smoothed out, i.e., the background material is de-accented. Such sentences cannot be rhythmically divided. They have strongly centered contours.[11]

[11] Bryzgunova's (1977, 1980) concept of intonational constructions reflects only a part of the contour of the sentence: namely the location of the main accent in the centre of the pitch movement, i.e., only the stressed syllable and the syllables immediately preceding and following it. However, different types of focus cannot be distinguished exclusively on the basis of the local tonal contour. It is necessary to compare intonational constructions with tonal movement of adjacent accents. Our approach allows us to analyse relational pitch, i.e., the relation to the global F0 course of the sentence.

The shape of a typical contrastive accent is created by the interaction of different prosodic parameters:

(5) (a) the accent type (combination of a rise and a beginning fall on the same syllable – the focus exponent),
(b) a higher vertical excursion of the F0 (extended pitch range on the accented syllable) as compared with NF,
(c) the flat remaining sentence declination which signals that this information is valid background material,
(d) an obvious lengthening on the accented syllable as compared with all other syllables in the sentence.

We were able to show that disambiguation of different focus types in sentences with identical word order is possible with the help of the context and intonation contours. Thus, it was shown that IS is reflected in intonation and that contrastive focus corresponds to a certain pitch contour. This allows us to describe intonation contours on the basis of the communicative intention of the speaker. With the help of discourse functions a new approach to intonation contours is possible, contrary to traditional Russian studies where intonation constructions only referred to sentence mood and to the presence or absence of emphasis (cf. Bryzgunova 1977, Xavronina and Krylova 1989).

4 Contrastive focus in perception: Three perception tests

"It is not possible, solely on the basis of a visual inspection of an F0 curve, to decide how it is converted by the auditory system into a melodic continuum, let alone that it would be possible to know what is communicatively relevant and what is not. This implies that our understanding of the listener's interpretation can only be achieved in a study dedicated to the perception of speech pitch, ..." (cf. 't Hart, Collier, Cohen 1990: 24f.)

Information that we find in the objective analysis of the speech signal is more complex than the information hearers use for the perception of speech (cf. 't Hart et al. 1990: 27). On the other side, linguistic signs must be available for discourse partners whose ability of differentiation is more restricted than that of a measuring device. From all the information revealed in the sound signal, the information encoded on the accented syllables is especially relevant for perception (cf. Makarova 2001). 't Hart et al. (1990) presume from the assumption that hearers perceive only a very restricted class of F0 changes – those which was produced intentionally by the speakers (cf. 't Hart et al. 1990: 68).

On the assumption that intonation on accented syllables is most relevant we will try to analyse the speech melody on positions which are important for the perception, i.e. on the focus exponents or sentence accents, respectively.[12]

With the help of perception tests we can check on which positions in utterances hearers perceive emphasis and thus, we can prove the hypothesis that contrastive accents are more highlighted than neutral sentence accents. Besides the identification of sentence accents we will consider the prominence of the accents in question.

The extracted parameters of the speech signal showed greater values for the prosodic parameters F0 and duration on the focus exponents for contrasted utterances compared with neutral ones. This leads us to the assumption that contrasted constituents are perceived to be more emphasized by the hearers, too.

Method. The recordings from the above described production experiment served as material for the perception tests. 20 native Russian speakers took part in the perception tests. They listened to the experimental items in context as recordings from the computer. At the same time they could read the items on a list. The sentence in question was bold faced. In all three perception tests they heard and saw the same recordings from the computer. In each test they had to carry out different tasks.

4.1 Identification of contrastive accent

The task in the first perception test was to concentrate on the bold faced sentence and to underline the word(s) which they found most highlighted.[13]

The results for sentences with CF are unambiguous. Sentence accents associated with CF were perceived by the subjects in 98.8% of all cases. The position of the contrasted word had no influence on this result. In no case was a second word underlined in addition to that with the contrastive accent.

The picture in sentences with neutral focus is not so clear cut. Only in a good half of the sentences (54.6%) the subjects identified the word associated with the focus exponent as the only sentence accent. In most of the deviating cases, another word was perceived as highlighted. There is a strong tendency for varying results in longer sentences. In a few cases, two words in the sentence were underlined. There is a significant difference between the amount of perceived neutral sentence accents and contrastive accents (cf. figure 7).

---

[12] Note that we use a relational model of intonation that considers the pitch contour on accented syllables in relation to the rest of the sentence.

[13] The subjects were instructed to underline at least one word and at most two words.

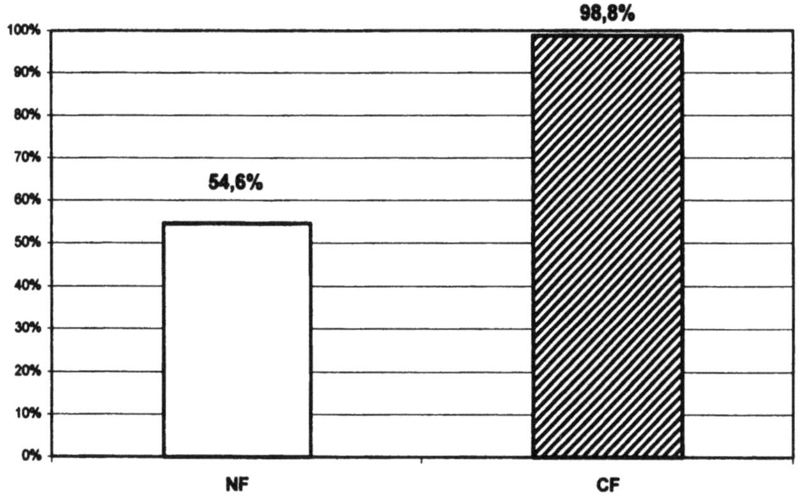

Figure 7: Identified sentence accents in experimental items with NF and CF

The results found in the first perception test show that it is easier to identify a contrastive accent than a neutral sentence accent. We predict that the more frequent identification of contrastive accents in comparison with neutral focus accents has to do with a higher prominence of contrasted words.

4.2 Prominence of contrastive accent

With the instruction in the second perception test a judgement about the degree of highlighting was required. The words in question carrying the focus exponents were underlined on the list according to the theory of IS. While listening to the sentence from the computer the subjects had to concentrate on the underlined word and to decide in which extent it was highlighted in comparison to the other words in the sentence. A five-grade scale served for the ranking:

(6) 1 not highlighted
2 a little bit highlighted
3 highlighted
4 strongly highlighted
5 very strongly highlighted

Here it should be noticed that we compared different sentence accents, i.e. focus exponents which are supposed to be highlighted. For that reason a relation 1:5 cannot be assumed. The question is whether neutral and contrastive accents differ in the degree of highlighting.

This is the case. The calculated average for sentence accents associated with CF is 4.42 in contrast to 2.24 for sentence accents associated with NF. Hence, there is a significant difference in the perception of the accent strength between the two (cf. figure 8).

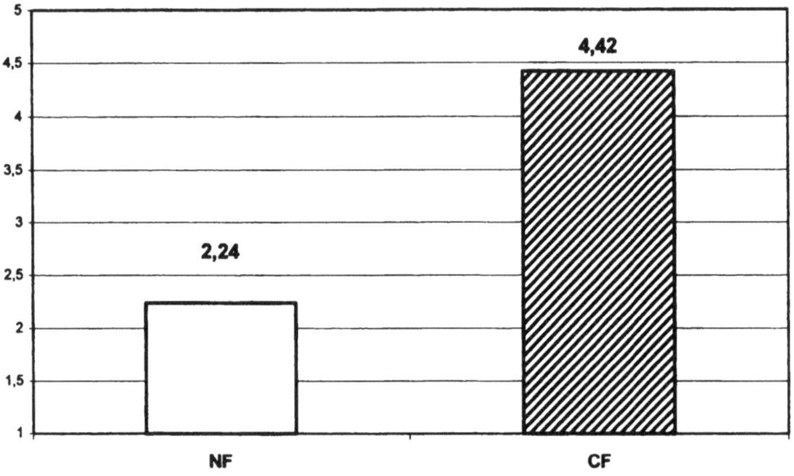

Figure 8: Average of the perceived degree of highlighting for sentence accents with CF and NF

4.3 Pattern of contrastive accent

In the third perception test, subjects received the same lists as for the second test. Now they had to concentrate on the melody of the accented words. There were 4 labels that they could use: they had to label an upwards arrow (↑) when they heard a rise on the accented syllable in the speaker's voice, a downwards arrow (↓) when they heard a fall, a double arrow (↑↓) when they heard a rise and a fall on the accented syllable and a dash (–) when they could not identify any pitch movement.[14]

Contrary to what could have been expected, subjects perceived the pitch movement on the contrastive accent either as a rise (57.7%) or as a combination of a rise and a fall (38.8%). There is no significant difference between the position of the contrasted word and the labelled pitch movement. The subjects were consistent in their judgements. If they heard a rise of the pitch on sentence initial contrasted words, they heard the same pattern in other positions in the sentence, too. But there is a very significant difference between the subjects. It seems that there are two kinds of subjects: one group (the larger one) only perceives a rise on the contrasted word. The other group seems to "hear more

[14] In case the subjects heard a pitch movement different from the given inventory, they were instructed to label it with appropriate arrows. In fact, all subjects managed with the given labels.

complex"; the combination of a rise and a fall of the pitch on the contrasted word corresponds exactly to the picture that we found in the speech signal.

The results for the neutral focus accents are different. The overwhelming majority of the subjects (89.8%) perceived a fall of the pitch on the neutral focus accent. 8.4% could not identify any pitch movement on the neutral focus exponent (cf. figure 9). The latter subjects belong to the group which "hears less complex".

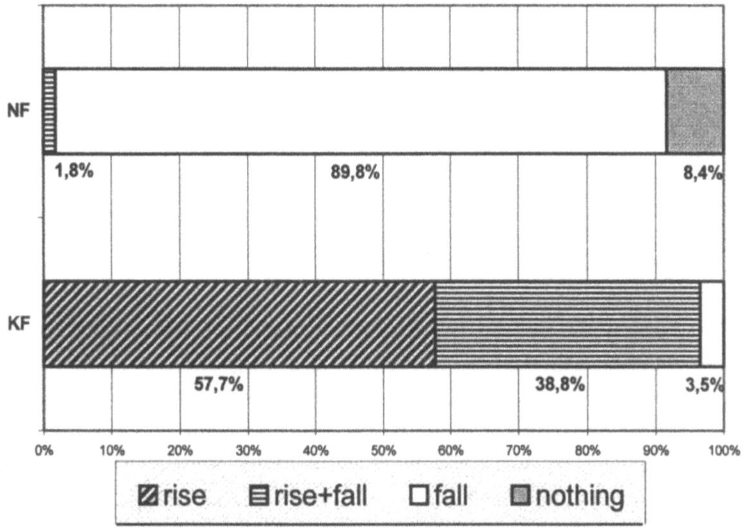

Figure 9: Identified Patterns of the Pitch Movement on Sentence Accents with CF and NF over all Subjects

5 Conclusions

The perception experiments showed that words that carry contrastive accent are significantly more often identified as emphasized than focus exponents in sentences with NF are. Furthermore, the degree of emphasizing is significantly higher with contrastive accents than with neutral sentence accents.

Obviously, subjects could identify changes of the melody on sentence accents. The fact that subjects consistently identify different patterns for contrastive and neutral sentence accents reveals evidence for the assumption that we deal with different categories here.

type of sentence accent	production experiment			perception tests		
	change of F0	overall pitch contour	syllable duration	1. identified sentence accent	2. strength of highlighting	3. perceived pitch movement
neutral accent (NF)	fall	rhythmically devided; other pitch accents besides the sentence accent	slightly lengthened	54.6%	2.24	↓ rsp. –
contrastive accent (CF)	combination of rise and fall	strongly centered contour; contrastive accent = intonation centre; remaining contour is smoothed out	significantly lengthened	98.8%	4.42	↑ rsp. ↑↓

Table 1: Results of the production and perception experiments[15]

The comparison between production and perception data shows a clear correlation between the observed F0 movement and the perceived pitch change (cf. table 1). This allows us to generalize the results. Obviously, the special contrast intonation facilitates the perception of corrections. Contrasted constituents in Russian[16] are linguistically encoded in a way which requires no additional effort for the interpretation.

From the analysis of both production and perception data we conclude that in Russian, there is a systematic differentiation between contrastive accent and neutral focus accent. This differentiation is relevant for the perception of contrast.

6 References

Alter, K. (1997): Fokusprosodie im Russischen: Phonologische und akustische Korrelate von Informationsstrukturierung. In: U. Junghanns and G. Zybatow (ed): Formale Slavistik, Frankfurt a. M.: Vervuert, 399-414.

Bannert, R. (1985): Fokus, Kontrast und Phrasenintonation im Deutschen. In: Zeitschrift für Dialektologie und Linguistik 3, 289-305.

[15] All reported findings refer to the focus exponent, i.e. the accented syllable of the corresponding focus.

[16] In this paper, we have dealt only with cases of CF. Intonation experiments with other contrasted constituents, such as verum focus (VF) and constrastive topics, show the same prosodic pattern of a contrastive accent in the speech signal as well as in the perception results (cf. Mehlhorn 2002). Whereas in sentences with CF and VF the contrastive accent is the only sentence accent, in sentences with contrastive topics we found a neutral sentence accent on the focus exponent and a more prominent contrastive accent on the contrastive topic.

Batliner, A. (1988): Der Exklamativ: Mehr als Aussage oder doch nur mehr oder weniger Aussage? Experimente zur Rolle von Höhe und Position des F0-Gipfels. In: H. Altmann (ed): Intonationsforschungen, Linguistische Arbeiten 200, Niemeyer: Tübingen, 243-271.

Bryzgunova, E. A. (1977): Zvuki i intonacija russkoj reči. Russkij jazyk: Moskva.

Bryzgunova, E. A. (1980): Intonacija. In: Russkaja Grammatika t. 1. Nauka, Akademija Nauk: Moskva, 96-122.

Culicover, P. W. and M. Rochemont (1983): Stress and focus in English. In: Language 59, 123-165.

Dietrich, R. (1990): Zu Form und Bedeutung der Kontrastintonation im Deutschen. In: Linguistische Berichte 129, Opladen: Westdeutscher Verlag, 415-430.

Drubig, H. B. (1998): Focus and Connectedness: Towards a Typology of Focus Constructions. Arbeitsbericht, Projekt "Typologie der Informationsstruktur", Universität Tübingen, Ms., 62.

Hoepelman, J., J. Machate, and R. Schnitzer (1991): Intonational Focusing and Dialogue Games. Journal of Semantics 8, 253-75.

Junghanns, U. (1997): Features and Movement. In: A. Alexiadou, N Fuhrhop, P. Law, and U. Kleinhenz (eds): ZAS Papers in Linguistics 9. Berlin: Zentrum für Allgemeine Sprachwissenschaft, Typologie und Universalienforschung, 74-88.

Junghanns, U. (2002): Informationsstrukturierung in slavischen Sprachen: Zur Rekonstruktion in einem syntax-zentrierten Modell der Grammatik. Habilitationsschrift. Universität Leipzig.

Junghanns, U. and G. Zybatow (1995): Fokus im Russischen. In: I. Kohlhof, S. Winkler, and H. B. Drubig (eds): Proceedings of the Göttingen Focus Workshop (17. DGfS, March 1-3, 1995), Arbeitsbericht Nr. 69 des Sonderforschungsbereich 340 "Theoretische Grundlagen für die Computerlinguistik". Stuttgart, Tübingen, 113-136.

Junghanns, U. and G. Zybatow (1997): Syntax and Information Structure of Russian Clauses. In: E. W. Browne, E. Dornisch, N. Kondrashova, and D. Zec. (eds): Formal Approaches to Slavic Linguistics 4: The Cornell Meeting 1995, Michigan Slavic Publications, Ann Arbor 289-319.

King, T. H. (1995): Configuring Topic and Focus in Russian. CSLI Publications: Stanford.

Kiss, K. É. (1995): Discourse configurational languages. Oxford Univ. Press: New York.

Makarova, V. (2001): Phonetic Approaches to Issues in Russian Intonation. In: G. Zybatow, U. Junghanns, G. Mehlhorn, and L. Szucsich (eds): Current Issues in Formal Slavic Linguistics. (= Linguistik international, 5), Peter Lang: Frankfurt a. M., Berlin u.a., 49-58.

Mehlhorn, G. (2002): Kontrastierte Konstituenten im Russischen. Experimentelle Untersuchungen zur Informationsstruktur. Peter Lang Verlag.

Molnár, V. (1998): Topic in Focus. On the Syntax, Phonology, Semantics, and Pragmatics of the So-called "Contrastive Topic" in Hungarian and German. In: Acta Linguistica Hungarica 45 (1/2), 89-166.

Nikolaeva, T. M. (1982): Semantika akcentnogo vydelenija. Moskva.

Rosengren, I. (1993): Wahlfreiheit mit Konsequenzen – Scrambling, Topikalisierung und FHG im Dienste der Informationsstrukturierung. In: M. Reis (ed): Wortstellung und Informationsstruktur, Linguistische Arbeiten 206. Niemeyer: Tübingen, 251-312.

Rudolph, E. (1996): Contrast. Adversative and Concessive Expressions on Sentence and Text Level. (Research in Text Theory), de Gruyter: Berlin, New York.

Steube, A. (2000): Ein kognitionswissenschaftlich basiertes Modell für Informationsstrukturierung (in Anwendung auf das Deutsche). In: J. Bayer, and Ch. Römer (ed): Von der Philologie zur Grammatiktheorie. Peter Suchsland zum 65. Geburtstag. Tübingen, 213-238.

Steube, A. (2001): Correction by Contrastive Focus. In: ZAS Papers in Linguistics 23, Berlin, 211-230.

Svetozarova, N. D. (1998): Intonation in Russian. In: D. Hirst and A. di Cristo (eds.): Intonation systems: A survey of twenty languages. Cambridge University Press, 261-274.

't Hart, J., R. Collier, and A. Cohen (1990): A perceptual study of intonation. An experimental-phonetic approach to speech melody. Cambridge University Press.

Xavronina, S. A. and O. A. Krylova (1989): Obučenie inostrancev porjadku slov v russkom jazyke. Russkij jazyk: Moskva, 16-39.

Britta Stolterfoht (Leipzig) and Markus Bader (Konstanz)

Focus Structure and the Processing of Word Order Variations in German*

1 Introduction

In contrast to English, German has a relatively free word order. The arguments of the verb can appear at different structural positions in a sentence. In our paper, we will focus on one specific type of word order variation, namely *scrambling*. One example is the scrambling of the object in front of the subject as illustrated in (1):

(1) (a) subject before object (SO)

Maria hat behauptet, dass **der** Onkel **den** Neffen begrüßt hat.

Mary has claimed that the uncle$_{nom}$ the nephew$_{acc}$ welcomed has

(b) object before subject (OS)

Maria hat behauptet, dass **den** Onkel **der** Neffe begrüßt hat.

Mary has claimed that the uncle$_{acc}$ the nephew$_{nom}$ welcomed has

'Mary claimed that the nephew welcomed the uncle.'

In (1a) the canonical word order, subject before object (SO), can be seen. (1b) shows the non-canonical, scrambled word order, object before subject (OS). In these examples, the syntactic functions are explicitly signalled by the case marking at the determiners, ***der*** versus ***den***. But this is only the case for masculine singular determiner phrases (DPs). Feminine or neuter DPs can be globally or locally ambiguous, as can be seen in examples (2) and (3).

(2) SO and OS (globally ambiguous)

Maria hat behauptet, dass die Tante die Nichte begrüßt hat.

Mary has claimed that the aunt$_{nom/acc}$ the niece$_{nom/acc}$ welcomed has

'Mary claimed that the aunt welcomed the niece.'

'Mary claimed that the niece welcomed the aunt.'

---

* *Acknowledgements:* We are grateful to Ina Bornkessel and Thomas Weskott for helpful comments on earlier versions of this article. The work was supported by the Leibniz Science Prize awarded to A.D.F. and a grant from the German Research Foundation (FR 519/17-3).

(3) (a) SO (locally ambiguous)
Maria hat behauptet, dass die Tante die Nichten begrüßt hat.
Mary has claimed that the aunt$_{nom/sg}$ *the nieces*$_{acc/pl}$ *welcomed has*$_{sg}$
'Mary claimed that the aunt welcomed the nieces.'
(b) OS (locally ambiguous)
Maria hat behauptet, dass die Tante die Nichten begrüßt haben.
Mary has claimed that the aunt$_{nom/sg}$ *the nieces*$_{acc/pl}$ *welcomed have*$_{pl}$
'Mary claimed that the nieces welcomed the aunt.'

In (2), there is no explicit case marking at the determiners. Both singular DPs can be either nominative or accusative; this results in a globally ambiguous sentence.

In the examples in (3), the DPs are also case ambiguous, but the first DP is marked for singular, the second for plural. The sentences are not ambiguous as a whole, but locally ambiguous. If we take the perspective of a person who reads the sentence in (3b) successively word by word, the sentence is ambiguous with respect to word order until the number information of the finite verb (the auxiliaries *hat* vs. *haben*) has been read. Prior research has established that processing difficulties arise at the auxiliary. Readers have a strong preference for the SO word order (e.g., Bader & Meng, 1999; Hemforth, 1993; Schriefers, Friederici & Kühn, 1995, among many others). What is the reason for this processing preference? In the following, it will be shown that different types of linguistic representations are responsible for this phenomenon. Not only syntactic, but also focus structural and prosodic information play a crucial role in the processing of scrambled word order.

Section 2 introduces the theoretical background for syntactic, focus structural and prosodic characteristics of scrambling. Section 3 briefly reviews the large number of studies that report evidence for the SO-preference in German. In addition, the few studies, including our own, that investigated focus structural aspects of scrambling in processing will be reported. In section 4, characteristics of focus particles will be discussed and used to formulate hypotheses for an experiment which is also described in this section. The last section will provide a summary of the results and some conclusions.

2 Syntactic, focus structural and prosodic characteristics of scrambling

Scrambling can be syntactically described as the optional change of the base order of phrases within the middlefield, the domain between the complementizer and the verbal head (e.g., Haider & Rosengren, 1998, among many others). If we look at the syntactic representations of the sentences in (3), the difference between the canonical and the scrambled word order in embedded clauses can be described as follows[1]: In (4b), the scrambled object is moved in front of the subject and leaves a trace in its base position. (4a) illustrates the base generated order without an empty category[2].

(4) (a) [$_{CP}$ Maria hat behauptet, [$_{CP}$ dass [$_{VP}$ die Tante [$_{V'}$ die Nichten [$_{V^0}$ begrüßt hat]]...
Mary has claimed that the aunt the nieces welcomed has

(b) [$_{CP}$ Maria hat behauptet, [$_{CP}$ dass [$_{VP}$ die Tante$_i$ [$_{VP}$ die Nichten [$_{V'}$ t$_i$ [$_{V^0}$ begrüßt haben]]...
Mary has claimed that the aunt the nieces welcomed have

The focus structural and prosodic representations of the two different word orders can be directly derived from the syntactic structure. It is assumed that the whole utterance can only be focused (maximal or *wide focus*) if the constituent carrying the nuclear accent (*focus exponent*) is in its base position and in the sister position of the verbal head (e.g., Haider & Rosengren 2002). According to the *Null Theory of Phrase Stress* (Cinque, 1993), a phrase's main stress is assigned to its most deeply embedded constituent. If there is no other focus structural information given (e.g., context), the focus projects. This stress pattern is associated with a wide focus reading. At least, the whole complement clause is in focus like in (5a).

(5) (a) Maria hat behauptet, dass [die Tante die NICHten begrüßt hat]$_F$.

(b) Maria hat behauptet, dass [die TANte]$_F$ die Nichten begrüßt hat.
Mary has claimed that the aunt the nieces welcomed has

(c) Maria hat behauptet, dass die Tante$_i$ [die NICHten]$_F$ t$_i$ begrüßt haben.
Mary has claimed that the aunt the nieces welcomed have

If the phrasal stress falls on a constituent higher in the structure, the focus does not project (Haider 1993, 2000). The sentence receives a narrow focus reading like in (5b). In (5c), which also has a narrow focus reading, the focus exponent is not the argument closest to the verb[3]. The most deeply embedded constituent has moved in front of the subject and has left behind a trace in its base position. Therefore, the stressed constituent takes a higher position in the structure.

---

1 The examples are the same as the sentences in (3), where the reader is referred to for translations.

2 Following Haider (1993), we adopt a movement account of scrambling. Furthermore, we assume that scrambling is an instantiation of adjunction and results in an A-chain. Note that these assumptions are not crucial for the development of our empirical hypotheses (for a base generation account of word order variation, cf. Fanselow, 2001).

3 Sentences containing a narrow focus are contextually more constrained than sentences with a wide focus reading (see e.g. Höhle, 1982). (5b) is only possible with a specific context like the focus question *Wer hat die Nichten begrüßt?* ('Who welcomed the nieces?'). (5c) is a suitable answer to the question *Wer hat die Tante begrüßt?* ('Who welcomed the aunt?') (see also footnote 5).

It c-commands the trace in the base position of the scrambled object. Accordingly, the focus does not project.[4]

But there are also cases of scrambled constituents that bear the nuclear accent. In (6), the focus also does not project.

(6) (a) Wen haben die Nichten begrüsst? 'Who was welcomed by the nieces?'
    (b) Maria hat behauptet, dass [die TANte$_i$]$_F$ die Nichten t$_i$ begrüßt haben.
    Mary has claimed that the aunt the nieces welcomed have

As far as example (6b) is grammatical, it contradicts the commonly held opinion that a focused object cannot precede the subject (see e.g., Abraham, 1992; Lenerz 1977). In accordance with Neeleman (1994), we assume that focus scrambling is possible and that (6b) is a grammatical sentence and an appropriate answer to the question (6a). Experimental support for this assumption comes from an ERP study by Bornkessel et al. (2003).

What this example shows, is the fact that the focus structure of a sentence cannot be fully determined by its syntactic structure[5]. Another example, which is not predicted by focus projection based on syntactic structure only, is illustrated in (7):

(7) (a) Maria hat behauptet, dass sie [die Nichten begrüßt hat]$_F$.
    Mary has claimed that she *the nieces welcomed has*
    (b) Maria hat behauptet, dass sie$_i$ [die Nichten t$_i$ begrüßt haben]$_F$.
    Mary has claimed that she the nieces welcomed have

(7a) and (7b) do not differ in terms of focus structure. Both sentences have a wide focus reading. The pronoun itself belongs to background information. It co-refers with the first DP of the sentence (*Maria*). In this case, the focus structural representation cannot be derived from the syntactic structure in the way just described. According to the *Null Theory of Phrase Stress*, the focus should not project. The theory wrongly predicts narrow focus on the constituent c-commanded by the dislocated pronoun.

In sum, we have seen that scrambled word order compared to canonical word order does not exhibit syntactic differences alone. The movement of a constituent goes along with a change of focus structure. We assume that focus structure is not constituted by syntactic structure alone. Contextual factors as

---

[4] This seems to be evidence for a movement account in contrast to a base generation account. The trace in the base position accounts for the fact that the nuclear accent in (5c) gives rise to a narrow focus (see Haider, 2000).

[5] We ignore the huge literature on the interaction of context with the syntax and focus of a sentence. We hope that this is justified by the fact that our experimental work investigated processing on sentence level only. We have nothing to say about processing of sentences in context (but see Weskott, 2004).

in (6) and the type of the moved constituent as in (7) also play a crucial role in determining the focus structure of a sentence. Additionally, we expect that the interaction of the described factors (and perhaps other types of linguistic information) leads to a focus structural representation of its own right.

What does that mean for the online process of sentence comprehension? How does the human sentence processor deal with scrambled structures? The following section introduces some assumptions on the processing of word order variations and presents psycholinguistic evidence.

3 The processing of word order variations

3.1 Syntactic processes

It is a commonly accepted assumption that the human parser is working *incrementally.* Incremental processing is best described by a constraint suggested by Frazier & Rayner (1987, 263):

(8) *Left-to-Right Constraint*

Each item is incorporated into a constituent structure representation of a sentence (essentially) as the item is encountered.

If the parser is integrating incoming constituents immediately, how does it deal with local ambiguities? One prominent view in parsing research, starting with Frazier & Fodor (1978), is the assumption that the parser assigns something like a *default* analysis to the ambiguous material. For ambiguous scrambled sentences, the default syntactic analysis could be specified as follows

(9) (a) $[_{CP}$ Maria hat behauptet, $[_{CP}$ dass $[_{VP}$ die Tante $[_{V'}$ die Nichten $[_{V^\circ}$ begrüßt ...
Mary has claimed that the aunt the nieces welcomed

(a') $[_{CP}$ Maria hat behauptet, $[_{CP}$ dass $[_{VP}$ die Tante$_i$ $[_{VP}$ *die Nichten* $[_{V'}$ t_i $[_{V^\circ}$ begrüßt haben]]...
Mary has claimed that the aunt the nieces welcomed have

The parser analyses the sentence fragment (9a) as a subject-before-object structure. When it arrives at the auxiliary, a reanalysis takes place. To arrive at the right interpretation of the sentence in (9a'), a scrambling chain has to be established. As it were, there is evidence that this could be the correct description of how the parser deals with ambiguities in scrambled orders. Several studies indicate that the parser prefers the subject before object reading in ambiguous regions and has severe problems with scrambled sentences like (9a'). This subject-first preference seems to be a very robust effect and was shown with different methods (self-paced reading: Bader, 1996; grammaticality judgements: Bader & Meng, 1999; eye movements: Hemforth, 1993;

Scheepers, 1996; and event-related potentials (ERPs): Bornkessel et al., 2002; Friederici, 1998; Friederici et al., 2001; Rösler et al.,1998; Schlesewsky et al., 2003).

To explain this parsing preference, different principles were formulated which can be combined in terms of *minimal structure building*[6]. The preferred syntactic representation determines the occurrence of reanalysis processes at the point of disambiguation. Most explanations of the subject-first preference consider only phrase structural differences between the canonical word order and the scrambled order. In the next section, an experiment will be introduced that investigated the influence of focus structural differences in word order variations and describes the starting point for the two experiments that will be discussed in more detail in the following sections.

3.2 Focus structural processes

Bader & Meng (1999) looked into the processing of scrambled sentences in comparison to sentences with moved pronouns.

(10)(a) Die Direktorin hat erzählt, dass die neue Lehrerin einige der Kollegen angerufen hat.
The director has said that the new teacher$_{fem}$ some of the colleagues phoned has
'The director said that the new teacher phoned some of the colleagues.'

(b) Die Direktorin hat erzählt, dass die neue Lehrerin$_i$ einige der Kollegen t_i angerufen haben.
The director has said that the new teacher$_{fem}$ some of the colleagues phoned have
'The director said that some of the colleagues phoned the new teacher.'

(11)(a) Die Direktorin hat erzählt, dass sie einige der Kollegen angerufen hat.
The director has said, that she some of the colleagues phoned has
'The director said that she phoned some of the colleagues.'

(b) Die Direktorin hat erzählt, dass sie$_i$ einige der Kollegen t_i angerufen haben.
The director has said, that she some of the colleagues phoned have
'The director said that some of the colleagues phoned her.'

In a reading experiment with a speeded grammaticality judgement task, the authors found a significant difference in the error rates between OS-sentences with referential DPs (10b) and sentences with pronouns (11b)[7].

---

[6] Starting from the *Active Filler Hypothesis* (Frazier, 1987, Clifton & Frazier, 1989), De Vincenzi (1991) formulated a parsing principle that applies also to subject-object ambiguities in German embedded clauses: *Minimal Chain Principle* – 'Avoid postulating unnecessary chain members at Surface-Structure, but do not delay required chain members.'

[7] Further evidence for DP type effects in the processing of word order variations comes from studies by Kaan (1998, 2001) who investigated ambiguous relative clauses in Dutch.

The authors interpret this difference as the result of an additional focus structural revision for the sentences with referential DPs. They assume that the sentence processor not only assigns a default syntactic structure to the incoming material, but, additionally, assigns a default focus structural representation which should be the widest focus possible.

(12)(a) ..., dass [die neue Lehrerin einige der Kollegen angerufen ...]$_F$.
..., that the new teacher$_{fem}$ some of the colleagues phoned ...
(b) ..., dass die neue Lehrerin [einige der Kollegen$_i$]$_F$ t_i angerufen haben.
..., that the new teacher$_{fem}$ some of the colleagues phoned have

(13)(a) ..., dass sie [einige der Kollegen angerufen ...]$_F$.
..., *that she some of the colleagues phoned ...*
(b) ..., dass sie [einige der Kollegen$_i$ t_i angerufen haben]$_F$.
..., *that she some of the colleagues phoned have*

In (12b), the default wide focus reading has to be changed into a narrow focus when the human sentence processor arrives at the point of disambiguation. This is not necessary for sentences with pronouns like (13b). The default wide focus assignment is compatible with the OS structure.

To get further evidence for this focus structural explanation, it may be assumed that the measurement of event-related brain potentials (ERPs) is a useful method. ERPs are measures of electrical activity in the brain obtained using electrodes placed on the scalp. ERPs are a continuous on-line measurement with high temporal resolution. In addition, ERPs are multidimensional. It is possible to differentiate ERP patterns along the following parameters: polarity (negative vs. positive), topography (electrode site at which an effect appears) and latency (time at which an effect is visible).

Figure 1 shows an idealized waveform. You can see different negative and positive language related ERP components which appear at different time points. Note that negativity is plotted upwards and positivity is plotted downwards. The N400 correlates with different types of semantic processing (for a neurophysiologically based model of language comprehension, see Friederici, 2002). But let us concentrate on the positivity around 600 ms (P600). This component has been correlated with syntactic reanalysis during the processing of garden-path sentences (Hagoort et al., 1993; Osterhout & Holcomb, 1992). A P600 has also been observed in German scrambled sentences (Friederici, 1998; Friederici et al., 2001). Under the assumptions that (a) the focus structure of a sentence has a representation of its own and (b) the processing cost connected to scrambled sentences is the result of two different processes, namely syntactic reanalysis and focus structural revision, different ERP effects should be observed: beside the ERP correlate of syntactic processing (P600), there should be another, qualitatively different ERP effect.

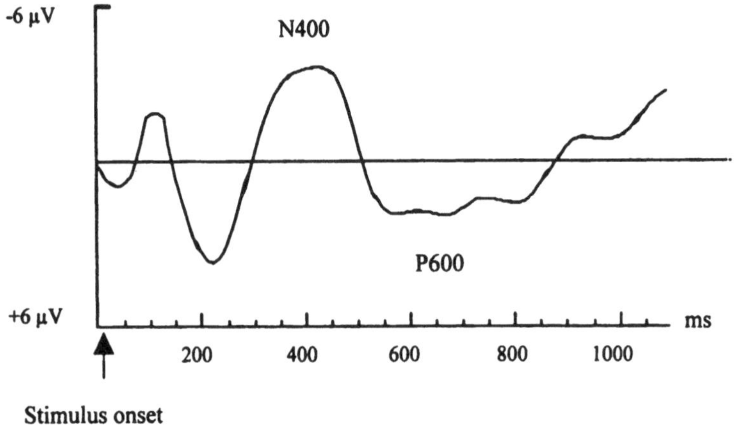

Figure 1: ERP correlates of language comprehension.

3.3 Experiment 1

We investigated ambiguous sentences with scrambled referential DPs and moved pronouns in comparison to their canonical counterparts in a reading study (see Table 1).

referential DP, subject before object (SO)
Maria hat behauptet, dass die Tante die Nichten begrüßt hat als die Schule zuende war.
Mary has claimed, that the aunt the nieces welcomed has when the school over was
referential DP, object before subject (OS)
Maria hat behauptet, dass die Tante die Nichten begrüßt haben als die Schule zuende war.
Mary has claimed, that the aunt the nieces welcomed have when the school over was
pronoun, subject before object (SO)
Maria hat behauptet, dass sie die Nichten begrüßt hat als die Schule zuende war.
Mary has claimed, that she the nieces welcomed has when the school over was
pronoun, object before subject (OS)
Maria hat behauptet, dass sie die Nichten begrüßt haben als die Schule zuende war.
Mary has claimed, that she the nieces welcomed have when the school over was

Table 1: Example of different versions of one experimental sentence

To avoid wrap-up effects in the ERP, the sentences continued after the auxiliary with a local or temporal modifier.

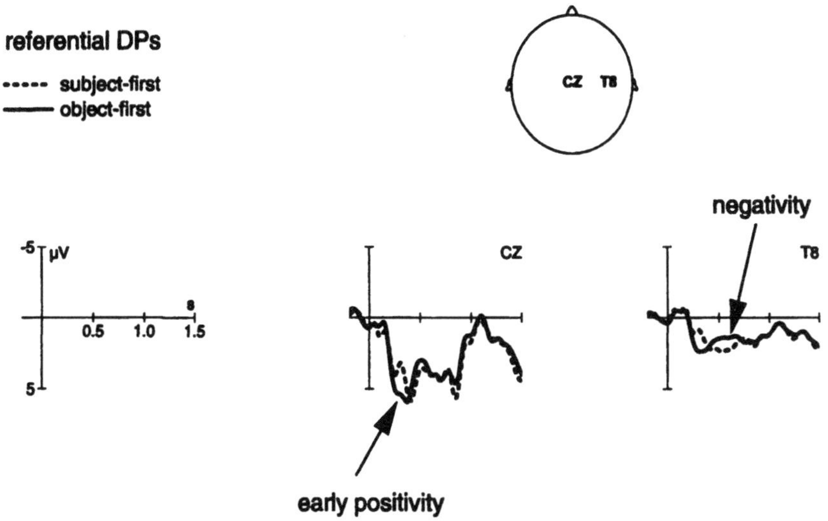

Figure 2: Referential DPs: grand averages for sentences with subject-first vs. object-first word order, time-locked to the disambiguating auxiliary (*hat* vs. *haben*, 1500 ms post onset).

We found two different ERP effects for the OS-sentences with referential DPs: an early positivity around 300 ms and a negativity around 550 ms (see Figure 2). For the sentences with moved pronouns, two positive effects were found: An early positivity around 300 ms like for the scrambled sentences and a late positivity around 700 ms (see Figure 3).

The early positivity, found for both DP types, was interpreted as an instantiation of a P600 and, therefore, as a correlate of syntactic reanalysis of the preferred SO-structure[8]. The late positivity, which was only observed for the sentences with moved pronouns, could not explicitly be correlated with a specific process so far. This effect will be evaluated and discussed in the context of Experiment 2 in section 4.

[8] For an explanation of the particular latency of the positivity, see Stolterfoht et al., 2003b).

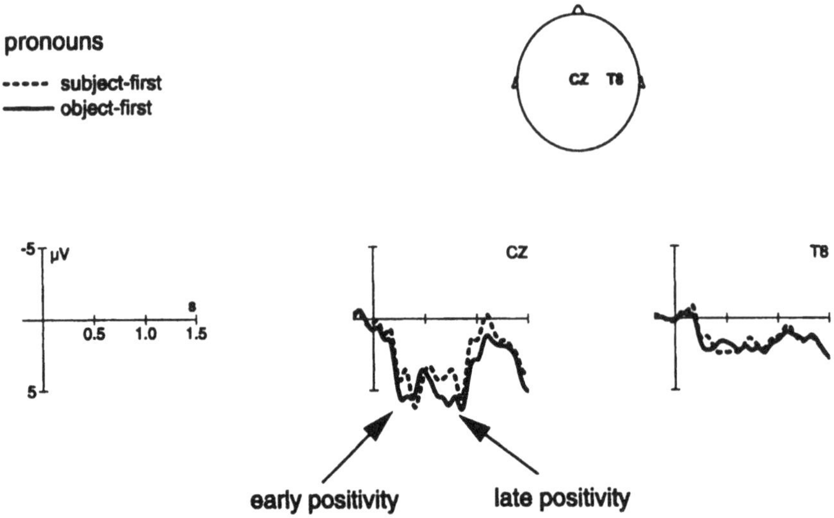

Figure 3: Pronouns: grand averages for sentences with subject-first vs. object-first word order, time-locked to the disambiguating auxiliary (*hat* vs. *haben*, 1500 ms post onset).

The negativity, clearly dissociated by latency and polarity from the positive effects, was only found for scrambled sentences (and not for sentences with pronoun movement), that is, for sentences for which a focus structural revision has to be done. Therefore, this could be the correlate of focus structural processing. The default wide focus reading in (14) has to be changed into a narrow focus in (15a).

default focus structure

(14) Maria hat behauptet, dass [die Tante$_i$ die NICHten t_i begrüßt ...]$_F$.

focus structural revision

(15)(a) Maria hat behauptet, dass die Tante$_i$ [die NICHten]$_F$ t_i begrüßt haben.
Mary has claimed that the aunt the nieces welcomed have

focus structural and prosodic revision

(b) Maria hat behauptet, dass [die TANte$_i$]$_F$ die Nichten t_i begrüßt haben.
Mary has claimed that the aunt the nieces welcomed have

In section 2, we argued that (15b) is also a possible focus structural representation of a scrambled sentence. If we compare (14) and (15b), not only a focus structural revision has to take place, but also a prosodic change has to be done: The sentence accent on *die Nichten* has to be shifted to the scrambled object *die Tante*. As a result, the negativity that was found in Experiment 1 could also be the correlate of focus structural **and** prosodic revision. Evidence for the latter interpretation comes from a study in which we could differentiate between focus structural and prosodic revision processes by using bare argument ellipses. We found a negativity with similar temporal and topographical characteristics for sentences that required a focus structural as well as a prosodic revision (Stolterfoht et al., 2003a).

To find further evidence for an ERP correlate of focus structural and prosodic processing, we did an ERP study which will be described in section 4[9]. In this study, effects of focus structure were investigated by the use of focus particles. The following section also will discuss some characteristics of these elements in connection to word order variations.

4 Focus particles and scrambling

4.1 Some characteristics of focus particles

Focus particles like *nur* ('only'), *auch* ('also') and *sogar* ('even') interact with the focus structure of a sentence. (14) shows one type of focus structural pattern for sentences with focus particles.

(14)(a) Ich glaube, dass Hans nur $[\text{ANna}]_F$ besucht hat.

(b) Ich glaube, dass Hans auch $[\text{ANna}]_F$ besucht hat.

I believe that Hans only/also Anna visited has.

'I believe that Hans visited only/also Anna.'

Here, the constituent to the right of the particle bears the nuclear stress of the sentence which is associated with narrow focus. This seems to be a typical pattern for sentences with focus particles (FPs). It can be described by two constraints formulated by Büring & Hartmann (2001, 236f):

(15)(a) FPs must be left-adjoined to an f-node of their focus[10].

(b) FPs are as close to the focus as possible.

---

[9] In the following, focus structural processing/revision shall be understood as synonymous with focus structural and prosodic processing/revision.

[10] There are exceptions to this principle, e.g., the stressed additive particle AUCH ('also') has to appear to the right of the 'added' constituent (Reis & Rosengren, 1997):

(i) Ich glaube, dass Hans [Anna] AUCH besucht hat.

If we compare the processing of scrambled sentences with and without a focus particle, the following difference appears , illustrated in (16) and (17):

(16)(a) ..., [dass die Tante die Nichten begrüßt ....]$_F$.
...., *that the aunt the nieces welcomed ....*
(a') ..., dass die Tante$_i$ [die Nichten]$_F$ t$_i$ begrüßt *haben.*
...., *that the aunt the nieces welcomed have.*

(17)(a) ..., dass die Tante nur [die Nichten]$_F$ begrüßt ....
...., *that the aunt only the nieces welcomed ....*
(a') ..., dass die Tante$_i$ nur [die Nichten]$_F$ t$_i$ begrüßt *haben.*
...., *that the aunt only the nieces welcomed have.*

(16a) again shows the preferred SO word order and the default wide focus assignment in the processing of ambiguous sentences. When the parser arrives at the point of disambiguation (the sentence final auxiliary), it has to reanalyse the syntactic structure (SO ⇒ OS). In addition, the sentence processor has to do a focus structural revision (wide focus ⇒ narrow focus) to arrive at the representation in (16a'). In the same processing scenario for (17), the sentence with a focus particle, only a syntactic reanalysis has to take place in order to arrive at the representation (17a'). The focus particle assigns narrow focus to the second DP, independently of word order. Consequently, there is no need for a focus structural revision[11].

This characterization of the focus structure of scrambled sentences with a focus particle leads us to the following hypotheses about the processing of such sentences measured by ERPs: If the negativity described in section 3.2 is indeed correlated with focus structural processes, it should disappear in scrambled sentences with focus particles. If focus structural processes are independent of syntactic processing, the correlate of syntactic processing (early positivity) should remain unaffected by the focus structural manipulation.

4.2 Experiment 2

We investigated ambiguous sentences with scrambled referential DPs in comparison to their canonical counterparts in a reading study[12]. In contrast to Experiment 1, the second DPs were preceded by a focus particle (see Table 2).

[11] That focus particles can influence sentence processing was shown by Bader (2000) for German and by Ni et al. (1996), Clifton et al. (2000) and Sedivy (2002) for English.

[12] Sentences with pronouns were also included in this experiment. The results for these sentences are reported in Stolterfoht et al. (2001, 2002).

referential DP, subject before object (SO)										
Maria hat behauptet,	dass	die Tante	nur die Nichten	begrüßt	hat	als	die Schule	zuende	war.	
Mary has claimed,	*that*	*the aunt*	*only the nieces*	*welcomed*	*has*	*when*	*the school*	*over*	*was*	
referential DP, object before subject (OS)										
Maria hat behauptet,	dass	die Tante	nur die Nichten	begrüßt	haben	als	die Schule	zuende	war.	
Mary has claimed,	*that*	*the aunt*	*only the nieces*	*welcomed*	*have*	*when*	*the school*	*over*	*was*	

Table 2: Example of different versions of one experimental sentence

To avoid wrap-up effects in the ERP, the sentences continued after the auxiliary with a local or temporal modifier.

We found two different ERP effects for the sentences with non-canonical word order: An early positivity around 300 ms and a late positivity around 700 ms.

As in Experiment 1, the early positivity is interpreted as the correlate of a syntactic reanalysis process. In line with our hypotheses, this process is not influenced by the focus structural manipulation. There seems to be no interaction of syntactic and focus structural processes.

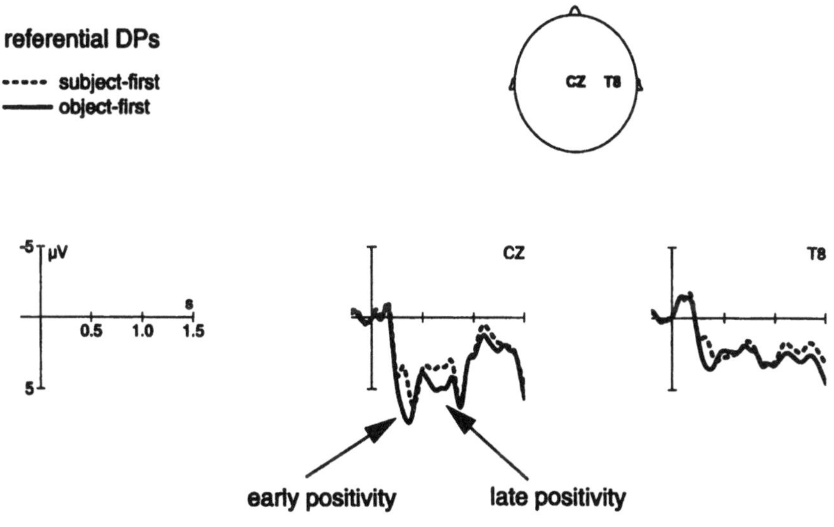

Figure 4: Grand averages for sentences with subject-first vs. object-first word order, time-locked to the disambiguating auxiliary (*hat* vs. *haben*, 1500 ms post onset).

In contrast, the late positivity seems to be influenced by the presence or absence of a focus particle. In the present study, scrambled sentences with focus particles revealed a late positivity. This process seems to interact with focus structural processing. In the previous study, the sentences with scrambled DPs without focus particles did not show this effect. Instead, the sentences with moved pronouns evoked a late positivity. This seems to be an effect of word order which is only present if no focus structural revision is necessary.

There is an ongoing debate weather the late positivity is really a pure syntactic process. It is a late process that seems to be influenced by other types of linguistic information (for example semantic information, see Gunter et al., 2000) and also by experimental manipulations like the type of the task (see Hahne, 1998; Hahne & Friederici, 2002) or the proportion of a specific type of sentence (see Hahne, 1998; Hahne & Friederici, 1999). Further research is needed to clarify the exact interactions of this component with other kinds of linguistic and non-linguistic processes.

The focus structural manipulation of Experiment 2 appeared to be effective. According to our prediction, the negativity found in Experiment 1 did not occur. This result provides further evidence for the correlation of the negativity with focus structural processing.

6 Conclusions

The main result of our two experiments is that syntactic processing and focus structural processing can be differentiated during online sentence comprehension. In both studies, we found an ERP effect which was correlated with the reanalysis of syntactic structure. In Experiment 1, we found an additional negative effect which we interpret as the result of a focus structural revision for sentences with referential DPs. In Experiment 2, the manipulation of focus structure by the means of focus particles had the expected effect: the correlate of focus structural revision was not observed. This is explained by the fact that the presence of a focus particle, which assigns focus to its adjacent constituent, makes a focus structural revision unnecessary. These results provide further experimental evidence for the correlation of the negativity with focus structural processes. In addition, the observation that syntactic movement is accompanied by a change of the focus structural representation obtains experimental support.

Further research is needed to clarify whether the late positive ERP effect reflects the interaction of syntactic and focus structural processes.

All in all, our results indicate that, beside the construction of a syntactic representation, the assignment of focus structure to a sentence plays a crucial role in sentence processing.

7 References

Abraham, W. (1992): Wortstellung und das Mittelfeld im Deutschen. In: W. Abraham (ed): Erklärende Syntax des Deutschen. Tübingen: Narr, 27-52.

Bader, M. (1996): Sprachverstehen: Syntax und Prosodie beim Lesen. Opladen: Westdeutscher Verlag.

Bader, M. (2000): On reanalysis: Evidence from German. In: B. Hemforth and L. Konieczny (eds): German Sentence Processing. Dordrecht: Kluwer, 187-246.

Bader, M. and M. Meng (1999): Subject-Object Ambiguities In German Embedded Clauses: An Across-the-board Comparison. Journal of Psycholinguistic Research 28, 121-143.

Bornkessel, I., M. Schlesewsky, and A. D. Friederici (2002): Grammar Overrides Frequency: Evidence from the Online Processing of Flexible Word Order. Cognition 85, B21-B30.

Bornkessel, I., M. Schlesewsky, and A.D. Friederici (2003): Contextual Information Modulates Initial Processes of Syntactic Integration: The Role of Inter- vs. Intrasentential Predictions. Journal of Experimental Psychology: Learning, Memory, and Cognition 29 (5), 971-882.

Büring, D. and K. Hartmann (2001): The Syntax and Semantics of Focus-sensitive Particles In German. Natural Language and Linguistic Theory 19, 229-281.

Cinque, G. (1993): A Null Theory of Phrase and Compound Stress. Linguistic Inquiry 18, 239-297.

Clifton, C., J. Bock, and J. Radó (2000): Effects of the Focus Particle Only and Intrinsic Contrast on Comprehension of Reduced Relative Clauses. In: A. Kennedy, R. Radach, D. Heller, and J. Pynte (eds): Reading as a Perceptual Process. Amsterdam: Elsevier, 591-619.

Clifton, C., and L. Frazier (1989): Comprehending sentences with long-distance dependencies. In: G. N. Carlson and M. K. Tanenhaus (eds): Linguistic Structure in Language Processing. Dordrecht: Kluwer, 273-317.

De Vincenzi, M. (1991): Syntactic Parsing Strategies in Italian. Dordrecht: Kluwer.

Fanselow, G. (2001): Features, q-Roles, and Free Constituent Order. Linguistic Inquiry 32(3), 405-437.

Frazier, L. (1987): Syntactic Processing: Evidence from Dutch. Natural Language and Linguistic Theory 5, 519-559.

Frazier, L. and J. D. Fodor (1978): The Sausage Machine: A New Two-Stage Parsing Model. Cognition 6, 291-325.

Frazier, L. and K. Rayner (1982): Making and Correcting Errors During Sentence Comprehension: Eye Movements In: the Analysis of Structurally Ambiguous Sentences. Cognitive Psychology 14, 178-210.

Frazier, L. and K. Rayner (1987): Parameterizing the Language Processing System: Left- vs. Right-branching within and across Languages. In: J. A. Hawkins (ed): Explaining Language Universals. Oxford: Blackwell, 247-279.

Friederici, A. D. (1998): Diagnosis and Reanalysis: Two Processing Aspects the Brain may differentiate. In: J. D. Fodor, and F. Ferreira (eds), Reanalysis in Sentence Processing. Dordrecht: Kluwer, 177-200.

Friederici, A. D. (2002): Towards a Neural Basis of Auditory Sentence Processing. Trends In Cognitive Science 6(2), 78-84.

Friederici, A. D., A. Mecklinger, K. M. Spencer, K. Steinhauer, and E. Donchin (2001): Syntactic Parsing Preferences and their On-line Revisions: a Spatio-Temporal Analysis of Event-related Brain: Potentials. Cognitive Brain Research 11, 305-323.

Gorrell, P. (1995): Syntax and Parsing. Cambridge: Cambridge University Press.

Gunter, T. C., A. D. Friederici, and H. Schriefers (2000): Syntactic Gender and Semantic Expectancy: ERPs Reveal Early Autonomy and Late Interaction. Journal of Cognitive Neuroscience 12:4, 556-568.

Hahne, A. (1998): Charakteristika syntaktischer und semantischer Prozesse bei der auditiven Sprachverarbeitung. Leipzig: MPI Series in Cognitive Neuroscience.

Hahne, A. and A. D. Friederici (1999): Elektrophysiological Evidence for Two Steps in Syntactic Analysis: Early Automatic and Late Controlled Processes. Journal of Cognitive Neuroscience 11(2), 194-205.

Hahne, A. and A. D. Friederici (2002): Differential Task Effects on Semantic and Syntactic Processes as Revealed by ERPs. Cognitive Brain Research 13, 339-356.

Hagoort, P., C. Brown and J. Groothusen (1993): The Syntactic Positive Shift as an ERP-measure of Syntactic Processing. Language and Cognitive Processes 8, 439-483.

Haider, H. (1993): Deutsche Syntax – Generativ. Tübingen: Narr.

Haider, H. (2000): Scrambling – What's the State of the Art. In: S.M. Powers and C. Hamann (eds): The Aquisition of Scrambling and Cliticization. Dordrecht: Kluwer, 19-40.

Haider, H. and I. Rosengren (1998): Scrambling. Sprache und Pragmatik 49, 1-104.

Haider, H. and I. Rosengren (2002): Scrambling – Non-triggered Chain Formation in OV-languages. MS. Salzburg University and Lund University.

Hemforth, B. (1993): Kognitives Parsing: Repräsentationen und Verarbeitung grammatischen Wissens, Sankt Augustin.

Höhle, T. (1982): Explikationen für 'normale Betonung' und 'normale Wortstellung'. In: W. Abraham (ed): Satzglieder im Deutschen. Tübingen: Narr.

Huynh, H. and L. S. Feldt (1979): Conditions under which the Mean Square Ratios in Repeated Measurement Designs have Exact F-distributions. Journal of the American Statistical Association 65, 1582-1589.

Inoue, A. and J. D. Fodor (1995) : Information-paced Parsing of Japanese. In: R. Mazuka and N. Nagai (eds): Japanese Sentence Processing. Hillsdale: Erlbaum, 9-63.

Kaan, E. (1998): Sensitivity to NP-type: Processing Subject-object Ambiguities in Dutch. Journal of Semantics 15, 335-354.

Kaan, E. (2001): Effects of NP type on the Resolution of Word Order Ambiguities. Journal of Semantics 15, 335-354.

Lenerz, J. (1977): Zur Abfolge nominaler Satzglieder im Deutschen. Tübingen: Narr.

Ni, W., S. Crain and D. Shankweiler (1996): Sidestepping Garden Paths: Assessing the Contributions of Syntax, Semantics and Plausibility in Resolving Ambiguities. Language and Cognitive Processes 11(3), 283-334.

Neeleman, A. (1994): Complex Predicates. OTS Dissertation Series: Utrecht.

Osterhout, L. and P. J. Holcomb (1992): Event-related Brain Potentials Elicited by Syntactic Anomaly. Journal of Memory and Language 31, 785-804.

Reis, M. and I. Rosengren (1997): A Modular Approach to the Grammar of Additive Particles: the Case of German 'Auch'. Journal of Semantics 14, 237-309.

Rösler, F., T. Pechmann, J. Streb, B. Röder, and E. Hennighausen (1998): Parsing of Sentences in a Language with Varying Word Order. Journal of Memory and Language 38, 150-176.

Scheepers, C. (1996): Menschliche Satzverarbeitung: Syntaktische und thematische Aspekte der Wortstellung im Deutschen. Doctoral dissertation, University of Freiburg.

Schlesewsky, M., I. Bornkessel, and S. Frisch (2003): The Neurophysiological Basis of Word Order Variations in German. Brain and Language 86, 116-128

Schriefers, H., A. D. Friederici, and K. Kühn (1995): The Processing of Locally Ambiguous Clauses in German. Journal of Memory and Language 34, 499-520.

Sedivy, J. C. (2002): Invoking Discourse-Based Contrast Sets and Resolving Syntactic Ambiguities. Journal of Memory and Language 46, 341-370.

Stolterfoht, B., A. Hahne, A. D. Friederici and M. Bader (2001): Word Order Variations In German: Revisions of Syntactic and Focus Structure. Poster at the conference Architectures and Mechanisms of Language Processing (AMLaP), Saarbrücken.

Stolterfoht, B., A. Hahne, A. D. Friederici, and M. Bader (2002): Word order variations – syntactic, focus structural and prosodic revision processes. Paper at the Fifteenth Annual CUNY Conference on Human Sentence Processing, New York City.

Stolterfoht, B., A. D. Friederici, K. Alter, and A. Steube (2003a): The difference between the processing of implicit prosody and focus structure during reading: evidence from event-related brain potentials. Poster at the Sixteenth Annual CUNY Conference on Human Sentence Processing, Boston.

Stolterfoht, B., A. Hahne, A. D. Friederici, and M. Bader (2003b): Syntactic and Focus Structural Revision: The Processing of Subject-Object Ambiguities in German. Poster at the Annual Meeting of the Cognitive Neuroscience Society (CNS), New York City.

Weskott, T. (this volume): Towards a Scalar Notion of Information Structural Markedness.

Carla Umbach, Ina Mleinek, Christine Lehmann, Thomas Weskott, Kai Alter, and Anita Steube

Intonational Patterns in Contrast and Concession

1 Introduction

This paper details an experimental study dealing with the interaction between the use of the German *aber* and specific intonational sentence patterns. It is the second in a series of experimental investigations into the interaction of intonation and meaning conducted by the project "Intonation and Meaning" which is a subproject of the Leipzig Linguistic Research Group.[1]

This study is part of the general investigation of contrast in information structure and discourse structure, which is one of the major topics of the research group. It is widely held that the notion of contrast plays an important role in both information structure and discourse structure. In the field of information structure, we have to distinguish contrastive focus from presentational or informational focus, and we have to account for the specific properties of contrastive topics as opposed to ordinary ones. In discourse structure, contrast interacts with various discourse relations signalled by all kinds of discourse markers.

In the Leipzig Linguistic Research Group, the notion of contrast has been discussed from the point of view of syntax, semantics and prosody, taking Slavic languages (Russian, Polish, Slovakian, Czech) into account in addition to German (see the articles in Steube & Umbach 2001 and in Steube 2002). The topics of research included, among others, the intonational differences between contrast and correction in Polish and Slovakian (Adamíková & Fehrmann 2001), the intonation of correction in German (Steube 2001a), the characteristics of the "hat-contour" pattern in German and in Russian (Steube 2001b, Mehlhorn 2001), and the influence of intonation on the interpretation of the German contrastive conjunction *aber* (Umbach 2001, to appear).

The study reported in this paper addresses the question of whether the contrastive (adversative)[2] use and the concessive use of German *aber* are distinguished by intonation. In Lang (2001) it has been claimed that the contrastive

[1] funded by the Deutsche Forschungsgemeinschaft (DFG)

[2] The term *contrastive* and the term *adversative*, which is common in the German literature, are used synonymously in this paper.

use and the concessive use of German *aber* correspond to different intonation patterns. According to Lang, in the contrastive use the topic given by the preceding context is elaborated in a symmetric way. Therefore, each conjunct of the *aber*-sentence comprises a contrastive topic and a focus. As compared to this, in the concessive use the topic is elaborated in an asymmetric way where the second conjunct is fully focussed. Different from Lang's hypothesis, the focus-based account of *but/aber* in Umbach (2001)/(to appear) does not couple contrast and concession with symmetry and asymmetry of elaboration. However, similar to Lang (2001), it predicts an intonational difference relating to the way of elaboration. Still, it is an open question whether this difference is reflected in the data.

The aim of the present study is to set out the connection between the theoretical considerations and our experimental approach in an exemplary fashion. In the experiment to be discussed below, subjects were presented sentences that were embedded into contexts which varied with respect to the interpretation of the *aber*-construction, i.e. contrastive vs. concessive. Subjects were asked to read the sentences aloud, and their productions were recorded and subject to a phonological and statistical analysis. Since this study is the first that investigated the issue of the contrastive vs. concessive reading in German from an empirical perspective, it has a rather exploratory character. Our main concern is to establish the type and number of factors that may influence the prosodic realisation of the two interpretations alluded to above.

The paper is organized as follows: Section 2 deals with the theoretical background and presents the hypotheses that guided the phonological analysis of the data. In section 3, the sentence material, the experimental procedure and the phonological properties of the data will be described in detail. In section 4, a descriptive statistical analysis is given which is followed by a discussion. Finally, section 5 presents our conclusions and points to some issues that have to be accounted for in further research.

2 Theoretical background

It is well known that German *aber*-sentences as well as English *but*-sentences allow for a concessive interpretation. In the concessive interpretation, a concessive marker, e.g., German *trotzdem* or English *nevertheless*, may be added without affecting the meaning of the sentence. Consider, for example, (1)(a) and (b):

(1) (a) Es regnete, aber Ben ging spazieren.
(It was raining, but Ben went for a walk.)
(b) Es regnete, aber Ben ging trotzdem spazieren.
(It was raining, but Ben went for a walk nevertheless.)

In her seminal paper in (1971) Lakoff distinguished between a semantic opposition use of *but* (*John is tall but Bill is short*) and a denial-of-expectation use (*John is tall but he's no good at basketball*). In the recent literature it is commonly held that the contrast expressed by *but/aber* results from a denial-of-expectation, the first conjunct triggering an expectation which is refuted by an inference from the second conjunct (cf., e.g., Lang 1984, Winter & Rimon 1994, Grote et al. 1997, Brauße 1998). The expectation is given by some kind of defeasible rule licensed by contextual or world knowledge. Concessive interpretations are regarded as a special case, where it is not an inference from the second conjunct but the second conjunct itself, which leads to a contradiction, compare (2)(a) and (b).

(2) (a) contrastive

"P *but* Q": $(P \rightarrow_D \neg R)$ & $(Q \rightarrow R)$

expectation: "Normally, P implies not-R"

(b) concessive

"P *but* Q [*nevertheless*]: $(P \rightarrow_D \neg Q)$ & Q

expectation: "Normally, P implies not-Q"

The examples in (3) and (4) demonstrate the inferences involved in the contrastive and the concessive use according to the standard approach.. In (3), hardly any context allows for a concessive interpretation (you may, however, imagine a situation where restaurants are advised to be open as long as there is a hungry person in town). The expectation triggered by the first conjunct will be the one in (3)(b) contradicting the inference resulting from the second conjunct, cf. (3)(c).[3] In (4), as compared to (3), the expectation resulting from the first conjunct directly contradicts the proposition in the second conjunct.

(3) contrastive

(a) We are hungry but the restaurants are closed.

(b) Normally, if we are hungry there is some food available.

(c) Restaurants are closed, so there is no food available.

(4) concessive

(a) It was raining, but Ben went for a walk [nevertheless].

(b) Normally, if it is raining, people don't go for a walk.

(c) Ben went for a walk.

[3] Note that, if we assume the expectation to be "Normally, if we are hungry, there is some restaurant open.", it would directly refute the proposition in the second conjunct, thus complying with the concessive schema in (2)(b). Hence the schema would predict a concessive reading although it is excluded by the context.

In the remainder of this section we will first present the hypothesis in Lang (2001), then outline the focus-based analysis in Umbach (2001, to appear), and finally compare the predictations made by these accounts.

2.1 Lang's hypothesis

According to the standard account sketched above, the contrastive reading and the concessive reading of a *but/aber*-sentence are seperated by the general context (background knowledge, knowledge inferred from the previous discourse etc.) Contrary to this, Lang (2001) claims that, (at least) in German, these readings are primarily separated by prosodic means. The context has to be in accordance with the prosodic marking, in particular, the immediately preceding discourse has to be such that it licences the specific intonation contour. This hypothesis is demonstrated by the example in (5):

(5) (a) contrastive

A: Was machen denn deine Eltern?
(So how are your parents?)

B: Es geht ihnen unterschiedlich:
(Different things:)

L*H L*H H% L L*H H*L L%

[[[Mein VAter/]$_T$[ist ernsthaft KRANK/]$_F$ ^{IP}] [[aber] [meine MUtter/]$_T$[geht ARbeiten\]$_F$ ^{IP}] ^{U}]

(My father is sick but my mom is going to work.)

(b) concessive

A: Was machen denn deine Eltern?
(So how are your parents?)

B: Ich bin entsetzt:
(I'm really annoyed:)

L*H L*H H H* H*L L%

[[Mein VAter/]$_T$ [ist ernsthaft KRANK/]$_F$ [aber meine MUtter geht ARbeiten\]$_F$ ^{U}]

(My father is sick, but my mom is going to work.)

Lang's hypothesis is based on his theory of coordination (cf. Lang 1984, 2002), which, in short, requires conjuncts to be parallel with respect to syntax, semantics, and prosody. Syntactic parallelism accounts for various well-formedness requirements. Semantic parallelism imposes two conditions: first, coordinated elements have to be semantically independent, neither of them subsuming the other, and secondly, there has to be a "common integrator", i.e. a concept subsuming both conjuncts. This is demonstrated in (6): In (a) semantic independence is violated because the meaning of *Tiere* subsumes the meaning of *Elefanten*. Therefore, (6)(a) will be infelicitous unless the hearer takes elephants to be a kind of animals not included in ordinary animals. In (b) the need for a common integrator leads to the interpretation of *Bank* as being a bench, excluding the interpretation as a financial organisation.

(6) (a) ?? Hans malt gerne Tiere und Elefanten.
(Hans likes to draw animals and elephants.)
(b) Hans hat einen Tisch und Peter hat eine Bank.
(Hans owns a table and Peter owns a bench.)

Note that the effects demonstrated in (6) also occur when we consider the alternatives evoked by focus, e.g. *??Hans malt nur Tiere, keine Elefanten.* Obviously, the alternatives constituting the domain of *only* have to comply with both semantic independence and the common integrator requirement. Actually, Lang's coordination conditions seem to be genuine conditions on alternatives, applying to coordination because coordinated elements constitute mutual alternatives.

Parallelism of the conjuncts is also required with respect to intonation, i.e. conjuncts should have the same topic-focus structure. It is possible, however, to induce non-parallel topic-focus structures in the conjuncts overwriting, in return, semantic and syntactic parallelism constraints. This accounts for the difference in (5)(a) and (b). (For detailed predictions about the prosodic structure cf. Section 3). In (5)(a) the sentence constitutes a symmetric elaboration of the discourse topic "the parents", first elaborating on one part of the topic ("my father") and then elaborating on the other part ("my mother"). Accordingly, each conjunct contains a contrastive topic and a VP-wide focus. In (5)(b), in contrast, the sentence constitutes an asymmetric elaboration where the conjuncts in combination give the reason for B's annoyance. Thus it is assumed that B's annoyance provides the discourse topic (and Common Integrator). Asymmetry of elaboration is reflected by the fact that the second conjunct is fully focussed.

Lang's hypothesis about the contrastive and the concessive reading of *aber*-sentences is as follows: The contrastive reading of an *aber*-sentence presupposes parallelism of conjuncts, thus inducing symmetric discourse elaboration. The concessive reading presupposes non-parallel conjuncts inducing asymmetric elaboration. Although following the standard account in assuming that a contrast expresses a denial of expectation, Lang's hypothesis proposes a different way to distinguish between the contrastive and the concessive reading. Instead of attributing the distinction to the context of use, it is primarily attributed to intonation, and instead of employing different inference patterns (where one is a special case of the other), different (non-overlapping) types of discourse elaboration are employed.

2.2 Concessive "over-interpretation"

In Umbach (2001)/(to appear) a focus-based account of the semantics and pragmatics of *but/aber* is presented which differs from the standard accounts because it is not based on the denial-of-expectation idea. Instead, it starts from two novel observations: (i) *but/aber* is similar to focus-sensitive operators such as *only,* because the contrast evoked by *but/aber* relates to the alternatives evoked by the focus, and (ii) any *but/aber*-sentence has to comprise a confirmation and a denial with respect to an implicit question referring to the alternatives under discussion. The latter is called "denial condition". It is demonstrated in (7): If the question is answered by confirming (or denying) both conjuncts, the use of *but* is not acceptable. If, however, one part of the question is confirmed and the other part denied, the use of *but* is perfect (and the use of *and* would be marked).

(7) Adam: Did John clean up his room and wash the dishes?
Ben: (a) # [yes], John cleaned up his room, but [yes] he washed the dishes.
(b) [yes], John cleaned up his room, but [no] he didn't wash the dishes.

Taking focus-sensitivity and the denial condition into account, the use of *but* imposes two conditions which can be outlined as follows: By using *but* an alternative is added to the set of alternatives under discussion, as in the case of *and* and *also*. However, unlike *and* and *also,* this alternative will result in a false proposition when combined with the common background, therefore requiring negation. Note that the denial condition must not be misunderstood as introducing a negation. Instead, *but* imposes an exhaustive reading on the first conjunct, similar to the adverb *only*. The affinity between *but* and *also/only* has been pointed out by Sæbø (2002). Adapting his terminology, the meaning of *but/aber* can be characterized as being "anti-additive", comprising both additivity and exclusion. Exclusion is trivial, if the second conjunct is explicitly negated. But it may also be given by entailment.

On the focus-based account, *but/aber*-sentences are classified as either "simple contrast" or "double contrast". Simple contrast cases involve one pair of alternatives, either individuals, or predicates, or propositions, cf. (8)(a)-(c).[4] The double contrast cases include two pairs of alternatives, which may occur parallel or crossed, cf. (9)(a), (b). In the simple contrast cases negation will either be explicit or be reconstructed by predicate negation (note that in the case of individual alternatives negation is obligatory, since individuals cannot be negated). In the double contrast cases negation comes as an entailment. (9)(a), for example, clearly entails that John did not wash the dishes.

[4] The intonation patterns may be more complex, cf. Umbach (to appear).

(8) simple contrast

(a) predicates: John cleaned up the \ROOM, but he didn't wash the \DISHES.

(b) individuals: \JOHN cleaned up the room, but \BILL didn't.

(c) propositions: It is \RAINING, but we are not going to stay at \HOME.

(9) double contrast

(a) parallel: /JOHN cleaned up the \ROOM, but /BILL did the \DISHES.

(b) crossed: /JOHN cleaned up the \ROOM, but it was \BILL who did the /DISHES.

This analysis differs from standard accounts of *but/aber* in that there is no recourse to a previously given hearer expectation which is denied by the use of *but/aber*. Instead, it is assumed that any sentence is linked to the preceding discourse by an explicit or implicit question, which in the case of *but/aber* has to be partly confirmed and partly denied. On the other hand, it is well-known that negated sentences have a general tendency to trigger the expectation that the corresponding affirmative proposition holds (cf. Givón 1978). Given the denial condition, *but/aber*-sentences include an (explicit or implicit) negation, thereby triggering the expectation that both alternatives hold simultaneously. Thus the idea that there is an expectation denied by the use of *but/aber* is finally confirmed. However, contrary to the standard account, the expectation is due to the general implicature of negation.

The focus-based account facilitates a clear separation of contrast and of concession. Following König (1991), concession is interpreted as incausality: "P *although* Q" iff "not (not-P *because* Q)", cf. (10):

(10)(a) Bill is rich although he lost a lot of money.

(b) It is not the case that ((Bill is not rich) because (he lost a lot of money)).

It is commonly known that, although the semantic meaning of *and* is a mere conjunction, *and*-sentences are often interpreted in a causal manner. For example, (11)(a) may be read as (11)(b). However, interpreting the conjunction *and* as a causal relation is clearly a case of over-interpretation, not included in the meaning of *and*.

(11)(a) It is raining and Mary is happy.

(b) It is raining and Mary is happy because of that.

Similarly, a *but*-conjunction as in (12)(a) may be interpreted as a concession. However, as in the case of *and*, this interpretation is not licensed by the meaning of *but*, which is a plain conjunction (plus the Denial Condition). Instead, this interpretation is induced by causal over-interpretation, too. However, in the case of *but* there is an inherent negation. For this reason, causal over-interpretation of *but* results in incausality, i.e. concession. This is demonstrated by the example in (12): In (b), according to the Denial Condition, the negation is reconstructed. In (c) the conjunction is supplemented with a causal relation which combines with the negation resulting in incausality, i.e. a concessive relation. Hence causal overinterpretation of (12)(a) results in (d).

(12)(a) It is raining but Mary is happy.
(b) It is raining but it is not the case that Mary is not happy.
(c) It is raining but it is not the case that Mary is not happy because of that.
(d) It is raining but Mary is happy in spite of that.

According to this analysis, there is no "concessive *but*", just as there is no "causal *and*". The meaning of *but* does not include incausality, just as the meaning of *and* does not include causality. At the same time, *but* is perfectly compatible with a concessive connective, just as *and* is compatible with a causal connective.

2.3 Comparison

The analyses in Lang (2001) and Umbach (to appear) differ considerably in their view of the concessive use of *but/aber*. According to the former, a concession is a special case of denial-of-expectation, where the expectation directly contradicts with the proposition stated in the second conjunct. According to the latter, it results from causal overinterpretation of the contrast. At the same time, both analyses assume that the information structure of the sentences has to respond to the topic set in the preceding discourse. Let us consider Lang's prototypical example in (5), repeated in (13). Lang's distinction between symmetric and asymmetric *but/aber*-sentences coincides to some degree with the distinction of simple contrast and double contrast made in the focus-based account. In (13)(a), assuming that the discourse topic to be elaborated is given by the parents, we expect a double contrast. In (13)(b), if the topic is provided by B' annoyance, we expect a simple contrast involving propositional alternatives. Thus the information structures predicted by the focus-based account roughly agree with Lang's prediction: The double contrast case in (13)(a) requires contrastive topics, whereas the simple contrast propositional case in (b) requires sentence-wide focus for at least one of the conjuncts.[5] So both accounts do predict similar intonation contours for (a) and (b), respectively.

---

[5] To be more precise, the focus-based account predicts that the second conjunct of (13)(b) is fully rhematic, which excludes a separate theme/topic, but allows for background material within the rheme.

(13) A: Was machen denn deine Eltern?
(So how are your parents?)
(a) contrastive – symmetric – double contrast
B: Es geht ihnen unterschiedlich:
(Different things:)
Mein /VATER ist \KRANK, aber meine /MUTTER geht \ARBEITEN.
(My father is sick but my mom is going to work.)
(b) concessive – asymmetric – simple contrast
B: Ich bin entsetzt:
(I'm really annoyed:)
[Mein Vater ist \KRANK]$_F$ aber [meine Mutter geht \ARBEITEN]$_F$.
(My father is sick, but my mom is going to work.)

However, in contrast to Lang's hypothesis, the focus-based account does not predict, that asymmetric, i.e simple contrast proposition cases must be interpreted as a concession. Since the concessive interpretation of *aber/but*-sentences is regarded as over-interpretation, it may or may not be induced by the context, independent of the respective information structure. Actually, (14) demonstrates a simple contrast proposition case where world knowledge precludes a concessive reading. Furthermore, on the focus-based account even symmetric, i.e. double contrast cases may be (over-)interpreted as a concession. The example in (15) shows a double contrast case which, according to the context, suggests a concessive reading.

(14) Kommissar: Ihr Mann kam also um fünf nach Hause und da lag ein Paket im Flur?
(detective: So your husband came home at five and there was a package lying in the hall?)
Zeugin: Mein Mann ist um fünf nach Hause gekommen, aber der Flur war [#trotzdem] leer.
(witness: My husband came home at five but the hall was empty [#nevertheless].)

(15) (context: Hanna loves to accompany her brother when he is feeding the animals.)
A: Was machen die Kinder?
(What are the children doing?)
B: /Anton füttert die Tiere, aber /Hanna ist [trotzdem] zu ihrer Freundin gegangen.
(Antony is feeding the animals but Hanna is staying with her girlfriend [nevertheless].)

To conclude: Whereas according to Lang's hypothesis symmetricity is coupled with adversativity and asymmetricity with concessivity, respectively, the focus-based account admits concessive readings in any of these cases. Still, both Lang (2001) and Umbach (to appear) predict that symmetric/double contrast cases such as (13)(a) and asymmetric/simple contrast cases such as (13)(b) differ in intonation.

3 Phonological analysis

The study presented in this paper aimed first and foremost at the verification of Lang's (2001) hypothesis that the contrastive/adversative and the concessive use of German *aber* are distinguished by prosodic means. It was set up according to the clear predictions concerning the intonational patterns in Lang (2001) and is rather explorative, our main concern being to establish the type and number of influencing factors. The study consists in a speech production task and provides acoustic analyses and a perceptual evaluation. In addition, there are post-hoc interviews verifying the intended readings.

3.1 Contexts and target sentences

In composing the contexts and target sentences, we closely followed Lang's original example (see section 2.1, examples 5a/b), which is also part of our corpus. In addition, we included four other target sentences. However, one of the items had to be removed afterwards, because it turned out that the subjects had difficulties to find a consistent interpretation (see section 3.3). The target sentences were integrated in an adversative and a concessive context, thus we finally worked with eight contexts similar to the one discussed in section 2.1 (see examples 5). One of the items is shown below:

(16)	Context:	Wie verstehst du dich mit deiner neuen Mitbewohnerin?
		(How do you get along with your new room-mate?)
(a)	adversative:	Wir sind sehr verschieden:
		(We differ in several respects.)
	Target:	Ich gehe früh schlafen, aber sie hört bis in die Nacht Musik.
		(I usually go to sleep very early, but she listens to music until midnight.)
(b)	concessive:	Ich bin ziemlich genervt:
		(I'm really annoyed:)
	Target:	Ich gehe früh schlafen, aber sie hört bis in die Nacht Musik.
		(I usually go to sleep very early, but she listens to music until midnight.)

We investigated the question of whether the difference between the versions are acoustically encoded, i.e. result in different intonational patterns. Lang provides a number of clear predictions of the prosodic features of the adversative and the concessive reading spelled out within the ToBI system, see example (5a/b). Below, the ToBi annotations in (5a/b) have been carried over the example in (16):

Adversative version:

L*H L*H H% L L*H H*L L%

[[ICH/]$_T$ [gehe früh SCHLAfen/]$_F$^{IP}] [[aber] [SIE/]$_T$ [hört bis in die Nacht MuSIK\]$_F$^{IP}]^U].

Concessive version:

L*H L*H H H* H*L L%

[[ICH/]$_T$ [gehe früh SCHLAfen/]$_F$ [aber sie hört bis in die Nacht MuSIK\]$_F$^{U}].

The ToBI labelling focusses on at least five relevant intonational differences (i-iii, v) between the adversative and the concessive readings, (cf. Table 1). The crucial predictions can be summarised as follows: The difference in the intonational patterns is located around the boundary between the two conjuncts in both readings. The first three points account for the boundary itself (iii) and the temporally right adjacent pitch, i.e. the tonal distribution on the connector (ii) and on the first lexical items in the second conjunct (i). In considering point (iv), it is unclear whether an optional deletion of the connector is due to phonological deletion rules or related to optional lexical. Point (v) deals with possible intonational phrasing properties which might be related to the patterns proposed in (iii). The question of whether this is a result of the difference between the adversative and the concessive realisations is left open.

	Difference points	Adversative version	Concessive version
(i)	Pitch accent in the beginning of the second conjunct	L*H	H*
(ii)	(lexical) tone of the connector	L	H
(iii)	IP boundary tone at the end of the first conjunct	H%	?
(iv)	Status of the connector	optional	obligatory
(v)	Delimitation of IP	conjunct wise	sentence wise

Table 1: Intonational patterns supposed to differentiate between adversative and concessive readings following Lang (2001: 125)

Based on these assumptions, we conducted a speech production study investigating the intonational parameters (i-iii). In addition to the acoustic analysis of the local pitch contour, the investigation included perceptive evaluations and the statistical analysis of the acoustic.

In the following sections, the experimental design (3.2), the acoustic and proto-typical intonational patterns and the perceptional observations are presented, (3.3). Finally, we briefly discuss the results of the post-hoc interviews, cf. (3.4).

3.2 Experimental design

Eleven female native German speakers were asked to read the 2x4 contexts. Thus, the corpus of the production study resulted in 88 target sentences (44 for each condition). After recording, the speakers were asked how they understood the examples and what exactly the difference between the respective adversative and the concessive variants was.

The contexts including the target sentences were recorded and digitised with a DAT-recorder at 16bit/44.1kHz sampling rate. The target sentences were cut out of the contexts by means of Cool Edit and acoustically and prosodically analyzed using WinPitch and PitchWorks.

3.3 Acoustic analyses

First, we looked at the labelled F0-contours of three subjects out of eleven in PitchWorks. They did not show systematic patterns which would suggest a prosodic disambiguation of the readings. For example, the decisive word *krank* in Lang's original example (example 5 in section 2) shows falling and rising patterns. These patterns are neither consistent for the conditions nor for the speakers. They even cancel each other out. This is demonstrated below:

subject 1/ adversative condition (Translation see example (5) a / b)

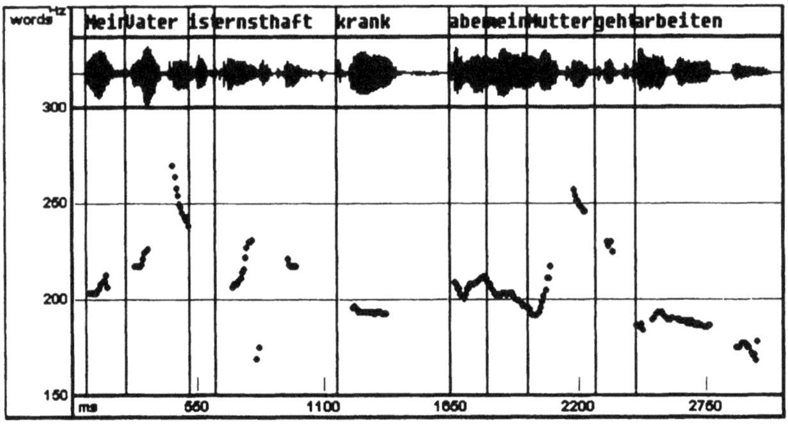

subject 1/ concessive condition

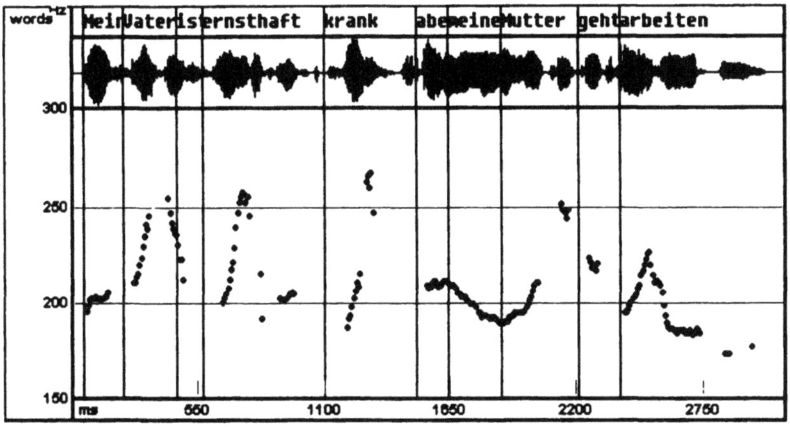

subject 2/ adversative condition

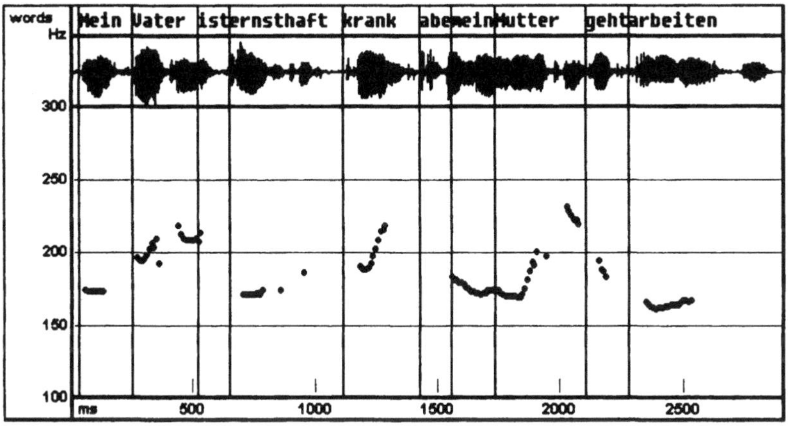

subject 2/ concessive condition

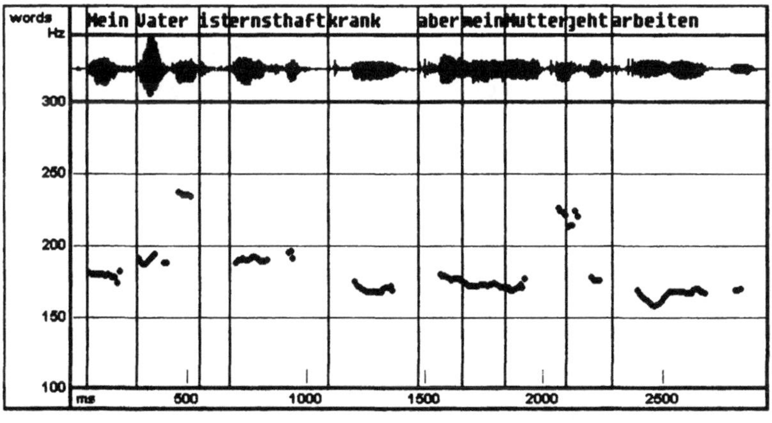

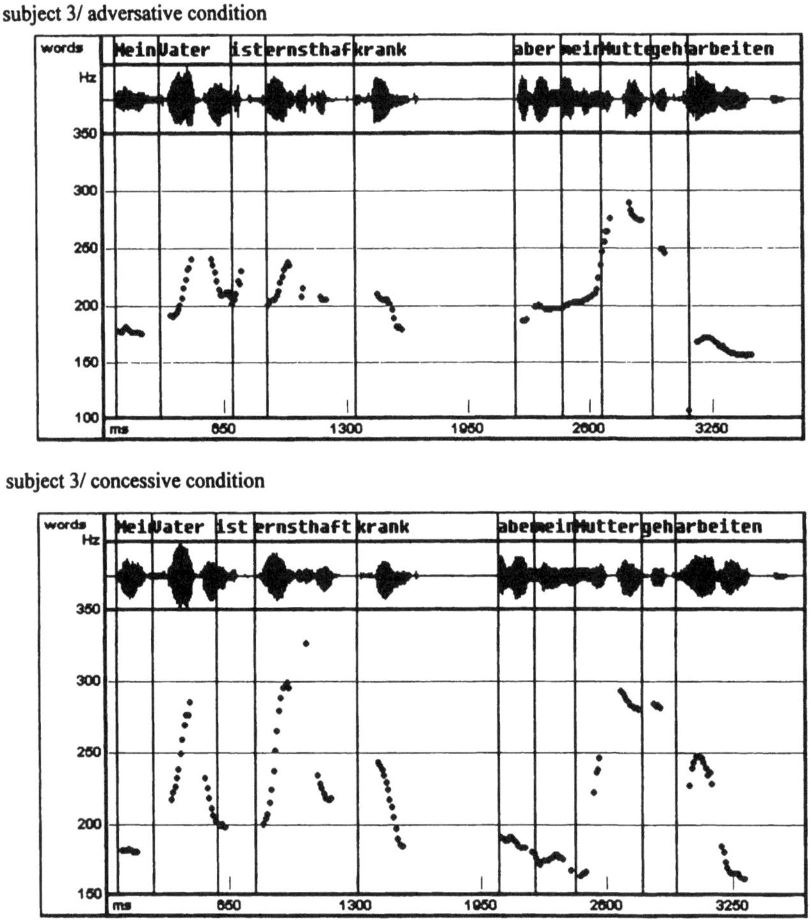

Figure 1: Single F0-contours for Lang's example in both versions

From these contours no tendency or thesis can be derived. They are even partly contradictory. At this point of the analysis, we had to take the possibility into account that there might be no correlation at all between the signal and the reading. For this reason, the target sentences of the 11 female speakers were perceptually evaluated.

We found that 9 out of 11 (female) speakers were mostly able to encode the semantic difference in a prosodic way. We noticed, however, there was one item where the speakers obviously failed encode the semantic difference prosodically. Thus we were not able to assign the prosodic signal to one of the two versions. This item was removed from our corpus.

We now tried to assign prosodic parameters to the semantic conditions. That was possible for 7 out of 11 (female) subjects. Judging from perceptive evaluation, these subjects use the same strategies, for example: rise of the fundamental frequency immediately before the phrase boundary in condition (a) or its fall in condition (b); greater stress on the sentence topic in the second conjunct in condition (b); the F0-contour on the focus of the second conjunct in condition (b) no longer fell for some speakers; finally, there are differences in the behaviour for pauses. However, it is unclear in what way and to what degree these perceptible distinctions are relevant for the distinction of the two versions.

With the help of the perceptual evaluation, we defined measurable parameters which could serve as correlates for differences between the versions. Actually, these parameters are closely connected to Lang's hypothesis. They include:

1. the direction of the pitch movement prior to the focus accent of the first conjunct = Onset of the focused word
2. the accent itself = Peak of the accented syllable
3. the boundary = Offset of the focussed word
4. the onset of the connector *aber*

For further analysis, we focussed on 4 items produced by the 7 (female) speakers who apparently behaved consistently. Thus we had 56 target sentences (28 sentences in each condition) for further prosodic observations and for statistic comparisons.

We defined suitable measuring points in F0 and corresponding time values (depending on the sentence length between 19 and 28 per target sentence) covering the whole contour as exactly as possible. Then we determined the mean average values of these measuring points. This is shown below by the prototypical F0-contours for all 4 items (the numbering in the signal reflects the above defined parameters 1 to 4; the accented syllable of the focused word in the first conjunct is marked by capital letters):

1 (a) (C) Was machen denn deine Eltern?
(So how are your parents?)
Es geht ihnen unterschiedlich.
(Different things:)
Mein Vater ist ernsthaft <u>KRANK</u>, aber meine Mutter geht arbeiten.
(My father is sick, but my mom is going to work.)

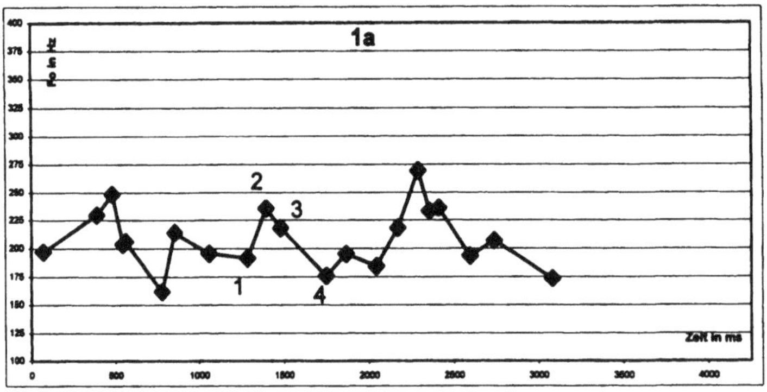

1 (b) (C) Was machen denn deine Eltern?
(So how are your parents?)
Ich bin ziemlich entsetzt.
(I'm really annoyed:)
Mein Vater ist ernsthaft <u>KRANK</u>, aber meine Mutter geht arbeiten.
(My father is sick, but my mom is going to work.)

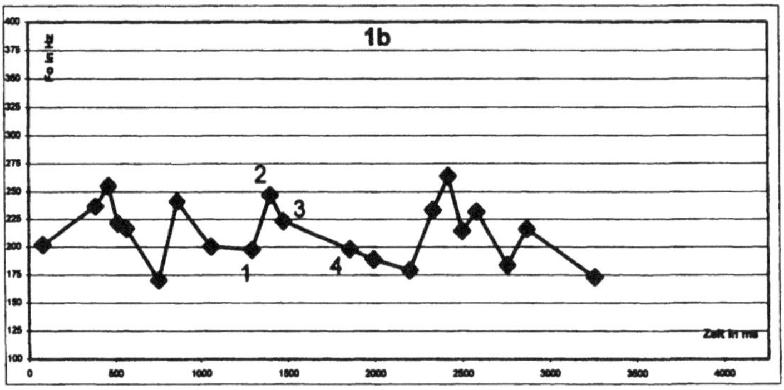

2 (a) (C) Wie verstehst du dich mit deiner neuen Mitbewohnerin?
(How do you get along with your new room-mate?)
Wir sind sehr verschieden.
(We differ in several respects.)
Ich gehe früh <u>SCHLAfen</u>, aber sie hört bis in die Nacht Musik.
(I usually go to sleep very early, but she listens to music until midnight.)

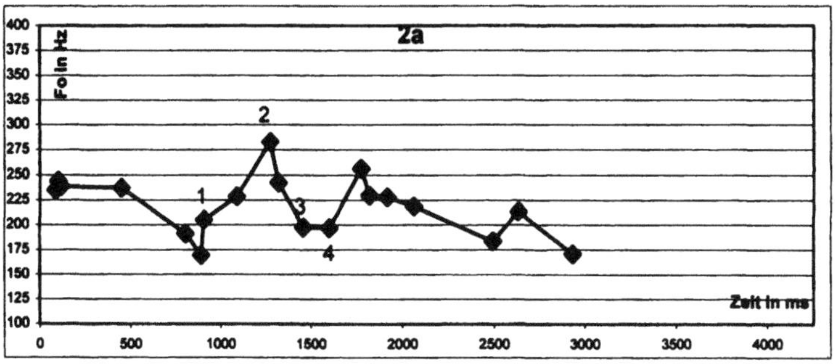

2 (b) (C) Wie verstehst du dich mit deiner neuen Mitbewohnerin?
(How do you get along with your new room-mate?)
Ich bin ziemlich genervt.
(I'm really annoyed:)
Ich gehe früh <u>SCHLAfen</u>, aber sie hört bis in die Nacht Musik.
(I usually go to sleep very early, but she listens to music until midnight.)

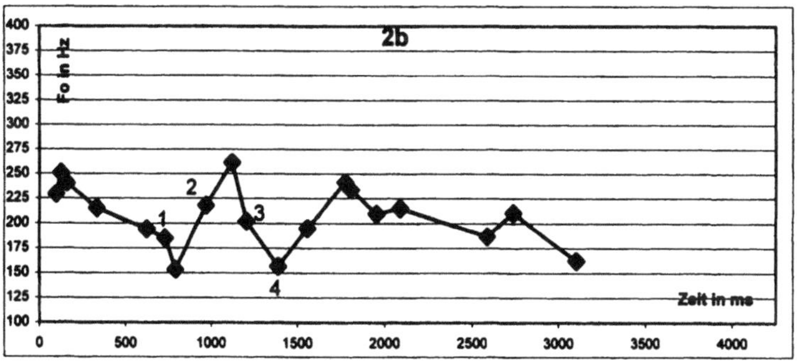

3 (a) (C) Was machen denn die Kinder gerade?

(What are the children doing at the moment?)

Paula hat in 2 Wochen eine wichtige <u>PRÜfung</u>, aber Peter will in Urlaub fahren.

(Paula has an important exam in two weeks, but Peter wants to go on vacation.)

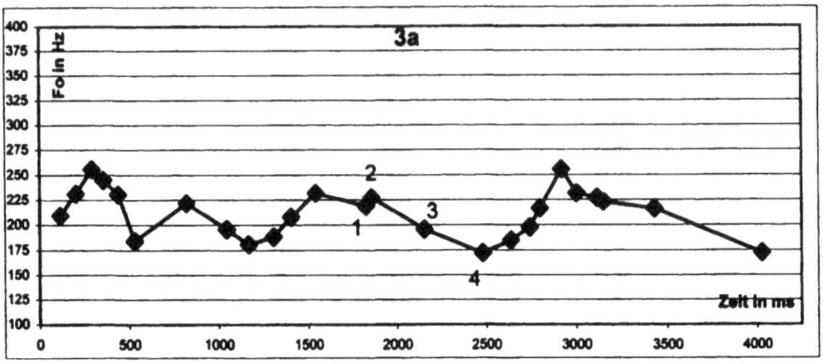

3 (b) (C) Warum streiten sich die beiden denn?

(Why do they argue?)

Paula hat in 2 Wochen eine wichtige <u>PRÜfung</u>, aber Peter will in Urlaub fahren.

(Paula has an important exam in two weeks, but Peter wants to go on vacation

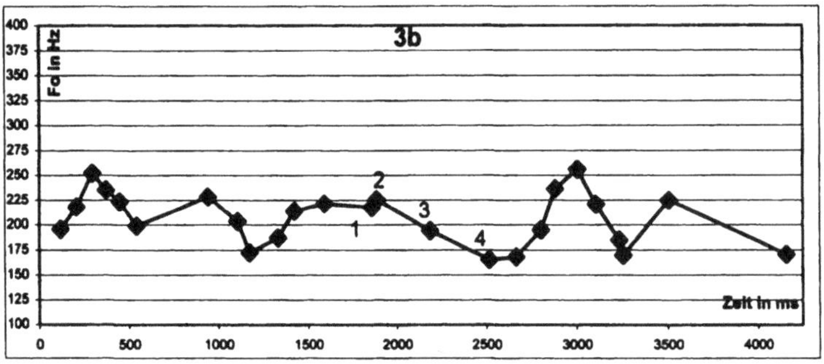

4 (a) (C) Was machen denn Peter und Paul dieses Wochenende?
(What do Peter and Paul do this weekend?)
Paul hat FREUNde eingeladen, aber Peter fährt zu einem Fußballspiel.
(Paul has invited friends, but Peter will go to a soccer game.)

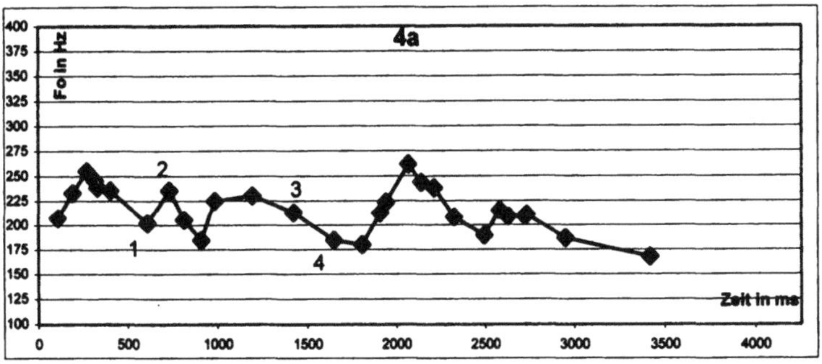

4 (b) (C) Warum ist sie denn enttäuscht?
Why is she disappointed
Paul hat FREUNde eingeladen, aber Peter fährt zu einem Fußballspiel.
(Paul has invited friends, but Peter will go to a soccer game.)

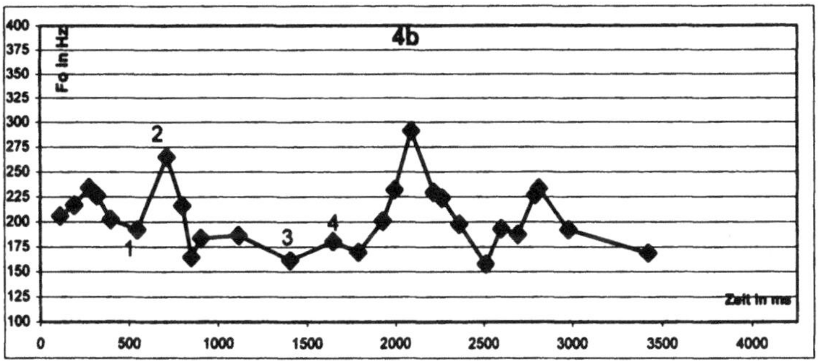

Figure 2: Prototypical F0-contours for all 4 items in both versions (a and b). The diagrams show the realisation of the time wave form (upper level) and the pitch contour (lower level). (a) stands for the adversative readings and (b) for the concessive readings.

Based on the perceptual evaluation, we expected an intonational difference between the concessive and the adversative target sentences. However, an explorative comparison of the F0-contours per condition did not reveal any systematic difference. In figure (1) in the first row, Lang's original example (cf. example 5) is presented for the two different conditions. The visual examination of the proto-typical F0-contours shows close similarity within one item and also within the versions. This applies to the other items as well. The only divergence to be seen appeared in the concessive reading of item 4. This leads to the conclusion that the thesis of Lang, which says that the semantic difference between the adversative and the concessive version correlates with a prosodic difference (at least in German), cannot be verified.

Finally, we conducted a combined inspection of both the auditory signals and the accompanying F0-contours. Based on the auditory evaluation we found some examples matching with the hypothesis in section 2. In single cases some speakers realised the hypothesized prosodic differentiation between the two readings, indicating a certain tendency for an opposition between versions: In five comparisons, we detected a clear high boundary in the adversative version, thus marking a difference between both readings (cf. parameter (iii) in Table 1). However, in at least three cases we also found the exact reversed realisation. Other correlates like the direction of tonal movement (cf. parameter 2 mentioned above) show similar distributions. The number of clearly distinguished examples revealed by this method is 11 of a total of 56, which equals random distributions.

No profound empirical conclusion can be drawn from these observations. A clear distinction based on both auditory evaluation and visual inspection of F0-contours, which is a prerequisite for prosodic analysis, does not reach confidence level.

However, in a more detailed statistical analysis, points (iii) and (iv) in the signal (the boundary and the connector) were evaluated for seven speakers and 4x2 items. We tried to find out whether at least these points, for which Lang made clear predictions (see ToBI annotation of examples (5a,b), and parameters (ii) & (iii) in Table 1), would show statistically relevant distinctions. The statistical analysis is described in section four.

3.4 Post-hoc interviews

In addition to the production task, we conducted post-hoc interviews aiming at the question of whether the subjects acknowledge the intended semantic difference between the versions and how they interpret the difference. Through the interviews we wanted to make shure that the presented triggered the intended readings. The interviews confirmed that, in each of the presented items, there is a clear semantic difference. Moreover, the subjects agreed to a high degree in their description of the contexts. The adversative variants were characterized as neutral, unbiased, less contrastive; conjuncts appear to be loosely connected. In contrast, the concessive variants were characterized as emotional, biased, containing an implizit reproach, highly contrastive; conjuncts appear to be closely connected. Three subjects actually suggested to insert *obwohl (although)* or *trotzdem (nevertheless)* into some of the concessive contexts.

From the interviews we learned that the failure in finding prosodic differences between the readings cannot be the result of inadequate test material. As mentioned in the beginning of this section, there was one item which was judged as being unclear. But this item had been removed from the data.

Still, the characterization of the concessive variant as being emotional or biased was surprising. According to Lang (2001), both the contrastive/adversative and the concessive reading of an *aber*-sentence express a denial of expectation, the difference consisting in the respective inference pattern (cf. section 2.1). According to the focus-based account in Umbach (to appear), the concessive reading results from an (in-)causal interpretation of the conjunction (cf. 2.2). Although this is a clear semantic distinction, it does not explain the characterization of the concessive contexts as being emotional. It may be argued that the concessive contexts unintentionally resemble Lang's original example, which is emotional. In any case, the question of how a concession is interpreted seems to be an interesting topic for further research.

4 Descriptive statistical analysis

A descriptive *post-hoc* analysis was performed on these data which took Lang's (2001) hypothesis as a heuristic. That is, we looked for a point in the sound signal where the two conditions of the items should clearly differ if that hypothesis was correct. Before turning to that analysis, however, a methodological remark is in place.

The exploratory analysis essentially hinges on two reliability conditions concerning the data patterns which do not seem to be fulfilled trivially by data stemming from this kind of production experiment. Note that these two conditions are independent from the hypothesis in question; they must be satisfied in order to relate the data to the hypothesis in the first place.

First of all, it has to be assumed that subjects exhibit a consistent behavior with respect to the distinctions at hand, independently of how that behavior relates to the hypothesis. This is to say that a given speaker should exhibit a behavior that is consistent *across* items, i.e. she should reliably produce a prosodic pattern in the adversative condition and the concessive condition, respectively, and that this pattern should be found in more or less all the items in the respective conditions.[6]

Secondly, one has to assume that speakers from a given sample do not differ essentially in the manner in which they encode the respective readings – again, independently of how that encoding fits with the hypothesis. This assumption predicts a given sample of speakers to reliably encode e.g. the adversative reading more or less in the same fashion, and the concessive reading more or less in the same fashion, too (*modulo* the personal characteristics of the speakers), irrespective of whether these fashions are the same or different for the conditions.

4.1 Results

With these two reliability requirements in mind, the data were screened and subjected to an exploratory descriptive analysis. We chose to analyze the region of the connective, since it was the element that reappeared in all 4 items in all conditions. This warranted the comparability of the F_0-values. Furthermore, this is the region where one would expect the conditions to differ considerably (s. section 2 above). The data consisted of the F_0-value for the offset of the last syllable of the first conjunct, and the F_0-value for the onset of the connective "aber". Table 2 shows the descriptive data for the F_0-values for the offset of the first conjunct in both conditions; condition 0 is the adversative, condition 1 the concessive interpretation. The rows show the performance of the 7 subjects on the items by condition successively; the columns show the scores for the 4 different items. The first reliability assumption made above should result in an approximately consistent pattern of data in the respective rows. The second assumption would predict that every second value in the columns should center around some mean value.

[6] This in turn depends on intra-personal consistency, i.e. that a speaker, when reading an item in one condition repeatedly, follows the same strategy in both prosodic realizations, yielding more or less the same behavioral pattern, i.e. producing similar F_0 scores. Since this assumption was not tested here, nothing can be said in favor of it, nor against it. Note that this condition on reliability (called "test-retest reliability" in test theory, i.e. the relationship between the scores that a person achieves when doing the same test twice) is tacitly assumed to be satisfied in most (psycho-)linguistic experimental studies because the sources of (intra-personal) variance are taken to be accidental, i.e. not ascribable to any systematic influence. We follow this assumption here and suppose that variance will decrease with higher test power, e.g. by testing more subjects.

subject	cond.	item 1	2	3	4	means	std.dev.
1	0	191	178	180	181	182.50	5.80
	1	254	244	182	117	199.25	63.41
2	0	209	265	161	181	204.00	45.18
	1	217	196	160	156	182.25	29.33
3	0	240	237	178	232	221.75	29.35
	1	211	228	181	163	195.75	29.23
4	0	212	130	203	233	194.50	44.80
	1	175	115	166	181	159.25	30.14
5	0	171	235	152	159	179.25	37.99
	1	172	220	160	160	178.00	28.57
6	0	323	370	324	320	334.25	23.89
	1	247	126	182	174	182.25	49.75
7	0	182	282	171	183	204.50	51.95
	1	289	286	329	179	270.75	64.23
means	0	218.29	242.43	195.57	212.71		
	1	223.57	202.14	194.29	161.43		
std.dev.	0	51.41	76.62	58.87	54.88		
	1	42.77	62.18	60.25	21.82		

Table 2: F_0-values for the offset of the 1st conjunct

However, as a thorough look at Table 2 reveals, the data exhibit a huge degree of variance *both* across items *and* subjects. Take for example the performance of subject 1 for item 1 (the first two data rows of Table 1), where the F_0-value for condition 1 clearly falls below that of condition 0; a similar pattern is obtained for item 2. But the performance for the two conditions of item 3 do not show any difference. And for item 4, there is a difference between the values, but it points in the opposite direction when compared to that of items 1 and 2. And the same inconsistency across items can be found in nearly all subjects, with the notable exception of subject 6, which is the only subject exhibiting a consistent pattern across items. Also note that the means across both subjects and items show a vastly inconsistent picture, which of course carries over to the relation between the two conditions. To give but one more example: if we consider the first data column of Table 2, we find all possible patterns for the data patterning over the two conditions of item 1 across the subjects: *condition (0) < condition (1)* (subjects 1, 2, and 7), *condition (0) > condition (1)* (subjects 3, 4 and 6), and *condition (0) ≈ condition (1)* (subject 5); the means of the two conditions however are nearly identical (μ (cond 0) = 218.29; μ (cond 1) = 223.57), and conceal this highly unsystematic variance. Even if we take standard deviation as an indicator of variance for the performance of a subject or item, we do not seem to get a similar patterning across items and/or subjects. This indicates that the patterning across items (the rows) does not reappear across subjects, which would be expected if it had been certain properties of the single items that influenced the subjects to produce a particular prosodic difference between the conditions with one item, but not with the other. One might suspect that the reason for the huge variance of the F_0-values between both subjects and items as witnessed by the standard deviation values has to be sought in the fact that the dependent variable in question belonged to different items which contained different lexical material, i.e. the offset of the first conjunct consisted of different lexical material. However, if we turn to the values for the onset of the connective "aber", we face the same diagnosis, as Table 3 reveals.

		item					
subject	cond.	1	2	3	4	means	std.dev.
1	0	204	191	145	199	184.75	27.04
	1	212	110	201	173	174.00	45.72
2	0	188	209	148	181	181.50	25.30
	1	189	152	145	149	158.75	20.73
3	0	100	194	206	154	163.50	47.82
	1	214	191	213	222	210.00	13.29
4	0	104	130	196	198	157.00	47.40
	1	175	115	105	176	142.75	38.04
5	0	193	198	152	159	175.50	23.36
	1	190	206	128	175	174.75	26.81
6	0	251	259	209	202	230.25	28.91
	1	209	115	180	185	172.25	40.21
7	0	191	201	150	198	185.00	23.71
	1	198	207	186	184	193.75	10.78
means	0	175.86	197.43	172.29	184.43		
	1	198.14	156.57	165.43	180.57		
std.dev.	0	54.81	37.72	29.69	20.30		
	1	14.42	44.38	40.07	21.81		

Table 3: F_0-values for the onset of the connective "aber":

Here we also found the F_0-values to vary dramatically across both items and subjects, as the standard deviation values reveal. Although the lexical material was the very same (i.e., the /a/ of "aber"), which should warrant a certain degree of uniformity of encoding, it was prosodically realized in a massively heterogeneous manner. Again, the only subject performing consistently across items was subject 6. No consistent pattern across subjects could be found for any of the items.

If we finally look at the difference between the two values – a measure which should mirror the tonal movement between the two points in the sound string – the inconsistent picture found in the tables above, unsurprisingly, carries over to Table 4. The values are the result of subtracting the F_0-values from Table 2 (those measured at the offset of the last constituent of the first conjunct) from those in Table 3 (those measured at the onset of the connective). That is, a positive value stands for a rising tonal movement between the two points, whereas a negative represents a fall.

		item					
subject	cond.	1	2	3	4	means	Std.dev.
1	0	13	13	-35	18	2.25	24.94
	1	-42	-134	19	56	-25.25	83.00
2	0	-21	-56	-13	0	-22.50	23.95
	1	-28	-44	-15	-7	-23.50	16.18
3	0	-140	-43	28	-78	-58.25	70.11
	1	3	-37	32	59	14.25	41.11
4	0	-108	0	-7	-35	-37.50	49.37
	1	0	0	-61	-5	-16.50	29.76
5	0	22	-37	0	0	-3.75	24.47
	1	18	-14	-32	15	-3.25	23.99
6	0	-72	-111	-115	-118	-104.00	21.52
	1	-38	-11	-2	11	-10.00	20.74
7	0	9	-81	-21	15	-19.50	43.92
	1	-91	-79	-143	5	-77.00	61.32
means	0	-42.43	-45.00	-23.29	-28.29		
	1	-25.42	-45.57	-28.86	19.14		
std.dev.	0	64.58	43.26	44.90	51.93		
	1	36.70	47.05	59.13	27.38		

Table 4: Difference between the F_0-values for the onset of "aber" and the offset of the 1st conjunct:

Comparing the subjects (rows) and items (columns) yields the by-now familiar picture: neither did subjects encode the concessive and adversative reading reliably across items (apart from subject 6, who quite consistently produced a fall in both conditions, but one that was about a half smaller in condition 1), nor did the patterns obtained from different speakers show any kind of recurrent structure. We have to conclude that the variance between items *and* between subjects was so huge that the reliability assumptions that we formulated as preconditions for testing Lang's hypothesis are simply not satisfied by the data we collected. Figure 3 illustrates this finding graphically.

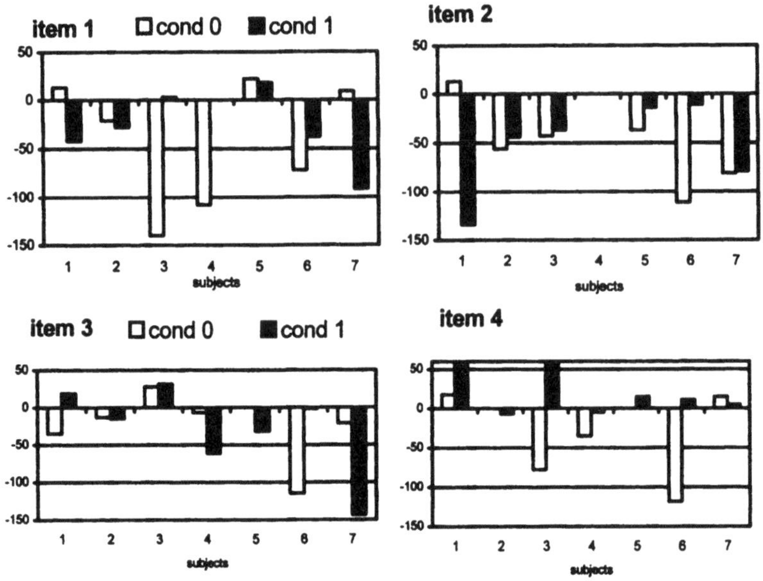

Figure 3: Differences between the F_0-values for the onset of "aber" and the offset of the 1st

4.2 Discussion

What is the reason for the variation our data showed? At the moment, we can only speculate about the answer to that question.

First of all, it may well be that the most basic reliability assumption mentioned in footnote 6 above may not be fulfilled in the present study, i.e. the assumption that there is an *intra*-personally reliable behavior underlying the prosodic realization of *any* sentence, i.e. a behavior that is consistent over time. This could e.g. be due to the fact that the concessive condition involved a good deal of emotional or evaluative attitude on part of the speakers, which of course may perhaps have varied over the course of the experiment. This explanation however would predict that the concessive conditions (cond 1) show a higher degree of variance than the contrastive ones (cond 0). This prediction however is not borne out by the data. Hence we may conclude that either there was a further factor influencing the consistency of performance, or, alternatively, that the variance exhibited by the performance in condition 1 infected the performance of condition 0.

A further source of variation may – as in most experiments – be sought in the sample of subjects that took part, and the size of that sample. That is, it is conceivable that there are samples of speakers which show a lesser degree of *inter*-personal variance, i.e. samples exhibiting a prosodic encoding that complies to the two conditions formulated above, and hence is more apt for putting

Lang's hypothesis to test. For example, it may be possible to find more subjects like subject 6 by some independent criterion, although it is far from clear what such a criterion would have to consist in. But if we recall the fact that the data for the seven subjects reported above are a subset of our sample which was selected by the criterion of *percepted consistency of encoding* (s. section 3.3), this possibility is seriously cast into doubt. A final stance on this issue cannot be taken here, since it may be that a bigger sample (with say, N=30), together with a carefully balanced item set, may yield a less blurry and more conclusive picture.

This finally brings us to two further sources of the variation between items: the evaluative quality of the concessive readings, and the discourse structure underlying the four items investigated here.

The first point concerns the "affective load" that our subjects attributed to the concessive readings, i.e. the degree of indignation that they subjectively associated to that reading. It may well be that the emotional quality of this condition makes it highly susceptible to inter-personal variation of encoding. Not having controlled for this property systematically, we cannot preclude that it may have resulted in a larger variance.

A similar observation holds for the second point, the discourse structure of the texts that our subjects were presented. All of the items contained an elaborative relation between the target sentence and an elaborandum given by the context. But the details of the elaboration relation are far from obvious. According to Lang (2001), the contrastive/adversative use of *aber* requires a symmetric elaboration, whereas the concessive use is based on an asymmetric one. This predicts in the case of item 1 that, in the contrastive condition, the two topics of the target conjunction ("My father ..., but my mother ...") elaborate the expression "your parents", establishing an elaborative relation between the discourse referent "parents" on the one hand, and "father" and "mother" on the other. In the concessive condition, it is assumed that the conjoined sentence elaborates on the fact that the speaker is annoyed ("Ich bin entsetzt"), thus establishing an elaboration relation between the speaker's annoyance and the reason he gives. However, as shown in section 2.2, the concessive reading need not correlate with an asymmetric elaboration, cf. example (15). It may therefore be argued that, in the concessive condition, speakers made use of either a symmetric or an asymmetric elaboration, which could explain the prosodic variation we found.

Note, moreover, that the items differ with respect to the type of elaborandum or "common integrator" provided by the context (cf. section 2). In item 1 and item 3 we find group antecedents ("the parents", "the children") to be elaborated by the topics of the conjuncts. Opposed to this, the elaborandum of item 2 is given explicitly: "you" and "your roommate". This means that the topics of the two conjuncts ("I" and "she") have explicit antecedents in the context that they can connect or bind to. Item 4 shows a structure deviating from the other ones: in condition 0, it features explicit antecedents for the topics ("Peter" and "Paula"), whereas in condition 1, there is no element that the topics of the conjuncts can relate to. It is clear from what was said so far that the factor "discourse structure" was not systematically controlled for in this study. However, if we assume for the sake of argument that it should exert some kind of influence on the prosodic realization, the data do not show any systematic pattern that would entitle us to conclude that discourse structure is a candidate for the source of variation, for the simple reason that the inter-individual variance prohibits drawing any conclusion pertaining to this issue.

To conclude: at first sight, the differences in prosodic realization associated to the different interpretations of *aber*-conjuncts seem a promising subject for straightforward empirical validation. But as we have argued, a study aiming at this difference faces a number of problems necessitating a more intricate design. Pointing to the relevant theoretical and methodological problems, the present study contributes to the intonational investigation of German *aber*-constructions and facilitates follow-up studies.

5 References

Adamíková, M. and D. Fehrmann (2001): Prosodische Differenzierung von Kontrast- und Korrekturkonstruktionen im Slovakischen und Polnischen. In: A. Steube and C. Umbach (eds), 81-112.

Brauße, U. (1998): Was ist Adversativität? *ABER* oder *UND*. Deutsche Sprache 26 (2), 138-159.

Givón, T. (1978): Negation in Language: Pragmatics, Function, Ontology. In P. Cole (ed): Syntax and Semantics 9: Pragmatics. Academic Press, New York, 69-112.

Grote, B., N. Lenke, and M. Stede (1997): Ma(r)king Concessions in English and German. Discourse Processes 24, 87-117.

König, E. (1991): Concessive relations as the dual of causal relations. In: D. Zaefferer (ed): Semantic universals and universal semantics. Groningen-Amsterdam studies in semantics 12, Foris, 190-209.

Lakoff, R. (1971): If's, and's and but's about conjunction. In: C. Fillmore and D. Terence Langendoen (eds): Studies in linguistic semantics. de Gruyter, New York, 114-141.

Lang, E. (1984): The semantics of coordination. SLCS 9, Amsterdam, Benjamins.

Lang, E. (2001): Kontrastiv vs. implikativ: Interpretationseffekte intonatorischer Distinktionen bei Koordination. In: A. Steube and C. Umbach (eds), 113-138.

Lang, E. (2002): Kontrastiv vs. implikativ II: Interpretationseffekte einer intonatorischen Distinktion bei elliptischen Sprichwörtern. In: A. Steube (ed), 187-212.

Lang, E. and C. Umbach (2002): Kontrast in der Grammatik: spezifische Realisierungen und übergreifender Konnex. In: A. Steube (ed), 145-186.

Mehlhorn, G. (2001): Produktion und Perzeption von Hutkonturen im Deutschen. In: A. Steube and C. Umbach (eds), 31-57.

Sæbø, K. J. (2002): Presupposition and Contrast: German aber as a Topic Particle. Paper presented at the Sinn & Bedeutung 2002, Konstanz.

Sanders, T., W. Spooren, and L. Noordman (1992): Toward a Taxonomy of Coherence Relations. Discourse Processes 15, 1-35.

Steube, A. (2001a): Correction by Contrastive Focus. Theoretical Linguistics 27 (2/3), 215-249.

Steube, A. (2001b): Grammatik und Pragmatik von Hutkonturen. In: A. Steube and C. Umbach (eds), 7-29.

Steube, A. (ed) (2002): Sprachtheoretische Grundlagen der Kognitionswissenschaft: Sprachliches und nichtsprachliches Wissen. Linguistische Arbeitsberichte 79, Leipzig.

Steube, A. and C. Umbach (eds) (2001): Kontrast - lexikalisch, semantisch, intonatorisch. Linguistische Arbeitsberichte 77, Leipzig.

Umbach, C. (2001): Contrast and Contrastive Topic. In: I. Kruijff-Korbayova and M. Steedman (eds): Proceedings of the ESSLLI 2001 Workshop on Information Structure, Discourse Structure and Discourse Semantics. 2-13. The University of Helsinki.

Umbach, C. (to appear): Contrast and Information: A focus-based analysis of but. To appear in: Linguistics.

Winter, Y. and M. Rimon (1994): Contrast and Implication in Natural Language. Journal of Semantics 11, 365-406.

Dorothee Fehrmann (Leipzig)

Prosody in Contrast
Prosodic Distinction of Contrast and Correction Readings of Polish Adversative Coordinate Structures

1 Introduction

This paper[1] is concerned with adversative coordinate structures in Polish that contain a negative marker in the first conjunct, as the one in example (1):[2]

(1)	Piotr	**nie**	ma samochodu,	**ale**	(ma)	motocykl.
	$\text{Peter}_{\text{nom}}$	**S-Neg**	has car_{gen}	$\textbf{Conj}_{\text{adv}}$	(has)	$\text{motorbike}_{\text{acc}}$

Depending on the embedding context, such a coordinate structure can have two interpretations, illustrated in (1a) and (1b) below. The different readings become obvious in the English and German translations as well as in the Polish paraphrases given below.

---

[1] This paper is a revised version of a working paper published in Linguistische Arbeitsberichte 77 (Adamíková and Fehrmann 2001) summarising the progress of our work in the Research group "Linguistic Foundations of Cognitive Science – Linguistic and Extra-linguistic Knowledge", project "Contrast and Correction" (Lang, Zybatow, Adamíková, Fehrmann), sponsored by the DFG. In that paper we analysed Polish and Slovak examples. The results of our analyses were also included in another research report published in inguistische Arbeitsberichte 79 (Alter 2002). I would like to thank my colleagues from the Slavic Department of the University of Leipzig and from the Research Group for helpful discussions. Special thanks to Uwe Junghanns for his careful proofreading of an earlier version of this paper.

[2] Besides the notational conventions customary in the literature, the following abbreviations are used in the glosses throughout the paper:

S-Neg	–	sentential negation
C-Neg	–	constituent negation
Conj_{adv}	–	adversative conjunction
$\text{Conj}_{\text{corr}}$	–	corrective conjunction
$\text{Conj}_{\text{contr}}$	–	contrastive conjunction

(1a)	(1b)
A: How are you getting to the station?	A: Peter's got a new Honda.
B: Peter is taking me there.	B: Really? Peter's got a new car?
A: Really? But he hasn't got a car!	A: Listen, dad!
B: *Piotr* ***nie*** *ma samochodu,* ***ale*** *motocykl.*	*Piotr* ***nie*** *ma samochodu,* ***ale*** *motocykl.*
(E) Peter hasn't got a car, but he's got a motorbike.	(E) Peter hasn't got a car, but a motorbike.
(Ger) Peter hat kein Auto, *aber* ein Motorrad.	(Ger) Peter hat kein Auto, *sondern* ein Motorrad.
CONTR(AST)	**CORR(ECTION)**
Paraphrases:	
(1a') specific connector:	(1b') specific conjunction[3]:
Piotr nie ma samochodu, ma *jednak* motocykl.	Piotr nie ma samochodu, *tylko* motocykl.
Peter S-Neg has car$_{gen}$ has *Conj$_{contr}$* motorbike$_{acc}$	Peter S-Neg has car$_{gen}$ *Conj$_{corr}$* motorbike$_{acc}$
(1a'') specific adverbials/particles:	(1b'') constituent negation:
Piotr *wprawdzie* nie ma samochodu, ale ma motocykl.	Piotr ma *nie* samochód, ale motocykl.
Peter *though* S-Neg has car$_{gen}$ Conj$_{adv}$ has motorbike$_{acc}$	Peter has *C-Neg* car$_{acc}$ Conj$_{adv}$ motorbike$_{acc}$
Piotr nie ma samochodu, ale *za to* ma motocykl.	
Peter S-Neg has car$_{gen}$ Conj$_{adv}$ *instead* has motorbike$_{acc}$	
(1a''') non-reduced second conjunct:	(1b''') asyndetic connection:
Piotr nie ma samochodu, ale *ma* motocykl.	Piotr nie ma samochodu. Ma motocykl.
Peter S-Neg has car$_{gen}$ Conj$_{adv}$ *has* motorbike$_{acc}$	Peter S-Neg has car$_{gen}$. pro$_{1.sg\text{-}nom}$ has motorbike$_{acc}$

Figure 1: Interpretations of Polish adversative coordinate structures with a negative marker in the first conjunct

Following Lang (1977, 1984) I call the two types of adversative constructions "contrast" (CONTR) and "correction" (CORR), respectively.

In the CONTR-reading two independent propositions expressed in the conjuncts C_1 and C_2 are opposed to each other, e.g. "Peter's not-having a car" and "Peter's having a motorbike". The proposition in C_2 denies directly or implicitly a possible conclusion that could be drawn from C_1, namely that Peter cannot give person B a lift to the station ("denial of expectation"-*but* – Lakoff 1971). In other words, C_1 gives an argument against the question under discussion ("Quaestio" – Brauße 1998), C_2 gives an argument in favour of this question. The establishing of the relation of CONTR between the two of them is induced by the special meaning of the adversative conjunction that operates on the propositions denoted by the conjuncts.

In the CORR-reading on the other hand, the operation taking place is a substitution of one (false or incorrect) proposition (the non-negated counterpart of C_1 "Peter's got a car") by another, namely C_2 ("Peter's got a motorbike"), replacing one element of C_1 – the *corrigendum* ("car") – by an alternative

[3] The Polish colloquial CORR-conjunction *tylko* is etymologically linked to the homonymous degree particle *tylko* – *only*.

entity given in C_2 – the *corrigens*[4] ("motorbike"), so that the proposition becomes true.[5]

While the semantic concept of the relation of CORR is restricted to a well defined group of constructions, the relation of CONTR subsumes a wide range of sub-relations, such as "adversative", "concessive", "compensatory" etc. I am not going to outline those relations here, but note that the interpretation of the CONTR-examples used in this paper is mainly adversative.

Following Lang (1984), different types of negation are involved. Whereas in the CONTR-reading the negation, which may be present in C_1 (but is not obligatory for this type of interpretation), is part of the meaning of C_1, expressing a normal sentential negation, the obligatory overt negation in C_1 in the case of CORR is a so-called *focusing negation* or *substitution negation* ("*replazive Negation*" – cf. Jacobs 1982, 1991), which is associated with a contrastively focused constituent in its scope (narrow focus), implying thereby the existence of an alternative entity to replace this constituent so that the proposition becomes true.

The interpretation of the adversative constructions under investigation (and coordinate structures in general, as shown among others by Lang – cf. Lang 1991, Lang 2000 in response to Sweetser 1990) is not only a matter of pragmatics but is determined by their grammatical structure, including information provided by syntax, lexicon, and intonation.

With respect to the two types of adversative constructions in question, there are languages that use distinct connectors for CONTR and CORR (named A/S-type languages after the initials of German *aber* and *sondern*) on the one hand, and, on the other hand, languages which use one and the same connector for both, distinguishing the two readings by means of syntactic structure – non-reduction vs. reduction or asyndetic adding of the second conjunct (A-type languages). This can be seen in the English (A-type) and German (A/S-type) sentences translating example (1).

But there are also languages which cannot be assigned to either of the two types. Polish[6] – along with other West Slavonic languages – is one such language. Though potentially making use of both lexical as well as syntactic means for a distinction, as can be seen in (1a'), (1a''), (1a'''), (1b'), (1b''), and (1b''') in figure 1, these languages prefer ambiguous constructions like (1) which is repeated here:

---

[4] The terms *corrigens* and *corrigendum*, used here as in Lang 1984, can alternatively denote the entire propositions, e.g. in Steube 2002.

[5] In corrections, the speaker can protest against the meaning of a whole sentence or parts of it or against the correctness, adequateness, grammatical or phonological form etc. of such parts down to single endings or sounds (metalinguistic negation – cf. Horn 1985). Our examples are restricted to truth-functional negation.

[6] Gehrmann (1992b:139) claims that Polish could be assigned to what Lang calls the A-type, but only in principle.

(1) Piotr **nie** ma samochodu, **ale** (ma) motocykl.
Peter$_{nom}$ **S-Neg** has car$_{gen}$ **Conj$_{adv}$** (has) motorbike$_{acc}$
(a) Peter hasn't got a car, but he's got a motorbike. (CONTR)
(b) Peter hasn't got a car, but a motorbike. (CORR)

These constructions are characterised as follows:

1. They are connected by the conjunction *ale* which is underspecified as for CONTR or CORR.
2. The conjunct C_1 contains an overt sentential negation (S-Neg)[7].
3. In C_2 all identical elements are elliptically deleted[8].

I assume the syntactic structure as shown in figure 2 for Polish adversative constructions with both CONTR as well as CORR readings.[9]

As for our concerns, these constructions are syntactically and lexically underspecified. Therefore I investigated the question whether prosody – as the remaining one among the interacting grammatical modules determining conceptual interpretation – makes a clear distinction between the two types of adversative constructions in these languages – a hypothesis first proposed by Lang and Adamíková (cf. Adamíková 1996).

[7] Along with Witkoś (1996, 1999) and Błaszczak (2001), I assume that Polish S-Neg, realised by the proclitic element *nie*, heads its own projection NegP located in the syntactic structure above VP and cliticises on to the finite verb which therefore moves to Neg°. Polish C-Neg (constituent negation), though formally identical to S-Neg *nie*, is a non-clitic phrasal category that adjoins to the constituent which is negated. S-Neg licenses negative concord and genitive of negation, C-Neg does not.

[8] In Polish, non-reduction of C_2 is accepted in CORR only up to a certain degree.

[9] With Munn (1987) and Wilder (1997), I assume that the conjunction of a coordinate structure is a head, called $\&_{adv}°$ here. Following Munn (1992) and Schwabe (2000), $\&_{adv}°$ heads the second conjunct forming an &P that adjoins to the first conjunct. I follow Wilder (1997) in assuming that only extended maximal projections in the sense of Grimshaw (1991) can be coordinated. Therefore the second conjunct is always a full CP with elliptical deletions. For a discussion of the format of coordination in Polish adversative constructions see Fehrmann (to appear).

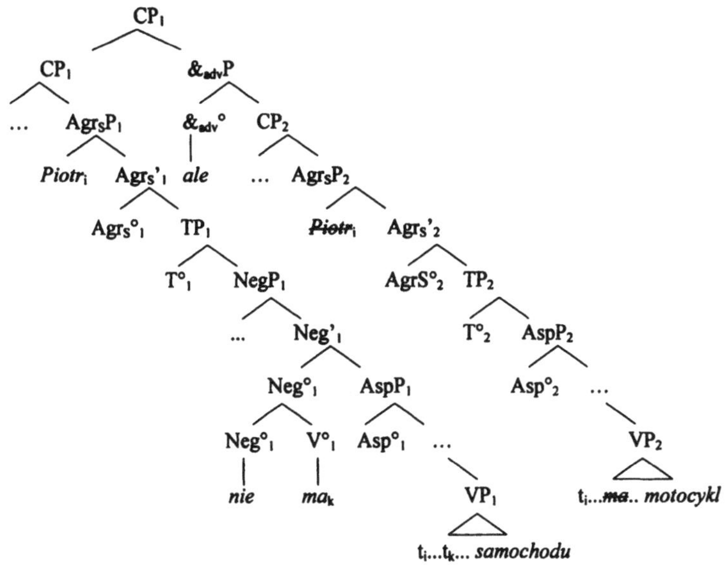

Figure 2: Syntactic Structure for example (1)

Prosody is influenced, among other factors, especially by information structure (IS). Thus, in connection with prosodic realisations of CONTR and CORR, I was looking for differences in

1. the domains of IS and
2. the structuring of the resulting units (into focus and background, on the one hand, and, on the other, into topic and comment).[10]

What I expected was:

(H-1) The relative autonomy of the propositions expressed in the two conjuncts of a CONTR-construction should result in a division of the whole construction into two informational and intonational units, whereas a CORR-construction should form one informational and intonational unit because of the structural and factual interdependency of its conjuncts and the substitutional character of the negation in C_1, sig-

[10] I will be mainly concerned with focus-background structure here. Differences in topic-comment structure lead to a clear distinction between CONTR and CORR, the former allowing the contrasted constituent (XP_1) affected by the negation to occupy a contrastive topic position, which seems impossible or at least slightly deviant in syndetic CORR-constructions (cf. Jacobs 1996:26 for German and Fehrmann 2001 for Polish). I am not going to analyse such constructions here, since they are clearly distinguished syntactically by different word order.

nalling the incompleteness of the sentence and implying a continuation (C_2).

(H-2) According to the concept of CORR and the definition of the involved negation as "replacive" and focusing, CORR-constructions should be associated with one and only one IS, namely parallel contrastive focusing of the lexically contrasting constituents[11] XP_1 (the corrigens) and XP_2 (the corrigendum) in their conjuncts. For CONTR we should expect no obligatory IS-parallelism.

2 Information structure

2.1 Theoretical framework

I follow the theories that define IS as a pragmatically induced structuring of the elements of an utterance (Reis and Rosengren, Steube, Zybatow and Junghanns etc.), which is realised at the sentence level by grammatical means like word order (syntax), stress (phonology), and pronominalizations, articles etc. (lexicon). The IS of a sentence reflects how the sentence and its elements fit into the context. There are at least two divisions of IS – focus-background structure (FBS) and topic-comment structure (TCS). In FBS we have to distinguish between new information or neutral focus (Fn) and contrastive focus (Fc). The focus part of the sentence does not always have to be absolutely new information. It is better characterised as the most relevant or important information in the given context.

For Polish I adopt most of the assumptions of Junghanns and Zybatow (1997) originally made for Russian. They match with observations on Polish word order e.g. in Szwedek (1981), Grzegorek (1984) and Duszak (1987). Following Junghanns (2002), [+F] in Slavic is a non-checking syntactic feature that is assigned to a syntactic constituent thus marking the focus domain. The element inside the focus domain that realises the focus accent is called the focus exponent. It is assigned a phonological [+P]-feature which corresponds to a pitch accent. The preferred position for Fn in Polish is the right periphery of the sentence, which may require IS-induced leftward movement of non-focused constituents. The Fn-accent is typically realised as a falling tone embedded in the continuous decline of the fundamental frequency (F0) and coinciding with the final fall of F0 at the end of the sentence. Fc can occur in any position in the sentence and is marked by a contrastive pitch accent. I do not

[11] I use the terms XP_1 and XP_2 for the contrasting constituents abstracting from their individual categorial status. This is, of course, a simplification. The elements in question can be of X°-category, too. In the examples analysed in this paper, however, the contrasting constituents are all phrasal.

analyse [+F] as an operator, nor do I assume a functional category for focus where the [+F]-feature would have to be checked in the course of the syntactic derivation. Nevertheless, focus can be associated with a focus sensitive operator. My assumptions on Polish IS are laid out in more detail in Fehrmann (1997).

Most models of IS consider simple sentences only. Not much work has been done so far on IS and its prosodic realisation in complex sentences, except the numerous studies on "hat contours" showing up in coordination (cf. e.g. Mehlhorn and Zybatow 2000), Féry and Hartmann (2001) who investigate German Gapping and Right Node Raising, and Hetland (1993). It still remains a question what the syntactic unit is that undergoes IS in the case of a complex sentence – each sentence separately or the complex sentence as a whole.

2.2 Some notes on the information structure of adversative coordinate structures

Recall that the information structure of a sentence depends on the context or situation in which it is uttered as well as on the speaker's intentions. In the case of adversative constructions the contextual relations determining their IS are multi-dimensional and hold on different levels. In addition to the preceding and the following utterances, the conjuncts themselves function as context for each other, and inferences deriving from them may contribute to the context as well.

Thus, in a CONTR-construction that is structured in a non-parallel fashion, as in example (2), C_2 is usually contrasted to a possible conclusion from C_1 (here, that John's parents wouldn't want him to go to Grammar School because of his bad marks) which is directly denied by C_2:

(2) John's got bad marks, but his parents, nevertheless, want him to go to Grammar School.

In a parallel structure like (3), C_2 usually implicitly denies a possible conclusion from C_1 by giving an argument against it. From *John's being intelligent* expressed in C_1 one would possibly draw the conclusion, that he will make it at Grammar School, but from C_2 (*He is lazy*) one would not. Here, the constituents denoting the arguments pro and con given in C_1 and C_2 are contrasted.

(3) A: What do you think: Will John make it at Grammar School?
B: I'm afraid he won't. He is **intelligent**, but he is **lazy**.

The same may hold for a parallel structure with a negation in C_1, like the ones we are analysing in Polish. Here, the negated predicate functions as the pro-argument:

(4) A: What do you think: Will John make it at Grammar School?
B: I'm afraid he won't. He **isn't dumb**, but he **is lazy**.

In such a construction, the speaker's intention can also be to reject a previously suggested argument by negating it in C_1 and giving an alternative pro-argument in C_2 that does hold. Here, the two pro-arguments given by the non-negated counterpart of C_1 (*He is **dumb***) on the one hand, and C_2 (*He is **lazy***) on the other, are contrasted:

(5) A: I can't figure out why John doesn't make it at Grammar School. Is he really too dumb?
B: He isn't **dumb**, but he is **lazy**.

This is very close to the interpretation of a construction where the syntactic constituent denoting the pro-argument in C_1 is promoted to the position of a contrastive topic (CT). The comment, containing a sentential negation, indicates that this argument does not hold. Such constructions are possible in Polish, as well as in other Slavic languages or in German. There is a double contrast expressed by the predicates *dumb* and *lazy* functioning as one "contrasting pair" and negation and affirmation as the other pair.

(6) A: I can't figure out why John doesn't make it at Grammar School. Is he really too dumb?

B: (a)	**[Głupi]$_{CT}$**	to	on	**nie**	**jest,**	ale	(jest)	**leniwy.**
	dumb$_{nom}$	Prt	he$_{nom}$	**S-Neg**	**is**	Conj$_{adv}$	(is)	**lazy$_{nom}$**
(b)	**[Głupi]$_{CT}$**	to	on	**nie**	**jest,**	ale	**[leniwy]$_{CT}$**	**tak.**
	dumb$_{nom}$	Prt	he$_{nom}$	**S-Neg**	**is**	Conj$_{adv}$	**lazy$_{nom}$**	**yes**

This is similar to parallel structures with a double lexical contrast:

(7) **John** is **sad**, but **his wife** is **quite happy**.

In a CORR-construction, the substituted and the replacing constituent (*corrigendum* and *corrigens*) are contrasted:

(8) A: John is too dumb to go to Grammar School. Just have a look at his last report!
B: Oh, you're not quite right. John isn't **dumb**, but **lazy**.
That's why he's got such bad marks on his last report.

When functioning in an argumentation, the CORR-construction as a whole figures as an argument, with C_1 denying a false assumption that was explicitly expressed or implied in a previous utterance and used as an argument for some possible conclusion and C_2 giving the argument against this conclusion:

(9) A: Why aren't you satisfied with your exam results? Peter said you got a grade B.
B: Oh, no. I didn't get a B, but a D.

In contrast to the CONTR-construction in (5) where one pro-argument is substituted by another, in the CORR example (9) an argument for some conclusion is substituted by an argument against it (or vice versa).

These are only some of a great variety of possible relations between the conjuncts of an adversative construction. For more see Lang (1984, 1988, 1991, 2000).

Besides the speaker's intention of contrasting or correcting, the IS of an adversative structure is influenced by the contextual boundness/non-boundness of its elements (i.e. their relation to previously established discourse referents).

The information given in the conjuncts of the coordinate structure can be all new. In example (10) the predicates of the conjuncts denote new information:

(10) A: Will John make it at Grammar School?
B: I'm afraid, he won't. He is intelligent, but he is lazy.

The speaker can take up a previously uttered (or implied) argument in C_1 of the coordinate structure corresponding to C_1 (including the negation) as in (11) or to the non-negated counterpart of C_1 as in (12):

(11) A: I can't figure out why John doesn't make it at Grammar School.
At least <u>he isn't dumb</u>.
B: <u>He isn't dumb</u>, but he is lazy.

(12) A: I can't figure out why John doesn't make it at Grammar School.
Do you think he is <u>dumb</u>?
B: He isn't <u>dumb</u>, but he is lazy.

Note also that in all examples the person John is contextually bound and therefore functioning as the topic of the sentence.

3 Experimental design

In order to substantiate the hypothesis about the prosodic determination of the interpretation of adversative coordinate structures in West Slavonic languages, a speech production experiment was carried out.[12] The aim of the experiment was to compare the prosodic realisations of lexically and syntactically identical adversative constructions having both the CONTR and the CORR reading. To get minimal pairs, mini-dialogues were made up like the ones in (1a) and (1b) above, in which the target sentences were embedded in contexts evoking the different readings.

The target sentences were constructed taking into consideration the conditions for coordination and contrast in general, e.g. parallelism of the conjuncts as well as parallelism of the embedding structure (coordination of "likes" only) – expressed e.g. in Ross's (1967) Coordinate Structure Constraint and its modification by Williams (1978), compatibility, distinctness, satisfying a Common Integrator – Lang (1977, 1984, 1991), Lang and Umbach (2002) and the special conditions for CORR (Lang 1988), which are structurally far more restricted than CONTR.

Consequently, the target sentences show the following structural characteristics:

- coordination by means of a conjunction – the underspecified adversative conjunction *ale*,
- an overt negation marker in C_1 which is a sentential negation (S-Neg),
- structural parallelism of the conjuncts (with respect to constituent structure and word order),
- reduction of identical elements in C_2,
- sentence final position of the lexically contrasting constituents XP_1 and XP_2 in their conjuncts – on the one hand, to make sure that XP_1 is in the scope of negation (i.e. c-commanded by Neg°), on the other hand, because this is the preferred focus position for Fn and a possible position for Fc in Polish.

The lexically contrasting constituents XP_1 and XP_2 varied as to their syntactic category and function. I tested NP/DP as direct object and in predicative position, AP in attributive and predicative position, PP as prepositional object and adverbial adjunct, finite VP and finite V°.

I tried to vary the dialogues with respect to the anchoring of the elements of the target sentence in discourse, so that the information contained in C_1 was sometimes all new, sometimes all familiar or partly familiar to the participants of the communication – either via explicit mentioning or via inference. For each minimal pair I tried to keep this condition constant. But this was not al-

[12] The experiment was carried out for Slovak and Polish by M. Adamíková and myself and was based on the first experiment investigating the issue under discussion by Adamíková (1996). In the following I will report the Polish data only. For Slovak see Adamíková (2000a, 2000b) and Adamíková and Fehrmann (2001).

ways possible due to the two-fold function of the embedding dialogues: in the first place they had to evoke the intended CONTR- or CORR-reading of the target sentence. But they also formed the context for the information structuring of the target sentence. In addition, there is always a chance of interpreting the context in a different way than the intended one.

All in all I tested 15 Polish adversative constructions with both readings. The 30 dialogues were recorded with 9 native speakers (all female, in their early twenties). The test persons were presented with the transcribed dialogues (each on an extra sheet) in a pseudo-randomised order and instructed to first acquaint themselves with the respective text before reading it aloud in order to produce as natural speech as possible. The dialogues were recorded with a DAT recorder and then digitalised. The target sentences were cut out using the COOL programme and analysed in PitchWorks.

According to the hypothesis, I expected the conjuncts of a CONTR-construction to be prosodically realised as two separate intonation phrases (IPh) with phonological IPh-boundary markers[13] in between, which should be absent in the case of CORR. As to accent realisation, in CORR there should always be contrastive pitch accents on XP_1 and XP_2, whereas in CONTR, I expected varying accent structures corresponding to various information structures.

I analysed the following phonological parameters relevant for (i) phrasing and (ii) the realisation (placement and type) of sentence accent(s)[14] in Polish:

(i) phrasing:
1. F0-parameter:
1.1. F0 at the end of C_1 and the beginning of C_2 (boundary tones)
1.2. F0-resetting
2. durational parameter:
2.1. pause insertion
2.2. prefinal lengthening
(ii) accent realisation:
1. F0-parameter (pitch accents):
1.1. position of pitch accents
1.2. type of F0-change
2. duration of accented syllables

[13] I regard as IPh-boundary markers – following Alter and Mleinek and Richter (2001:318) – boundary tones, prefinal lengthening, pause insertion and F0-resetting. The role of properties of segmental phonology such as blocking of voice and articulatory place assimilation or stop assimilation for marking prosodical domains hasn't been taken into consideration for our data.

[14] It is generally assumed that Polish as an intonational language marks accents mainly by variation of the fundamental frequency F0 (significant rise/fall of F0) - pitch accents - accompanied by durational properties, which are in inverse proportion to intensity (cf. Skorek 1997).

Intensity should play a role for accent realisation, too, but hasn't been tested yet.

For the phonological description of intonation patterns I used a simplified application of Pierrehumbert's (1980) model of tonal sequencing.[15] Tonal movements (i.e. changes of the fundamental frequency of the speech signal) are described in terms of two different tones – H (high) and L (low) and combinations thereof. L% and H% mark IPh-boundary tones.

4 Results

At first glance, prosody does not seem to play the crucial role I expected in distinguishing CONTR and CORR.

4.1 Only in less than 50 % of my examples (6 out of 15) did the majority of the speakers produce a prosodic differentiation between the minimal pairs.

4.2 As for these six examples, only in two of them could I detect a systematic differentiation, i.e. for a given example, the majority of the speakers used the same or similar means of differentiation.

In the remaining cases, the speakers used different, sometimes even contrary ways to differentiate between the CONTR and CORR readings. Consider the following example:

CONTR (po-12)		CORR (po-12')	
A:	How do you know that Marek has taken the documents, since he's gone straight from home to the conference?	A:	Marek has come back from his holiday. I've just talked to him. He is excited.
		B:	And how does he look? Has he got a tan?
B:	*He hasn't been at the office, but he's phoned.* He said he'd taken them.	A:	I don't know. *He hasn't been at the office, he's phoned.* I'll meet him only in the afternoon.

Po:	*Nie*	*było*	*go*	*w*	*biurze,*	*ale*		*zadzwonił.*
	S-Neg	$was_{3.sg\text{-}n}$	him_{gen}	in	office	$Conj_{adv}$	$pro_{3.sg\text{-}nom}$	called

As can be seen in the exemplary intonation contours given in figure 3 below, some speakers (e.g. Ro) produce CONTR with a highly contrastive accent (LH*L) on XP_1 (*w BIUrze*) which is much more prominent than the rise-fall on the prosodic word formed by the negation marker and the finite verb $[_{Neg^\circ}$ Neg° V°] (*nie BYło*), whereas in CORR the accent on XP_1 (L*H) is less prominent, so that the LH*L on $[_{Neg^\circ}$ Neg° V°] at least equals it. In the case of CONTR,

[15] Cf. Féry (1993) or GToBI as described in Benzmüller and Grice (1997).

speaker Ro completes C_1 with an L-tone and begins C_2 on the same low level with no intonational break in between. CORR is realised by speaker Ro with a rising ("continuative") intonation at the conjunct boundary which starts on the accented syllable of XP_1 (L*H on *BIUrze*) and continues on the last syllable of C_1 and the first syllables of C_2.

Other speakers (e.g. Bu) do it exactly the other way round. Some subjects do not differentiate at all, producing in both readings either a highly contrastive LH*L on XP_1 as the most prominent accent of C_1 and an L-tone at the end of C_1 (e.g. Wa) or two equally prominent accents on $[_{Neg°}$ Neg° V°] and XP_1 and a rising tone on the last syllable of C_1 that goes up to a very high level from which C_2 continues in a subsequent decline (e.g. Ko).

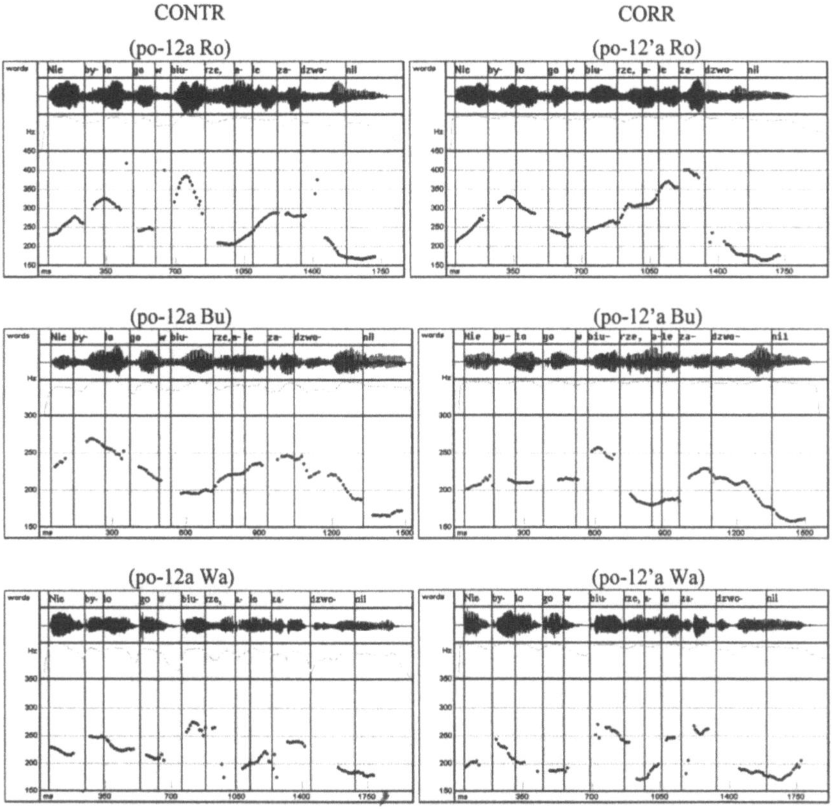

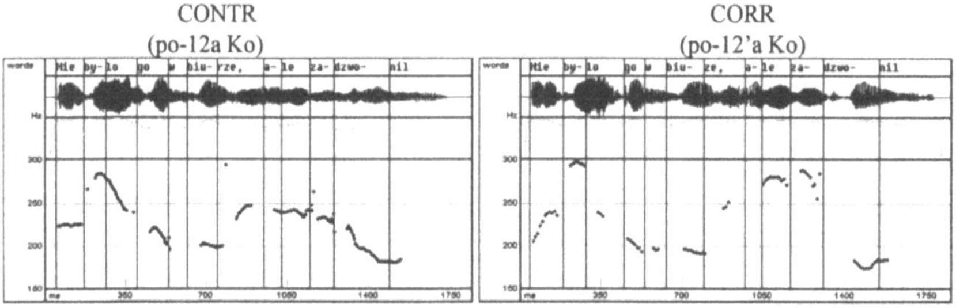

Figure 3: Different strategies for encoding CONTR and CORR for example (po-12/12') across speakers

This means that there was a lot of variation across the speakers for a given example. One might suspect that this is due to individual preferences. But then, one would expect that one and the same speaker consistently uses the same strategies across the examples. However, a comparison of the prosodic patterns produced by the respective speakers across the examples reveals that a given speaker did not encode the difference between CONTR and CORR in a consistent way.

4.3 A comparison of the examples where at least a certain number of speakers produced a relatively systematic distinction shows that the ways of differentiation may diverge or even be contrary between the examples. Compare the differentiation between (po-07) and (po-07') with the differentiation between (po-14) and (po-14') in figure 4:

(po-07/07')	CONTR (po-07)	CORR (po-07')
most prominent pitch accent(s) in C_1	XP_1: L* or L*H	$[_{\text{Neg}^\circ}$ Neg° V°] : LH*L
Phrasing	no IPh-boundary markers	no IPh-boundary markers

(po-14/14')	CONTR (po-14)	CORR (po-14')
most prominent pitch accent(s) in C_1	$[_{\text{Neg}^\circ}$ Neg° V°]: LH*L	1. $[_{\text{Neg}^\circ}$ Neg° V°]: H* or LH*L 2. XP_1: LH* or L
Phrasing	IPh-boundary between C_1 and C_2: L%, pause insertion, resetting	no IPh-boundary markers

Figure 4: Means of differentiation used by the majority of speakers for a given example

For the intonation contours cf. figures 5, 6 and 11, 12 in 4.4.

4.4 Prosody and information structure

4.4.1 It turns out that the various prosodic realisations are correlated to certain information structures of the target sentences. IS, and especially FBS, determines the placement and type of sentence accent(s) and has influence on phrasing, too.

Thus, in the CORR-example (po-07'), given as (1b) in the introduction and repeated below, with the corrected proposition „Peter's got a car" mentioned in the immediately preceding context, the obvious reaction of the speakers was to reject this proposition by means of focusing the negated *verum*-component (verum focus – Fv)[16] in C_1 (backward related Fc), the one and only prominent pitch accent in C_1 resulting as contrastive LH*L on the prosodic word formed by the negation marker *nie* and the finite verb $[_{Neg^\circ}$ Neg° V°] (*NIE ma*)[17] and the rest of C_1 being pronounced with the "flat" intonation typical for sentences with Fc[18]. The proposition is then corrected in C_2, with the *corrigens*-constituent being contrastively focused (backward related Fc) resulting in an LH*L-accent on *moTOcykl.*[19] The conjuncts have a non-parallel information structure reflected in the intonation contour. Compare intonation contour (po-07'b Ro) in figure 6 below.[20]

In the corresponding CONTR-sentence (po-07) on the other hand, the negated proposition expressed in C_1 had been mentioned before, so the IS of the adversative construction would be most probably determined by the intention of the speaker to contrast the two arguments of the discourse, resulting in parallel focusing of the constituents that bear the minimal lexical contrast – *samoCHOdu* in C_1 (forward related Fc) and *moTOcykl* in C_2 (backward related

[16] The so called "verum focus" (Fv) was first described by Höhle (1992) for German. It is a special kind of Fc – with the truth or falsity of the sentence being in focus. Following a suggestion by Szucsich (2002:203), I assume that it is located in Neg°. For a unified functional structure of negated and non-negated sentences, a Pol-category has been proposed (polarity phrase – Drubig 1994, position phrase – Haftka 1994) which is specified for the [+/-neg]-feature. For expository purposes, I will, in this article, use the label Neg° for the [+neg]-specified Pol°.

[17] Whether the focus accent of a Fv is realised on the negative marker *nie* or on the verb depends on the number of syllables of the complex formed by the verb and the negative marker, which counts as a prosodical word. In Polish word stress is on the penultimate syllable. Thus, in case of a single-syllable verb, the accent will be realised on *nie*, (e.g. *NIE ma* in po-07'b Ro in figure 6). The accent will be realised on the verb in case the verb consists of more than one syllable (e.g. *nie dosTAłem* in po-05g Ro in figure 9). Nevertheless, what is focused is always the negative *verum* component.

[18] Cf. Zybatow and Mehlhorn (2000) and Mehlhorn (2001) for Russian.

[19] In the intonation contour for CORR (po-07'b Ro) shown below, the contrastive accents on $[_{Neg^\circ}$ Neg° V°] in C_1 and on the corrigens in C_2 are emphatically strengthened by speaker Ro, resulting in a very strong rise of the fundamental frequency up to 600 Hz.

[20] I provide only examplary intonation contours produced by individual speakers, because the calculation of average values from a certain number of speakers did not seem appropriate due to excessive variety in several parameters.

Fc). In the intonation contour shown in figure 5 below (po-07b Ro), the focus accents are both realised as HL* – the HL* tone on *samoCHOdu* in C_1 being followed by a beginning rise of the F0 on the final syllable continued in C_2 ("continuative" intonation signalling incompleteness), the HL* tone on *moTO-cykl* in C_2 coinciding with the final fall of the F0 completed on the final syllable.

The C_1-conjunct was pronounced by nearly all speakers with reduced stress and a relatively flat intonation contour because it repeats an utterance from the immediately preceding context. (The target sentences in the dialogues are typed in italics, the relevant context sentences are underlined. In the labelled targets given under the intonation contours, capitals indicate the accented syllables.)

CONTR (po-07)	CORR (po-07')
A: How are you getting to the station?	A: Peter's got a new Honda.
B: Peter is taking me there.	B: Really? Peter's got a new car?
A: Really? But he hasn't got a car!	A: Listen, dad!
B: *Peter hasn't got a car, but he's got a motorbike.*	*Peter hasn't got a car, but a motorbike.*

Po:	*Piotr*	*nie*	*ma*	*samochodu,*	*ale*	*motocykl.*
	$Peter_{nom}$	S-Neg	has	car_{gen},	$Conj_{adv}$	$motorbike_{acc}$

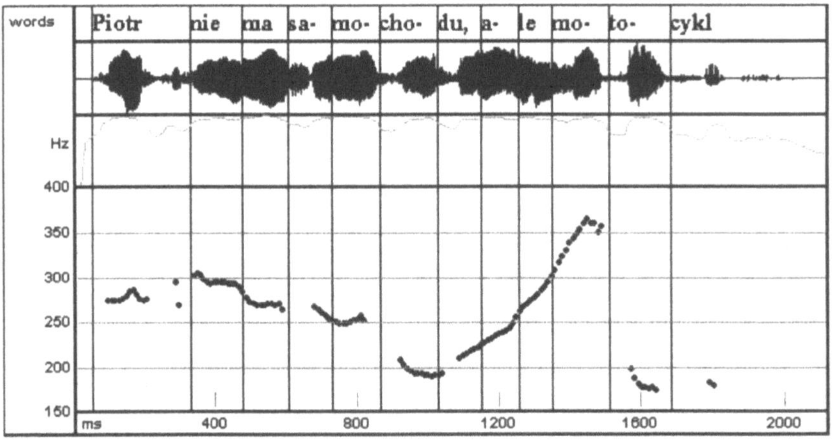

HL* HL*

Piotr nie ma [samoCHOdu]$_F$, ale [moTOcykl]$_F$.

Figure 5: (po-07b Ro) CONTR

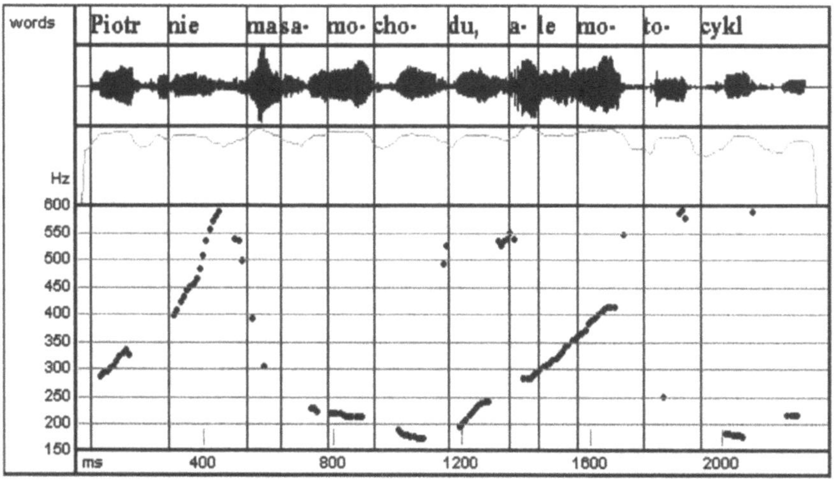

LH*L LH*L

Piotr $[_{Neg°}$NIE ma$]_{Fv}$ samochodu , ale [moTOcykl$]_{F}$.

Figure 6: (po-07'b Ro) CORR

In the minimal pair (po-04/04') with the same information structural difference the Fc-accents on XP_1 and XP_2 in CONTR (po-04) are alternatively realised by speaker Wr as LH*L in both conjuncts, the accent in C_1 being pronounced with reduced stress (cf. figures 7, 8 below).

CONTR (po-04)	CORR (po-04')
A: Let's paint the swing for the children! B: But how? We should paint it yellow, but the stuff you bought isn't yellow. A: *This isn't yellow, but it's orange.* It's a warm color, too. The children will like it.	A: Let's paint the swing for the children! B: But how? We should paint it yellow. *And this isn't yellow, but orange.*

Po: *To*	*nie*	*jest*	*żółty*	*kolor,*	*ale*	*pomarańczowy.*
$Pron_{dem\text{-}nom}$	S-Neg	is	$yellow_{nom}$	$color_{nom}$	$Conj_{adv}$	$orange_{nom}$

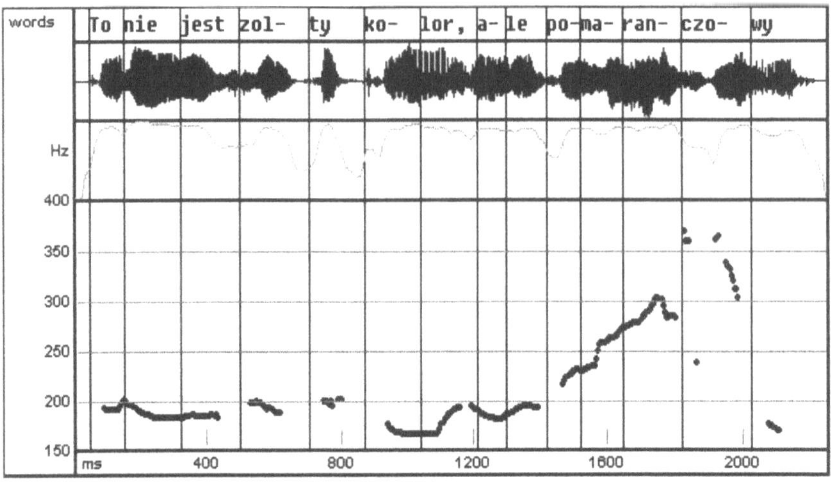

LH*L LH*L

To nie jest [ŻÓŁty kolor]$_F$, ale [pomarańCZOwy]$_F$

Figure 7: (po-04a Wr) CONTR

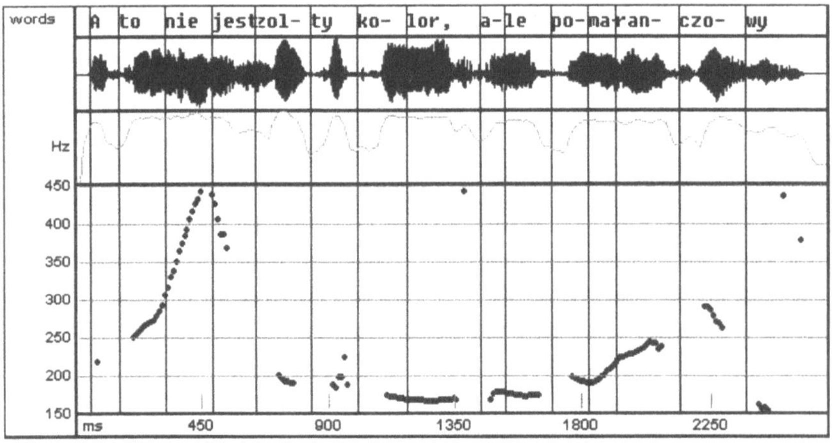

LH*L LH*L

A to [NIE jest]$_{Fv}$ żółty kolor, ale [pomarańCZOwy]$_F$

Figure 8: (po-04'a Wr) CORR

4.4.2 But neither CONTR nor CORR are bound to a specific IS each. Whereas in the minimal pairs (po-07/07') and (po-04/04') in the CORR-examples C_1 rejects a previous utterance by negated Fv, in the minimal pairs (po-05g/05'g) and (po-14/14') this is the case in the CONTR-sentences, cf. figures 9, 10, 11,12 below.

CONTR (po-05g)	CORR (po-05'g)
A: Hi Wojtek. How are you? How did the exam go? I'm dead sure <u>you've got a grade A</u>! B: *I didn't get an A, but I got a B.* I'm quite happy with it.	A: Hi Wojtek. How are you? How did the exam go? B: Don't ask. *I didn't get an A, but a B.* I would have needed the A to get an overall "excellent".
Po: *Nie* *dostałem* *piątki, ale* *czwórkę.* pro$_{1.sg\text{-}nom}$ S-Neg got fife$_{gen}$ Conj$_{adv}$ four$_{acc}$	

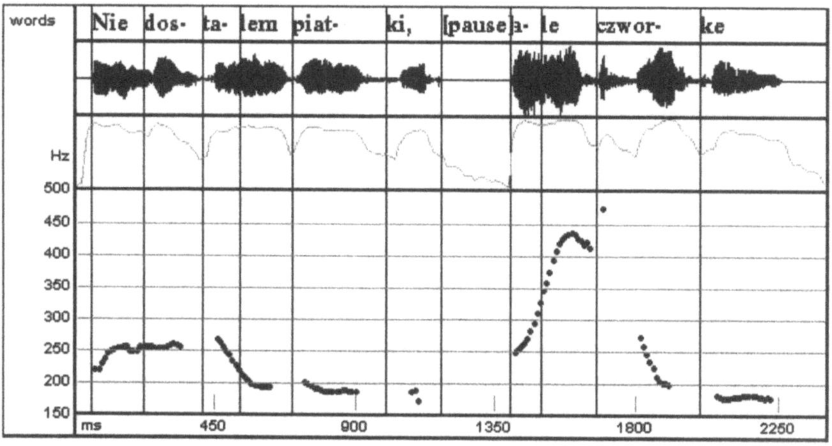

H*L L- L% HL*

[Nie dos TAłem]$_{Fv}$ piątki, ale [CZWÓRkę]$_F$

Figure 9: (po-05g Ro) CONTR

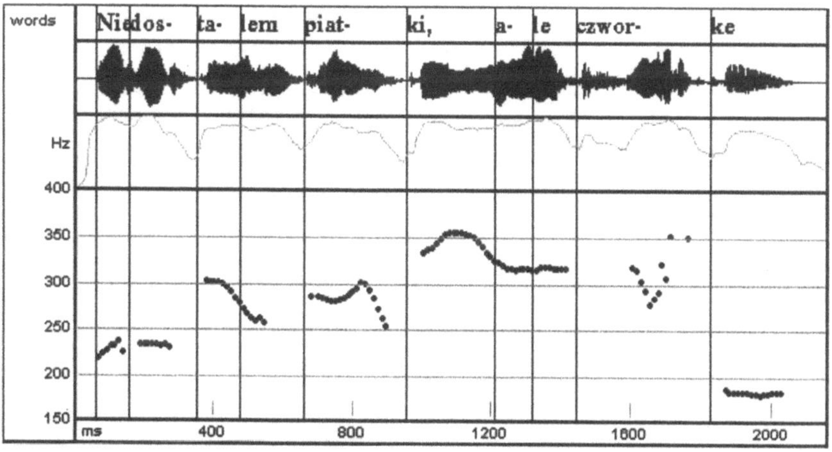

LH*L LH* LH*L

Nie dosTAłem [PIĄTki]$_F$, ale [CZWÓRkę]$_F$

Figure 10: (po-05'g Ro) CORR

In the CONTR-examples speaker B rejects an assumption made by the interlocutor A which is explicitly expressed in his previous utterance in the case of (po-05g) above (namely, that person B got a grade A) or can be inferred from it in the case of (po-14) below (person B has the newspaper). We find the typical LH*L or H*L accent on [$_{\text{Neg}°}$ Neg° V°][21] in C_1, expressing Fv (backward related Fc), the rest of the intonation contour of C_1 being flat and ending with a low boundary tone L%. After a significant pause, C_2 begins with a rising tone continued on the following syllable(s). In C_2 the speaker gives a compensation which is focused (falling tone HL* on the contrasted constituent *CZWÓRkę* in (po-05g) and *czasoPISmo* in (po-14) (backward related Fc). The conjuncts are pronounced as two intonation phrases (IPh), which is marked by the boundary tone at the end of C_1 (L%) and the beginning of C_2 (%H), the inserted pause (225 ms in (po-05g Ro) above and 550 ms in (po-14b Ro) below) and the register resetting before C_2.

In the CORR-examples (po-05'a above) and (po-14' below) IS is determined by the speaker's intention to correct. This leads to contrastive focusing of the *corrigendum* (forward related Fc) and *corrigens* (backward related Fc) in both conjuncts (LH* on *PIĄTki* in C_1 of (po-05'g), HL* on *gaZEty* in C_1 of (po-14'), LH*L on *CZWÒRkę* (po-05'g) and *czasoPISmo* (po-14') in C_2). Additionally there is a rise of the F0 on [$_{\text{Neg}°}$ Neg° V°] (*nie dosTAłem* resp. *NIE mam*) in the CORR-examples, which is perceived as less prominent than the accent on XP_1. This will be explained below. The two conjuncts are uttered as one IPh.

CONTR (po-14)	CORR (po-14')
A: Could I have something to read? Maybe today's newspaper. B: *I don't have the newspaper, but I have a magazine.* Would you like it?	A: We don't copy newspapers. B: *I don't have a newspaper, but a magazine.* Could you make a copy of that?

Po:	*Nie*	*mam*	*gazety,*	*ale*	*(mam)*	*czasopismo.*
$pro_{1.sg\text{-}nom}$	S-Neg	have	$newspaper_{gen}$	$Conj_{adv}$	(have)	$magazine_{acc}$

[21] In (po-05g) the Fv accent is realised on the finite verb, not on the negation marker *nie*, because the complex formed by the negation and the verb consists of more than one syllable (see footnote 17).

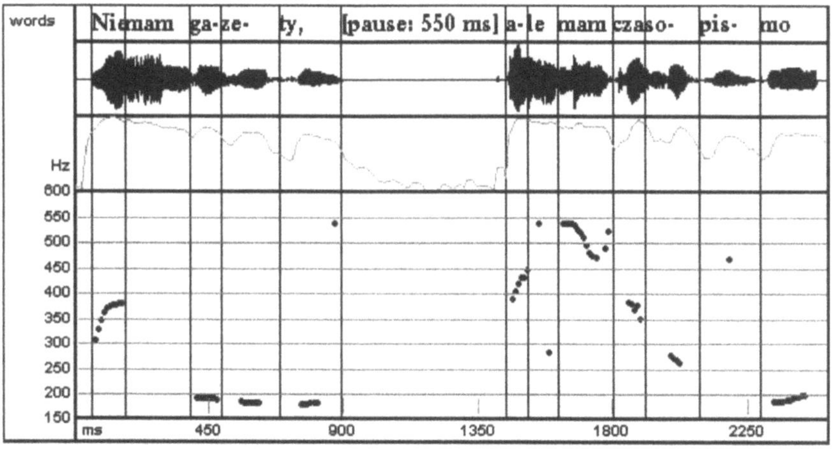

LH*L L-L% [pause] %H L*

[NIE mam]$_{Fv}$ gazety, ale mam [czasoPISmo]$_F$

Figure 11: (po-14b Ro) CONTR

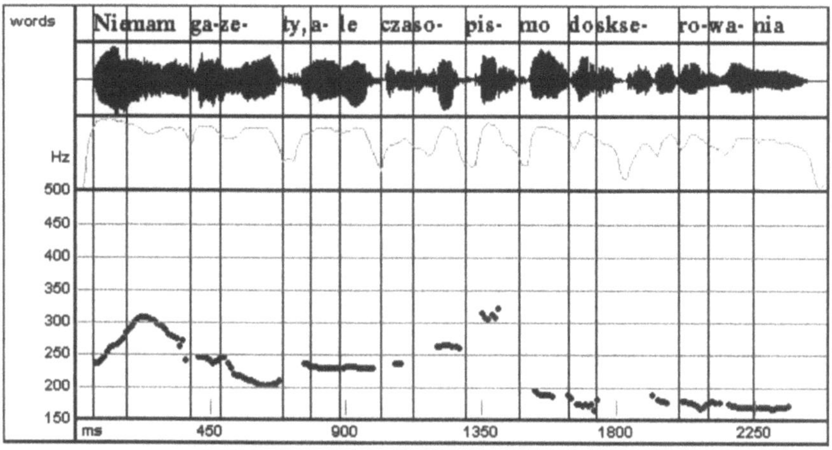

HL* LH*L

Nie mam [gaZEty]$_F$, ale [czasoPISmo]$_F$ (do skserowania).

Figure 12: (po-14'a Ro) CORR

4.4.3 However, certain contexts leave room as to how the intentions on part of the speaker can be realised.

So, in CONTR-example (po-04), where most of the speakers preferred parallel focusing of the contrasted constituents (or a de-accentuation of C_1 as background information) (cf. figure 7 above), speaker Wa pronounced the C_1-conjunct with an LH*L pitch accent on [$_{Neg°}$ Neg° V°] expressing a Fv in order to confirm the truth of the argument (*This isn't yellow*) that had been given before, cf. (po-04a Wa) in figure 13 below.

For CORR (po-04'), the majority of the speakers preferred a Fv in C_1, refusing thereby an assumption inferred from the previous context (figure 8 above). Nevertheless, speaker Wa stresses her intention to correct by contrastively focusing the corrigendum in C_1 (LH*L on *ŻÓŁty*), cf. figure 14 below.

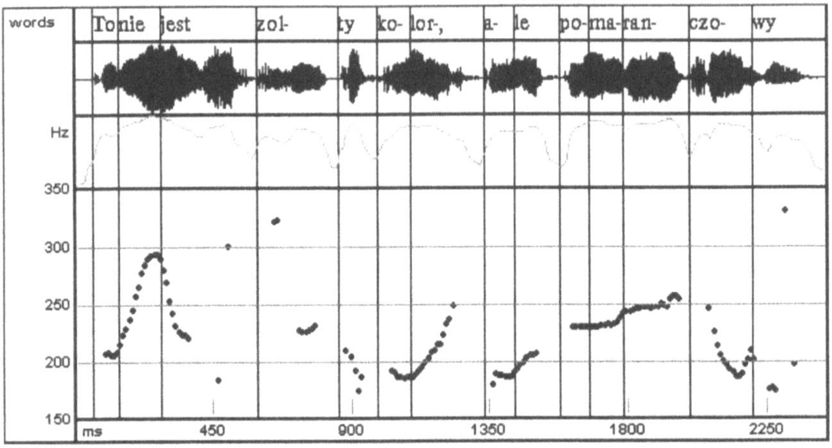

LH*L HL*

To [NIE jest]$_{Fv}$ żółty kolor, ale [pomarańCZOwy]$_F$

Figure 13: (po-04a Wa) CONTR (compare with po-04a Wr in figure 7 above)

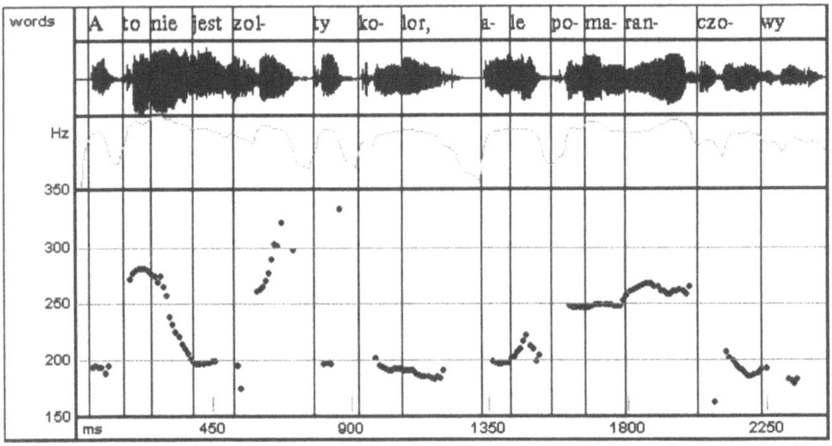

LH*L HL*

A to nie jest [ŻÓŁty kolor]$_F$, ale [pomarańCZOwy]$_F$

Figure 14: (po-04'a Wa) CORR (compare with po-04'a Wr in figure 8 above)

Thus, the speaker need not necessarily reject an assertion that has been made in the immediately preceding context by using a Fv in C_1 of the adversative construction. Instead s/he is free to emphasise the contrasting constituents in both conjuncts. This can be observed in (po-07/07'), (po-05g/po-05'g) and (po-14/14'), too.[22] Our hypothesis (H-2) about the invariant placement of sentence accent(s) in CORR based on parallel contrastive focusing of the corrigendum and the corrigens in their conjuncts has not been confirmed. CORR can also be realised with the sentence accent in C_1 on the phonological word formed by the proclitic negation marker and the finite verb, which means that the negative verum-element is focused in order to reject an assertion that was made in the preceding discourse. Differing from CONTR, however, is the continuative intonation at the boundary of the conjuncts. There is no IPh-boundary between the conjuncts in the case of CORR. In CONTR with Fv in C_1, the conjuncts are always very clearly pronounced as two distinct IPhs.

4.5 Default intonation contour

4.5.1 For most of the examples and most of the speakers, CONTR and CORR show an analogous intonation contour (IC), as shown in the examples (po-02/02') in figures 15 and 16 below. I will call it the default-IC, which is characterised as follows:

Phrasing:
We observe a continuative intonation at the end of C_1 (beginning or continued rise of the F0 that is further continued at the beginning of C_2). There are no IPh-boundary markers such as boundary tones, pause insertion, prefinal lengthening – except F0-resetting, which can be observed in nearly all of the recorded examples with any IS. The IC of the whole construction resembles rather a "continuous overall contour" („konnexe Gesamtkontur") – a term taken from Lang (2001:127). I regard it as one IPh only.

Accents:
Accent placement:
There are three prominent pitch accents in the whole IC, which are of nearly the same prominence – two in the first conjunct (on $[_{Neg°}$ Neg° V°] and on the contrasted constituent XP_1), and a third one in the second conjunct on the contrasted constituent XP_2.
Accent type:

[22] In another speech experiment, the speakers had to pronounce one and the same target sentence (po-05) in varying contexts with different anchoring of the elements of the target sentence in the preceding contexts – for the CONTR-reading as well as for the CORR-reading. These experiments have proved our assumption about the determination of prosody by information structure, but also a certain freedom of choice for the speaker with respect to IS.

[$_{Neg^\circ}$ Neg° V°] – LH*L
[XP_1] – varying, often L*H[23] (cf. po-02a/02'_a Ko), or LH*, sometimes LH*L
[XP_2] – varying, often LH*L (cf. po-02a/02'a_ Ko) or HL* (cf. po-05/05'a Sta)

<table>
<tr><th>CONTR (po-02a)</th><th>CORR (po-02'a)</th></tr>
<tr><td>A: We need somebody for our concert tomorrow night. Zbyszek has fallen ill.
B: What about Adam? He doesn't play the oboe, but he plays the flute.
So he could help you out, if you don't manage to find an oboe player quickly.</td><td>A: We need somebody for our concert tomorrow night. Zbyszek has fallen ill.
B: What about Adam?
A: Oh, no.
He doesn't play the oboe, but the flute.
Zbyszek is our oboe player, you know.</td></tr>
<tr><td colspan="2">Po: On [$_{Neg^\circ}$ [$_{Neg^\circ}$ NIE] [$_{V^\circ}$ gra]] [$_{XP1}$ na oBOju], ale [$_{XP2}$ na FLEcie]
he$_{nom}$ S-Neg plays on oboe , Conj$_{adv}$ on flute</td></tr>
</table>

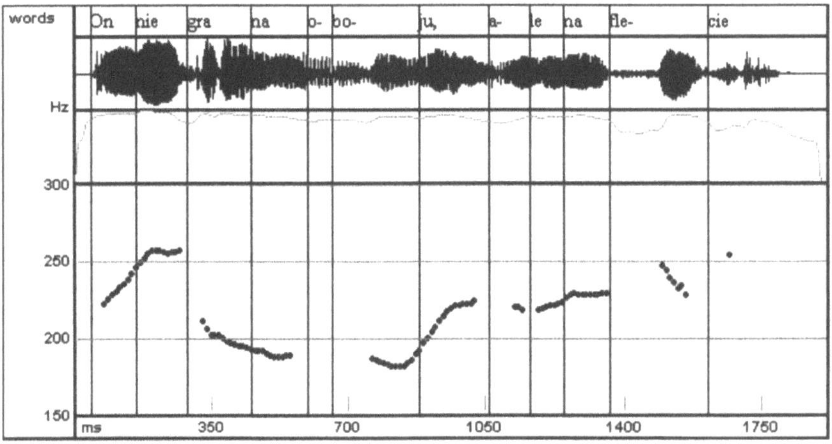

LH*L L*H LH*L
On NIE gra na oBOju, ale na FLEcie

Figure 15: (po-02a Ko) CONTR

[23] L*H seems to be the typical focus accent on the right periphery of a non-final conjunct. This is consistent with observations on prosody of complex sentences in Polish in Skorek (1997), who does not invoke any concept of IS or focus. When such an accent can be interpreted as contrastive, has not been studied yet. For now we can only conclude from the interpretational side whether it signals a contrastive or neutral focus. LH*L, however, is clearly contrastive, as shown e.g. in Zybatow and Mehlhorn (2000) for Russian.

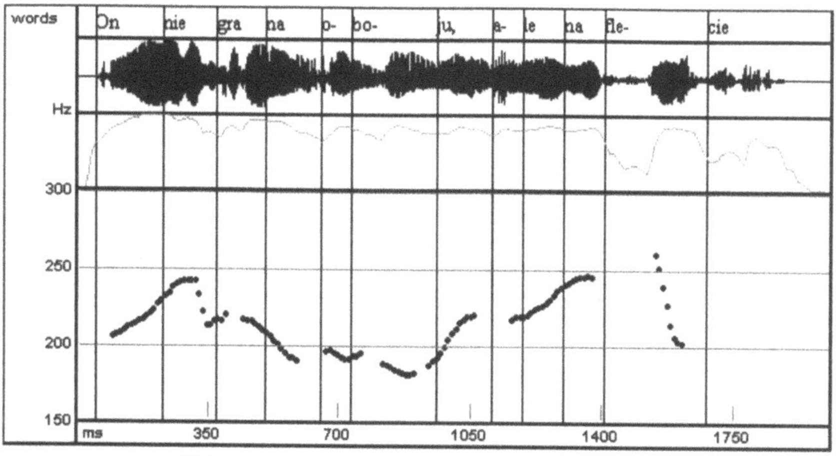

LH*L L*H LH*L
On NIE gra na oBOju, ale na FLEcie

Figure 16: (po-02'a Ko) CORR

Also compare (po-05a/05'a) by speaker Sta in figures 17 and 18 below:

<table>
<tr><td>CONTR (po-05a)</td><td>CORR (po-05'a)</td></tr>
<tr><td>A: Hi Wojtek. How are you? How did the exam go?
B: Not bad. I didn't get an A, but I got a B. I'm quite happy with it.</td><td>A: Hi Wojtek. How are you? How did the exam go?
B: Don't ask. I didn't get an A, but a B. I would have needed the A to get an overall "excellent".</td></tr>
<tr><td colspan="2">Po: [pro]$_{T}$ [$_{Neg°}$ [$_{Neg°}$ Nie] [$_{V°}$ doSTAłem] [$_{XP1}$ PIĄTki]], ale [$_{XP2}$ CZWÓRkę].
pro$_{1.sg\text{-}nom}$ S-Neg got fife$_{gen}$, CONJ$_{adv}$ four$_{acc}$</td></tr>
</table>

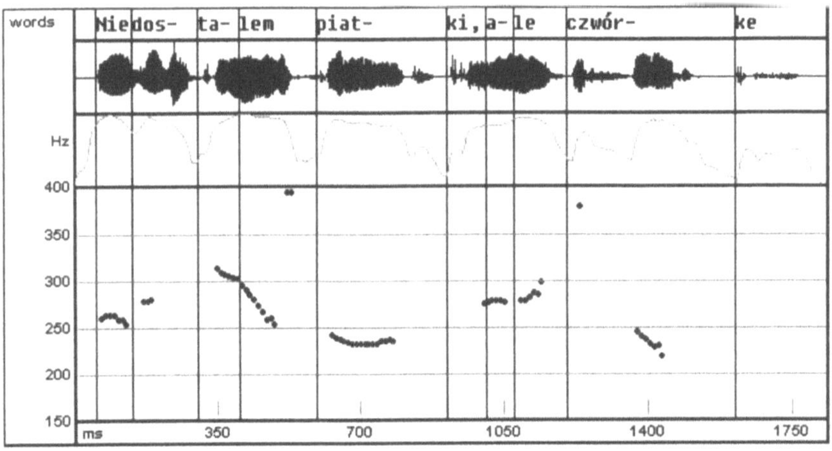

LH*L L*H HL*

Nie dosTAłem PIĄTki, ale CZWÓRkę

Figure 17: (po-05a Sta) CONTR

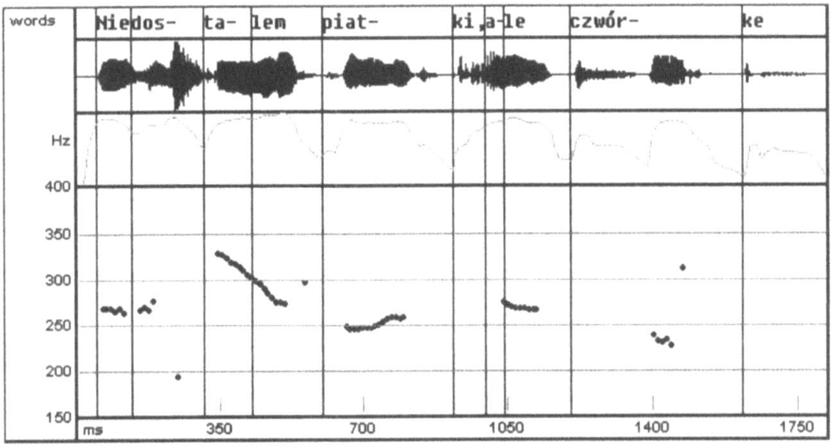

LH*L L*H HL*

Nie dosTAłem PIĄTki, ale CZWÓRkę

Figure 18: (po-05'a Sta) CORR

Why do CONTR and CORR in most cases share this intonation contour? In my opinion, it is because – differently from what Lang (2001) found in his comparison of concessive and contrastive (adversative) interpretations of German "*aber*"-constructions – in case the default- IC is used, there is no evident difference in the information structure of CONTR with negated C_1 and CORR.

Then, what is the IS underlying the prosodic default realisation of CONTR and CORR? For the examples realised by the default-IC the information structure of the conjuncts is determined by the speaker's intention of contrasting or correcting, which is compatible with the embedding context. As for FBS, the conjuncts constitute the relevant context for each other.

In CORR this results in parallel contrastive focusing of the constituents that represent the *corrigendum* affected by the negation in C_1 (XP_1) and the *corrigens* in C_2 (XP_2). The frequently observed additional pitch accent on $[_{Neg°}$ Neg° V°] can be explained as additional stressing of the operator (NEG) associated with the contrastively focused constituent.[24]

In CONTR, according to the definition given in the introduction, the arguments for and against the issue under discussion are contrasted. This should result in parallel contrastive focusing of the negative $PolP_1$ – the default focus domain for negated sentences (cf. Junghanns (in press) and Hajíčová 1993) – and the affirmative $PolP_2$. Though the focus domain is different from that of CORR, the focus exponents realising the focus accent are the same as in CORR, namely the constituents bearing the minimal lexical contrast - XP_1 and XP_2. But because of the lexical contrast involved, the speaker is free to assign a minimal Fc to the lexically differing constituents, alternatively.[25] [26] In this case, not only are the focus exponents the same in CONTR and CORR, but also the focus domains. The additional accent on $[_{Neg°}$ Neg° V°] in CONTR can be explained in the same way as for CORR. It is a means of emphasizing (in addition to the focus) the operator associated with the minimal focus, which is motivated by the relation to the preceding context (rejection of an assumption explicitly mentioned or implicitly contained in the preceding utterance(s)).

Compare now the IS-differences in Lang's examples with the matching IS of CONTR and CORR. (For the labelling of prosodic units I use Lang's notation here, where U means utterance, and IP – intonation phrase.)

---

[24] The problem of explaining the additional pitch accent on $[_{Neg°}$ Neg° V°] is discussed in more detail in Adamíková and Fehrmann (2001). To clarify the status of this accent in Polish and other Slavic languages, negated non-complex sentences have to be tested. It may turn out, that the significant pitch on $[_{Neg°}$ Neg° V°] is independent from its possible association with Fc and may occur in every negated sentence as a typological characteristics of these languages.

[25] Steube (2002:223) claims that Fc is "independent of the information structural change of new information into familiar". And Molnár (2002) regards contrast as an "autonomous concept of information structuring" which finds its reflection in prosody (cf. also Molnár 2001) – an assumption that is shared by Lang and Umbach (2002).

[26] In this case, the interpretation of CONTR is comparable to the one that we find in (5) in section 2.2 above. For (po-02) this means that the *oboe* is not the relevant instrument, since Adam does not play it. But he plays the *flute* and, thus, can help them out at the concert. This is in line with Adamíková (2003a), who comes to similar results for her Slovak data. She analyses them using Jacobs' Relational Focus Theory.

(po-02) CORR:

LH*L L*H H H*L L%

[[[On]$_T$ NIE gra [$_{PP}$ na oBOju]$_{Fc}$ ale [$_{PP}$ na FLEcie]$_{Fc}$ ^{U}]^{IP}]

He$_{nom}$ S-Neg plays on oboe Conj$_{adv}$ on flute

He doesn't play the oboe, but the flute.

(po-02') CONTR:

LH*L L*H H H*L L%

a) [[[On]$_T$ NIE gra [$_{PP}$ na oBOju]$_{Fc}$ ale [$_{PP}$ na FLEcie]$_{Fc}$ ^{U}]^{IP}]

b) [[[On]$_T$ [$_{PolP}$ NIE gra na oBOju]$_{Fc}$ ale [$_{PolP}$ na FLEcie]$_{Fc}$ ^{U}]^{IP}]

He$_{nom}$ S-Neg plays on oboe Conj$_{adv}$ on flute

He doesn't play the oboe, but he plays the flute.

Compare this with Lang's (2002:124) examples (1-a) and (1-b), given here as (13a) and (13b):[27]

(13a) Contrastive (adversative):

A: Was machen denn deine Eltern? (How are your parents?)

B: Es geht ihnen unterschiedlich: (Well, mom is OK, but dad is not:)

L*H L*H H% L L*H H*L L%

[[[Mein VAter]$_T$ [ist ernsthaft KRANK]$_F$ ^{IP}] [aber [meine MUTter]$_T$ [geht ARbeiten]$_F$ ^{IP}]^U]

my$_{nom}$ father$_{nom}$ is seriously ill Conj$_{adv}$ my$_{nom}$ mother$_{nom}$ goes working$_{inf}$

My father is seriously ill, but my mother is working.

(13b) Concessive:

A: Was machen denn deine Eltern? (How are your parents?)

B: Ich bin ziemlich entsetzt: (I'm quite upset:)

L*H L*H H H* H*L L%

[[Mein VAter]$_T$ [ist ernsthaft KRANK]$_F$ aber [meine MUTter geht ARbeiten]$_F$ ^{U}]

my$_{nom}$ father$_{nom}$ is seriously ill Conj$_{adv}$ my$_{nom}$ mother$_{nom}$ goes working$_{inf}$

My father is seriously ill, but my mother is working.

(Though my father is seriously ill, my mother is working.)

The default-IC is the most frequent pattern for CORR. It was produced in all tested CORR examples at least by some speakers and is accepted in all CORR-contexts, as speech perception experiments show. For CONTR it was used very often, too, but not to the same extent.

[27] I have translated the relevant contexts into English.

CORR is further restricted in that it is always pronounced as one IPh with a continuative (rising or progredient) intonation at the boundary of the conjuncts, when connected syndetically. CONTR is more variable in this respect, too.

4.5.2 However, when the construction is realised with the IS typical for the default case outlined above, sometimes speakers (in fact, very few) make a slight distinction between CONTR and CORR. The tendency of this distinction can be described as follows.
(i) Though there are two prominent pitch accents in the first conjunct as is typical for the default-IC, in CONTR it is more often the accent on XP_1 which is slightly more prominent than the one on $[_{Neg°}$ Neg° V°], whereas in CORR we observe the opposite.
(ii) The pitch accent on XP_2 in the second conjunct tends to be perceived as more contrastive in CORR than in CONTR.
(iii) In the CONTR-examples speakers sometimes tended to produce an IPh-boundary between the conjuncts by means of prefinal lengthening or insertion of a short pause detected in none of the CORR-examples.

	CONTR	CORR
relative prominence of the accents in C_1	$[_{Neg°}$ Neg° V°] < XP_1	$[_{Neg°}$ Neg° V°] > XP_1
type of the accent on XP_2 in C_2	XP_2 less contrastive (often HL*)	XP_2 more contrastive (often LH*L)
phrasing between C_1 and C_2	reinforcement of IPh-boundary by: - prefinal lengthening - pause insertion (- boundary tones)	no IPh-boundary

Figure 19: Tendency to differentiate between CONTR and CORR with the default-IS. (Here "<" and ">" denote the relative prominence relation between two accents.)

Accordingly, in (po-05a/05'a) produced by speaker Ko (see figures 20 and 21 below), the duration of the final syllable of C_1 (*-ki-* in the focused XP_1 *piątki*) is 300 ms in CONTR, but only 140 ms in CORR, while the first syllable of XP_1 as well as the whole C_1 and the whole utterance have nearly the same duration in both readings (*-piąt-*: 350 ms resp. 360 ms; C_1: 1280 ms resp. 1150 ms; C_1+C_2: 1970 ms resp. 1870 ms). Additionally, in CONTR the pitch accent on XP_1 was perceived as more prominent than the one on $[_{Neg°}$ Neg° V°] by the majority of subjects in a perception experiment. In CONTR they judged both accents as equally prominent.

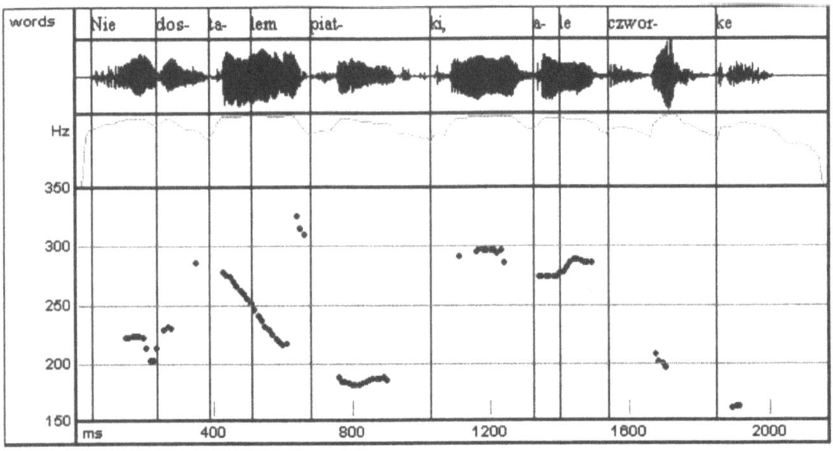

LH*L L*H HL*

Nie dosTAłem [PIĄTki]$_F$, ale [CZWÓRkę]$_F$

Figure 20: (po-05a Ko) CONTR

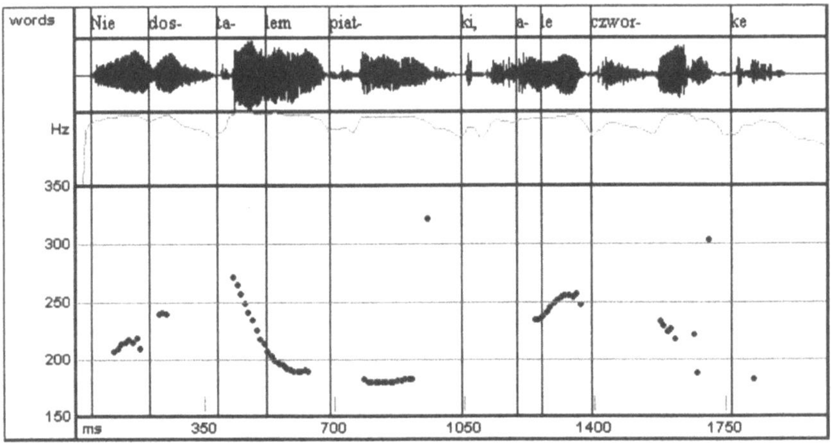

LH*L L*H HL*

Nie dosTAłem [PIĄTki]$_F$, ale [CZWÓRkę]$_F$

Figure 21: (po-05'a Ko) CORR

	CONTR	CORR
accent perception	Neg+V < XP_1	Neg+V = XP_1
phrasing: duration of the last syllable of C_1	300 ms (prefinal lengthening) → IPh-boundary?	140 ms → no IPh-boundary

Figure 22: Differentiation between CONTR and CORR in (po-05/05'a) made by speaker Ko

Speaker Wr (see figures 23 and 24 below) also lengthens the final syllable of C_1 in CONTR (up to 300 ms compared to 160 ms in CORR) and additionally inserts a pause of 130 ms:

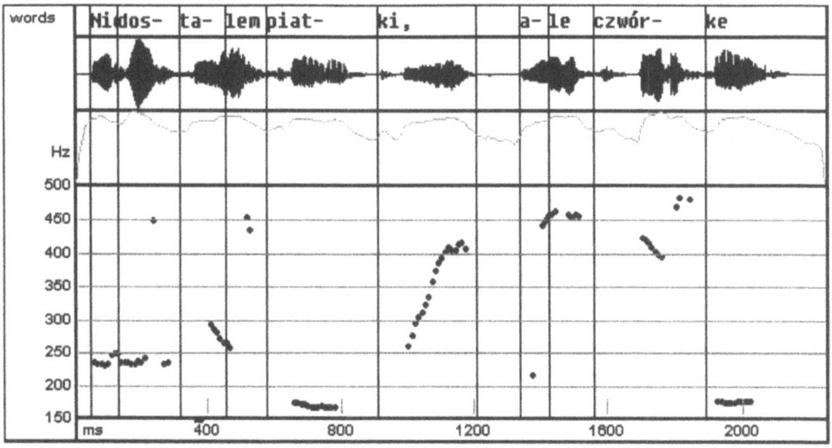

LH*L L*H HL*

Nie dosTAłem [PIĄTki]F, ale [CZWÓRkę]F

Figure 23: (po-05a Wr) CONTR

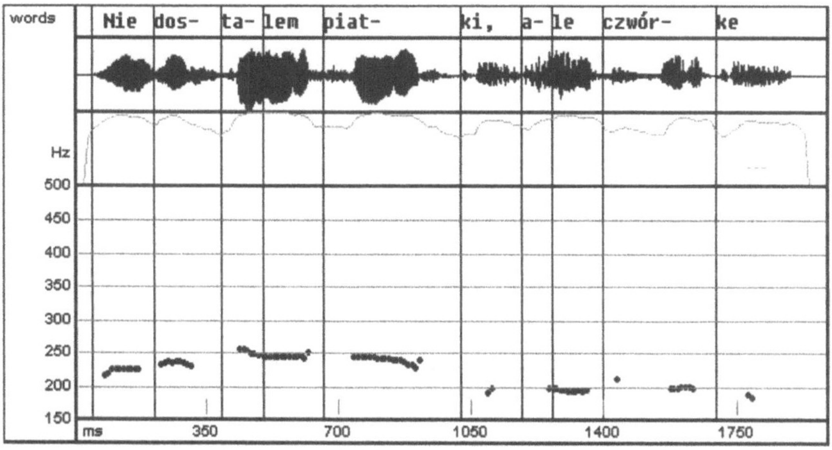

LH*L L*H HL*

Nie dosTAłem [PIĄTki]F, ale [CZWÓRkę]F

Figure 24: (po-05'a Wr)[28] CORR

---

[28] It is striking that the pitch range in the intonation contour of CORR example (po-05'a) produced by speaker Wr is much narrower than in the respective CONTR example, as well as in others of our exmples. The accents are marked by intensity and duration rather than by F0 modulation. I think that this is due to the negative emotive involvement of the speaker who isn't satisfied with his/her exam results at all. Similar effects have been stated for Russian by Richter (2003:203).

	CONTR	CORR
phrasing:		
- duration of the last syllable of C_1	300 ms (prefinal lengthening)	160 ms
- pause duration	130 ms	Ø (no pause)
	→ IPh-boundary?	→ no IPh-boundary

Figure 25: Differentiation between CONTR and CORR in (po-05/05'a) made by speaker Wr

Compare with (po-05a/05'a Sta) in figures 17 and 18 above where no difference can be detected.

4.5.3 The differentiation via phrasing is especially evident in the case of non-parallel information structuring of the two conjuncts – as has been mentioned above in 4.4.3. A CONTR-construction with Fv in C_1 and focused XP_2 in C_2 is characterised by a significant pause between the conjuncts and an L% boundary tone at the end of C_1 - see examples (po-05g Ro) in figure 9 and (po-14b Ro) in figure 11 above. Sometimes C_2 begins with an %H boundary tone as in (po-05k Ro) in figure 26 below. Because C_2 functions here as an independent utterance, it is usually syntactically non-reduced. The reduced case is highly marked, but, nevertheless, possible.

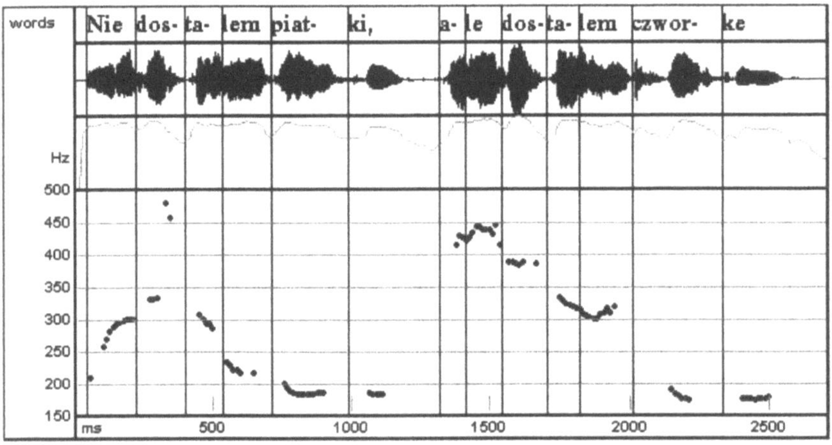

H*L L- L% %H HL*
[Nie dosTAłem]$_{Fv}$ piątki, ale dostałem [CZWÓRkę]$_F$

Figure 26: (po-05k Ro) CONTR

In a CORR-construction, when coordinated by a conjunction, the second conjunct has to be integrated prosodically into the whole utterance even in the case of non-parallel information structuring – see (po-07'b Ro) in figure 6 and (po-04'a Wr) in figure 8 above. Otherwise it can only be added asyndetically as an independent (and non-reduced) sentence as in (po-05'c Ro) in figure 27 below:

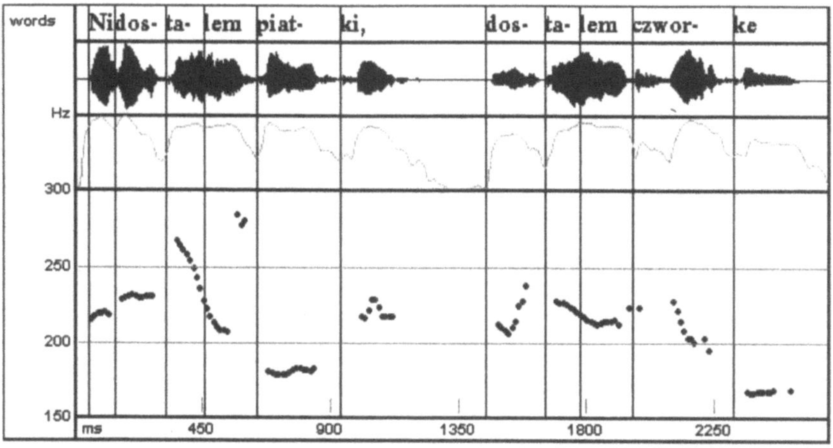

H*L L- L% %H HL*

[Nie dosTAłem]$_{Fv}$ piątki. Dostałem [CZWÓRkę]$_F$

Figure 27: (po-05'c Ro) CORR

4.6 In sum, the tested examples sometimes show differences in phrasing that correlate with the distinction into CONTR and CORR, and sometimes they exhibit variation in the placement and type of sentence accent(s) that do not go along with the two types of coordinate structures, but rather are due to different information structures depending on the embedding context and the speaker's intentions, as well as to free variation of focus accent realisation. There is no one-to-one mapping between the semantico-conceptual reading and IS. Various information structures are compatible with both readings.

In the majority of examples we find no prosodical distinction between CONTR and CORR.

5 Conclusions

A prosodic differentiation between CONTR and CORR constructions is not obligatory in Polish. However, prosody can help to single out the relevant conceptual interpretation which is primarily determined by the context.

CORR-constructions are correlated with a specific prosodic pattern more regularly than CONTR. The intonation contour that is typical for CORR consists of one intonation phrase only and is based on the parallel contrastive focusing of corrigendum and corrigens and the additional stressing of the phonological word formed by the proclitic negation marker (as the operator associated with a minimal Fc) and the finite verb. It is used for the realisation of CONTR, too, and is accepted in CONTR-contexts. This intonation contour gets the semantico-conceptual interpretation induced by the context and can be regarded as the default prosodic realisation.

Phonology provides only a limited inventory of formal means for expressing a diversity of relations. Therefore it is not surprising to find syncretism in usage. CONTR and CORR, which often display identical syntax and information structure, need not necessarily be distinguished prosodically, either.

All in all, the results of the speech production and speech perception experiments suggest that the intonational patterns of adversative coordinate structures are determined much more by the information structure of the conjuncts than by the conceptual interpretation type.

In addition, the prosodical realisation is influenced by independent factors such as emphasis, emotion, hesitation, etc. induced by the context or the attitude of the individual speakers, which provides a special problem for an objective comparison of the accent realisation and phrasing phenomena. Further research is necessary here.

6 References

Adamíková, M. (1996): KONTRAST- und KORREKTUR-Konstruktionen im Deutschen und ihre Entsprechungen im Slowakischen. MA Thesis, Berlin: Humboldt-Universität.

Adamíková, M. (2000a): Lexikalische, syntaktische und prosodische Mittel der Differenzierung von KONTRAST und KORREKTUR-Konstruktionen am Beispiel des Slovakischen. In: H. Weydt and S. Poljakova (eds): Linguistik online 6, 2/00. http://www.linguistik-online.com .

Adamíková, M. (2000b): Kontrast und Korrektur im Interaktionsbereich von Lexikon, Syntax und Prosodie am Beispiel des Slovakischen. In: K. Böttger, M. Giger, and B. Wiemer (eds): Beiträge der europäischen Slavistischen Linguistik 3 (POLYSLAV), Die Welt der Slaven (= Sammelbände 4), München, 1-9.

Adamíková, M. (2003a): Sentential Negation and Focus in Slovak Adversative Constructions. In: P. Kosta et al. (eds) Investigations into Formal Slavic Linguistics (=Linguistik International 10). Frankfurt a. M., 157-168.

Adamíková, M. and D. Fehrmann (2001): Prosodische Differenzierung von Kontrast- und Korrekturkonstruktionen im Slovakischen und Polnischen. In: A. Steube and C. Umbach (eds): Kontrast – lexikalisch, semantisch, intonatorisch. Linguistische Arbeitsberichte 77, Leipzig, 81-112.

Alter, K. (2002): Realisierung von Verarbeitung von Korrektur: Zum Zusammenhang von Bedeutung und Intonation. In: A. Steube (ed): Sprachtheoretische Grundlagen der Kognitionswissenschaft: Sprachliches und nicht sprachliches Wissen. Linguistische Arbeitsberichte 79 ,Leipzig, 255-274.

Alter, K., I. Mleinek, and N. Richter (2001): Prosodic Phrasing and Accentuation in Russian. In: G. Zybatow, U. Junghanns, G. Mehlhorn, and L. Szucsich (eds): Current Issues in Fromal Slavic Linguistics, Frankfurt/M. et al.: Lang, 317-328.

Benzmüller, R. and M. Grice (1997): Trainingsmaterialien zur Etikettierung Deutscher Intonation mit GToBI. In: Phonus 3. Institute of Phonetics, University of the Saarland, 9-34.

Błaszczak, J. (2001): Investigation into the interaction between the indefinites and negation. In: Studia grammatica 51, Berlin: Akademie-Verlag.

Braußе, U. (1998): Was ist Adversativität? *aber* oder *und*? Deutsche Sprache 26 (2), 138-159.

Drubig, H. B. (1994): Island Constraints and the Syntactic Nature of Focus and Association with Focus. In: Sprachtheoretische Grundlagen für die Computerlinguistik. Arbeitspapiere des Sonderforschungsbericht 340, vol 51, Universität Stuttgart/Tübingen.

Duszak, A. (1987): The dynamics of Topics in English and Polish. Warszawa: Wydawnictwo UW.

Fehrmann, D. (1997): Sekundärprädikate und Informationsstruktur im Polnischen. In: U. Junghanns, and G. Zybatow (eds): Formale Slavistik. Frankfurt/M.: Vervuert, 371-386.

Fehrmann, D. (2001): Kontrastive Topiks in adversativen Konstruktionen mit Kontrast- vs. Korrekturinterpretation im Polnischen. Paper presented at the 4th International Conference on Formal Description of Slavic Languages (FDSL-4), Potsdam, November 2001.

Fehrmann, D. (to appear): The format of coordination for Polish adversative constructions with a Contrast and a Correction reading. To appear in: Proceedings of the 5th International Conference on Formal Description of Slavic Languages (FDSL-5), Leipzig, November 2003, Frankfurt a. M.: Lang

Féry, C. (1993): German Intonational Patterns (= LA 285), Tübingen: Niemeyer.

Féry, C. and Hartmann, K. (2001): Focus and prosodic structures of German Gapping and Right Node Raising (Ms.)

Gehrmann, M. (1988): Adversative Konjunktionen des Polnischen im Vergleich zum Deutschen. LS/ZISW/A 183, 107-201.

Gehrmann, M. (1992a): Typy konstrukcji adwersatywnych w języku polskim. In: Studia gramatyczne X, Kraków, 119-132.

Gehrmann, M. (1992b): Korektor a kontrast: dwa typy konstrukcji adwersatywnych w języku polskim i niemieckim (studium konfrontatywne). In: Studia gramatyczne X, Kraków, 133-147.

Grimshaw, J. (1991): Extended Projection. Ms. Brandeis University.

Grzegorek, M. (1984): Thematization in English and Polish: a study in word order. Poznań: Wydawnictwo Naukowe UAM.

Haftka, B. (1994): Wie positioniere ich meine Position? Überlegungen zu funktionalen Phrasen im deutschen Mittelfeld. In: B. Haftka (ed): Was determiniert Wortstellungsvariationen? Studien zu einem Interaktionsfeld von Grammatik, Pragmatik und Sprachtypologie. Opladen: Westdeutscher Verlag, 139-159).

Hajičová, E. (1993): Issues of Sentence Structure and Discourse Patterns In: Theoretical and Computational Linguistics 2, Praha.

Hetland, J. (1993): Über Argumentstruktur, Fokus und Satzadverbiale. In: I. Rosengren (ed): Satz und Illokution 2. Linguistische Arbeitsberichte 279, Tübingen: Niemeyer, 109-126.

Höhle, T. (1992): Über Verum-Fokus im Deutschen. In: J. Jacobs (ed): Informationsstruktur und Grammatik . Linguistische Berichte, Sonderheft 4, 112-141.

Horn, L. R. (1985): Metalinguistic Negation and Pragmatic Ambiguity. Language 61 (1/1985), 121-174.

Jacobs, J. (1982): Syntax und Semantik der Negation im Deutschen. München.

Jacobs, J. (1991): Negation. In: A. v. Stechow and D. Wunderlich (eds): Semantik. Semantics (= HSK 6), Berlin/New York: de Gruyter, 560-596.

Jacobs, J. (1996): Bemerkungen zur I-Topikalisierung. In: Sprache und Pragmatik 41, 1-48.

Junghanns, U. (2002): Informationsstrukturierung in slavischen Sprachen: Zur Rekonstruktion in einem syntaxzentrierten Modell der Grammatik. Habilitationsschrift, Leipzig.

Junghanns, U. (in print): Scope conflicts involving sentential negation in Czech. In: S. Brown and A. Przepiórkowski (eds): Negation in Slavic. Bloomington: Indiana: Slavica Publishers.

Junghanns, U. and G. Zybatow (1997): Syntax and Information Structure of Russian Clauses. In: E. W. Browne et al. (eds): Annual Workshop of Formal Approaches to Slavic Linguistics. The Cornell Neeting 1995. Michigan Slavic Materials 39, Ann Arbor: Michigan Slavic Publications, 289-319.

Lakoff, R. (1971): IFs, ANDs and BUTs about conjunction. In: Ch. J. Fillmore and T. D. Langendoen (eds): Studies in Linguistic Semantics. New York etc.: Holt, Rinehart and Winston, 114-149.

Lang, E. (1977): Semantik der koordinativen Verknüpfung In: studia grammatica XIV, Berlin: Akademie-Verlag.

Lang, E. (1984): The Semantics of Coordination In: Studies in Language Companion Series 9, Amsterdam/Philadelphia: John Benjamins B.V.

Lang, E. (1988): Syntax und Semantik der Adversativkonnektive, Einstieg und Überblick. Unpubl. Ms., Berlin.

Lang, E. (1991): Koordinierende Konjunktionen. In: A. v. Stechow, and D. Wunderlich (eds): Semantik. Semantics (= HSK 6), Berlin/New York: de Gruyter, 597-623.

Lang, E. (2000): Adversative Connectors on Distinct Levels of Discourse: A Reexamination of Eve Sweetser's Three-level Approach. In: E. Couper-Kuhlen, and B. Kortmann (eds): Cause – Condition – Concession – Contrast. Cognitive and Discourse Perspectives. Berlin/New York: de Gruyter, 235-256.

Lang, E. (2001): Kontrastiv vs. implikativ: Interpretationseffekte intonatorischer Distinktionen bei Koordination. In: A. Steube and C. Umbach (eds): Kontrast – lexikalisch, semantisch, intonatorisch. Linguistische Arbeitsberichte 77, Leipzig, 113-138.

Lang, E. (2002): Kontrastiv vs. implikativ II: Interpretationseffekte einer intonatorischen Distinktion bei elliptischen Sprichwörtern. In: A. Steube (ed): Sprachtheoretische Grundlagen der Kognitionswissenschaft: Sprachliches und nichtsprachliches Wissen. Linguistische Arbeitsberichte 79, Leipzig, 187-212.

Lang, E. and C. Umbach (2002): Kontrast in der Grammatik: spezifische Realisierungen und übergreifender Konnex. In: A. Steube (ed): Sprachtheoretische Grundlagen der Kognitionswissenschaft: Sprachliches und nichtsprachliches Wissen. Linguistische Arbeitsberichte 79, Leipzig, 145-186.

Mehlhorn, G. (2001): Kontrastierte Konstituenten im Russischen. Experimentelle Untersuchungen zur Informationsstruktur. PhD diss., Universität Leipzig.

Mehlhorn, G. and G. Zybatow (2000): Alte und neue Hüte der russischen Informationsstruktur. In: J. Dölling, and T. Pechmann (eds): Prosodie – Struktur – Interpretation. Linguistische Arbeitsberichte 74, Leipzig, 25-42.

Molnár, V. (2001): Contrast from a Contrastive Perspective. In: I. Kruijff-Korbayová, and M. Steedman (eds): Information Structure, Discourse Structure and Discourse Semantics, 95-110.

Molnár, V. (2002): Contrast - from a contrastive perspective. Paper presented at the 3rd Leipzig Workshop on Contrast and Information Structure, University of Leipzig, February 2002.

Munn, A. (1987): Coordinate Structure and X-bar Theory. In: McGill Working Papers in Linguistics 4.

Munn, A. (1992): A Null Operator Analysis of ATB Gaps. In: The Linguistic Review 9, 1-26.

Nikolaeva, T. M. (1969): Intonazija sloshnogo predloshenija v slavjanskich jasykach. Moskva: Nauka.

Pierrehumbert, J. (1980): The Phonetics and Phonology of English Intonation. PhD diss., MIT.

Richter, N. (2003): Evaluative utterances in Russian and their prosodic realisation. In: R. Blankenhorn, J. Błaszczak, and R. Marzari (eds): Beiträge der Europäischen Slavistischen Linguistik. München: Sagner, 199-204.

Rosengren, I. (1993): Wahlfreiheit mit Konsequenzen – Scrambling, Topikalisierung und FHG im Dienste der Informationsstrukturierung. In: M. Reis (ed): Wortstellung und Informationsstruktur. Tübingen, 251-312.

Ross, J. R. (1967): Constraints on Variables in Syntax. PhD diss., MIT.

Schwabe, K. (2000): Coordinate Ellipsis and Information Structure. In: K. Schwabe, and N. Zhang (eds): Ellipsis in Coordination, Tübingen: Niemeyer, 247-269.

Skorek, J. (1997): Fonologia suprasegmentalna języków rosyjskiego I polskiego. Wyższa Szkoła Pedagogiczna im. Tadeusza Kotarbińskiego w Zielonej Górze, Zielona Góra.

Steube, A. (1999): Ein kognitionswissenschaftlich basiertes Modell für Informationsstrukturierung (in Anwendung auf das Deutsche). In: J. Bayer and Chr. Römer (eds): Von der Philologie zur Grammatiktheorie. Tübingen: Niemeyer.

Steube, A. (2002): Correction by Contrastive Focus. In: Theoretical Linguistics 27 (2/3), 215-249.

Sweetser, E. (1990): From Etymology to Pragmatics. Metaphorical and Cultural Aspects of Semantic Structure. Cambridge: University Press.

Szucsich, L. (2002): Nominale Adverbiale im Russischen. Syntax, Semantik und Informationsstruktur. In: Slavistische Beiträge, München: Sagner; 414.

Szwedek, A. (1981): Word Order, Sentence Stress and Reference in English and Polish. Bydgoszcz: Wydawnictwo WSP.

Wilder, Ch. (1997): Some Properties of Ellipsis in Coordination. In: A. Alexiadou and T. A. Hall (eds): Studies on Universal Grammar and Typological Variation. Linguistik Aktuell 13 / Linguistics Today 13), Amsterdam/Philadelphia: John Benjamins, 59-107.

Williams, E. (1978): Across-the-board Rule Application. In: Linguistic Inquiry 9, 31-43.

Witkoś, J. (1996): On NegP and the structure of the Polish clause. Papers and Studies in Contrastive Linguistics 31, 65-96.

Witkoś, J. (1999): The Syntax of Clitics: Steps Towards a Minimalist Account. Poznań: Motivex.

Zybatow, G. and G. Mehlhorn (2000): Experimental evidence for Focus Structure in Russian. In: T. H. King and I. A. Sekerina (eds): Annual Workshop on Formal Approaches to Slavic Linguistics. The Philadelphia Meeting 1999. Michigan Slavic Publications: Ann Arbor, 414-434.

Short Portraits of the Authors

Alter, Kai
Dr. phil. habil.; senior lecturer at the Newcastle University Medical School, School of Neurology, Neurobiology and Psychiatry; Newcastle Auditory Group;
Research interests: cognitive neuroscience, brain research, auditory processing, processing of prosody and its interfaces

Bader, Markus
PhD in 1995 from the University of Stuttgart;
lecturer in the Department of Linguistics of the University of Konstanz;
Research interests: human language comprehension, in particular parsing and interpretation; syntactic theory; metrics

Fehrmann, Dorothee
research assistant of the Research group "Linguistic Foundations of Cognitive Science - linguistic and extralinguistic knowledge";
Research interests: syntax, information structure, and prosody, especially in Slavic, in a Chomskyan framework.

Gyuris, Beáta
PhD in 2003 from the Loránd Eötvös University, Budapest;
Research fellow at the Research Institute for Linguistics of the Hungarian Academy of Sciences;
Research interests: the semantics of quantification, of aspect, and the study of information structure

Haftka, Brigitta
Dr. phil.; retired; worked on several projects on German grammar at the Academy of Sciences of the GDR and at the Zentrum für Allgemeine Sprachwissenschaft (ZAS) Berlin;
Research interest: German and general syntax, topology, information structure

Hruska, Claudia
PhD student at the Max Planck Institute for Human Cognitive and Brain Sciences; member of the Junior Research Group

Eva Hajičová

Professor of Charles University in Prague; head of the Center of Computational Linguistics, Faculty of Mathematics and Physics; chairperson of the Prague Linguistic Circle;
Research interests: Czech and English studies, theoretical and computational linguistics, syntax and its relations to semantic

Lang, Ewald

Professor of Semantics at Humboldt-University Berlin;
Research interests: interfaces in grammar, sentence vs. discourse, coherence

Lühr, Rosemarie

Professor of Indo-European linguistics at the University of Jena/Germany; member of the Saxon Academy of Sciences at Leipzig
Research interests: syntax, etymology, the conception of the lexicon

Max, Ingolf

extraordinary Professer, Dr. phil. habil. in 1999; research and teaching positions at the Universities of Prague, Konstanz, Bloomington/In/USA, Irvine/Ca/USA and Jena; currently lecturer in the field of logic and philosophy of science at the University of Leipzig;

Mehlhorn, Grit

PhD in Slavic Linguistics in 2002 from the University of Leipzig, Germany; currently in a research and teaching position at the University of Stuttgart, Department of German Linguistics;
Research interests: L2 acquisition of prosody and the interface of prosody and information structure

Mleinek, Ina

graduate student in Slavic linguistics at the University of Leipzig; member of the Research group "Linguistic Foundations of Cognitive Science - linguistic and extralinguistic knowledge";
Research interests: information structure and prosody in Russian and German.

Sgall, Petr

Professor emeritus of Charles University, working in the Centre of Computational Linguistics, Faculty of Mathematics;
Research interests: syntax and its relations to semantics, typology, spoken Czech.

Späth, Andreas
Dr. phil. habil. in 2004 from theUniversity of Leipzig;
research assistant of the Research Group "Linguistic Foundations of Cognitive Science" in the field of intonation and meaning;
Research interests: syntax and semantics, information -and event structure

Steube, Anita
Professor emeritus of General Linguistics, Department of Linguistics at the University of Leipzig;
Research interests: formal grammars and theory of texts

Stolterfoht, Britta
research fellow at the Max Planck Institute for Human Cognitive and Brain Sciences, Leipzig;
Research interests: syntax and information structure in language comprehension

Toepel, Ulrike
PhD student at the Max-Planck-Institute for Cognitive and Brain Sciences in Leipzig, Germany;
Research interests: Electrophysiological correlates of information structural processing, intonation on sentence level and beyond, neural correlates of German Sign Language (DGS)

Trautwein, Martin
PhD in 2003 from the University of Leipzig;
research fellow at the Institute for Formal Ontology and Medical Information Science, University of Leipzig;
Research interests: semantics and knowledge representation, semantics of time, theories of truth and reference

Umbach, Carla
Dr. ing.; Institute of Cognitive Science, University of Osnabrueck;
Research interests: semantics and pragmatics, esp. information structure and discourse structure, presuppositions and context-dependency

Thomas Weskott,
PhD in 2002 from the University of Leipzig;
Research assistant at the Collaborative Research Center 632 "Informationsstruktur" at the University of Potsdam/Germany;
research interests: formal pragmatics and language processing

Index

D

E

F

W

Bei Fragen zur Produktsicherheit wenden Sie sich bitte an:
If you have any questions regarding product safety,
please contact:

Walter de Gruyter GmbH
Genthiner Straße 13
10785 Berlin
productsafety@degruyterbrill.com